Children's Writer's Word Book

Children's Writer's Word Book

E verything you need to ensure your writing speaks to your young audience, including:

- word lists, separated by grade (K-6)
- thesaurus of listed words
- reading levels for synonyms
- advice and tips on word usage in children's writing

ALIJANDRA MOGILNER

Writer's Digest Books

CINCINNATI, OHIO

Children's Writer's Word Book. Copyright © 1992 by Alijandra Mogilner, Ph.D. Printed and bound in the United States of America. All rights reserved. No part of this book may be reproduced in any form or by any electronic or mechanical means including information storage and retrieval systems without permission in writing from the publisher, except by a reviewer, who may quote brief passages in a review. Published by Writer's Digest Books, an imprint of F&W Publications, Inc., 1507 Dana Avenue, Cincinnati, Ohio 45207. First edition.

This hardcover edition of *Children's Writer's Word Book* features a "self-jacket" that eliminates the need for a separate dust jacket. It provides sturdy protection for your book while it saves paper, trees and energy.

96 95 94 93   5 4 3 2

Library of Congress Cataloging in Publication Data

Mogilner, Alijandra
   Children's writer's word book / by Alijandra Mogilner.
      p. cm.
   Includes bibliographical references.
   ISBN 0-89879-511-7
   1. English language — Glossaries, vocabularies, etc. 2. Children's literature — Author-ship. 3. Children — Books and reading. 4. Children — Language. 5. Vocabulary.
   I. Title.
   PE1691.M57 1992
   428.1 — dc20   92-17778
                                     CIP

Edited by Donna Collingwood
Designed by Sandy Conopeotis

About the Author

Alijandra Mogilner started writing on a bet and sold her first piece of children's writing to the Children's Television Workshop publication "3-2-1 Contact" in 1982. She holds a Ph.D. in anthropology from the University of Mexico at Mexico City and currently teaches a class in writing for publication at the University of California at San Diego. She is married with three children and lives in California.

Acknowledgments

Usually the acknowledgments start with family and friends who helped put a book together. However, this is one time when the editorial staff deserves top billing. The first team consisted of Jean Fredette, who believed in the idea enough to take on the project; Julie Whaley, who was patient enough to stay with me through the unexpected; and editorial director Bill Brohaugh whose enthusiasm was contagious. Donna Collingwood "inherited" the project and shaped the finished product. Others helped put the pieces together, filled in the blanks, and did a remarkably difficult job in a short time. They included Lynn Perrigo, Tracy Schneller, Lynn Haller, Beth Johnson, Deb Garvey and Bev Tabe. Production editor Sandy Grieshop was my final link before publication and saw the book through to completion. After all the horror stories of "orphaned" books and editorial staffs from the dark side, I want the reader to know there are positive and giving people in the industry. Everyone at Writer's Digest Books has my deepest thanks.

Closer to home I would like to thank Leif Fern, Ph.D., publisher of Kabyn Books and professor of education at San Diego State University. His wonderful series on creative and developmental writing for children, "The Writing Kabyn," is a guide through uncharted territory. I would also like to thank my family for their support and patience. Writers Cynthia Richmond and Lynn Ford helped, as did my young friends who were my ultimate "reality checks," especially David and Tayopa Mogilner, Clint Smith, Micha Easley, Lainya, Cervantes and Ahnsaan Magana, Carolyn Pisciuneri, and David Conde. Thank you all.

Dedication

To Joanna Foley who started me writing for children. She was my first children's editor and the best editor of any type I have ever worked with. Her subtle changes and kind suggestions always made me wish I had written it that way in the first place. This book is, in great measure, her doing. If you ever have the good fortune to work with her, treasure what she gives you.

Contents

Introduction

One of the wonderful things about dreaming of becoming a children's writer is that it is such a possible dream. Successful writers not only gain financially, but they also gain a loyal and generous readership. I can think of no more gracious and enthusiastic an audience than young readers. Children identify strongly with characters in their books and often want the same book read to them over and over again. That could be your book—the one that's dog-eared and tattered from being someone's cherished companion.

To achieve your dream and become an author for this special audience, you first must understand the unique style necessary in children's writing. The clarity, simplicity and rhythm that should be present in a children's book or story can be difficult to master. However, it's these very ingredients that will make your book one that is read over and over again.

Children's Writer's Word Book will help you choose words children will both understand and be challenged by, words that will help them perceive the world as it is and imagine worlds that could be. You, as a writer of children's literature, have a special commitment; along with the joy of creating for your readers comes the responsibility of writing honestly and clearly. This book will help you meet that responsibility. Anyone working in children's literature, young adult literature and educational writing will find it an invaluable tool.

Educators will find the book useful in creating classroom materials, such as vocabulary lists, as well as for creative writing projects with students. Teachers and day-care professionals can use the lists as a reference when developing spelling lists and other classroom material.

The above professionals and aspirants will refer again and again to specific word lists to spur ideas. The lists can stimulate creativity and verify your perception of what's appropriate. The book is for anyone who works with or would like to reach children and beginning readers, whether writing a story for fifth-grade boys or an adult reading text to improve literacy skills.

As adults, we often forget that children can comprehend more than they can articulate, and we end up communicating to them below their level, leaving them bored. Or, the opposite can happen: children are growing up faster than we did and act very sophisticated although their vocabulary skills are undeveloped. Striking the balance between writing below or above their level is tricky. This book helps make the levels clear.

Children's Writer's Word Book is a desk reference, intended to be kept close by for frequent and immediate access. When you need to know if a word you want to use is appropriate for your young audience, or how long your sentences should be, the answer is there.

As a writer and teacher, I often needed to know what level a particular word or idea was and didn't know where to look. That's when I got the idea for a book I could turn to any time I had a question of this nature. As the idea evolved, it became focused on three areas: lists of specific words commonly introduced at each graded reading level, a thesaurus of these words listing synonyms with the level at which each is usually introduced, and a discussion of standard practices related to word usage in children's writing.

The grade level at which the words presented here are introduced is usually derived from more than one graded source. When there was a discrepancy between standard sources, the words are listed under the grade in which they were most frequently introduced. If there was no clear consensus, the words in this book have a bias in favor of the earliest usage. If that sounds a little inexact, it is—the ultimate judge is the child and every child is different, as are school districts and parents. All of these factors contribute to a child's comprehension and vocabulary.

In your word choices and in your decisions about theme and concept, you'll frequently be using your own judgment. This book will help make that judgment more certain.

The words in the lists were compiled from several basic word lists and other sources, then subjected to my own testing. Certified reading specialists who work with children in the California school system checked the lists. Then, several panels of grade-school children reviewed words I was uncertain about. Beyond this word-by-word analysis, I received more general help from professors of education at San Diego State University and others from the University of California at San Diego, where I teach writing at the extension.

The lists include those words that educators and publishers generally agree should become a permanent part of children's word knowledge. Sources used to create the word lists are listed in the appendix.

HOW TO USE THIS BOOK

Children's Writer's Word Book is a fast reference book—presenting word lists and a thesaurus set up to help no matter how you write. In publishing, the classifications of children's literature are broader than the grade-by-grade method employed here. However, before generalizing, you must first understand some of the fine distinctions in ages, grade levels and word usage. Because a picture book is for children ages two to eight, it's apparent the two-year-old will be listening to, not reading, the story. Somewhere in that span of six years, the child begins recognizing words; later she can recall the spelling of some of the words when the book is not in front of her. Obviously, this process of selection is different in each child.

So, when you're writing a picture book, look for words at or below the third-grade level. Limit the amount of third-grade-level words you use because they are understood by the fewest picture-book readers. Publishers' categories are further explained in the section titled "Some Things You'll Need to Know."

Except at the kindergarten and first-grade levels, all permutations and tenses of a word are assumed to be introduced at the same time, with exceptions noted on the list. Even at the first-grade level, regular conjugations of a verb are introduced together. For example, only the word *choice* is given in the listings but its presence indicates that *choose, chose* and *chosen* may all be used. Word families, such as *chemical, chemist* and *chemistry* or *absorb, absorbed, absorbent, absorbing* and *absorption* are also introduced together. When a first-grade word changes radically, it may become a second-grade word; for example, *reason* is a first-grade word, but *unreasonable* would be considered second grade because both a prefix and a suffix are appended to the root word. This is where that ever-sharpening judgment will come into play.

Subjects are also grouped. For example, the early history of the United States is usually taught during the fifth grade and any words relating to that period are appropriate for the ten- to twelve-year-old child.

Word lists are least exact at the pre-reader/kindergarten and first-grade levels for several reasons. Children are first learning to read and they learn selectively, based on what they're most interested in. Also, many children in this age group are not yet in a formalized educational setting. And, finally, regional, religious and family influences are stronger than classroom influences at this stage.

Many unusual nouns and even made-up words are introduced in children's books and all of them cannot (and should not) be presented here. Richard Scarry's books are often accompanied by elaborate illustrations that clearly identify these objects with pickle cars joining jeeps in a delightful hodgepodge that has nothing to do with reality. Dr. Seuss's words are often only nonsense (Zizzer-Zazzer-Zuzz or Fiffer-feffer-feff) and are meant to teach alphabet and sound skills. These joyful exercises in experimental language are presented carefully and underscore the idea that you can do almost anything you like if you do it in a context the reader can understand. Take a look at these books. You will see that they are carefully crafted and other conventions, such as sentence length, are carefully adhered to.

Using the Graded Lists

The introductions to the word lists discuss the special requirements of children's writing and the standard practices in that field. They cover optimal sentence lengths for particular age groups, when contractions and possessives are introduced and other such topics.

Words are grouped by grade—kindergarten through sixth. A short introduction to each grade gives you general guidelines for writing for that grade. Writing samples integrating this information with the appropriate vocabulary follow each list. These lists are best used as a springboard to create stories. Look through the second-grade word list. Certain words will pop out at you. Take the first word that you stop at and create a sentence. A story may follow, or try another word. The possibilities are limited only by your imagination.

Let's go to the kindergarten word list and use it as an example of developing a short passage. The following mini-story, *A Trip to the Store*, was developed from that list.

> Mother said: Tell the family to get in the car. We're going to the store to pay the bill. I have some extra money. You can buy the hat you want. Your brother can have a book.
>
> Ben asked: Can I buy a cat?
>
> Mother said: No, you can't.
>
> Tom asked: Can we get some food?
>
> Mom asked: What do you want?
>
> Ben and Tom yelled: Pizza!
>
> Mom said: OK, pizza it is.

Using the Thesaurus

Children's Writer's Word Book's thesaurus is similar to other thesauruses except it features only words understood by children from kindergarten to sixth grade.

If you have already written a story, or are in the middle of writing one, and are not certain if a particular word is appropriate for your intended audience, look up the word alphabetically and see if it "fits" what you are doing. If the word is listed but is too far off the mark, you will find other choices listed.

I wanted to make sure the following story was appropriate for second-grade readers:

> Lockheed is a company that makes rockets and jet planes. So, of course, when they need to deliver messages, they use airmail. However, they don't use an airplane to do it. They use pigeons! That's because Robert Nelson came up with an old-fashioned idea to solve a modern problem.

The only inappropriate words in this paragraph were *old-fashioned*, a third-grade word, and *deliver*, a fifth-grade word. I used the thesaurus to find an appropriate substitute for *deliver* and in the revision it became *send*, a first-grade word.

I simply dropped the word *fashioned* from *old-fashioned*. It changed the meaning slightly, but the story wasn't hurt in the process.

Clauses and phrases are usually given the grade of the highest-level word in the phrase. Sometimes a phrase may have all first-grade- or kindergarten-level words, but, as a concept, may not be understood at that level. Consider the phrase a level above. For example, in the phrase *as best he could*, all words are level K. But, as a phrase, it may not be understood by a kindergarten reader, so bump it up to the first-grade level.

In the phrase *on cloud nine*, *on* and *nine* are level K, and cloud is level one, so the phrase would be considered first-grade level. However, because it's an idiom, it may not be understood by a first-grade reader. Again, judgment is needed.

Guidelines for Using Words Not on This List

The words presented in the word lists and thesaurus should be considered a part of a child's basic and permanent reading vocabulary. That is, at the appropriate level children should know the word well enough to know how to pronounce the word and recognize the important meaning, or meanings, of the word when they see it. There will probably be many other words you wish to use that do not fall into this category and, thus, are not on these lists.

To check if such words are appropriate for your intended readers, look up similar words, or words in the same subject area, and get an idea if the reader will understand the one you want to use. Take, for example, this excerpt from a science story written for ten- to twelve-year-olds about foods we will eat in the future.

Many changes are already being made in the kind of food we eat. Many of you use imitation "bacon bits" or drink imitation milk. The new products are usually made out of soybeans, sunflower seeds or alfalfa. That is because they are high-protein crops.

Most of the words used in this story, including the plants, are listed in the thesaurus; however, *soybean* is not. The introduction to the graded word lists notes that almost all foods and plants have been introduced by fourth grade. So, we know it's safe to use *soybean* in this article.

You may not find the word you are looking for if it is a different conjugation, tense or form of one listed. Look for the most basic form of the word. I have tried to use the present tense of the words here, but there are some exceptions.

English has many compound words and most of them are not presented here. As a general rule, compound words are first introduced in second grade. After that, almost any compound word is acceptable as long as the two parts are already known to the reader. For example, the word *wildlife* is not listed in the thesaurus;

however, *wild* is a second-grade word and *life* is introduced in first grade. Therefore, *wildlife* is all right to use in the second grade and beyond. If you have any question about a word, look up the two parts to see if they will be familiar to your audience. A few compound words, such as *myself* and *cannot*, can be used before second grade. The general rule here is that the compound word should be made up of easily recognizable words. The child must be familiar enough with the word that he/she will recognize it even though it is combined with another word.

Sometimes a whole story will hinge on an unusual word or idea. In fact, you are often telling the story, or writing the article, precisely because it is about something foreign, rare or unusual. When you use those words, they should be given with enough information so that the reader will understand their meaning and can enjoy reading about it. For example:

> In Mexico, a small town is called a *pueblo*. Maria Lopez is a little girl who lives in a pueblo called Toco. Her parents are farmers. Every day Maria helps her parents. . . .

When appropriate, I have noted sources that may be of further help in the section "Recommended Reading."

The material in this book reflects my own years of experience as a children's writer. Much of it is information given to me over ten years by kind and patient editors. I hope *Children's Writer's Word Book* becomes a key to opening the door to your own success and helps you realize your dream. Writing for children has been a real joy for me and I hope it brings you the same kind of satisfaction.

Alphabetical List

Following is a complete list of all the words included in the graded lists, arranged alphabetically. This list is most useful for simply determining the level of a word. You'll turn to this again and again while writing.

a *K*
abacus *5th*
abandon *4th*
abbey *6th*
abbot *6th*
abbreviate *6th*
abdomen *6th*
abduct *6th*
abhor *6th*
abide *5th*
ablaze *6th*
able *3rd*
aboard *2nd*
abode *5th*
abolish *5th*
abolition *5th*
abominable *6th*
about *K*
above *K*
abroad *5th*
abrupt *5th*
absence *5th*
absent *5th*
absolute *3rd*
absorb *5th*
abstain *6th*
abstract *6th*
absurd *6th*
abundant *5th*
abuse *6th*
accent *6th*
accept *3rd*
access *6th*

accessory *6th*
accident *4th*
accommodate *6th*
accompany *3rd*
accomplish *2nd*
according *4th*
account *3rd*
accumulate *6th*
accurate *6th*
accuse *4th*
accustom *4th*
ace *2nd*
ache *5th*
achieve *5th*
acid *4th*
acknowledge *5th*
acorn *4th*
acquaint *4th*
acquire *4th*
acquit *6th*
acre *3rd*
acrobat *5th*
across *1st*
act *K*
action *1st*
active *3rd*
actor *2nd*
actual *3rd*
acute *6th*
A.D. *5th*
ad *4th*
adapt *4th*
add *K*

adder *5th*
addict *5th*
addition *3rd*
address *K*
adept *4th*
adhere *6th*
adhesive *6th*
adjective *6th*
adjoin *6th*
adjourn *6th*
adjust *5th*
administer *6th*
admiral *5th*
admire *5th*
admit *4th*
adobe *4th*
adolescent *5th*
adopt *3rd*
adore *4th*
adorn *6th*
adrift *6th*
adult *1st*
advance *2nd*
advantage *3rd*
adventure *3rd*
advertise *4th*
advice *3rd*
affair *2nd*
affect *4th*
affection *4th*
afford *3rd*
afire *2nd*
aflame *2nd*

afloat *2nd*
afraid *1st*
after *K*
afternoon *1st*
afterward *4th*
again *K*
against *1st*
agate *4th*
age *1st*
agent *5th*
aggress *6th*
aggressive *6th*
agile *6th*
agitate *5th*
ago *1st*
agony *5th*
agree *2nd*
agriculture *4th*
ahead *1st*
aid *2nd*
aide *5th*
aim *3rd*
air *K*
Air Force *1st*
aircraft *1st*
airfield *2nd*
airplane *1st*
airport *1st*
airtight *5th*
alabaster *4th*
alarm *3rd*
alas *4th*
albatross *5th*

album *1st*
alcohol *5th*
alder *3rd*
ale *2nd*
alert *5th*
alfalfa *3rd*
algae *5th*
alias *6th*
alibi *6th*
alien *5th*
alight *5th*
alike *1st*
alive *3rd*
alkaline *6th*
all *K*
Allah *5th*
allege *6th*
allergic *5th*
allergy *5th*
alley *6th*
allied *6th*
alligator *1st*
allow *2nd*
allowance *5th*
alloy *6th*
almond *2nd*
almost *K*
aloe *4th*
alone *K*
along *1st*
aloud *4th*
alphabet *2nd*
already *1st*
also *K*
altar *4th*
alter *4th*
alternate *5th*
although *2nd*
altitude *5th*
alto *6th*
alum *6th*
aluminum *6th*

always *K*
a.m. *6th*
am *K*
amateur *5th*
amaze *5th*
amazon *5th*
ambassador *5th*
amber *5th*
ambergris *5th*
ambition *4th*
ambulance *6th*
ambush *6th*
amen *4th*
amend *4th*
amethyst *4th*
amid *4th*
amiss *3rd*
ammonia *6th*
ammunition *6th*
among *1st*
amount *2nd*
amphibian *3rd*
ample *5th*
amplify *6th*
amuse *4th*
an *K*
anarchy *5th*
ancestor *5th*
anchor *4th*
anchovy *4th*
ancient *3rd*
and *K*
anemone *3rd*
anew *3rd*
angel *4th*
anger *1st*
angle *3rd*
angry *1st*
anguish *6th*
animal *K*
animate *6th*
ankle *4th*

announce *3rd*
annoy *5th*
annual *4th*
anoint *6th*
another *1st*
answer *K*
ant *K*
anticipate *6th*
antique *6th*
antler *4th*
anvil *6th*
anxiety *4th*
anxious *4th*
any *K*
anybody *1st*
anyone *1st*
anything *1st*
anyway *1st*
apart *3rd*
apartment *1st*
ape *K*
ape (copy) *5th*
apologize *6th*
apology *6th*
apparatus *6th*
apparent *3rd*
appeal *3rd*
appear *2nd*
appearance *2nd*
appetite *4th*
apple *K*
applesauce *3rd*
apply *2nd*
appoint *3rd*
appreciate *5th*
approach *3rd*
approve *4th*
April *1st*
apron *3rd*
apt *5th*
aquarium *2nd*
Arab *5th*

arch *4th*
archaeology *5th*
archer *5th*
arctic *3rd*
ardent *6th*
are *K*
area *3rd*
arena *5th*
aren't *1st*
argue *3rd*
arid *6th*
arise *4th*
aristocrat *6th*
arithmetic *3rd*
ark *2nd*
arm *K*
armadillo *1st*
armload *2nd*
armor *4th*
Army *1st*
around *1st*
arouse *4th*
arrange (ment) *3rd*
array *5th*
arrest *3rd*
arrive *2nd*
arrogant *6th*
arrow *2nd*
arrowhead *4th*
art *K*
artichoke *4th*
article *2nd*
artificial *6th*
artist *2nd*
as *K*
ascend *4th*
ash *3rd*
ashamed *4th*
ashore *2nd*
aside *3rd*
ask *K*
asleep *3rd*

aspect *5th*
aspen *4th*
asphalt *5th*
assault *4th*
assemble *4th*
assert *6th*
assertive *6th*
assign *5th*
assist *4th*
assistance *4th*
assistant *4th*
associate *5th*
association *5th*
assort *5th*
assume *5th*
assure *3rd*
asteroid *6th*
asthma *6th*
astonish *4th*
astound *4th*
astray *3rd*
astride *6th*
astrology *5th*
astronaut *4th*
astronomy *4th*
at *K*
ate *K*
athlete *5th*
atmosphere *4th*
atom *5th*
atop *3rd*
attach *5th*
attack *3rd*
attain *6th*
attempt *2nd*
attend *3rd*
attention *2nd*
attire *6th*
attitude *5th*
attract *5th*
audible *6th*
August *1st*

aunt *1st*
austere *5th*
author *3rd*
authority *3rd*
autobiography *6th*
autograph *6th*
automatic *6th*
automobile *3rd*
autumn *3rd*
avenge *5th*
avenue *3rd*
average *3rd*
aviation *6th*
avocado *3rd*
avoid *3rd*
await *5th*
awake (n) *3rd*
award *5th*
aware *3rd*
away *K*
awe *6th*
awful *3rd*
awhile *5th*
awkward *6th*
ax *K*

babble *6th*
babe *5th*
baboon *1st*
baby *K*
bachelor *6th*
back *K*
backbone *4th*
background *4th*
backing *1st*
backpack *4th*
backward *4th*
backwoods *4th*
bacon *4th*
bad *K*
badge *5th*
badger *2nd*

bag *1st*
bagpipe *3rd*
bait *3rd*
bake *1st*
balance *3rd*
balcony *6th*
bald *6th*
ball *K*
ballad *5th*
ballast *4th*
ballet *4th*
balloon *1st*
ballot *6th*
bamboo *3rd*
ban *K*
banana *2nd*
band *1st*
bandit *3rd*
bane *5th*
baneberry *4th*
bang *3rd*
banister *5th*
bank *1st*
banner *3rd*
banquet *4th*
banyan *4th*
bar *3rd*
barbecue *5th*
barber *2nd*
bare *3rd*
bareback *4th*
bargain *4th*
barge *5th*
bark *3rd*
barley *4th*
barn *K*
barnacle *3rd*
barometer *5th*
baron *4th*
barrel *4th*
barren *4th*
barrier *6th*

base *1st*
baseball *1st*
basement *3rd*
bashful *4th*
basic *2nd*
basin *4th*
basis *2nd*
basket *1st*
basketball *1st*
bass *1st*
bat *K*
batch *2nd*
bath *1st*
bathe *1st*
bathroom *1st*
bathtub *1st*
baton *5th*
batter *1st*
battery *5th*
battle *2nd*
bawl *5th*
bay *K*
bayonet *5th*
bayou *5th*
bazaar *5th*
B.C. *5th*
be *K*
beach *K*
beached *1st*
bead *K*
beagle *3rd*
beak *4th*
beam *3rd*
bean *1st*
bear *K*
beard *4th*
beast *3rd*
beat *1st*
beautiful *1st*
beautify *2nd*
beaver *1st*
because *K*

become *1st*
bed *K*
bedraggled *5th*
bedroom *3rd*
bee *K*
beech *4th*
beef *2nd*
been *K*
beep *K*
beer *5th*
beet *4th*
beetle *1st*
before *K*
befriend *6th*
beg *1st*
began *K*
begin *K*
beginner *2nd*
behalf *6th*
behave *4th*
behavior *4th*
behind *1st*
behold *3rd*
beige *3rd*
being *1st*
belief *1st*
believe *1st*
bell *K*
belle *6th*
bellow *4th*
belly *5th*
belong *1st*
beloved *4th*
below *1st*
belt *2nd*
bench *4th*
bend *K*
beneath *1st*
beneficial *3rd*
benefit *3rd*
bent *K*
berate *5th*

berry *1st*
beseech *5th*
beside *1st*
best *K*
bestow *5th*
bet *1st*
betray *5th*
better *K*
between *1st*
beverage *6th*
beware *6th*
bewilder *3rd*
beyond *1st*
bias *6th*
bib *1st*
Bible *4th*
bicycle *2nd*
bid *1st*
big *K*
bike *1st*
bill *1st*
billboard *3rd*
billiards *6th*
billion *5th*
bin *1st*
bind *2nd*
binoculars *6th*
biography *6th*
biosphere *6th*
birch *4th*
bird *K*
birthday *K*
biscuit *4th*
bishop *5th*
bison *4th*
bit *1st*
bite *1st*
bitter *3rd*
black *K*
blackberry *2nd*
blackbird *1st*
blackboard *3rd*

blackmail *4th*
blacksmith *4th*
blacktop *1st*
blade *2nd*
blame *2nd*
blank *4th*
blanket *3rd*
blast *2nd*
blaze *1st*
bleach *4th*
bleat *4th*
blemish *5th*
blend *5th*
bless *3rd*
blimp *5th*
blind *3rd*
blink *6th*
blister *5th*
blizzard *4th*
block *1st*
blond *5th*
blood *1st*
bloodhound *3rd*
bloodshed *4th*
bloodthirsty *4th*
bloom *4th*
blossom *4th*
blot *4th*
blotch *6th*
blouse *1st*
blow *1st*
blue *K*
blue jay *1st*
bluebell *2nd*
blueberry *2nd*
bluebird *1st*
bluebottle *3rd*
bluff *6th*
blunt *6th*
blur *4th*
blush *4th*
boar *5th*

board *1st*
boast *4th*
boat *1st*
bobbin *4th*
bobcat *1st*
bobolink *5th*
bodily *5th*
body *1st*
bodyguard *4th*
bog *5th*
boil *3rd*
bold *2nd*
bolt *4th*
bomb *5th*
bonbon *4th*
bond *3rd*
bondage *6th*
bone *1st*
bonfire *3rd*
bonnet *6th*
bonus *6th*
boo *K*
boob *2nd*
book *K*
bookcase *3rd*
bookkeeper *3rd*
bookstore *1st*
boom *1st*
boomerang *5th*
boon *5th*
boot *1st*
booth *5th*
borax *5th*
border *1st*
bore *2nd*
born *1st*
borrow *2nd*
boss *K*
both *K*
bother *2nd*
bottle *3rd*
bottom *1st*

bought *2nd*	breeches *5th*	brute *6th*	burlap *6th*
boulder *5th*	breed *4th*	bubble *2nd*	burn (ing) *3rd*
boulevard *4th*	breeze *4th*	buck *1st*	burnoose *5th*
bounce *6th*	brew *6th*	bucket *3rd*	burp *3rd*
bound *2nd*	bribe *5th*	buckeye *4th*	burro *1st*
boundary *4th*	brick *4th*	buckle *6th*	burrow *5th*
boundless *4th*	bride *4th*	buckskin *6th*	burst *3rd*
bouquet *6th*	bridesmaid *4th*	bud *1st*	bury *3rd*
bout *6th*	bridge *1st*	buddy *4th*	bus *K*
bow *1st*	brief *3rd*	budge *4th*	bush *2nd*
bowl *1st*	brier *6th*	budget *5th*	bushel *4th*
box *K*	brig *6th*	buffalo *1st*	business *2nd*
boxer *1st*	brigantine *6th*	buffet *6th*	bust *6th*
boy *K*	bright *1st*	bug *K*	bustle *6th*
boycott *6th*	brilliant *4th*	buggy *6th*	busy *1st*
boyfriend *4th*	brim *5th*	bugle *6th*	busybody *3rd*
boyhood *4th*	bring *K*	build *1st*	but *K*
brace *5th*	brink *6th*	building *1st*	butcher *4th*
bracelet *5th*	brisk *6th*	bulb *2nd*	butter *2nd*
bract *6th*	bristle *6th*	bulge *4th*	buttercup *3rd*
brag *3rd*	broad *3rd*	bulk *4th*	butterfly *1st*
Brahman *5th*	broadcast *5th*	bull *K*	buttermilk *3rd*
braid *2nd*	broadcloth *5th*	bulldog *1st*	button *1st*
brain *3rd*	broadsword *4th*	bulldozer *1st*	buttonhole *4th*
brake *1st*	brocade *5th*	bullet *4th*	buy *K*
branch *2nd*	broccoli *4th*	bulletin *3rd*	buyer *1st*
brand *2nd*	broil *4th*	bullfrog *1st*	buzz *5th*
brandish *6th*	bronco *6th*	bull's-eye *1st*	buzzard *4th*
brass *2nd*	bronze *4th*	bully *1st*	by *K*
brat *3rd*	brooch *4th*	bumble *4th*	
bravado *6th*	brood *4th*	bumblebee *5th*	cab *K*
brave *1st*	brook *2nd*	bump *2nd*	cabbage *4th*
bravo *6th*	broom *2nd*	bun *2nd*	cabin *1st*
bread *2nd*	broth *4th*	bunch *3rd*	cabinet *4th*
breadfruit *2nd*	brother *1st*	bundle *5th*	cable *1st*
break *1st*	brow *4th*	bung *6th*	cactus *2nd*
breakers *4th*	brown *K*	bunk *4th*	cadet *3rd*
breakfast *1st*	brownie *2nd*	bunny *K*	cafe *4th*
breakwater *4th*	brownstone *4th*	bunt *2nd*	cafeteria *5th*
breast *3rd*	bruise *5th*	burden *5th*	cage *1st*
breath *1st*	brush *2nd*	bureau *4th*	cake *K*
breathe *1st*	brutal *6th*	burglar *1st*	calamity *6th*

calcium *6th*	capitalize *3rd*	cat *K*	certificate *6th*
calculate *5th*	capitol *2nd*	catalog *5th*	certify *6th*
calendar *1st*	captain *2nd*	catbird *1st*	chagrin *5th*
calf *K*	caption *6th*	catch *1st*	chain *3rd*
calico *6th*	capture *3rd*	caterpillar *1st*	chair *1st*
call *K*	car *K*	cathedral *5th*	chalk *5th*
calm *3rd*	caramel *5th*	catholic *4th*	challenge *4th*
calories *3rd*	caravan *6th*	catnip *3rd*	chamber *5th*
came *K*	carbon *4th*	cattle *3rd*	chamberlain *5th*
camel *K*	carcass *5th*	cauldron *6th*	champion *4th*
cameo *4th*	card *1st*	cauliflower *4th*	chance *2nd*
camera *1st*	cardboard *2nd*	cause *2nd*	chancellor *6th*
camouflage *6th*	cardinal *3rd*	caution *5th*	chandelier *5th*
camp *1st*	care *K*	cautious *5th*	change *2nd*
campaign *3rd*	career *4th*	cavalry *6th*	channel *4th*
campfire *1st*	carefree *3rd*	cave *1st*	chant *5th*
campus *6th*	careful *1st*	cavity *5th*	chap *4th*
can *K*	careless *5th*	cayuse *6th*	chapel *4th*
canal *4th*	caretaker *4th*	cease *3rd*	chapter *3rd*
canary *1st*	cargo *5th*	cedar *2nd*	character *2nd*
cancel *6th*	carload *4th*	ceiling *4th*	characteristic *6th*
cancer *6th*	carnation *4th*	celebrate *4th*	charcoal *6th*
candidate *4th*	carnival *2nd*	celebrity *5th*	charge *2nd*
candle *2nd*	carol *3rd*	celery *4th*	chariot *6th*
candy *K*	carp *5th*	celestial *6th*	charity *4th*
cane *3rd*	carpenter *4th*	cell *1st*	charm *3rd*
canine *5th*	carpet *4th*	cellar *1st*	chart *1st*
cannibal *4th*	carriage *5th*	cellophane *5th*	chase *1st*
cannon *4th*	carrot *2nd*	cellular *5th*	chat *1st*
cannot *1st*	carry *K*	cement *4th*	chatter *1st*
canoe *4th*	cart *1st*	cemetery *6th*	chauffeur *6th*
canopy *6th*	carton *4th*	census *6th*	cheap *3rd*
can't *1st*	cartoon *2nd*	cent *1st*	cheat *3rd*
canter *5th*	cartridge *6th*	center *2nd*	check *1st*
canvas *6th*	carve *4th*	centigrade *2nd*	checkers *2nd*
canyon *4th*	case *2nd*	centimeter *2nd*	cheek *2nd*
cap *K*	cash *2nd*	central *3rd*	cheer *3rd*
capable *4th*	cask *4th*	century *2nd*	cheese *3rd*
capacity *6th*	casserole *4th*	cereal *6th*	chef *4th*
cape *4th*	cast *2nd*	ceremony *5th*	chemical *4th*
caper *4th*	castle *3rd*	certain *1st*	chemistry *4th*
capital *2nd*	casual *5th*	certainly *1st*	cherish *5th*

cherry *2nd*
chess *4th*
chest *2nd*
chestnut *4th*
chew *1st*
chick *2nd*
chickadee *5th*
chicken *K*
chief *1st*
child *K*
childhood *4th*
children *K*
chili *4th*
chill *3rd*
chime *6th*
chimney *2nd*
chin *1st*
chip *5th*
chipmunk *2nd*
chirp *2nd*
chivalry *6th*
chocolate *4th*
choice *3rd*
choir *5th*
choke *1st*
choose *3rd*
chop *2nd*
chord *5th*
chorus *5th*
chow *5th*
chowder *5th*
Christ *4th*
Christian *4th*
Christmas *K*
chrome *2nd*
chronicle *6th*
chubby *2nd*
chum *6th*
church *K*
churn *3rd*
chute *5th*
cider *2nd*

cigar *4th*
cigarette *4th*
cinch *6th*
cinnamon *2nd*
circle *K*
circuit *4th*
circular *4th*
circumstantial *6th*
circus *1st*
cite *6th*
citizen *3rd*
city *K*
civil *3rd*
civilization *4th*
claim *2nd*
clam *1st*
clambake *5th*
clamor *6th*
clamp *5th*
clan *5th*
clang *4th*
clank *4th*
clap *2nd*
clash *5th*
clasp *4th*
class *1st*
classic *5th*
classroom *1st*
clatter *5th*
clause *6th*
claw *1st*
clay *1st*
clean *K*
clear *2nd*
cleat *5th*
clergyman *6th*
clerk *2nd*
clever *3rd*
click *2nd*
client *6th*
cliff *2nd*
climate *4th*

climb *1st*
cling *4th*
clinic *1st*
clip *2nd*
cloak *4th*
clock *1st*
clog *5th*
close *K*
closet *2nd*
clot *5th*
cloth *1st*
clothes *1st*
cloud *1st*
clover *2nd*
clown *1st*
club *1st*
clue *2nd*
clump *3rd*
clumsy *6th*
cluster *4th*
clutch *4th*
clutter *4th*
coach *4th*
coal *2nd*
coarse *4th*
coast *2nd*
coat *1st*
coax *6th*
cob *1st*
cobra *1st*
cobweb *3rd*
cocaine *6th*
cock *4th*
cockpit *2nd*
cocoa *1st*
cocoon *2nd*
cod *1st*
code *3rd*
coffee *2nd*
coffin *6th*
cog *6th*
coil *5th*

coin *3rd*
coke *1st*
cold *K*
collapse *5th*
collar *4th*
collect *3rd*
college *4th*
collie *2nd*
collision *6th*
cologne *5th*
colonel *3rd*
colonial *4th*
colony *3rd*
color *K*
colorful *2nd*
colt *K*
column *4th*
comb *2nd*
combat *5th*
combine *3rd*
combustion *6th*
come *K*
comedian *5th*
comedy *5th*
comet *5th*
comfort *3rd*
comfortable *3rd*
comic *5th*
coming *K*
comma *2nd*
command *2nd*
commence *6th*
commend *6th*
comment *5th*
commentator *5th*
commercial *5th*
commissar *5th*
commission *2nd*
commit *4th*
committee *5th*
commodity *5th*
commodore *4th*

common *2nd*
commonwealth *5th*
commotion *5th*
communicate *5th*
communism *5th*
community *2nd*
commute *4th*
compact *5th*
companion *3rd*
company *2nd*
compare *3rd*
compartment *6th*
compass *4th*
compassion *5th*
compassionate *5th*
compel *3rd*
compensation *6th*
compete *4th*
competent *6th*
competition *5th*
complain *4th*
complete *3rd*
complex *6th*
complicate *6th*
compliment *5th*
comply *6th*
composition *4th*
compound *4th*
comprehend *5th*
compress *6th*
comprise *6th*
compromise *5th*
computer *1st*
comrade *4th*
con *3rd*
conceal *4th*
concede *6th*
conceited *5th*
conceive *4th*
concentrate *5th*
concern *3rd*
concession *6th*

conclude *3rd*
concord *6th*
concrete *4th*
condemn *4th*
condense *6th*
condition *3rd*
condor *3rd*
conduct *3rd*
cone *1st*
confederate *6th*
conference *4th*
confess *4th*
confide *6th*
confident *6th*
confidential *6th*
conflict *4th*
conform *6th*
confound *6th*
confront *5th*
confuse *4th*
congratulate *6th*
congregation *6th*
Congress *1st*
congress *4th*
connect *3rd*
conquer *4th*
conscience *4th*
conscious *6th*
conscript *6th*
conscription *6th*
consent *3rd*
consequence *4th*
conserve *5th*
consider *2nd*
consist *3rd*
console *5th*
conspicuous *5th*
constable *6th*
constant (ly) *4th*
constellation *5th*
consternation *6th*
constitute *4th*

construct *3rd*
concord *6th*
consul *5th*
consult *4th*
consume *4th*
contact *4th*
contagious *6th*
contain *5th*
contaminate *6th*
contemplate *6th*
contemporary *5th*
contempt *5th*
contend *5th*
content *3rd*
contest *4th*
continent *4th*
continue *2nd*
contract *3rd*
contrary *4th*
contrast *4th*
contribute *4th*
contrite *5th*
contrive *6th*
control *2nd*
controversy *6th*
convenient *4th*
convent *6th*
convention *6th*
conventional *6th*
conversation *5th*
convert *4th*
convey *4th*
convict *5th*
convince *4th*
cook *1st*
cookie *K*
cool *1st*
cooperate *5th*
cop *K*
copal *5th*
cope *6th*
copper *4th*
copy *3rd*

coral *3rd*
cord *4th*
cordial *6th*
core *6th*
cork *6th*
corn *2nd*
corner *2nd*
cornmeal *5th*
corny *2nd*
corporal *4th*
corporation *4th*
corps *6th*
correct *3rd*
correspond *5th*
corridor *5th*
corrupt *6th*
cosmetics *6th*
cost *K*
costume *4th*
cot *1st*
cottage *4th*
cotton *2nd*
couch *4th*
cough *5th*
could *K*
couldn't *1st*
council *5th*
count *K*
counter *5th*
countless *5th*
country *1st*
couple *3rd*
courage *4th*
course *3rd*
court *3rd*
courtesy *4th*
courtier *6th*
courtroom *3rd*
cousin *3rd*
cover *1st*
covert *6th*
covet *6th*

cow (animal) *K*
cow (intimidate) *6th*
cowardly *4th*
cowboy *4th*
cowpuncher *6th*
coyote *1st*
crab *K*
crack *4th*
cracker *4th*
crackle *3rd*
cradle *4th*
craft *2nd*
craftsmanship *6th*
crag *6th*
cram *5th*
cramp *6th*
crane *3rd*
crash *2nd*
crate *5th*
crater *3rd*
crave *6th*
crawfish *3rd*
crawl *1st*
crayfish *4th*
crayon *K*
crazy *4th*
creak *4th*
cream *1st*
crease *5th*
create *3rd*
creature *3rd*
credible *6th*
credit *5th*
credulous *6th*
creed *6th*
creek *4th*
creep *1st*
cremate *5th*
crepe *6th*
crescent *6th*
crest *4th*
crevice *6th*

crew *2nd*
crib *2nd*
cricket *1st*
crime *2nd*
criminal *4th*
crimson *5th*
cripes *1st*
critical *5th*
criticize *5th*
crocodile *1st*
Cro-magnon *5th*
crop *2nd*
cross (wise) *1st*
crotch *6th*
crouch *5th*
crow *2nd*
crowd *2nd*
crown *1st*
cruel *5th*
crunch *4th*
crush *4th*
cry *K*
crystal *3rd*
cub *K*
cube *4th*
cuddle *5th*
cue *2nd*
cuff *1st*
cultivate *6th*
culture *6th*
cunning *6th*
cup *K*
curb *3rd*
cure *4th*
curfew *6th*
curious *3rd*
curl *2nd*
current *3rd*
curse *3rd*
curtain *5th*
curve *3rd*
custom *6th*

customer *5th*
cut *K*
cute *1st*
cutlass *6th*
cutting *1st*
cylinder *6th*

dab *1st*
dad (dy) *K*
daft *6th*
daily *4th*
dairy *1st*
dam *K*
damage *5th*
damp *5th*
damsel *6th*
dance *1st*
dandy *1st*
danger *1st*
dangerous *6th*
dangle *5th*
dare *2nd*
dark *K*
darkness *1st*
dart *1st*
date *1st*
daughter *1st*
day *K*
daydream *2nd*
daylight *1st*
dazzle *5th*
dead *1st*
deal *2nd*
dear *1st*
debris *5th*
decapitate *6th*
decay *5th*
deceive *5th*
December *1st*
decide *1st*
decision *3rd*
deck *1st*

declare *5th*
decline *6th*
decode *5th*
decorate *3rd*
decoration *3rd*
dedicate *6th*
deduce *6th*
deed *1st*
deep *1st*
deer *K*
defeat *5th*
defend *5th*
defy *6th*
degree *5th*
deity *5th*
dejected *5th*
delay *5th*
delegate *5th*
delegation *5th*
deliberate *6th*
delicate *5th*
delicatessen *5th*
delight *3rd*
deliver *5th*
demand *5th*
demigod *6th*
demonstrate *6th*
demure *5th*
den *1st*
dent *1st*
deny *5th*
depart *5th*
department *2nd*
depend *3rd*
depose *6th*
deposit *5th*
depress *5th*
depression *6th*
depth *5th*
derelict *6th*
descend *6th*
desert *1st*

deserve *4th*
design *5th*
desire *5th*
desk *2nd*
desolate *6th*
desperate *5th*
despise *5th*
destiny *5th*
destroy *2nd*
destruction *5th*
destructive *5th*
detail *5th*
detective *4th*
determine *5th*
detest *6th*
dethrone *6th*
devastate *6th*
develop *5th*
device *4th*
devote *5th*
devotee *5th*
devour *5th*
dew *1st*
dial *5th*
dialect *5th*
diamond *4th*
diary *3rd*
did *K*
didn't *1st*
die *2nd*
diet *4th*
differ *4th*
different *1st*
difficult *5th*
dig *1st*
dill *1st*
dim *1st*
dime *1st*
diminutive *6th*
din *6th*
dinar *5th*
dine *1st*

dinner *1st*
dinosaur *K*
dip *1st*
diplomat *5th*
dire *6th*
direct (ion) *1st*
dirt *1st*
disabled *3rd*
disagree *2nd*
disappoint *5th*
disaster *6th*
disbelief *5th*
discard *6th*
discipline *6th*
discontinue *4th*
discourage *5th*
discover *1st*
discuss *5th*
disease *5th*
disguise *5th*
disgust *5th*
dish *1st*
dishearten *5th*
disintegrate *5th*
disk *2nd*
dispense *5th*
display *3rd*
dispose *5th*
disposition *5th*
dispute *6th*
distance *4th*
distant *4th*
distaste *6th*
distinctive *5th*
distinguish *6th*
distress *5th*
distribute *6th*
district *4th*
disturb *6th*
dive *1st*
divide *4th*
divorce *4th*

do *K*
dock *1st*
doctor *1st*
does *1st*
doesn't *1st*
dog *K*
doing *1st*
doll *K*
dolphin *1st*
domicile *5th*
dominant *5th*
dominate *5th*
done *1st*
donkey *K*
don't *1st*
door *K*
doorbell *1st*
doorway *2nd*
dope *1st*
dormitory *5th*
dose *1st*
dot *K*
double *3rd*
doubt (ful) *1st*
dough *5th*
doughnut *2nd*
dove *K*
down *K*
downhearted *5th*
downstairs *1st*
downtown *1st*
Dr. *K*
drag *3rd*
dragon *1st*
drain *5th*
drake *5th*
drama *5th*
drape *5th*
draught *6th*
draw *K*
dread *6th*
dream *K*

dress *K*
dresser *2nd*
drift *2nd*
drill *2nd*
drink *1st*
drip *2nd*
drive *K*
droop *5th*
drop *K*
dropped *1st*
drove *1st*
drown *1st*
drug *1st*
drum *5th*
dry *1st*
dubious *6th*
duck *K*
due *2nd*
dull *1st*
dumb *1st*
dummy *1st*
dump *2nd*
dumpling *4th*
dune *5th*
dungeon *5th*
duplicate *6th*
durable *6th*
during *1st*
dusk *5th*
dust *2nd*
duty *1st*
dwarf *4th*
dwell *4th*
dwelling *4th*
dye *2nd*
dynamic *5th*
dynamite *6th*

each *K*
eager *5th*
eagle *1st*
ear *1st*

earl *4th*	electronic *5th*	endeavor *4th*	erupt *4th*
early *1st*	elegant *5th*	endow *6th*	escape *1st*
earn *2nd*	element *3rd*	endure *4th*	escort *5th*
earnest *4th*	elephant *K*	enemy *2nd*	Eskimo *3rd*
earth *1st*	elevate *2nd*	energy *4th*	especially *4th*
earthenware *5th*	elevation *4th*	enforce *5th*	essay *5th*
earthquake *5th*	elevator *2nd*	engage *5th*	essential *6th*
ease *3rd*	elf *1st*	engine *3rd*	establish *3rd*
east *1st*	eliminate *5th*	engineer *4th*	estate *4th*
Easter *1st*	elk *K*	English *1st*	esteem *5th*
easy *K*	elm *2nd*	engrave *5th*	estimate *5th*
eat *K*	else *1st*	enjoy *2nd*	et cetera *6th*
eating *1st*	elsewhere *4th*	enlarge *5th*	etc. *6th*
eaves *6th*	elves *1st*	enlist *6th*	eternal *4th*
echo *4th*	embarrass *5th*	enliven *6th*	ethics *5th*
eclipse *5th*	emblem *5th*	enormous *4th*	eve *5th*
ecology *5th*	embrace *4th*	enough *1st*	even *1st*
economy *4th*	embroider *5th*	enrage (d) *6th*	evening *1st*
ecstasy *6th*	emerge *5th*	enrich *6th*	event *3rd*
eddy *6th*	emergency *5th*	enter *1st*	eventually *5th*
edge *1st*	emigrant *6th*	enterprise *5th*	ever *K*
edit (or) *3rd*	eminent *6th*	entertain *4th*	evergreen *4th*
educate *3rd*	emotion *4th*	enthusiasm *4th*	every *K*
education *3rd*	emperor *4th*	entire *3rd*	everybody *3rd*
eel *K*	emphasize *5th*	entitle *5th*	everyone *1st*
effect *3rd*	emphatic *6th*	entrance *3rd*	everything *1st*
effective *4th*	empire *4th*	entrap *3rd*	everywhere *2nd*
effort *2nd*	employ *5th*	envelope *5th*	evidence *5th*
egg *K*	empress *4th*	environment *6th*	evident *5th*
egret *3rd*	empty *3rd*	envy *4th*	evil *3rd*
eight *K*	enable *4th*	episode *6th*	evolution *6th*
eighteen *1st*	enamel *6th*	equal *2nd*	exact *2nd*
eighty *1st*	enchant *6th*	equator *6th*	exaggerate *6th*
either *2nd*	encircle *5th*	equipment *5th*	examine *5th*
ejaculate *6th*	enclose *4th*	equivalent *6th*	example *2nd*
elaborate *5th*	encode *5th*	era *6th*	exceed *4th*
elastic *6th*	encounter *4th*	erase *2nd*	excel *6th*
elbow *4th*	encourage *4th*	ere *4th*	excellent *1st*
elder (ly) *5th*	encrust *6th*	erect *4th*	except *1st*
elect *3rd*	encyclopedia *5th*	err *6th*	excess *5th*
electric *3rd*	end *K*	errand *4th*	exchange *4th*
electricity *3rd*	endanger *6th*	error *4th*	excite *4th*

exclaim *3rd*	fabric *5th*	fatal *4th*	few *K*
exclude *6th*	face *K*	fate *3rd*	fez *5th*
exclusive *6th*	facility *5th*	father *K*	fib *1st*
excuse *3rd*	fact *1st*	fathom *6th*	fiber *3rd*
execute *5th*	factor *5th*	fatigue *5th*	fiction *5th*
executive *5th*	factory *1st*	fault *3rd*	fiddle *4th*
exercise *1st*	faculty *6th*	fauna *6th*	fidelity *6th*
exert *6th*	fad *K*	favor *1st*	field *2nd*
exhaust *4th*	fade *1st*	favorite *3rd*	fierce *4th*
exhibit *4th*	Fahrenheit *4th*	fawn *1st*	fiery *5th*
exhilarate *6th*	fail *2nd*	fear *1st*	fife *5th*
exile *5th*	faint *3rd*	fearful *1st*	fifteen *1st*
exist *3rd*	fair *1st*	feast *1st*	fifth *1st*
exit *3rd*	fairy *4th*	feat *1st*	fifty *1st*
expand *5th*	faith *3rd*	feather *2nd*	fig *1st*
expect *2nd*	fake *1st*	feature *3rd*	fight *K*
expedition *4th*	falcon *3rd*	February *1st*	figure *2nd*
expel *6th*	fall *K*	fed *K*	filch *5th*
expense *3rd*	false *3rd*	federal *4th*	file *1st*
experience *4th*	falter *3rd*	fee *4th*	fill *K*
experiment *3rd*	fame *3rd*	feeble *4th*	film *4th*
expert *5th*	familiar *3rd*	feed *1st*	filter *5th*
expire *6th*	families *1st*	feel *K*	fin *1st*
explain *2nd*	family *K*	feeling *K*	final *3rd*
explode *3rd*	famine *6th*	feet *1st*	finance (s) *1st*
exploit *6th*	famous *2nd*	fell *1st*	find *K*
explore *4th*	fan *K*	fellow *1st*	finding *1st*
export *5th*	fancy *3rd*	female *4th*	fine *1st*
expose *4th*	fang *5th*	fence *1st*	finger *1st*
express *5th*	fantastic *6th*	fend *6th*	fingernail *4th*
exquisite *6th*	far *1st*	fern *5th*	fingerprint *5th*
extend *4th*	faraway *3rd*	ferret *5th*	finish *1st*
exterminate *6th*	fare *3rd*	ferry *6th*	fire *K*
extinct *5th*	farm *K*	fertile *5th*	firecracker *5th*
extra *1st*	farmer *K*	fertilizer *5th*	firefly *2nd*
extraordinary *5th*	farming *1st*	fervor *6th*	fireman *K*
extravagant *6th*	farther *3rd*	festive *5th*	fireworks *2nd*
extreme *5th*	fascinate *5th*	festivity *5th*	firm *2nd*
eye *K*	fashion *3rd*	fetch *4th*	first *1st*
eyeglasses *4th*	fast *1st*	fetish *5th*	fish *K*
	fasten *4th*	feud *6th*	fishing *1st*
fable *5th*	fat *1st*	fever *4th*	fishline *5th*

fist *2nd*	floor *K*	forego *5th*	fragile *6th*
fit *K*	flop *6th*	forehead *4th*	fragment *6th*
fitness *3rd*	flora *6th*	foreign *5th*	fragrant *5th*
fitting *2nd*	floss *2nd*	foreman *6th*	frail *6th*
five *K*	flotation *6th*	foresight *6th*	frame *3rd*
fix *1st*	flotsum *6th*	forest *1st*	framework *4th*
fixture *6th*	flounder *5th*	foretell *6th*	frank *4th*
fizz *5th*	flour *3rd*	forever *3rd*	frantic *5th*
flag *3rd*	flourish *4th*	forfeit *6th*	fraud *6th*
flagpole *5th*	flow *1st*	forge *5th*	freckles *1st*
flail *6th*	flower *K*	forget *1st*	free *K*
flair *6th*	fluid *6th*	forgive *2nd*	freedom *3rd*
flake *1st*	fluorescent *6th*	fork *1st*	freely *K*
flame *3rd*	flush *4th*	forlorn *6th*	freeze (ing) *4th*
flamingo *5th*	fluster *6th*	form *1st*	freight *4th*
flank *5th*	flute *5th*	formal *4th*	French *1st*
flannel *5th*	fly *K*	formation *4th*	frequent *4th*
flap *4th*	foal *2nd*	former *6th*	fresco *5th*
flare *6th*	foam *4th*	formidable *6th*	fresh *2nd*
flash *2nd*	focus *5th*	formula *6th*	freshwater *4th*
flat *2nd*	foe *4th*	forsake *6th*	fret *5th*
flatter *4th*	fog *1st*	fort *5th*	friar *5th*
flavor *4th*	fold *1st*	forth *2nd*	friction *6th*
flaw *2nd*	foliage *6th*	forthright *5th*	Friday *1st*
flax *6th*	folk *3rd*	fortnight *6th*	fried *5th*
flea *5th*	folklore *5th*	fortress *5th*	friend *1st*
flee *5th*	follow (ing) *1st*	fortunate *4th*	friendship *2nd*
fleece *6th*	folly *4th*	fortune *3rd*	fright *2nd*
fleet *6th*	fond *4th*	forty *1st*	frightened *5th*
flesh *3rd*	food *K*	forward *1st*	frigid *6th*
flew *1st*	fool (ish) *2nd*	fossil *4th*	fringe *5th*
flexible *6th*	foot *K*	foul *4th*	frizz *5th*
flicker *5th*	football *1st*	found *K*	fro *5th*
flight *2nd*	footstep *3rd*	foundation *5th*	frock *4th*
fling *6th*	for *K*	fountain *3rd*	frog *K*
flint *5th*	forbid (den) *4th*	four *K*	frolic *6th*
flip *2nd*	force *1st*	fourteen *1st*	from *K*
flipper *4th*	forceful *2nd*	fourth *1st*	front *1st*
flirt *6th*	ford *5th*	fowl *4th*	frontier *5th*
float *1st*	fore *6th*	fox *K*	frost *4th*
flock *2nd*	forecast *4th*	foxglove *5th*	frown *2nd*
flood *2nd*	forefather *6th*	fraction *4th*	froze *4th*

fruit *2nd*
fry *1st*
fuel *4th*
fugitive *4th*
fulfill *4th*
full *K*
fumble *5th*
fume *3rd*
fun *K*
function *4th*
fund *4th*
fundamental *4th*
funeral *4th*
fungus *5th*
funnel *3rd*
funny *1st*
fur *K*
furious *4th*
furnace *4th*
furnish *4th*
furniture *3rd*
furrow *6th*
further *2nd*
fury *4th*
fuse *4th*
fuss *1st*
future *5th*

gab *1st*
gag *1st*
gain *2nd*
gait *6th*
gale *2nd*
gallant *4th*
gallery *5th*
gallon *2nd*
gallop *4th*
gallows *6th*
gamble *5th*
game *K*
gang *1st*
gap *K*

gape *5th*
garage *6th*
garb *5th*
garbage *6th*
garden *K*
gargle *6th*
garland *6th*
garment *4th*
garnish *6th*
garrison *5th*
gas *1st*
gasp *4th*
gate *1st*
gather *1st*
gaunt *6th*
gave *K*
gay *1st*
gaze *5th*
gazelle *5th*
gear *1st*
gee *K*
gelatin *5th*
general *2nd*
generation *4th*
generous *4th*
genial *5th*
genius *4th*
gentle *3rd*
gentleman *3rd*
genuine *5th*
geographic *5th*
geography *5th*
geologist *5th*
geology *5th*
germ *6th*
German *2nd*
gesture *4th*
get *K*
getting *1st*
ghastly *6th*
ghost *K*
giant *2nd*

gift *K*
gigantic *5th*
gild *6th*
gill *4th*
gin *6th*
ginger *5th*
gingerbread *1st*
gingerly *6th*
giraffe *K*
girdle *6th*
girl *K*
girlfriend *4th*
give *K*
glacier *3rd*
glad *K*
glance *3rd*
gland *5th*
glare *4th*
glass *1st*
glasses *1st*
glaze *6th*
gleam *1st*
glee (ful) *5th*
glen *6th*
glide *4th*
glimmer *6th*
glimpse *4th*
glisten *6th*
glitter *4th*
globe *4th*
gloom *3rd*
glory *3rd*
glove *4th*
glow *1st*
glue *1st*
glum *4th*
gnarled *5th*
gnash *4th*
gnat *5th*
gnaw *1st*
gnome *6th*
go *K*

goal *4th*
goat *K*
gobble *4th*
goblin *4th*
god *1st*
goddess *1st*
godfather *3rd*
godmother *3rd*
goes *1st*
goggle *4th*
goggles *4th*
going *1st*
gold *K*
golden *K*
goldenrod *5th*
goldfinch *5th*
goldfish *K*
golf *4th*
gone *1st*
good *K*
good-bye *1st*
good-natured *5th*
good-night *2nd*
goose *K*
gooseberry *5th*
gopher *1st*
gorge *5th*
gorgeous *5th*
gorilla *1st*
gospel *6th*
gossip *5th*
got *K*
gourd *5th*
govern *2nd*
government *1st*
gown *4th*
grab *4th*
grace *3rd*
grade *2nd*
gradual *3rd*
graduate *4th*
graham *6th*

grain *3rd*
grammar *6th*
grand *2nd*
grandfather *1st*
grandmother *1st*
grant *2nd*
grape *2nd*
grapefruit *5th*
grapeshot *6th*
grapple *6th*
grasp *4th*
grass *K*
grasshopper *1st*
grateful *4th*
grave *3rd*
gravel *4th*
gravity *5th*
gravy *4th*
gray *1st*
graze *5th*
grease *5th*
great *K*
greed (y) *4th*
green *K*
greenery *3rd*
greenhouse *3rd*
greet *3rd*
grey *3rd*
greyhound *3rd*
grief *5th*
grim *4th*
grin *1st*
grind *4th*
grip *4th*
gripe *5th*
grizzly *4th*
groan *3rd*
grocery *4th*
groom *5th*
groove *5th*
grope *6th*
gross *3rd*

ground *1st*
group *1st*
grove *4th*
grow *K*
growl *4th*
grown-up *1st*
grub *5th*
grudge *5th*
grudgingly *5th*
gruel *6th*
gruff *1st*
grumble *5th*
grunt *3rd*
guarantee *6th*
guard *1st*
guess *1st*
guest *3rd*
guide *1st*
guidepost *6th*
guilt (y) *4th*
guitar *1st*
gulf *4th*
gully *6th*
gulp *1st*
gum *K*
gun *K*
gust *5th*
gut *1st*
gutter *6th*
guttural *6th*
guy *1st*
gym *1st*
gymnasium *5th*
gypsy *6th*

habit *3rd*
habitable *6th*
habitat *6th*
hackle *6th*
had *K*
hadn't *1st*
hail *4th*

hair *K*
hale *2nd*
half *1st*
half-mast *5th*
hall *1st*
halt *4th*
ham *K*
hamburger *4th*
hammer *2nd*
hamster *1st*
hand *K*
handcuffs *1st*
handkerchief *4th*
handle *2nd*
handsome *3rd*
hang *2nd*
happen *1st*
happy *K*
harbor *2nd*
hard *K*
harden *2nd*
hardship *5th*
hardy *5th*
hare *3rd*
hark *6th*
harm *3rd*
harmonize *4th*
harmony *4th*
harness *4th*
harp *4th*
harsh *5th*
harvest (ing) *4th*
has *K*
hasn't *1st*
haste *2nd*
hasty *2nd*
hat *K*
hatch *4th*
hate *2nd*
hateful *3rd*
haughty *6th*
haul *4th*

haunch *5th*
haunt *2nd*
have *K*
haven't *1st*
hawk *3rd*
hay *K*
hazard *6th*
he *K*
he'd *1st*
head *K*
headache *6th*
headquarters *3rd*
heal *3rd*
health *K*
heap *4th*
hear *K*
heard *K*
heart *K*
heartache *6th*
hearth *5th*
hearty *5th*
heat *1st*
heathen *6th*
heave *5th*
heaven *1st*
heavenly *2nd*
heavy *1st*
hectic *3rd*
hedge *4th*
heed *4th*
heel *3rd*
height *4th*
heir *4th*
hello *K*
helm *6th*
help *K*
helper *1st*
helping *1st*
hem *1st*
hemisphere *6th*
hemlock *6th*
hemp *5th*

hen *K*
hence *3rd*
her *K*
herald *3rd*
herb *5th*
herd *2nd*
here *K*
hereafter *6th*
here's *1st*
hermit *5th*
hero *1st*
heroic *5th*
herring *5th*
hers *K*
herself *1st*
hesitate *4th*
hew *6th*
hey *K*
hi *K*
hidden *1st*
hide *1st*
hideous *6th*
high *K*
higher *1st*
highway *4th*
hike *3rd*
hill *K*
hillside *4th*
him *K*
himself *1st*
hind *4th*
hinder *6th*
hindquarter *5th*
Hindu *5th*
hinge *5th*
hint *1st*
hip *1st*
hippo *K*
hippopotamus *3rd*
hire *3rd*
his *K*
hiss *3rd*

history *2nd*
hit *K*
hither *6th*
hive *2nd*
hoarfrost *6th*
hoarse *5th*
hoary *6th*
hoax *5th*
hobby *3rd*
hockey *3rd*
hoe *2nd*
hog *K*
hogan *2nd*
hoist *6th*
hold *1st*
hole *K*
holiday *K*
hollow *3rd*
holy *5th*
homage *6th*
home *K*
homespun *5th*
homework *1st*
honest *3rd*
honey *1st*
honeysuckle *5th*
honk *1st*
honor *1st*
hood *4th*
hoof (ves) *1st*
hook *4th*
hoop *5th*
hoot *1st*
hop *K*
hope *K*
hopped *1st*
horde *6th*
horizon *4th*
horizontal *6th*
horn *3rd*
hornet *5th*
horrible *1st*

horrid *4th*
horrify *4th*
horror *4th*
horse *K*
hose *6th*
hospital *3rd*
host *4th*
hostile *4th*
hot *K*
hotel *3rd*
hothouse *5th*
hound *2nd*
hour *1st*
house *K*
housekeeper *3rd*
housework *3rd*
hover *5th*
how *K*
however *1st*
howl *4th*
hue *6th*
hug *1st*
huge *1st*
hull *4th*
hum *1st*
human *3rd*
humble *4th*
humor *4th*
hump *3rd*
hunch *6th*
hundred *1st*
hunger *2nd*
hungry *2nd*
hunker *6th*
hunt *2nd*
hurl *5th*
hurry (ied) *1st*
hurt *K*
husband *1st*
hush *3rd*
hut *4th*
hydrogen *6th*

hyena *4th*
hymn *5th*
hysteria *6th*
hysterical *6th*

I *K*
ice *K*
iceberg *3rd*
icebox *1st*
I'd *1st*
idea *1st*
ideal *3rd*
identical *6th*
identify *4th*
identity *5th*
idiot *6th*
idle *4th*
idol (ize) *6th*
if *K*
ignite *6th*
ignorant *4th*
ignore *5th*
ill *1st*
I'll *1st*
illegal *1st*
illuminate *6th*
illusion *6th*
illustration *4th*
illustrious *6th*
I'm *1st*
image *4th*
imagine *2nd*
imitate *5th*
immaculate *6th*
immature *5th*
immediate *3rd*
immense *4th*
immigrant *6th*
immobile *6th*
immortal *4th*
imp *5th*
impart *6th*

impatient *5th*	inferior *5th*	insure *5th*	it's *1st*
imperial *5th*	infinite *5th*	intelligent *4th*	itself *2nd*
impetus *6th*	inflect *6th*	intend *6th*	I've *1st*
implement *6th*	influence *5th*	intense (ive) *6th*	ivory *3rd*
imply *5th*	inform *5th*	intent *5th*	ivy *2nd*
import *5th*	informal *5th*	intention *6th*	
important *1st*	information *5th*	interest *1st*	jab *1st*
impose *4th*	ingenious *6th*	interfere *4th*	jack *1st*
impossible *3rd*	ingredient *4th*	interior *5th*	jackal *5th*
impress *5th*	inhabit *6th*	internal *6th*	jackdaw *5th*
impression *5th*	inherit *5th*	international *5th*	jacket *3rd*
imprint *4th*	initial *6th*	interpret *5th*	jagged *5th*
imprison *6th*	initiate *5th*	interrupt *3rd*	jaguar *4th*
improve *3rd*	initiative *6th*	interval *6th*	jail *4th*
impulse *5th*	injure *5th*	interview *5th*	jam *K*
in *K*	injury *5th*	intestine *4th*	January *1st*
incapable *6th*	ink *2nd*	intimate *5th*	jar *K*
incense *5th*	inland *5th*	into *1st*	jasper *5th*
inch *1st*	inlet *4th*	intricate *6th*	jaunty *6th*
incident *5th*	inn *4th*	introduce *5th*	jaw *4th*
incline (d) *5th*	inner *5th*	intrude *6th*	jay *1st*
include *3rd*	innocent *5th*	invade (ing) *5th*	jealous *5th*
income *4th*	innumerable *5th*	invent *2nd*	jeans *1st*
inconvenient *6th*	inquire *3rd*	invest *5th*	jeep *1st*
increase *3rd*	insane *6th*	investigate *5th*	jeer *5th*
incredible *6th*	inscribe *5th*	invisible *6th*	jell *1st*
incredulous *6th*	inscription *6th*	invite *3rd*	jelly *1st*
indeed *1st*	insect *4th*	involve *6th*	jellybean *4th*
independent *3rd*	insert *6th*	inward *6th*	jellyfish *2nd*
index *6th*	inside *1st*	iris *5th*	jersey *5th*
Indian *1st*	insist *5th*	irk *6th*	jest *4th*
indicate *4th*	inspect *5th*	iron *2nd*	Jew *K*
indifferent *5th*	inspire *4th*	irregular *6th*	jewel (ry) *5th*
indignant *5th*	install *6th*	irritate *6th*	jibe *6th*
indispensable *6th*	instance *5th*	Islam *5th*	jingle *2nd*
individual *3rd*	instant *3rd*	island *2nd*	job *K*
indoor *6th*	instead *1st*	isn't *1st*	jog *2nd*
induce *5th*	instinct *5th*	issue *4th*	join (ed) *3rd*
indulge *5th*	institute *5th*	it *K*	joint *4th*
industry *5th*	instruct *4th*	itch *5th*	joke *1st*
infant *5th*	instrument *3rd*	item *5th*	jolly *4th*
infect *6th*	insult *5th*	its *K*	jostle *6th*

jot *1st*	king *K*	lair *5th*	lazy *4th*
journal *2nd*	kingbird *2nd*	lake *1st*	lead *1st*
journey *3rd*	kingdom *3rd*	lamb *K*	leaf *1st*
joust *6th*	kingfisher *5th*	lame *4th*	league *3rd*
jovial *5th*	kiss *K*	lament *6th*	leak *6th*
joy *1st*	kit *1st*	lamp *1st*	lean (ing) *3rd*
judge *1st*	kitchen *1st*	lance *4th*	leap *3rd*
jug *1st*	kite *K*	land *K*	learn *1st*
juice *K*	kitten *K*	landing *1st*	lease *6th*
July *1st*	knapsack *4th*	landslide *5th*	least *1st*
jump *K*	knave *5th*	lane *4th*	leather *1st*
jumped *1st*	knead *4th*	language *2nd*	leave (s) *1st*
June *1st*	knee *1st*	lanky *5th*	lecture *5th*
jungle *4th*	kneel *4th*	lantern *5th*	led *K*
junior *4th*	knew *1st*	lap *K*	ledge *5th*
junk *3rd*	knife *1st*	lapse *6th*	lee *5th*
jury *4th*	knight *2nd*	lard *6th*	leech *4th*
just *1st*	knit *4th*	large *K*	leek *5th*
justice *3rd*	knock *3rd*	lark *5th*	left *1st*
justification *5th*	knot *4th*	larkspur *5th*	leg *K*
juvenile *5th*	know (n) *1st*	lash *4th*	legal *5th*
	know-how *2nd*	lass *1st*	legend *5th*
kaiser *5th*	knowledge *2nd*	lasso *4th*	legion *6th*
kangaroo *1st*	knuckle *4th*	last *K*	legislation *5th*
karate *1st*	koala *K*	latch *6th*	legitimate *6th*
keen *4th*	Koran *5th*	late *K*	leisure *5th*
keep *K*		later *1st*	lemon *2nd*
keeper *1st*	lab *1st*	Latin *5th*	lend *K*
keg *1st*	label *3rd*	latitude *5th*	length *2nd*
kettle *4th*	labor *1st*	latter *3rd*	lens *1st*
key *K*	laboratory *4th*	laugh *1st*	Lent *4th*
keyboard *1st*	lace *4th*	launch *5th*	leopard *1st*
khaki *6th*	lack *1st*	laundry *6th*	less *1st*
kick *1st*	lad *K*	laurel *5th*	lessen *1st*
kid *K*	ladder *2nd*	lava *4th*	lesson *3rd*
kill *1st*	laden *6th*	lavender *2nd*	lest *4th*
kilo *6th*	ladle *4th*	lavish *6th*	let *K*
kilogram *2nd*	lady *1st*	law *1st*	let's *1st*
kilometer *2nd*	ladybird *2nd*	lawn *2nd*	letter (s) *1st*
kin *1st*	lag *1st*	lawyer *5th*	lettuce *4th*
kind *K*	lagoon *5th*	lay *1st*	levee *6th*
kindle *5th*	laid *2nd*	layer *4th*	level *3rd*

levy *6th*	liter *6th*	lope *5th*	mad *K*
liable *6th*	literal *6th*	lord *2nd*	madam *4th*
liberal *4th*	literature *5th*	lose *K*	made *K*
liberty *3rd*	litter *2nd*	loss *K*	madness *3rd*
library *3rd*	little *K*	lost *K*	magazine *3rd*
lice *2nd*	live *1st*	lot *K*	magic *1st*
license *5th*	lived *1st*	lotus *5th*	magician *5th*
lick *1st*	lives *1st*	loud *1st*	magistrate *6th*
lid *1st*	livestock *3rd*	lounge *6th*	magnet *3rd*
lie *1st*	living *1st*	love *K*	magnificent *4th*
lieutenant *4th*	lizard *1st*	loved *1st*	magnify *3rd*
life *1st*	llama *1st*	lovely *1st*	magnolia *5th*
lift *1st*	load *2nd*	low *K*	magpie *5th*
light *K*	loaf *4th*	lowland *6th*	maid *3rd*
lighthouse *2nd*	loan *4th*	loyal *5th*	maiden *4th*
lightweight *4th*	lobster *3rd*	luck *1st*	mail *1st*
like *K*	local *3rd*	lucky *K*	mailbox *1st*
likely *1st*	locality *4th*	lug *1st*	mailman *1st*
likes *1st*	locate *3rd*	luggage *4th*	maim *4th*
lilac *5th*	location *3rd*	lull *5th*	main *3rd*
lily *1st*	lock *1st*	lumber *1st*	mainland *5th*
limb *4th*	locket *3rd*	lumbering *1st*	maintain *4th*
limber *4th*	locomotive *5th*	lumberman *1st*	maize *2nd*
lime *4th*	locust *5th*	lump *4th*	majesty *4th*
limestone *4th*	lodge *4th*	lunatic *6th*	major *3rd*
limit *3rd*	loft *5th*	lunch *1st*	majority *3rd*
limp *5th*	lofty *5th*	lung *4th*	make *K*
limpet *3rd*	log *K*	lunge *6th*	maker *1st*
limpid *6th*	logger *4th*	lurch *5th*	making *K*
linden *5th*	logic *6th*	lure *5th*	male *4th*
line *K*	logo *4th*	lurk *5th*	malice *6th*
linen *4th*	loincloth *6th*	lush *6th*	malignant *6th*
linger *4th*	lone *2nd*	lust *6th*	malinger *6th*
link *5th*	lonely *2nd*	luster *4th*	mall *K*
lion *K*	long (ing) *1st*	luxury *4th*	mallard *4th*
lip *1st*	longitude *5th*	lye *2nd*	malt *2nd*
liquid *3rd*	look *K*	lynx *4th*	mama *1st*
liquor *5th*	looked *1st*	lyre *6th*	mammal *5th*
list *2nd*	looking *1st*		mammoth *5th*
listen *1st*	loom *5th*	ma'am *6th*	man *K*
listless *6th*	loop *5th*	machine (ry) *1st*	manage *4th*
lit *K*	loose *3rd*	mackerel *5th*	manager *4th*

mandarin 5th	master 1st	mellow 6th	milk 1st
mane 1st	mastiff 5th	melody 4th	mill 1st
mango 5th	mastodon 1st	melon 3rd	millimeter 2nd
manifest 5th	mat K	melt 2nd	million 3rd
mankind 4th	match (ing) 3rd	member 1st	mimic 6th
manly K	mate 4th	memory 3rd	mimosa 5th
manner 1st	material 5th	men 1st	mince 6th
mansion 5th	mathematical 5th	menace 5th	mind 1st
mantle 4th	mathematics 5th	mend 1st	mine 1st
manufacture 3rd	matter 1st	mental 5th	mineral 5th
manure 5th	mattress 6th	mention 5th	mingle 4th
manuscript 6th	mature 5th	menu 6th	miniature 6th
many K	maturity 6th	meow K	minimum 6th
map 1st	maxim 6th	merchandise 6th	minister 4th
maple 2nd	maximum 6th	merchant 3rd	mink 3rd
mar 6th	May 1st	mercury 6th	minnow 4th
marble 4th	may K	mercy 4th	minor 5th
March 1st	maybe 1st	mere 3rd	minority 6th
march 1st	mayonnaise 4th	merit 4th	minstrel 5th
mare 4th	mayor 4th	mermaid 4th	mint 5th
margin 5th	me K	merry 3rd	minuet 5th
marigold 5th	mead 6th	mesa 6th	minus 1st
marine 5th	meadow 3rd	mess 1st	minute 1st
Marines 1st	meal 3rd	message 1st	miracle 5th
mark 1st	mean 1st	met 1st	miraculous 6th
market 1st	mean (average) 5th	metal 3rd	mirror 4th
marquis 6th	meaning 3rd	meteor 5th	mirth 5th
marrow 5th	measure 2nd	meter 2nd	mischief 4th
marry 1st	meat 1st	method 2nd	miser 5th
marsh 5th	meatloaf 5th	metropolitan 6th	miserable 4th
marshal 5th	mechanic 5th	microphone 6th	misery 4th
marsupial 1st	mechanical 6th	microscope 4th	misfortune 5th
martyr 6th	mechanism 6th	middle 2nd	mislead 5th
marvel 4th	medal 6th	midge 5th	miss K
marvelous 4th	meddle 6th	midnight 3rd	mission 5th
mash 4th	mediate 5th	might (y) 1st	mist 1st
mask 2nd	medicine 4th	migrant 4th	mistake 1st
mason 5th	meditate 6th	mike 1st	mistreat 3rd
mass 3rd	medium 5th	mild 4th	mistress 4th
massacre 6th	meek 2nd	mile 1st	misuse 3rd
massive 5th	meet K	milestone 5th	mitten 1st
mast 4th	melancholy 6th	military 3rd	mix 1st

mixed *1st*	moor *5th*	multiply *2nd*	name *K*
mixture *4th*	moose *K*	mumble *4th*	nap *K*
mix-up *2nd*	mop *1st*	mums *4th*	napkin *5th*
moan *5th*	mope *5th*	municipal *6th*	napping *1st*
mob *4th*	moral *3rd*	murder *3rd*	narcissus *4th*
mobil *6th*	more *K*	murmur *4th*	narrate *6th*
mobilize *6th*	moreover *3rd*	muscle *4th*	narrow *2nd*
moccasin *2nd*	Mormon *4th*	muse *4th*	nasturtium *4th*
mock *4th*	morning *1st*	museum *4th*	nation *1st*
mock-up *6th*	morsel *5th*	mush *5th*	native *1st*
mode *5th*	mortal *4th*	mushroom *4th*	natural *2nd*
model *3rd*	mortgage *6th*	music *K*	naturalist *6th*
moderate *4th*	Moslem *5th*	musical *5th*	nature *1st*
modern *2nd*	mosque *5th*	musician *4th*	naught *5th*
modest *4th*	mosquito *4th*	musk *5th*	naughty *5th*
modify *5th*	moss *1st*	musket *5th*	navigate *5th*
moist *4th*	most *1st*	muskrat *5th*	Navy *1st*
moisture *3rd*	moth *1st*	muss *1st*	nay *4th*
mold *5th*	mother *K*	mussel *3rd*	Nazareth *4th*
mole *2nd*	motion *3rd*	must *1st*	Neanderthal *5th*
molecule *5th*	motivate *6th*	mustang *4th*	near (ing) *1st*
mom (my) *K*	motive *5th*	mustard *4th*	nearly *1st*
moment *1st*	motor *4th*	muster *6th*	neat *K*
momentum *6th*	motto *6th*	mute *6th*	nebula *4th*
monarch *5th*	mound *2nd*	mutiny *6th*	necessary *1st*
monastery *5th*	mount *2nd*	mutt *4th*	neck *1st*
Monday *1st*	mountain *2nd*	mutter *4th*	need *1st*
money *K*	mourn *4th*	mutton *5th*	needle *3rd*
mongoose *5th*	mouse *K*	mutual *5th*	negative *6th*
monk *4th*	mouth *1st*	muzzle *6th*	neglect *4th*
monkey *K*	move *K*	my *K*	neighbor *2nd*
monopoly *6th*	movement *2nd*	myriad *6th*	neighborhood *2nd*
Monsieur *4th*	movie *1st*	myrtle *4th*	neither *1st*
monster *1st*	Mr. *K*	myself *1st*	nephew *4th*
monstrous *5th*	Mrs. *K*	mystery *1st*	nervous *1st*
month *1st*	Ms. *K*	mystic *4th*	nest *1st*
monument *2nd*	much *1st*	myth *4th*	net *3rd*
moo *1st*	mud *1st*		nettle *4th*
mood *3rd*	muffin *4th*	nab *1st*	neutral *6th*
moon *1st*	mug *1st*	nag *1st*	never *K*
moonbeam *4th*	mulberry *4th*	nail *2nd*	nevertheless *4th*
moonlight *4th*	mule *2nd*	naked *4th*	new *K*

newspaper *1st*
next *K*
nibble *4th*
nice *1st*
nickel *1st*
niece *3rd*
night *1st*
nightingale *4th*
nine *K*
nineteen *1st*
ninety *1st*
nip *1st*
nitrogen *6th*
no *K*
noble *3rd*
nobody *1st*
nod *1st*
noise *1st*
noisy *5th*
nominate *5th*
none *1st*
nonetheless *5th*
nonfiction *5th*
nonsense *5th*
nook *6th*
noon *1st*
nor *3rd*
normal *5th*
north *1st*
nose *1st*
nostril *5th*
not *K*
notable *5th*
notch *5th*
note *1st*
nothing *1st*
notice *1st*
noticeable *3rd*
notify *3rd*
notion *5th*
nourish *6th*
novel *5th*

November *1st*
novice *5th*
now *K*
nuclear *6th*
nucleus *4th*
nuisance *6th*
number *K*
numeral *5th*
numerous *4th*
nun *1st*
nurse *K*
nut *K*
nutmeg *4th*
nuzzle *1st*
nymph *6th*

oak *1st*
oar *1st*
oarlock *4th*
oat *1st*
oath *5th*
oatmeal *5th*
obey *3rd*
object *1st*
objective *2nd*
obligation *6th*
oblige *6th*
obscure *6th*
observe *3rd*
obstacle *5th*
obstinate *5th*
obtain *5th*
obvious *5th*
occasion *3rd*
occupation *6th*
occupy *3rd*
occur *3rd*
ocean *1st*
o'clock *4th*
October *1st*
octopus *1st*
odd *4th*

odor *3rd*
of *K*
off *K*
offend *4th*
offensive *4th*
offer *2nd*
office *1st*
officer *1st*
official *3rd*
often *1st*
oh *1st*
oil *K*
O.K. *K*
okay *1st*
old *K*
older *1st*
olive *4th*
omen *6th*
ominous *6th*
omit *6th*
on *K*
once *1st*
one *K*
oneself *3rd*
onion *2nd*
only *K*
onto *1st*
onward *3rd*
onyx *5th*
opal *5th*
open *K*
opera *4th*
operate *3rd*
operation *3rd*
operator *5th*
opinion *3rd*
opossum *3rd*
opponent *5th*
opportunity *3rd*
oppose *3rd*
opposite *3rd*
oppress *6th*

or *K*
oracle *6th*
orange *K*
orbit *4th*
orchard *5th*
orchestra *6th*
orchid *4th*
ordain *6th*
order *1st*
ordinary *3rd*
ore *4th*
organ *4th*
organic *6th*
organism *6th*
organize *4th*
orient *5th*
original *3rd*
oriole *3rd*
ornament *4th*
orphan *5th*
osprey *5th*
ostrich *1st*
other *1st*
otherwise *3rd*
otter *1st*
ought *1st*
ounce *2nd*
our *K*
ourselves *3rd*
out *K*
outcome *4th*
outcry *4th*
outer *5th*
outer space *5th*
outlandish *6th*
outline *4th*
outrage *6th*
outright *6th*
outside *1st*
outstanding *2nd*
outward *6th*
outwit *6th*

oval *1st*	pane *5th*	passport *6th*	peer *1st*
oven *1st*	panel *6th*	past *1st*	peg *1st*
ovenbird *2nd*	pang *6th*	paste *1st*	pelican *1st*
over *K*	panic *1st*	pastel *4th*	pellet *6th*
overflow *5th*	panther *3rd*	pastime *6th*	pen *1st*
overlook *4th*	pantry *5th*	pastor *4th*	penalty *5th*
overseas *4th*	pants *1st*	pasty *5th*	pencil *1st*
oversee *1st*	papa *1st*	pat *K*	penetrate *5th*
overtake *5th*	paper *K*	patch *4th*	penguin *1st*
overthrow *2nd*	papier-mache *6th*	patent *4th*	peninsula *6th*
overwhelm *5th*	paprika *4th*	path *1st*	penny *1st*
owe *3rd*	papyrus *4th*	pathetic *6th*	pension *6th*
owl *K*	parade *2nd*	patient *4th*	people *K*
own *1st*	paradise *4th*	patriot *4th*	pepper *4th*
ox *K*	paragraph *6th*	patrol *1st*	peppermint *4th*
oxygen *4th*	parakeet *5th*	patron *5th*	perceive *6th*
oyster *4th*	parallel *5th*	patter *6th*	percent *4th*
ozone *5th*	paralysis *6th*	pattern *3rd*	perch *4th*
	paralyze *6th*	pause *3rd*	perfect *3rd*
pace *3rd*	paranormal *5th*	pave *5th*	perform *4th*
pack *1st*	parcel *4th*	pavilion *5th*	perfume *3rd*
package *4th*	pardon *4th*	paw *1st*	perhaps *1st*
packet *5th*	parent *3rd*	pay *K*	peril *5th*
pad *K*	parish *6th*	paying *1st*	period *2nd*
paddle *1st*	park *1st*	payment *1st*	periodic *4th*
page *1st*	parlor *4th*	pea *1st*	perish *4th*
pageant *6th*	parrot *1st*	peace *1st*	permanent *5th*
pagoda *5th*	parsley *4th*	peach *1st*	permit *3rd*
paid *2nd*	parsnip *4th*	peacock *1st*	perpetual *6th*
pail *2nd*	parson *6th*	peak *4th*	perplex *6th*
pain *2nd*	part *1st*	peal *6th*	persecute *6th*
paint *2nd*	partial *6th*	peanut *3rd*	persimmon *4th*
pair *1st*	particle *5th*	pear *4th*	persist *5th*
pal *K*	particular *4th*	pearl *4th*	person *1st*
palace *1st*	partition *6th*	peasant *4th*	personal *3rd*
pale *3rd*	partner *5th*	pebble *4th*	personality *5th*
paleontologist *5th*	partridge *1st*	peck *1st*	perspire *6th*
pallet *5th*	part-time *3rd*	peculiar *4th*	persuade *5th*
palm *4th*	party *K*	peddler *5th*	pest *1st*
pamphlet *6th*	pass *K*	peek *2nd*	pester *2nd*
pan *K*	passenger *4th*	peel *2nd*	pestilence *6th*
panda *K*	passion *6th*	peep *4th*	pet *1st*

petal *5th*	pine *1st*	pleat *5th*	pomp *6th*
petrify *4th*	pineapple *4th*	pledge *5th*	pond *1st*
petroleum *6th*	pinecone *2nd*	plentiful *2nd*	ponder *6th*
petticoat *6th*	pink *1st*	plenty *1st*	pony *K*
petty *6th*	pint *2nd*	pliers *3rd*	poodle *4th*
pewter *5th*	pioneer *4th*	plight *6th*	pool *1st*
Pharaoh *6th*	pious *6th*	plod *5th*	poor *K*
phase *6th*	pipe *1st*	plop *1st*	pop *K*
pheasant *4th*	pipeline *6th*	plot *4th*	popcorn *1st*
phenomenon *6th*	pirate *5th*	plow *4th*	Pope *5th*
philosophy *5th*	pistol *5th*	pluck *1st*	poplar *4th*
phone *2nd*	pit *1st*	plug *5th*	poppy *2nd*
phonograph *5th*	pitch *2nd*	plum *4th*	popular *3rd*
photograph *5th*	piteous *6th*	plumber *5th*	population *3rd*
phrase *5th*	pity *3rd*	plume *6th*	porch *3rd*
physical *5th*	pivot *5th*	plump *6th*	porcupine *2nd*
physics *6th*	pizza *K*	plunder *5th*	pore *6th*
piano *4th*	place *1st*	plunge *4th*	pork *6th*
pick *1st*	plague *5th*	plural *4th*	porpoise *1st*
picket *3rd*	plain *2nd*	plus *1st*	porridge *5th*
pickle *1st*	plait *5th*	ply *6th*	port *3rd*
picnic *5th*	plan *1st*	p.m. *6th*	porter *5th*
picture *K*	plane *1st*	poach *6th*	portion *4th*
pie *K*	planet *4th*	pocket *1st*	portrait *5th*
piece *1st*	plank *5th*	pod *1st*	position *2nd*
piecemeal *6th*	plant *K*	poem *3rd*	positive *2nd*
pier *4th*	plantation *5th*	point *1st*	possess *3rd*
pierce *4th*	plaque *5th*	poise *6th*	possible *1st*
pig *K*	plaster *4th*	poison *3rd*	post *1st*
pigeon *1st*	plastic *3rd*	poke *1st*	postcard *1st*
pike *4th*	plate *K*	polar *3rd*	postpone *6th*
pile *1st*	plateau *6th*	pole *K*	pot *K*
pilgrim *5th*	platform *4th*	police *1st*	potato *4th*
pill *1st*	platter *6th*	policeman *1st*	pouch *1st*
pillar *5th*	play *K*	policy *5th*	poultry *6th*
pillbox *2nd*	player *1st*	polish *4th*	pounce *5th*
pillow *4th*	playground *1st*	polite *4th*	pound *2nd*
pilot *5th*	plea *5th*	political *4th*	pour *3rd*
pimento *4th*	plead *5th*	politics *4th*	poverty *5th*
pimple *5th*	pleasant *3rd*	poll *5th*	powder *3rd*
pin *K*	please *K*	pollute *3rd*	power *1st*
pinch *4th*	pleasure *2nd*	pomegranate *4th*	powerful *2nd*

practical *4th*
practice *1st*
prairie *4th*
praise *4th*
prank *5th*
pray (er) *3rd*
preach *4th*
precaution *5th*
precede *6th*
precious *4th*
precipice *6th*
precise *5th*
predict *6th*
preen *2nd*
preface *6th*
prefer *3rd*
prehistoric *5th*
prehistory *5th*
prejudice *6th*
preliminary *6th*
premise *6th*
preoccupy *5th*
prepare *1st*
prescribe *6th*
present *K*
preserve *4th*
preside *6th*
president *1st*
press *1st*
pressure *4th*
presume *6th*
pretend *2nd*
pretext *5th*
pretty *1st*
prevail *5th*
prevent *3rd*
previous (ly) *5th*
prey *4th*
price *K*
prick *5th*
pride *2nd*
priest *4th*

prim *5th*
primary *5th*
prime *5th*
primitive *5th*
prince *1st*
princess *1st*
principal *3rd*
principle *4th*
print *1st*
prior *5th*
prison *3rd*
private *3rd*
privateer *6th*
privilege *5th*
prize *3rd*
pro *5th*
probably *4th*
problem *1st*
proceed *4th*
process *4th*
procession *4th*
proclaim *4th*
procure *5th*
prod *6th*
produce *2nd*
product *4th*
production *4th*
profess *5th*
profession *5th*
professor *4th*
profile *5th*
profit *4th*
profound *6th*
program *4th*
progress *4th*
prohibit *6th*
project *4th*
prolong *5th*
promenade *5th*
prominent *5th*
promise *1st*
promote *5th*

promotion *5th*
prompt *4th*
pronghorn *5th*
pronounce *4th*
proof *4th*
prop *5th*
propel *6th*
proper *3rd*
property *3rd*
prophet *4th*
proportion *4th*
propose *4th*
proprietor *6th*
prospect *4th*
prosper *5th*
protect (ion) *4th*
protein *5th*
protest *4th*
proud *2nd*
prove *1st*
provide *3rd*
province *6th*
provision *4th*
provoke *6th*
prow *5th*
prowess *6th*
prowl *2nd*
prudent *6th*
prune *3rd*
pry *6th*
psalm *6th*
psychic *6th*
psychology *6th*
pub *1st*
public *1st*
publication *4th*
publicity *4th*
publicize *4th*
publish *4th*
pudding *4th*
puff *2nd*
pull *K*

pulp *6th*
pulse *5th*
puma *4th*
pump *4th*
pumpkin *K*
punch *4th*
punish *4th*
pup *K*
pupil *4th*
puppy *K*
purchase *3rd*
pure *3rd*
Puritan *1st*
purple *K*
purpose *1st*
purse *4th*
pursue *5th*
pursuit *5th*
push *1st*
push-up *1st*
pushy *1st*
put *K*
putting *1st*
puzzle *4th*
pyramid *5th*

quack *K*
quail *1st*
quaint *5th*
quake *4th*
Quaker *1st*
qualify *4th*
quality *4th*
quantity *4th*
quarrel *4th*
quarry *6th*
quart *2nd*
quarter *1st*
quay *5th*
queen *K*
queer *4th*
quench *6th*

query *6th*
quest *3rd*
question *1st*
quick *1st*
quicksand *1st*
quiet *K*
quill *6th*
quilt *6th*
quit *1st*
quite *1st*
quiver *4th*
quoit *6th*
quote *5th*

rabbi *4th*
rabbit *K*
raccoon *1st*
race *1st*
rack *1st*
radiant *6th*
radiate *6th*
radical *6th*
radio *1st*
radioative *6th*
radish *1st*
radius *6th*
raft *6th*
rafter *6th*
rag *1st*
rage *4th*
ragged *5th*
raid *6th*
rail *2nd*
railroad *2nd*
rain *1st*
raindrops *2nd*
rainfall *2nd*
raise *1st*
rake *1st*
rally *5th*
ram *K*
ramble *6th*

ramp *6th*
rampart *6th*
ran *K*
ranch *5th*
random *6th*
range *3rd*
ranger *1st*
rank *3rd*
ransom *6th*
rap *1st*
rapid *4th*
rapture *6th*
rare *4th*
rascal *5th*
rash *6th*
raspberry *2nd*
rat *K*
rate *1st*
rather *1st*
ratify *6th*
ratio *6th*
rattle *2nd*
rattlesnake *1st*
ravage *6th*
rave *5th*
raven *1st*
ravenous *6th*
ravine *5th*
ravish *6th*
raw *1st*
ray *1st*
razor *6th*
reach *1st*
react *5th*
read *K*
ready *1st*
real *1st*
reality *5th*
realize *2nd*
realm *4th*
reap *4th*
rear *3rd*

reason (able) *1st*
reassure *6th*
rebuke *4th*
recall *3rd*
receipt *5th*
receive *1st*
recent *3rd*
reception *5th*
recess *2nd*
recipe *4th*
recite *5th*
reckless *5th*
reckon *5th*
reclaim *6th*
recline *6th*
recognize *3rd*
recollect *6th*
recommend *5th*
recompense *6th*
reconcile *6th*
record *2nd*
recount *6th*
recourse *6th*
recover *4th*
recreation *5th*
recruit *6th*
rectangle *1st*
recur *6th*
red *K*
redeem *6th*
redouble *6th*
reduce *3rd*
redwood *4th*
reed *4th*
reef *5th*
reel *5th*
refer *5th*
refine *6th*
reflect *4th*
reflex *6th*
reform *5th*
refrain *6th*

refresh *6th*
refrigerator *2nd*
refuge *5th*
refuse *2nd*
refute *5th*
regain *6th*
regal *6th*
regard *4th*
regiment *5th*
region *4th*
register *4th*
registration *5th*
regret *5th*
regular *3rd*
regulate *5th*
rehearse *6th*
reheat *6th*
reign *4th*
reindeer *K*
reins *1st*
reject *5th*
rejoice *4th*
relate *4th*
relation *4th*
relative *4th*
relax *4th*
relay *6th*
release *5th*
relic *5th*
relief *4th*
relieve *4th*
religion *4th*
relish *6th*
reluctant *6th*
rely *5th*
remain *1st*
remark *4th*
remedy *4th*
remember *1st*
remind *3rd*
remnant *6th*
remonstrate *6th*

remorse *6th*	resource *5th*	rid *1st*	romance *5th*
remote *5th*	respect *2nd*	riddle *1st*	roof *1st*
remove *2nd*	respecting *4th*	ride *K*	room *K*
renaissance *5th*	respiration *6th*	ridge *5th*	roost *2nd*
rend *4th*	respite *6th*	ridicule *6th*	rooster *1st*
renew *4th*	respond *5th*	ridiculous *6th*	root *3rd*
renounce *6th*	responsible *4th*	riding *1st*	rope *1st*
renown *5th*	rest *1st*	rifle *4th*	rose *1st*
rent *K*	restaurant *5th*	rig *1st*	rot *1st*
repair *4th*	restless *4th*	right *K*	rotate *6th*
repeat *4th*	restore *5th*	rigid *5th*	rote *4th*
repel *6th*	restrain *5th*	rim *1st*	rough *4th*
repent *6th*	restrict *6th*	ring *1st*	round *K*
replace *5th*	result *2nd*	rinse *3rd*	roundhouse *1st*
replenish *6th*	resume *5th*	riot *6th*	rouse *4th*
reply *1st*	retain *5th*	rip *K*	roust *5th*
report *1st*	retire *4th*	ripe *1st*	route *4th*
repose *6th*	retort *5th*	ripen *1st*	routine *6th*
represent *4th*	retreat *4th*	ripple *4th*	rove *6th*
reproach *6th*	retrieve *6th*	rise *1st*	row *K*
reproduce *5th*	return *1st*	risk *4th*	royal *3rd*
reptile *4th*	reveal *4th*	rite *6th*	rub *1st*
republic *4th*	revenge *5th*	ritual *6th*	rubber *1st*
repulse *6th*	revenue *6th*	rival *4th*	rubbish *5th*
reputation *5th*	reverence *4th*	river *K*	ruby *6th*
request *4th*	reverend *4th*	road *K*	rude *2nd*
require *1st*	reverse *5th*	roadbed *1st*	ruffle *6th*
requisition *6th*	review *4th*	roam *4th*	rug *1st*
rescue *4th*	revive *6th*	roar *1st*	rugged *5th*
research *5th*	revolt *5th*	roast *4th*	ruin *5th*
resemble *4th*	revolution *5th*	rob *K*	rule *K*
resent *5th*	revolve *5th*	robe *4th*	rum *1st*
reserve *3rd*	revolver *5th*	robin *K*	rumble *3rd*
reside *5th*	reward *4th*	robot *K*	rumbled *3rd*
residence *5th*	rhinoceros *3rd*	robust *5th*	rumor *5th*
resident *5th*	rhubarb *4th*	rock *K*	run *K*
resign *5th*	rhyme *6th*	rocket *K*	running *1st*
resin *5th*	rhythm *5th*	rod *1st*	rural *5th*
resist *4th*	rib *1st*	roe *5th*	rush *2nd*
resolution *5th*	ribbon *4th*	rogue *5th*	russet *4th*
resolve *5th*	rice *1st*	role *6th*	rust *2nd*
resort *5th*	rich *K*	roll *1st*	rustle *3rd*

rut *1st*
rye *4th*

Sabbath *6th*
saber *5th*
saber-toothed *5th*
sable *5th*
sack *1st*
sacred *4th*
sacrifice *4th*
sad *K*
saddle *4th*
sadness *1st*
safe *K*
saffron *4th*
sag *1st*
saga *6th*
sage *4th*
sagebrush *4th*
said *K*
sail *1st*
sailor *3rd*
saint *3rd*
sake *3rd*
salamander *3rd*
salary *3rd*
sale *1st*
salesperson *6th*
sally *5th*
salmon *3rd*
saloon *6th*
salt *1st*
salute *4th*
salvation *6th*
same *K*
sample *5th*
sanction *6th*
sand *1st*
sane *6th*
sap *1st*
sapling *5th*
sapphire *6th*

sardine *4th*
sash *6th*
sassafras *4th*
satellite *6th*
satin *6th*
satisfy *3rd*
Saturday *1st*
satyr *6th*
sauce *5th*
saunter *6th*
sausage *4th*
saute *4th*
savage *5th*
save *1st*
savior *6th*
savor *6th*
savory *6th*
saw *K*
sawmill *1st*
say *K*
scabbard *6th*
scale *3rd*
scamper *4th*
scandal *6th*
scant *6th*
scar *5th*
scarce *4th*
scare (d) *1st*
scarecrow *1st*
scarf *6th*
scarlet *4th*
scatter *3rd*
scene *1st*
scent *3rd*
schedule *6th*
scheme *5th*
scholar *5th*
school *K*
schoolwork *1st*
science *3rd*
scientist *3rd*
scissors *5th*

scoff *6th*
scold *5th*
scoop *4th*
scope *6th*
scorch *6th*
score *1st*
scorn *4th*
scorpion *5th*
scour *6th*
scourge *6th*
scout *1st*
scow *6th*
scramble *4th*
scrap *3rd*
scrapbook *3rd*
scrape *4th*
scratch *4th*
scream *1st*
screech *5th*
screen *1st*
screw *3rd*
screwdriver *3rd*
scroll *5th*
scrub *6th*
scuff *5th*
scull *6th*
sculptor *4th*
sculpture *4th*
scurvy *6th*
scuttle *4th*
sea *K*
seal *K*
seam *5th*
search *1st*
season *2nd*
seat *1st*
second *1st*
secret *1st*
secretary *4th*
section *4th*
secure *3rd*
see *K*

seed *1st*
seek *1st*
seem *1st*
seen *1st*
seep *4th*
seesaw *1st*
seize *3rd*
seldom *4th*
select *4th*
self *3rd*
selfish *5th*
sell *K*
Senate *1st*
senate *4th*
send *K*
senior *6th*
sensation *5th*
sense *3rd*
sensible *6th*
sensitive *5th*
sensitivity *5th*
sent *K*
sentence *1st*
sentiment *5th*
sentinel *5th*
sentry *5th*
separate *3rd*
September *1st*
sequoia *2nd*
serene *6th*
serf *6th*
serge *6th*
sergeant *5th*
series *4th*
serious *4th*
sermon *5th*
serpent *5th*
servant *3rd*
serve *1st*
service *1st*
session *6th*
set *K*

settle *2nd*
seven *K*
seventeen *1st*
seventy *1st*
several *1st*
severe *4th*
sew *2nd*
sex *3rd*
shabby *4th*
shade *2nd*
shadow *3rd*
shaft *4th*
shaggy *5th*
shake *1st*
shale *6th*
shall *1st*
shallow *4th*
shaman *5th*
shame *3rd*
shape *1st*
share *2nd*
shark *1st*
sharp *1st*
shatter *5th*
shave *1st*
shawl *6th*
she *K*
sheaf *6th*
shear *5th*
sheep *K*
sheer *5th*
sheet *1st*
shelf *6th*
shell *1st*
shellfish *5th*
shelter *4th*
shepherd *4th*
sherbet *5th*
sheriff *4th*
shield *4th*
shift *4th*
shimmer *5th*

shine *1st*
shiny *3rd*
ship *1st*
shipment *5th*
shipwreck *5th*
shirk *6th*
shirt *1st*
shiver *1st*
shock *1st*
shoe *K*
shoemaker *1st*
shoot *3rd*
shop *1st*
shoplift *3rd*
shore *1st*
short *1st*
shortly *1st*
shot *1st*
should *1st*
shoulder *1st*
shouldn't *1st*
shout *1st*
shove *5th*
shovel *1st*
show *1st*
shower *4th*
showroom *4th*
shred *5th*
shrewd *6th*
shriek *4th*
shrill *5th*
shrine *5th*
shrink *5th*
shroud *6th*
shrub *4th*
shrug *4th*
shudder *4th*
shun *6th*
shut *1st*
shutter *4th*
shuttle *5th*
shy *K*

sick *K*
sickle *6th*
side *K*
sidekick *1st*
sidewalk *1st*
siege *5th*
sieve *5th*
sift *4th*
sigh *3rd*
sight *1st*
sign *1st*
signal *4th*
signature *6th*
significant *6th*
signify *6th*
silent *3rd*
silk *3rd*
silkworm *3rd*
silly *1st*
silver *1st*
similar *4th*
simmer *4th*
simple *1st*
simulate *6th*
sin *1st*
since *1st*
sincere *4th*
sinew *6th*
sing *1st*
single *3rd*
sink *3rd*
sip *1st*
sir *1st*
sire *4th*
sister *1st*
sit *K*
site *5th*
sitting *1st*
situation *4th*
sit-up *1st*
six *K*
sixteen *1st*

sixth *1st*
sixty *1st*
size *1st*
skate *1st*
skateboard *1st*
skeleton *4th*
sketch *5th*
skill *2nd*
skim *6th*
skin *1st*
skinny *1st*
skip *2nd*
skirt *3rd*
skull *5th*
skunk *K*
sky *K*
skyline *5th*
skyrocket *3rd*
slab *5th*
slam *5th*
slant *6th*
slap *2nd*
slash *6th*
slate *1st*
slaughter *5th*
slave *3rd*
slay *4th*
sled *5th*
sledge *6th*
sleek *3rd*
sleep *K*
sleeve *5th*
slender *4th*
slice *5th*
slide *2nd*
slight *4th*
slim *5th*
slip *3rd*
slipper *5th*
slit *5th*
slither *4th*
slob *5th*

slope *3rd*

sloth *5th*

slouch *6th*

slow *1st*

slug *5th*

slugger *5th*

slumber *4th*

slump *5th*

sly *4th*

smack *6th*

small *K*

smart *1st*

smash *3rd*

smear *3rd*

smell *3rd*

smile *1st*

smite *5th*

smog *5th*

smoke *1st*

smooth *2nd*

smother *6th*

smuggle *6th*

snack *2nd*

snail *1st*

snake *1st*

snap *2nd*

snare *6th*

snarl *5th*

snatch *4th*

sneak *4th*

sneer *6th*

sneeze *5th*

sniff *4th*

snooze *4th*

snore *6th*

snorkel *5th*

snort *5th*

snout *5th*

snow *K*

snowball *K*

snowman *K*

snowstorm *3rd*

snuff *6th*

snug *6th*

snuggle *5th*

so *K*

soak *5th*

soap *4th*

soar *6th*

sob *1st*

sober *4th*

soccer *1st*

social *1st*

society *3rd*

sock *1st*

socket *6th*

socks *1st*

sod *6th*

sodden *6th*

soft *K*

soil *2nd*

soldier *3rd*

sole *4th*

solemn *5th*

solid *3rd*

solitary *5th*

solution *5th*

solve *4th*

sombrero *6th*

some *K*

somebody *1st*

someday *1st*

someone *1st*

something *1st*

sometimes *1st*

somewhere *1st*

son *K*

song *K*

sonic *2nd*

sonnet *6th*

soon *K*

sooth *5th*

sore *4th*

sorrow *4th*

sorry *2nd*

sort *1st*

soul *3rd*

sound *1st*

soup *1st*

sour *2nd*

source *4th*

south *1st*

sovereign *4th*

space *1st*

spade *6th*

span *6th*

spank *2nd*

spar *5th*

spare *3rd*

spark *3rd*

sparkle *5th*

sparrow *5th*

spasm *6th*

speak *1st*

spear *4th*

spearhead *5th*

special *2nd*

species *5th*

specific *5th*

specimen *5th*

speck *4th*

spectacle *5th*

spectator *5th*

spectrum *6th*

speculate *6th*

speech *2nd*

speed *3rd*

spell *1st*

spend *2nd*

sphere *6th*

spice *3rd*

spider *K*

spike *4th*

spill *1st*

spin *1st*

spinach *2nd*

spine *4th*

spire *6th*

spirit (s) *2nd*

spiritual *5th*

spit *3rd*

spite *3rd*

splash *1st*

splendid *4th*

splendor *4th*

splinter *6th*

split *4th*

splotch *5th*

spoil *4th*

spoke *1st*

sponge *3rd*

spool *2nd*

spoon *1st*

sport *1st*

sportsman *1st*

spot *1st*

spout *5th*

sprawl *6th*

spray *2nd*

spread *2nd*

spring *K*

sprinkle *3rd*

sprint *5th*

spruce *3rd*

spur *4th*

spurt *5th*

sputter *3rd*

spy *4th*

squadron *6th*

square *2nd*

squash *2nd*

squat *5th*

squawk *2nd*

squeak *2nd*

squeeze *5th*

squid *3rd*

squire *4th*

squirm *2nd*

squirrel *1st*	steed *4th*	strand *5th*	stupid *4th*
squirt *4th*	steel *2nd*	strange (r) *1st*	sturdy *3rd*
stab *5th*	steep *2nd*	strangle *6th*	stutter *1st*
stable *4th*	steer *4th*	strap *5th*	style *3rd*
stack *3rd*	stem *2nd*	strategy *6th*	subdue *6th*
staff *4th*	step *1st*	straw *2nd*	subject *1st*
stag *1st*	stereoscope *5th*	strawberry *2nd*	sublime *6th*
stage *3rd*	stern *4th*	stray *3rd*	submarine *5th*
stagger *4th*	stew *2nd*	streak *5th*	submerge *5th*
stain *4th*	stick *K*	stream *1st*	submit *4th*
stair *2nd*	sticker *K*	street *1st*	subsequent *6th*
stake *1st*	sticky *K*	strength *1st*	subside *6th*
stalagmite *5th*	stiff *3rd*	strenuous *6th*	substance *5th*
stale *2nd*	still *1st*	stress *6th*	substantial *5th*
stalk *4th*	stimulate *6th*	stretch *4th*	substitute *5th*
stall *5th*	sting *4th*	stricken *6th*	subtle *6th*
stallion *4th*	stink *2nd*	strict *6th*	subtract *1st*
stalwart *6th*	stir *3rd*	stride *5th*	suburb *6th*
stamen *6th*	stitch *6th*	strife *5th*	success *2nd*
stammer *6th*	stock *1st*	strike *2nd*	succession *6th*
stamp *2nd*	stockade *6th*	string *1st*	such *1st*
stampede *5th*	stocking *4th*	strip *3rd*	suck *1st*
stand *K*	stomach *2nd*	stripe *1st*	suckling *6th*
standard *3rd*	stomp *4th*	strive *5th*	sudden *1st*
stanza *5th*	stone *2nd*	stroke *1st*	suffer (ing) *2nd*
staple *6th*	stood *K*	stroll *5th*	suffice *6th*
star *K*	stool *2nd*	strong *K*	sufficient *3rd*
starch *6th*	stoop *5th*	structure *4th*	suffocate *6th*
stare *3rd*	stop *K*	struggle *1st*	sugar *1st*
starfish *1st*	stoplight *1st*	strut *5th*	suggest *2nd*
start *1st*	stopped *1st*	stubble *6th*	suggestion *2nd*
startle *4th*	store *K*	stubborn *5th*	suit *1st*
starve *5th*	stork *2nd*	stuck *4th*	suitcase *1st*
state *1st*	storm *2nd*	stud *6th*	suitor *5th*
station *1st*	story *K*	student *3rd*	sulky *5th*
statue *4th*	stout *4th*	studio *5th*	sullen *5th*
stature *6th*	stove *1st*	study *1st*	sulphur *4th*
stay *1st*	stovepipe *4th*	stuff *1st*	sultan *5th*
steady *3rd*	stow *6th*	stumble *4th*	sum *1st*
steak *2nd*	straight *3rd*	stump *3rd*	sumac *4th*
steal *3rd*	strain *4th*	stun *4th*	summer *K*
steam *2nd*	strait *5th*	stunt *6th*	summit *5th*

summon *4th*	sustain *5th*	tail *1st*	tee *1st*
sun *K*	swagger *5th*	tailor *4th*	teen *2nd*
Sunday *1st*	swallow *1st*	taint *6th*	teenager *3rd*
sundown *2nd*	swamp *4th*	take *K*	teeth *1st*
sundry *6th*	swarm *4th*	taken *1st*	telegram *4th*
sunlit *2nd*	swarthy *6th*	tale *3rd*	telephone *2nd*
sunny *1st*	sway *3rd*	talent *2nd*	telescope *4th*
sunrise *2nd*	swear *4th*	talk *K*	television *5th*
sunset *1st*	sweat *3rd*	tall *K*	tell *K*
suntan *2nd*	sweater *3rd*	tame *4th*	telling *1st*
super *1st*	sweep *4th*	tan *K*	temper *4th*
superb *6th*	sweet *K*	tangle *3rd*	temperature *5th*
superintendent *5th*	sweetmeat *5th*	tank *5th*	temple *3rd*
superior *4th*	sweetness *2nd*	tankard *6th*	temporary *5th*
supernatural *5th*	sweets *1st*	Taoist *5th*	tempt *4th*
superstition *5th*	swell *3rd*	tap *K*	temptation *5th*
supervise *6th*	swift *4th*	tape *1st*	ten *K*
supper *2nd*	swim *K*	taper *5th*	tenant *5th*
supple *6th*	swine *5th*	tapestry *6th*	tend *K*
supply *1st*	swing *1st*	tar *1st*	tendency *5th*
support *4th*	swish *2nd*	target *5th*	tender *3rd*
suppose *2nd*	switch *4th*	tariff *5th*	tenement *6th*
suppress *5th*	swoop *4th*	taro *4th*	tense *5th*
supreme *5th*	sword *4th*	tarpaulin *6th*	tent *1st*
sure *K*	sycamore *4th*	tarry *5th*	term *3rd*
surf *4th*	syllable *6th*	tart *5th*	terminate *6th*
surface *3rd*	symbol *5th*	task *3rd*	terrace *5th*
surge *5th*	sympathy *4th*	taste *1st*	terrible *1st*
surgeon *5th*	symphony *6th*	taught *2nd*	terrier *5th*
surly *6th*	symptom *6th*	taunt *5th*	terrific *5th*
surmise *6th*	syrup *4th*	tavern *5th*	terrified *3rd*
surmount *6th*	system *2nd*	tawny *6th*	terrify *3rd*
surpass *6th*		tax *K*	territory *3rd*
surplus *6th*	tab *K*	taxi *1st*	terror *3rd*
surprise *1st*	table *K*	tea *1st*	test *3rd*
surrender *5th*	tablecloth *4th*	teach (ing) *1st*	tether *6th*
surround (ing) *3rd*	tablespoon *4th*	teacher *1st*	text *6th*
survey *5th*	tack *1st*	team *1st*	texture *6th*
survive *5th*	tackle *4th*	tear *2nd*	than *K*
suspect *5th*	tact *6th*	tease *3rd*	thank *1st*
suspend *5th*	tactics *6th*	teaspoon *2nd*	that *K*
suspicion *4th*	tag *K*	tedious *6th*	thatch *4th*

that's *1st*	threat *5th*	tint *5th*	tornado *6th*
the *K*	three *K*	tiny *2nd*	torrent *5th*
theater *3rd*	three-fourths *5th*	tip *1st*	tortoise *3rd*
thee *2nd*	thresh *6th*	tiptoe *4th*	torture *5th*
their *K*	threshold *5th*	tire *2nd*	toss *2nd*
them *K*	threw *1st*	tissue *5th*	total *2nd*
theme *4th*	thrift *6th*	title *3rd*	tote *5th*
themselves *1st*	thrill *4th*	to *K*	totter *6th*
then *K*	thrive *6th*	toad *2nd*	touch (ing) *1st*
thence *4th*	throat *1st*	toast *5th*	tough *5th*
theory *5th*	throb *5th*	tobacco *4th*	tour *3rd*
there *1st*	throne *4th*	today *K*	tourist *5th*
therefore *1st*	throng *5th*	toe *K*	tournament *5th*
thermometer *6th*	through *1st*	toenail *4th*	tow *1st*
these *K*	throughout *2nd*	together *1st*	toward *1st*
they *K*	throw *1st*	toil *4th*	towel *6th*
they'll *1st*	thrush *5th*	toilet *2nd*	tower *3rd*
they're *1st*	thrust *4th*	token *5th*	towhead *4th*
thick *2nd*	thud *3rd*	told *K*	town *K*
thicket *4th*	thunder *3rd*	tolerate *5th*	toxic *2nd*
thief *3rd*	Thursday *1st*	toll *6th*	toy *K*
thigh *3rd*	thus *1st*	tomato *4th*	trace *3rd*
thin *1st*	thy *3rd*	tomb *5th*	track *1st*
thing *K*	thyme *4th*	tomfoolery *5th*	tractor *K*
things *K*	thyself *5th*	tomorrow *1st*	trade *1st*
think *1st*	tick *1st*	ton *1st*	tradition *5th*
third *1st*	ticket (s) *1st*	tone *3rd*	traffic *5th*
thirsty *2nd*	tide *1st*	tongue *3rd*	tragedy *5th*
thirteen *1st*	tie *1st*	tonic *2nd*	trail *2nd*
thirty *1st*	tiger *K*	tonight *1st*	train *K*
this *K*	tight *1st*	too *1st*	trained *1st*
thistle *4th*	tile *1st*	took *1st*	trait *6th*
thorn *3rd*	till *1st*	tool *1st*	traitor *4th*
thorough *4th*	tilt *5th*	toolbox *5th*	tramp *4th*
those *1st*	timber *5th*	toot *1st*	trample *5th*
thou *1st*	time *1st*	tooth *1st*	tranquil *6th*
though *1st*	timid *5th*	toothpaste *2nd*	transfer *5th*
thought *1st*	tin *1st*	top *K*	transform *5th*
thoughtful *2nd*	tinge *5th*	topic *5th*	transit *6th*
thousand *1st*	tingle *4th*	topple *6th*	translate *5th*
thrash *4th*	tinker *5th*	torch *5th*	transmit *6th*
thread *2nd*	tinkle *5th*	torment *5th*	transom *6th*

transparent *5th*
transport *5th*
trap *1st*
trash *2nd*
travel *1st*
traverse *5th*
tray *1st*
treacherous *6th*
tread *4th*
treason *4th*
treasure *4th*
treat *2nd*
treatment *5th*
treaty *4th*
treble *6th*
tree *K*
tremble *3rd*
tremendous *4th*
tremor *6th*
trench *5th*
trend *2nd*
trespass *6th*
trial *4th*
triangle *1st*
tribe *3rd*
tribunal *6th*
tribute *5th*
trick *1st*
trickery *5th*
tricycle *K*
tried *K*
trifle *5th*
trigger *6th*
trim *4th*
trinket *6th*
trio *2nd*
trip *1st*
tripod *6th*
triumph *5th*
troll *1st*
troop *3rd*
trophy *6th*

tropic *6th*
tropical *5th*
trot *5th*
troth *6th*
trouble *1st*
troublemaker *1st*
trough *6th*
trousers *5th*
trout *4th*
truant *6th*
truce *6th*
truck *1st*
trudge *5th*
true *K*
trunk *4th*
trust *1st*
truth *1st*
try *K*
tryout *2nd*
tub *1st*
tube *3rd*
tuck *1st*
Tuesday *1st*
tuft *3rd*
tug *1st*
tulip *2nd*
tumble *4th*
tummy *K*
tumor *6th*
tumult *6th*
tune *1st*
tunic *6th*
tunnel *2nd*
turban *5th*
turbulent *5th*
turf *5th*
turkey *K*
turmoil *5th*
turn *1st*
turnip *3rd*
turquoise *5th*
turret *5th*

turtle *K*
tusk *5th*
tussle *6th*
tutor *6th*
TV *K*
twain *6th*
twang *6th*
twelve *1st*
twenty *1st*
twice *3rd*
twig *4th*
twine *3rd*
twinkle *4th*
twirl *3rd*
twist *1st*
two *K*
type *1st*
typewriter *1st*
typical *6th*
tyranny *6th*
tyrant *5th*

udder *5th*
ugh *4th*
ugly *4th*
ultimate *6th*
umbrella *2nd*
umpire *1st*
unanimous *6th*
unbidden *6th*
uncanny *6th*
uncertain *1st*
uncle *1st*
under *K*
underground *4th*
understand *1st*
undertaking *1st*
undoubtedly *5th*
unfit *1st*
unhappy *1st*
unidentified *5th*
uniform *1st*

union *3rd*
unique *6th*
unison *6th*
unit *5th*
unite *5th*
unity *5th*
universal *4th*
universe *4th*
university *4th*
unless *2nd*
unlimited *3rd*
unpaid *2nd*
unreal *1st*
unruly *6th*
until *1st*
unto *3rd*
unusual *3rd*
unzip *1st*
up *K*
uphill *1st*
uphold *6th*
upholster *6th*
upholstery *6th*
upon *1st*
upper *3rd*
upright *4th*
uproar *5th*
upset *3rd*
upstairs *3rd*
uptown *1st*
upward *4th*
uranium *6th*
urchin *3rd*
urge *4th*
urgent *6th*
us *K*
use *K*
used *K*
useful *2nd*
useless *2nd*
usher *6th*
usual *3rd*

utensil *6th*
utilize *6th*
utter *4th*

vacant *6th*
vacation *2nd*
vacuum *5th*
vague *5th*
vain *4th*
vale *4th*
valiant *6th*
valley *2nd*
valuable *4th*
value *2nd*
valve *6th*
vamoose *6th*
van *K*
vanish *3rd*
vanity *5th*
vanquish *6th*
vapor *3rd*
various *4th*
vary *4th*
vase *5th*
vast *4th*
vault *5th*
veal *4th*
veer *6th*
vegetable *2nd*
vehicle *6th*
veil *3rd*
vein *4th*
velvet *4th*
vengeance *6th*
venison *5th*
vent *4th*
venture *4th*
verdict *6th*
verge *6th*
verse *4th*
version *6th*
vertical *6th*

very *K*
vessel *4th*
vest *3rd*
vet *1st*
veteran *6th*
veterinarian *4th*
vex *5th*
vexation *5th*
vibrant *5th*
vibrate *5th*
vice *4th*
vicinity *6th*
vicious *6th*
victim *4th*
victory *4th*
view *1st*
viewpoint *5th*
vigor *5th*
vigorous *5th*
Viking *5th*
vile *6th*
village *2nd*
villain *5th*
vine *1st*
vinegar *6th*
violent *5th*
violet *2nd*
violin *4th*
virgin *6th*
virtually *6th*
virtue *4th*
visible *4th*
vision *4th*
visit *1st*
vital *5th*
vivid *6th*
vocabulary *6th*
voice *1st*
void *6th*
volcano *4th*
volume *3rd*
volunteer *5th*

vote *2nd*
vow *4th*
voyage *4th*
vulture *3rd*

waddle *5th*
wade *4th*
waft *5th*
wag *1st*
wage *3rd*
wagon *2nd*
wail *5th*
waist *4th*
wait *K*
wake *1st*
walk *K*
walked *1st*
walking *1st*
wall *K*
wallet *6th*
wallow *6th*
walnut *1st*
walrus *1st*
waltz *6th*
wan *6th*
wand *3rd*
wander *3rd*
want *K*
wanted *1st*
war *1st*
warble *6th*
ward *5th*
wardrobe *6th*
ware *5th*
warehouse *5th*
warm *1st*
warn *3rd*
warning *3rd*
warp *4th*
warrant *5th*
warrior *4th*
wary *5th*

was *K*
wash *1st*
wasn't *1st*
wasp *2nd*
waste *1st*
wasteland *6th*
watch *1st*
watchful *2nd*
water *K*
watercress *4th*
watermelon *3rd*
wave *K*
waver *5th*
wax *K*
way *K*
wayfarer *6th*
we *K*
weak *3rd*
weakness *3rd*
wealth *3rd*
weapon *4th*
wear *1st*
weary *4th*
weasel *3rd*
weather *1st*
weave *4th*
wed *K*
wedding *1st*
wedge *4th*
Wednesday *1st*
weed *1st*
week *K*
weep *4th*
weevil *5th*
weigh *1st*
weight *1st*
weird *1st*
welcome *1st*
weld *6th*
welfare *5th*
well *K*
we'll *1st*

well built *2nd*
went *K*
were *K*
we're *1st*
west *1st*
westward *3rd*
wet *K*
whale *1st*
wharf *5th*
what *K*
whatever *1st*
wheat *1st*
wheel *1st*
wheeze *5th*
when *K*
whence *4th*
whenever *3rd*
where *1st*
whereas *4th*
wherefore *4th*
whereupon *4th*
whether *1st*
which *1st*
whiff *5th*
while *1st*
whim *6th*
whimper *5th*
whine *5th*
whip *4th*
whippoorwill *4th*
whir *6th*
whirl *4th*
whisk *4th*
whiskey *6th*
whisper *1st*
whistle *4th*
white *K*
White House *K*
who *K*
whoever *1st*
whole *1st*
wholesome *5th*

wholly *5th*
whom *2nd*
whoop *6th*
whose *2nd*
why *K*
wick *1st*
wicked *4th*
wide *1st*
widespread *5th*
widow *4th*
width *4th*
wield *6th*
wife *1st*
wig *1st*
wigwam *5th*
wild *2nd*
wildcat *2nd*
wilderness *4th*
wile *6th*
will *K*
willing *5th*
willow *2nd*
wilt *4th*
win *K*
wince *5th*
wind *1st*
window *1st*
wine *1st*
wing *1st*
wink *2nd*
winter *K*
wipe *1st*
wire *3rd*
wise *1st*
wish *K*
wit *1st*
witch *K*
with *K*
withal *6th*
withdraw *2nd*
wither *5th*
within *1st*

without *1st*
witness *3rd*
wizard *6th*
wobble *4th*
woe *4th*
wolf *K*
woman *K*
women *K*
wonder *1st*
wonderful *1st*
wont *5th*
won't *1st*
woo *6th*
wood *1st*
woodbine *3rd*
woodchuck *2nd*
woodpecker *2nd*
wool *3rd*
word *K*
work *K*
worked *1st*
worker *1st*
workman *1st*
world *1st*
worm *K*
worn *3rd*
worrisome *5th*
worry *1st*
worse *1st*
worship *4th*
worst *3rd*
worth *3rd*
worthless *3rd*
would *1st*
wouldn't *1st*
wouldst *5th*
wound *3rd*
wow *K*
wrap *3rd*
wrath *4th*
wreath *4th*
wreck *4th*

wren *5th*
wrench *6th*
wrest *6th*
wrestle *6th*
wretched *6th*
wriggle *5th*
wring *5th*
wrinkle *3rd*
wrist *5th*
writ *6th*
write *K*
writer *1st*
writhe *6th*
written *3rd*
wrong *1st*
wrought *5th*

yam *1st*
yank *2nd*
yard *K*
yarn *2nd*
yawn *5th*
ye *4th*
yea *K*
yeah *1st*
year *1st*
yearly *2nd*
yearn *6th*
yeast *2nd*
yell *K*
yellow *K*
yelp *6th*
yeoman *5th*
yes *K*
yesterday *3rd*
yet *1st*
yew *2nd*
yield *4th*
yip *1st*
yoke *6th*
yon *4th*
yonder *4th*

yore *6th* yourself *2nd* zealous *6th* zinc *5th*
you *K* youth *2nd* zebra *K* zip *K*
you'll *1st* yucca *1st* zephyr *6th* zipper *K*
young *1st* yule *2nd* zero *K* zone *4th*
your *K* zest *6th* zoo *K*
you're *1st* zeal *6th* zigzag *3rd*

Introduction to the Graded Word Lists

What subjects students learn and when they learn them is fairly standard across the country. What is presented in the following grade-by-grade summaries are the common practices not only in vocabulary but also in subjects like history and science since many words are inherent to these subjects.

For example, the early history of the United States is traditionally taught during fifth grade, and any words or subjects relating to that period are appropriate for the ten- to twelve-year-old. Virtually any related word may be used at the level the subject is introduced.

While that makes vocabulary questions easier, historical accuracy beomes more important. The early-American period allows marvelous adventures, mysteries and historical stories, but the facts must be correct. Most children's publishers are very stringent in this area.

In each grade that follows, I'll highlight what the child is learning in school as far as vocabulary and other subjects of study. This will give you a background that will help you make decisions as you write.

Kindergarten (5)

Social Changes. At one time, kindergarten was considered primarily a socialization process. Those days are gone — in many areas of the country, children actually have to pass a reading test to "graduate" into first grade. Teachers now must teach reading skills, and there is a growing demand for stories for classroom use.

In the Classroom. Because many kindergartners have been through some type of preschool, they are able to read materials previously considered appropriate for first to third graders.

Health education usually begins in kindergarten. Children are often given toothbrushes and encouraged to brush their teeth at school. Nutrition is discussed in terms of eating a good breakfast and drinking milk.

Holidays such as Halloween, Christmas and Easter may seem too advanced for this level, but are, in fact, commonly used. Like many complicated picture books, they are understood in context and become recognized by "sight" reading words rather than "phonic" ones. Mother's Day, Valentine's Day, February as Black History Month and President's Day have all come into major focus in schools. Even though they are not vacation holidays, a great deal of time is devoted to talking, writing and arts and crafts projects in celebration of these days. Poetry and short stories with minor holiday themes are a part of classroom learning.

Dinosaurs are popular with young children, but they are treated in a simplified manner here and formally introduced in fourth or fifth grade. They make good subjects for shape books or picture and coloring books. At this level, if you use the scientific names for the different species, be sure they're compatible with current opinions. Dinosaurs are also a focus in the classroom and are the basis of art projects, music and developing reading and writing skills.

Cooking also is often used in the same way and provides hands-on experience that can lend extra dimensions to classroom learning.

Specific Vocabulary Development. The kindergarten student's vocabulary centers around one syllable words, under six letters. The numbers one to ten and the primary colors are introduced in kindergarten. Seasons are also introduced (autumn is known as fall). Kindergartners know words like *the* and *a* as well as *tree* and, of course, *boy* and *girl*. They do not understand contractions yet, and possessives are not commonly used either. The months and days of the week are not introduced until first grade.

The animals most commonly introduced at the kindergarten level are included in the following word list. Groups of animals and plants are particularly flexible.

Please see the first- through third-grade lists for other animals that are introduced at the earliest levels.

Publishing. Schools primarily use picture books and magazines, which traditionally address the two- to eight-year-old child. Picture stories are also good for this group, although traditionally meant for the first- to third-grade child. The major book format for this age is the "picture story." Whether meant to be read aloud by an adult or alone by the child, the story line is carried more by text than by pictures in the picture story. These stories should have lots of action.

Books meant to be read by adults to the youngest listeners should take no more than twenty minutes to read; ten to fifteen minutes is preferred. The sentence length can vary, but should be such that the child being read to can follow it easily. If the sentences are long, they should have breaks and pictures to keep the child in the story. The self-reader should have a sentence length of five to six words.

Dialogue at this level is often set off by a full colon, rather than by quotation marks:

Mother said: See the sun. Today will be fun.

Stories about other holidays that take into account our nation's cultural diversity are often eagerly sought. You may find Chinese New Year, Chanukah and Kawanza have little or no competition in the marketplace, yet they provide a healthy market for the children's writer and excellent formats for creative writing exercises in class. Magazines, book publishers and even newspapers often look for holiday material for children, and it's easiest to sell stories about holidays that get less media coverage than Christmas and Easter.

Writing Samples. The following is a picture story meant for the adult to read to the kindergarten child.

There is one girl. One. And she wants to have fun.
• • •
She can roll a ball,
• • •
color,
• • •
draw,
• • •
ride a bus,
• • •
play with the cat.
• • •
She can walk the dog
• • •

or play with her doll.

• • •

But one, just one,

• • •

cannot play bat the ball,

• • •

or go fish

• • •

or run, red, run.

• • •

One, just one,

• • •

cannot play house

• • •

or school

• • •

or store.

• • •

It is best to have two when you go to the zoo

• • •

or go for a walk

• • •

or just want to talk.

• • •

It is a good thing she has a brother.

Sentence length changes must be made in order to make it a self-reader:

There is one girl. One.

• • •

And she wants to have fun.

• • •

She can roll a ball.

• • •

She can color.

• • •

She can ride a bus.

• • •

She can play with the cat.

• • •

She can walk the dog.

• • •

Or play with her doll.

. . .

But one cannot play ball.

. . .

Or play go fish.

. . .

Or play run, red, run.

. . .

One cannot play house.

. . .

Or play school.

. . .

Or play store.

. . .

You need two for the zoo.

. . .

Or to go for a walk.

. . .

Or just to talk.

. . .

She is glad she has a brother.

The sentences are not actually complete, but a period is used to show a complete thought. This is less daunting to a young reader.

KINDERGARTEN WORD LIST

a	animal	bad	begin	bring
about	answer	ball	bell	brown
above	ant	ban	bend	bug
act	any	barn	bent	bull
add	ape	bat	best	bunny
address	apple	bay	better	bus
after	are	be	big	but
again	arm	beach	bird	buy
air	art	bead	birthday	by
all	as	bear	black	cab
almost	ask	because	blue	cake
alone	at	bed	boo	calf
also	ate	bee	book	call
always	away	been	boss	came
am	ax	beep	both	camel
an	baby	before	box	can
and	back	began	boy	candy

cap	door	five	gun	I
car	dot	floor	had	ice
care	dove	flower	hair	if
carry	down	fly	ham	in
cat	Dr.	food	hand	is
chicken	draw	foot	happy	it
child	dream	for	hard	its
children	dress	found	has	jam
Christmas	drive	four	hat	jar
church	drop	fox	have	jet
circle	duck	free	hay	job
city	Easter	freely	he	juice
clean	easy	frog	head	jump
close	eat	from	health	keep
cold	eel	full	hear	key
color	egg	fun	heard	kid
colt	eight	fur	heart	kind
come	elephant	game	hello	king
coming	elk	gap	help	kiss
cookie	end	garden	hen	kite
cop	ever	gave	her	kitten
cost	every	gee	here	koala
could	eye	get	hers	lad
count	face	ghost	hey	lamb
cow	fad	gift	hi	land
crab	fall	giraffe	high	lap
crayon	family	girl	hill	large
cry	fan	give	him	last
cub	farm	glad	hippo	late
cup	farmer	go	his	led
cut	father	goat	hit	leg
dad (dy)	fed	gold	hog	lend
dam	feel	golden	hole	let
dark	feeling	goldfish	holiday	light
day	few	good	home	like
deer	fight	goose	hop	line
did	fill	got	hope	lion
dinosaur	find	grass	horse	lit
do	fire	great	hot	little
dog	fireman	green	house	log
doll	fish	grow	how	look
donkey	fit	gum	hurt	lose

loss	now	pop	say	strong
lost	number	pot	school	summer
lot	nurse	present	sea	sun
love	nut	price	seal	sure
low	of	pull	see	sweet
lucky	off	pumpkin	sell	swim
mad	oil	pup	send	tab
made	O.K.	puppy	sent	table
make	old	purple	set	tag
making	on	put	seven	take
mall	one	quack	she	talk
man	only	queen	sheep	tall
manly	open	quiet	shoe	tan
many	or	rabbit	shy	tap
mat	orange	ram	sick	tax
may	our	ran	side	tell
me	out	rat	sit	ten
meet	over	read	six	tend
meow	owl	red	skunk	than
miss	ox	reindeer	sky	that
mom (my)	pad	rent	sleep	the
money	pal	rich	small	their
monkey	pan	ride	snow	them
moose	panda	right	snowball	then
more	paper	rip	snowman	these
mother	party	river	so	they
mouse	pass	road	soft	thing
move	pat	rob	some	things
Mr.	pay	robin	son	this
Mrs.	people	robot	song	three
Ms.	picture	rock	soon	tiger
music	pie	rocket	spider	to
my	pig	room	spring	today
name	pin	round	stand	toe
nap	pizza	row	star	told
neat	plant	rule	stick	top
never	plate	run	sticker	town
new	play	sad	sticky	toy
next	please	safe	stood	tractor
nine	pole	said	stop	train
no	pony	same	store	tree
not	poor	saw	story	tricycle

tried	very	well	wish	yell
true	wait	went	witch	yellow
try	walk	were	with	yes
tummy	wall	wet	wolf	you
turkey	want	what	woman	your
TV	was	when	women	zebra
two	water	white	word	zero
under	wave	White House	work	zip
up	wax	who	worm	zipper
us	way	why	wow	zoo
use	we	will	write	
used	wed	win	yard	
van	week	winter	yea	

First Grade ⁽⁶⁾

Social Changes. Although many first graders have been in all-day kindergarten, there are still some who are new to being away from home all day long. And all first graders are new to the sustained periods of concentration that are necessary in the first-grade classroom.

In the Classroom. While children learn the seasons and the numbers one to ten in kindergarten, the months, days of the week and numbers over ten generally wait until first grade to be introduced.

Almost all sports are introduced by name at this level. However, the technical details and rules are not generally introduced until third grade.

Most children in first grade can sound out any three- or four-letter word. However, many of these words (such as *eve* or *dim*) are introduced later since they are somewhat abstract.

Specific Vocabulary Development. The prefix *un* is introduced for the simplest of words such as *unhappy, unfit* or *undo*. The suffix *ing* is also introduced and words such as *fishing, walking* and *reading* are common. The past tense is also introduced. This includes irregular forms such as *know* to *knew* and *was* to *were* as well as the addition of a simple *ed* such as *ask* to *asked* and *walk* to *walked*.

Possessives are introduced at the very beginning of the year. *Dad's hat* and *mother's dress* appear along with the other changes mentioned above and give the writer a great deal more flexibility than when writing for the youngest self-readers.

Contractions such as *I'd, I'll, I'm, I've, we're, can't* and *won't* are introduced at this level.

Publishing. The desired sentence length is around five to six words. However, as with all writing, length should vary throughout your story. The longest sentence length used in a strictly graded text for this age is ten words. Parenthetical statements should be avoided. Sentence length is important because the early reader will become lost in the individual words and have trouble understanding the overall idea. The constraints on sentence length are eased by the ability to start sentences with such words as *and, because* and *but*. Sentences at this level need to be whole ideas but do not necessarily need to conform to strictly correct adult standards.

If the story is written for an adult to read to a child, sentence length is only restricted to that which is comfortably read aloud in one breath. The vocabulary should be such that the child can easily understand it.

There is a much larger periodical market for the primary group than there is for the very beginning reader. "Fillers," or very short articles or stories (usually under 500 words and often under 100), are popular. Games, riddles and stories about good health habits, safety, science and human interest pieces are especially welcome.

As mentioned, most sports are understood by name at this level and are especially popular in literacy books for older readers. There is a great appetite for stories and nonfiction articles about everything from baseball to karate; however, the technical details and rules are not generally introduced until the reader achieves third-grade reading skills.

Like sports, simple mysteries and "friendly" ghost stories are popular among first graders. Many, if not most, of the fiction stories published for this age are fantasies, but retelling such classics as *The Goose Girl* in modern dress is sure to garner rejection slips instead of praise.

Books for teens and adults learning to read often start at the first-grade level rather than kindergarten. Most of these books are presented much like those for the young reader but with fewer pictures than those for children, and many are presented in a standard paperback format. They primarily feature romance, sports, suspense, nonviolent mysteries and other high-interest subjects. They may also address such practical areas as working, social skills and legal problems and how to solve them. The vocabulary, length and style guidelines are the same as for the reading level it's written at.

Writing Samples. The following story employs a popular subject — ghosts; and popular genre — mysteries. It also takes on a common "problem" for kids — moving. The sentences are within the ten-word limit, and the words are mono-syllabic.

Another theme present is adaptation. First graders adapt to full days of school-work and Tommy adapts to new surroundings.

Tommy and the Ghost

Tommy looked at the old house. There was a ghost in that house. It was a little ghost, just like Tommy. He could see the top of its white head. He could see its eyes. But that was all. It had to be a small ghost.

"This is OK. A ghost is fun," he said. "Moving here may be OK."

Tommy did not like to move. He did not want to move from the city. But his father was a park ranger. He worked at a beach park now so they all had to move. \?

His father liked the beach. So did his brother Bob. His mother loved their house. Most houses for rangers are not new. This one was new and it was big. Tommy was the only one who did not want to live there.)?

"But a ghost is really OK," he said. "The old house is OK. The new house may be OK, too."

FIRST GRADE WORD LIST

across	bank	blaze	burglar	class
action	base	block	burro	classroom
adult	baseball	blood	busy	claw
afraid	basket	blouse	butterfly	clay
afternoon	basketball	blow	button	climb
against	bass	blue jay	buyer	clinic
age	bath	bluebird	cabin	clock
ago	bathe	board	cable	cloth
ahead	bathroom	boat	cage	clothes
Air Force	bathtub	bobcat	calendar	cloud
aircraft	batter	body	camera	clown
airplane	beached	bone	camp	club
airport	bean	bookstore	campfire	coat
album	beat	boom	canary	cob
alike	beautiful	boot	cannot	cobra
alligator	beaver	border	can't	cocoa
along	become	born	card	cod
already	beetle	bottom	careful	coke
among	beg	bow	cart	computer
anger	behind	bowl	catbird	cone
angry	being	boxer	catch	Congress
another	belief	brake	caterpillar	cook
anybody	believe	brave	cave	cool
anyone	belong	break	cell	cot
anything	below	breakfast	cellar	couldn't
anyway	beneath	breath	cent	country
apartment	berry	breathe	certain	cover
April	beside	bridge	certainly	coyote
aren't	bet	bright	chair	crawl
armadillo	between	brother	chart	cream
Army	beyond	buck	chase	creep
around	bib	bud	chat	cricket
August	bid	buffalo	chatter	cripes
aunt	bike	build	check	crocodile
baboon	bill	building	chew	cross (wise)
backing	bin	bulldog	chief	crown
bag	bit	bulldozer	chin	cuff
bake	bite	bullfrog	choke	cute
balloon	blackbird	bull's-eye	circus	cutting
band	blacktop	bully	clam	dab

dairy	doorbell	fact	fold	gopher
dance	dope	factory	follow (ing)	gorilla
dandy	dose	fade	football	government
danger	doubt (ful)	fair	force	grandfather
darkness	downstairs	fake	forest	grandmother
dart	downtown	families	forget	grasshopper
date	dragon	far	fork	gray
daughter	drink	farming	form	grin
daylight	dropped	fast	forty	ground
dead	drove	fat	forward	group
dear	drown	favor	fourteen	grown-up
December	drug	fawn	fourth	gruff
decide	dry	fear	freckles	guard
deck	dull	fearful	French	guess
deed	dumb	feast	Friday	guide
deep	dummy	feat	friend	guitar
den	during	February	front	gulp
dent	duty	feed	fry	gut
desert	eagle	feet	funny	guy
dew	ear	fell	fuss	gym
didn't	early	fellow	gab	hadn't
different	earth	fence	gag	half
dig	east	fib	gang	hall
dill	eating	fifteen	gas	hamster
dim	edge	fifth	gate	handcuffs
dime	eighteen	fifty	gather	happen
dine	eighty	fig	gay	hasn't
dinner	elf	file	gear	haven't
dip	else	fin	getting	heat
direct (ion)	elves	finance(s)	gingerbread	heaven
dirt	English	finding	glass	heavy
discover	enough	fine	glasses	he'd
dish	enter	finger	gleam	helper
dive	escape	finish	glow	helping
dock	even	first	glue	hem
doctor	evening	fishing	gnaw	here's
does	everyone	fix	god	hero
doesn't	everything	flake	goddess	herself
doing	excellent	flew	goes	hidden
dolphin	except	float	going	hide
done	exercise	flow	gone	higher
don't	extra	fog	good-bye	himself

hint	jeep	least	mailbox	Monday
hip	jell	leather	mailman	monster
hold	Jew	leave (s)	maker	month
homework	joke	left	mama	moo
honey	jot	lens	mane	moon
honk	joy	leopard	manner	mop
honor	judge	less	map	morning
hoof (ves)	jug	lessen	march	moss
hoot	July	let's	March	most
hopped	jumped	letter (s)	Marines	moth
horrible	June	lick	mark	mouth
hour	just	lid	market	movie
however	kangaroo	lie	marry	moving
hug	karate	life	marsupial	much
huge	keeper	lift	master	mud
hum	keg	likely	mastodon	mug
hundred	keyboard	likes	matter	muss
hurry (ied)	kick	lily	May	must
husband	kill	lip	maybe	myself
icebox	kin	listen	mean	mystery
I'd	kit	live	meat	nab
idea	kitchen	lived	member	nag
ill	knee	lives	men	napping
I'll	knew	living	mend	nation
illegal	knife	lizard	mess	native
I'm	know (n)	llama	message	nature
important	lab	lock	met	Navy
inch	labor	long (ing)	might (y)	near (ing)
indeed	lack	looked	mike	nearly
Indian	lady	looking	mile	necessary
inside	lag	loud	milk	neck
instead	lake	loved	mill	need
interest	lamp	lovely	mind	neither
into	landing	luck	mine	nervous
isn't	lass	lug	minus	nest
it's	later	lumber	minute	newspaper
I've	laugh	lumbering	mist	nice
jab	law	lumberman	mistake	nickel
jack	lay	lunch	mitten	night
January	lead	machine (ry)	mix	nineteen
jay	leaf	magic	mixed	ninety
jeans	learn	mail	moment	nip

nobody	palace	plan	quail	riddle
nod	panic	plane	Quaker	riding
noise	pants	player	quarter	rig
none	papa	playground	question	rim
noon	park	plenty	quick	ring
north	parrot	plop	quicksand	ripe
nose	part	pluck	quit	ripen
note	partridge	plus	quite	rise
nothing	past	pocket	raccoon	roar
notice	paste	pod	race	rod
November	path	point	rack	roll
nun	patrol	poke	radio	roof
nuzzle	paw	police	radish	rooster
oak	paying	policeman	rag	rope
oar	payment	pond	rain	rose
oat	pea	pool	raise	rot
object	peace	popcorn	rake	roundhouse
ocean	peach	porpoise	ranger	rub
October	peacock	possible	rap	rubber
octopus	peck	post	rate	rug
office	peer	postcard	rather	rum
officer	peg	pouch	rattlesnake	running
often	pelican	power	raven	rut
oh	pen	practice	raw	sack
okay	pencil	prepare	ray	sadness
older	penguin	president	reach	sag
once	penny	press	ready	sail
onto	perhaps	pretty	real	sale
order	person	prince	reason (able)	salt
ostrich	pest	princess	receive	sand
other	pet	print	rectangle	sap
otter	pick	problem	reins	Saturday
ought	pickle	promise	remain	save
outside	piece	prove	remember	sawmill
oval	pigeon	pub	reply	scare (d)
oven	pile	public	report	scarecrow
oversee	pill	Puritan	require	scene
own	pine	purpose	rest	schoolwork
pack	pink	push	return	score
paddle	pipe	push-up	rib	scout
page	pit	pushy	rice	scream
pair	place	putting	rid	screen

search	show	somewhere	subtract	third
seat	shut	sort	such	thirteen
second	sidekick	sound	suck	thirty
secret	sidewalk	soup	sudden	those
seed	sight	south	sugar	thou
seek	sign	space	suit	though
seem	silly	speak	suitcase	thought
seen	silver	spell	sum	thousand
seesaw	simple	spill	Sunday	threw
Senate	sin	spin	sunny	throat
sense	since	splash	sunset	through
sentence	sing	spoke	super	throw
September	sip	spoon	supply	Thursday
serve	sir	sport	surprise	thus
service	sister	sportsman	swallow	tick
seventeen	sitting	spot	sweets	ticket (s)
seventy	sit-up	squirrel	swing	tide
several	sixteen	stag	tack	tie
shake	sixth	stake	tail	tight
shall	sixty	starfish	taken	tile
shape	size	start	tape	till
shark	skate	state	tar	time
sharp	skateboard	station	taste	tin
shave	skin	stay	taxi	tip
sheet	skinny	step	tea	together
shell	slate	still	teach (ing)	tomorrow
shine	slow	stock	teacher	ton
ship	smart	stoplight	team	tonight
shirt	smile	stopped	tee	too
shiver	smoke	stove	teeth	took
shock	snail	strange (r)	telling	tool
shoemaker	snake	stream	tent	toot
shop	sob	street	terrible	tooth
shore	soccer	strength	thank	touch (ing)
short	social	string	that's	tow
shortly	sock	stripe	themselves	toward
shot	socks	stroke	there	track
should	somebody	struggle	therefore	trade
shoulder	someday	study	they'll	trained
shouldn't	someone	stuff	they're	trap
shout	something	stutter	thin	travel
shovel	sometimes	subject	think	tray

triangle	understand	war	whether	worked
trick	undertaking	warm	which	worker
trip	unfit	wash	while	workman
troll	unhappy	wasn't	whisper	world
trouble	uniform	waste	whoever	worry
troublemaker	unreal	watch	whole	worse
truck	until	wear	wick	would
trust	unzip	weather	wide	wouldn't
truth	uphill	wedding	wife	writer
tub	upon	Wednesday	wig	wrong
tuck	uptown	weed	wind	yam
Tuesday	vet	weigh	window	Yankee
tug	view	weight	wine	yeah
tune	vine	weird	wing	year
turn	visit	welcome	wipe	yet
twelve	voice	we'll	wise	yip
twenty	wag	we're	wit	you'll
twist	wake	west	within	young
type	walked	whale	without	you're
typewriter	walking	whatever	wonder	yucca
umpire	walnut	wheat	wonderful	
uncertain	walrus	wheel	won't	
uncle	wanted	where	wood	

Second Grade

Social Changes. One of the major changes common at this age is that most children have become less self-oriented than they were in kindergarten and even first grade. As a result, they have stopped generalizing characters, and individual personalities have become important in stories.

In the Classroom. A beginning study of the solar system is often part of second-grade curriculum. The continents and the cardinal directions, north, south, east and west, are generally taught in school, and there is usually some work with the world map.

Schools introduce their home state, other major states and a few foreign countries by this level. These countries include major powers and nations that are near neighbors of the United States both physically and culturally. The best-known states, such as New York, California, Florida and Texas, are familiar to the second grader as he learns about the continental United States. More explanation or description may be needed in introducing difficult names or lesser-known states. Canada and Mexico, which border the United States, and England, France and Germany are known at this level. Nations currently in the news are often familiar to the second grader also.

Foreign or unusual words begin to be introduced at this level. When including words that are not in the child's vocabulary, it is best to give the definition first and then the word. Readers tend to skip over unfamiliar words, getting the meaning from the context of the sentence. Giving the definition first makes it much easier to actually learn the new word. For example: A large open plain in Africa is called a *savanna*.

Specific Vocabulary Development. Compound words such as lookout, use-less and walkway are introduced in second grade. Any compound words that are made up of words the children already know and easily recognize may be used. Going beyond the standard list, you might name a Native American *Redhorse* or *Whitesnake* and still be well within the parameters of the age group. Some compound words in the word lists are listed at a higher grade level with this method than where they usually would be placed. These words are listed at the levels at which they were actually used in graded texts. However, if the meaning is clear and the word is easily read, it can be used at a lower level.

Publishing. From this point on, the protagonist of your story should be at least the same age, and preferably a little older, than the reader.

Since there are few illustrations in easy readers, you need to help your reader identify the characters and give them easy ways to remember each character. One way to do this is with a "tag." Tags are actions, gestures or physical attributes that easily identify the person for the reader. One character might constantly be pushing up his glasses when he talks, or another's red hair and freckles may make her memorable.

Mysteries, adventures and hero stories are very popular at this age. Vocabulary choice and sentence length are important because most books are aimed at self-readers. The ideal sentence length is still five or six words. However, some publishers have already increased the target sentence length to around ten words. Long passages of description are still unacceptable. There are many reasons to maintain a short sentence length, even if the publisher does not require it. The child reads one word at a time, then puts the words together to make a whole idea. The shorter the sentence is, the easier that process becomes. Thus, it is easier to understand. The inexperienced reader also gets a sense of accomplishment in successfully finishing and understanding a sentence.

Most books run between 1,000 and 1,500 words. The low end is 500 words and the high end is 2,000. Most magazines aimed at this age group use stories ranging from 300 to 500 words but welcome short pieces also. One thousand words is almost certain to be too long for a magazine. Check your writer's guidelines or *Children's Writer's and Illustrator's Market* for individual length requirements and remember—publishers generally list the maximum number of words they want.

The second grader seems to be caught in the middle as far as books and magazines are concerned. They are neither at the beginning nor the end of a period. Their interests, reading skills and ego sometimes make reading picture books unacceptable, and heavily illustrated picture stories are often overlooked because they seem too "babyish" to be seen reading. Even though the vocabulary goes beyond strictly second grade, at this point the "young reader" or "easy-to-read" book really comes into its own. The more adult presentation appeals to the seven- and eight-year-olds, and their reading skills are generally good enough that they no longer need the support provided by profuse illustrations.

Writing Samples. The following story asks the young reader to use her imagination. It also demonstrates how to introduce a new word, *barnacle*.

Let's Pretend

Let's pretend you have an aquarium. What would you put in it? Would you put a cat in it? No. Cats don't live in water. Would you put a dog in it? No. Dogs don't live in water. Would you put a barnacle in it? You could. Barnacles live in water. But they aren't very pretty. They are small grayish sea animals. Would you put a fish in it? Yes. Fish live in water. Most fish are pretty. Some fish are beautiful. I think I like fish best. I would put them in my aquarium.

SECOND GRADE WORD LIST

aboard	beginner	cardboard	coal	doorway
accomplish	belt	carnival	coast	doughnut
ace	bicycle	carrot	cockpit	dresser
actor	bind	cartoon	cocoon	drift
advance	blackberry	case	coffee	drill
affair	blade	cash	collie	drip
afire	blame	cast	colorful	due
aflame	blast	cause	comb	dump
afloat	bluebell	cedar	comma	dust
agree	blueberry	center	command	dye
aid	bold	centigrade	commission	earn
airfield	boob	centimeter	common	effort
ale	bore	century	community	either
allow	borrow	chance	company	elevate
almond	bother	change	consider	elevator
alphabet	bought	character	continue	elm
although	bound	charge	control	enemy
amount	braid	checkers	corn	enjoy
appear	branch	cheek	corner	equal
appearance	brand	cherry	corny	erase
apply	brass	chest	cotton	everywhere
aquarium	bread	chick	craft	exact
ark	breadfruit	chimney	crash	example
armload	brook	chipmunk	crew	expect
arrive	broom	chirp	crib	explain
arrow	brownie	chop	crime	fail
article	brush	chrome	crop	famous
artist	bubble	chubby	crow	feather
ashore	bulb	cider	crowd	field
attempt	bump	cinnamon	cue	figure
attention	bun	claim	curl	firefly
badger	bunt	clap	dare	fireworks
banana	bush	clear	daydream	firm
barber	business	clerk	deal	fist
basic	butter	click	department	fitting
basis	cactus	cliff	desk	flash
batch	candle	clip	destroy	flat
battle	capital	closet	die	flaw
beautify	capitol	clover	disagree	flight
beef	captain	clue	disk	flip

flock	hound	meek	pitch	skill
flood	hunger	melt	plain	skip
floss	hungry	meter	pleasure	slap
foal	hunt	method	plentiful	slide
fool (ish)	imagine	middle	poppy	smooth
forceful	ink	millimeter	porcupine	snack
forgive	invent	mix-up	position	snap
forth	iron	moccasin	positive	soil
fresh	island	modern	pound	sonic
friendship	itself	mole	powerful	sorry
fright	jellyfish	monument	preen	sour
frown	jingle	mound	pretend	spank
fruit	jog	mount	pride	special
further	journal	mountain	produce	speech
gain	kilogram	movement	proud	spend
gale	kilometer	mule	prowl	spinach
gallon	kingbird	multiply	puff	spirit (s)
general	knight	nail	quart	spool
German	know-how	narrow	rail	spray
giant	knowledge	natural	railroad	spread
good-night	ladder	neighbor	raindrops	square
govern	ladybird	neighborhood	rainfall	squash
grade	laid	objective	raspberry	squawk
grand	language	offer	rattle	squeak
grant	lavender	onion	realize	squirm
grape	lawn	ounce	recess	stair
hale	lemon	outstanding	record	stale
hammer	length	ovenbird	refrigerator	stamp
handle	lice	overthrow	refuse	steak
hang	lighthouse	paid	remove	steam
harbor	list	pail	respect	steel
harden	litter	pain	result	steep
haste	load	paint	roost	stem
hasty	lone	parade	rude	stew
hate	lonely	peek	rush	stink
haunt	lord	peel	rust	stomach
heavenly	lye	period	season	stone
herd	maize	pester	sequoia	Stone Age
history	malt	phone	settle	stool
hive	maple	pillbox	sew	stork
hoe	mask	pinecone	shade	storm
hogan	measure	pint	share	straw

strawberry	taught	toothpaste	useless	willow
strike	tear	toss	vacation	wink
success	teaspoon	total	valley	withdraw
suffer (ing)	teen	toxic	value	woodchuck
suggest	telephone	trail	vegetable	woodpecker
suggestion	thee	trash	village	yank
sundown	thick	treat	violet	yarn
sunlit	thirsty	trend	vote	yearly
sunrise	thoughtful	trio	wagon	yeast
suntan	thread	tryout	wasp	yew
supper	throughout	tulip	watchful	yourself
suppose	tiny	tunnel	well built	youth
sweetness	tire	umbrella	whom	yule
swish	toad	unless	whose	
system	toilet	unpaid	wild	
talent	tonic	useful	wildcat	

Third Grade

Social Changes. Third graders begin identifying themselves with the world around them through attachments to objects such as toys. They begin to clearly prefer one thing to another. It is just this discovery of taste preferences that creates devoted "fans." Whether it's G.I. Joe or the Little Mermaid, eight- and nine-year-old third graders are prime markets for toy manufacturers.

In the Classroom. Health, drug and sex education are started early throughout the United States and anti-drug messages are often a part of the third-grade curriculum. In our culture the word, *drug* has generally taken on the connotation of being a narcotic or other controlled substance. In most schools, however, the idea has expanded to include caffeine, tobacco and alcohol. It is wise to stay away from any positive portrayal of these substances, whether your work is aimed at an academic or popular market. The word *medicine* is generally used to specify the proper use of controlled substances.

Third graders do a lot of in-class reading and group reading. One of the popular classroom subjects is sports. The details, rules and technical aspects begin to be introduced at this level, and sports will remain a high-interest subject throughout all children's and young adult markets. Another ongoing interest is in mystery stories. While they are one of the most popular genres for young readers there are a few rules you need to know. Too much violence is generally unacceptable for any juvenile writing. For preteens, murder is out, and so are most dead bodies. The only corpses generally are ancient mummies that lend a safely creepy atmosphere to a story. For your youngest readers, such as those for this age, think about centering your mysteries around missing treasure or legends and secrets. Mysteries can actually hone academic skills in a fun way by acting as elaborate puzzles the reader must solve.

Specific Vocabulary Development. The prefixes *dis*, *ex* and *re* are added at this level. For example, *disable, disadvantage, disallow, redo, reset* or any other word already introduced may be used with these prefixes.

Hyphenated words such as *part-time, sit-ups, dry-eyed* and *age-old* are introduced in third grade.

The suffix *ment* is also introduced at this level: *excitement, encouragement.*

You may use the name of almost any body part at this level. Ankles, knees, shoulders and even abdomen join the simpler head, arms and legs previously introduced. Individual bones and muscles are not understood yet.

Publishing. By third grade, children have reached the end of the primary reading level. They have some experience both reading and choosing books and are beginning to have a good idea of what type of story they like to read.

Your book title helps sell your story both by catching the reader's attention and giving him some idea of what the book is about. Mysteries or adventures often announce themselves with their title at this level: *The Mystery of the Golden Door, The Adventure of Aben-Go-Down*. The title can also announce whether the main character is a boy or a girl: *Paula Makes a Mess, Norman Joins the Circus*. It is true that most book titles are finally chosen by the publisher, but a carefully selected title may be part of what sells your book (and tells your publisher you understand the market) in the first place.

Juvenile publishing is one of the few areas where the commercial rights covered in every book contract may actually be exercised. Commercial rights cover all use of your story or characters for toys, posters, magnets and a rather long list of other odd things. It doesn't happen often, but there are enough Bart Simpson, Speed Racer and Batman T-shirts out there to make one hopeful. If you have not reserved commercial rights, all contracts for such items will go through your publisher no matter how little they seem to resemble your book.

Writing Samples. The following writing sample demonstrates how to introduce words not in the vocabulary.

Every day Maria helps her family. She feeds the chickens and rolls up the bed mats from the dirt floor of their one-room house. She also makes a flat bread called *tortillas*. The tortillas are cooked on top of the stove.

One day Maria woke up early. She was sure something special was going to happen. Then she remembered what it was. Today the men from the town were going to buy bricks in the city. They would bring back the bricks to build an oven for the pueblo. Her father would go with them to help.

With an oven, they could make bread called *bolillos*. They are very much like french rolls. Maria knew that they could make sweet rolls called *pan dulces*. And they could even make cookies and cakes!

THIRD GRADE WORD LIST

able	adventure	anemone	arctic	atop
absolute	advice	anew	area	attack
accept	afford	angle	argue	attend
accompany	aim	announce	arithmetic	author
account	alarm	apart	arrange (ment)	authority
acre	alder	apparent	arrest	automobile
active	alfalfa	appeal	ash	autumn
actual	alive	applesauce	aside	avenue
addition	amiss	appoint	asleep	average
adopt	amphibian	approach	assure	avocado
advantage	ancient	apron	astray	avoid

awake (n)	brief	cobweb	current	faith
aware	broad	code	curse	falcon
awful	bucket	coin	curve	false
bagpipe	bulletin	collect	decision	falter
bait	bunch	colonel	decorate	fame
balance	burn (ing)	colony	decoration	familiar
bamboo	burp	combine	delight	fancy
bandit	burst	comfort	depend	faraway
bang	bury	comfortable	diary	fare
banner	busybody	companion	disabled	farther
bar	buttercup	compare	display	fashion
bare	buttermilk	compel	double	fate
bark	cadet	complete	drag	fault
barnacle	calm	con	Dutch	favorite
basement	calories	concern	ease	feature
beagle	campaign	conclude	edit (or)	fiber
beam	cane	condition	educate	final
beast	capitalize	condor	education	fitness
bedroom	capture	conduct	effect	flag
behold	cardinal	connect	egret	flame
beige	carefree	consent	elect	flesh
beneficial	carol	consist	electric	flour
benefit	castle	construct	electricity	folk
bewilder	catnip	content	element	footstep
billboard	cattle	contract	empty	forever
bitter	cease	copy	engine	fortune
blackboard	central	coral	entire	fountain
blanket	chain	correct	entrance	frame
bless	chapter	couple	entrap	freedom
blind	charm	course	Eskimo	fume
bloodhound	cheap	court	establish	funnel
bluebottle	cheat	courtroom	event	furniture
boil	cheer	cousin	everybody	gentle
bond	cheese	crackle	evil	gentleman
bonfire	chill	crane	exclaim	glacier
bookcase	choice	crater	excuse	glance
bookkeeper	choose	crawfish	exist	gloom
bottle	churn	create	exit	glory
brag	citizen	creature	expense	godfather
brain	civil	crystal	experiment	godmother
brat	clever	curb	explode	grace
breast	clump	curious	faint	gradual

grain	impossible	maid	odor	possess
grave	improve	main	official	pour
greenery	include	major	oneself	powder
greenhouse	increase	majority	onward	pray (er)
greet	independent	manufacture	operate	prefer
grey	individual	mass	operation	prevent
greyhound	inquire	match (ing)	opinion	principal
groan	instant	meadow	opossum	prison
gross	instrument	meal	opportunity	private
grunt	interrupt	meaning	oppose	prize
guest	invite	melon	opposite	proper
habit	ivory	memory	ordinary	property
handsome	jacket	merchant	original	provide
hare	join (ed)	mere	oriole	prune
harm	journey	merry	otherwise	purchase
hateful	junk	metal	ourselves	pure
hawk	justice	midnight	owe	quest
headquarters	kingdom	military	pace	range
heal	knock	million	pale	rank
hectic	label	mink	panther	rear
heel	latter	mistreat	parent	recall
hence	league	misuse	part-time	recent
herald	lean (ing)	model	pattern	recognize
hike	leap	moisture	pause	reduce
hippopotamus	lesson	mood	peanut	regular
hire	level	moral	perfect	remind
hiss	liberty	moreover	perfume	reserve
hobby	library	motion	permit	rhinoceros
hockey	limit	murder	personal	rinse
hollow	limpet	mussel	picket	root
honest	liquid	needle	pity	royal
horn	livestock	net	plastic	rumble
hospital	lobster	niece	pleasant	rustle
hotel	local	noble	pliers	sailor
housekeeper	locate	nor	poem	saint
housework	location	noticeable	poison	sake
human	locket	notify	polar	salamander
hump	loose	obey	pollute	salary
hush	madness	observe	popular	salmon
iceberg	magazine	occasion	population	satisfy
ideal	magnet	occupy	porch	scale
immediate	magnify	occur	port	scatter

scent	slope	strip	thunder	vest
science	smash	student	thy	volume
scientist	smear	stump	title	vulture
scrap	smell	sturdy	tone	wage
scrapbook	snowstorm	style	tongue	wand
screw	society	sufficient	tortoise	wander
screwdriver	soldier	surface	tour	warn
secure	solid	surround (ing)	tower	warning
seize	soul	sway	trace	watermelon
self	spare	sweat	tremble	weak
sense	spark	sweater	tribe	weakness
separate	speed	swell	troop	wealth
servant	spice	tale	tube	weasel
sex	spit	tangle	tuft	westward
shadow	spite	task	turnip	whenever
shame	sponge	tease	twice	wire
shiny	sprinkle	teenager	twine	witness
shoot	spruce	temple	twirl	woodbine
shoplift	sputter	tender	union	wool
sigh	squid	term	unlimited	worn
silent	stack	terrified	unto	worst
silk	stage	terrify	unusual	worth
silkworm	standard	territory	upper	worthless
single	stare	terror	upset	wound
sink	steady	test	upstairs	wrap
skirt	steal	theater	urchin	wrinkle
skyrocket	stiff	thief	usual	written
slave	stir	thigh	vanish	yesterday
sleek	straight	thorn	vapor	zigzag
slip	stray	thud	veil	

Fourth Grade

Social Changes. Fourth grade is a turning point in a child's development. They're more independent and self-reliant. Homework is now considered their responsibility, rather than one shared with parents. Most kids are able to read independently and many begin to read on their own.

In the Classroom. Astronomy, ecology, geology, paleontology and all other types of science and space are usually taught in fourth or fifth grade. Science fiction becomes a popular leisure reading subject because it combines the newly acquired academic knowledge with fast-paced adventure.

While many preschool and beginning books feature dinosaurs, they are formally introduced at this level. Don't be afraid to use their scientific names; the children probably knew them by heart by the time they were three.

Many words pertaining to American history are learned in fourth grade, as are the different states and the countries of the world. Many types of plants become familiar at this age also. The plants given in the word lists are the ones most commonly used in literature.

Local history is often introduced at this level. This means you can write about geographic areas such as the Rockies, the Great Plains or New England because a large number of children will be exposed to these topics.

Words pertaining to foods, cooking and measurements are introduced by this level and are frequently taught as part of "fun" projects in cooking. Children often make cookies or holiday foods in earlier grades, but now cooking is integrated with mathematics and sociology. Multicultural festivals at schools often attempt to pull together a great variety of skills in a creative, exciting way.

Native American history is also studied in many fourth-grade classrooms. It is good policy to use the correct names for indigenous groups, rather than using the anglicized or Spanish names. For example, it's just as easy for children to learn the name *Kummeai* for the peaceful Native American tribe that lived in San Diego as it is to learn the Spanish name *Degunios*. It's also just as easy to use the term *Native Americans* or *Native American Indians* as it is to say "Indians." Your awareness of ethnic language concerns will enrich the experience of your readers.

Publishing. Whether it's space, video games or baby-sitting, both fiction and nonfiction for this age should deal with the special interests and problems of the eight to twelve age group. Most books now range between 20,000 and 40,000 words. Typical magazine stories run between 700 and 2,000 words but most publications also use a page or two of special interest short-shorts under 100 words.

Even the most conservative publishers now use the ten-word sentence as a target, with a maximum length of about twenty words. Even if it's not required, you should not go too far beyond twenty words at a stretch because it becomes harder to follow. Almost all children are still reading one word at a time at this level, and they can actually forget the subject being talked about in a long sentence.

Be careful of using localized terminology, such as specific wildlife or customs unique to an area. For example, I once wrote a story on lighter-than-air vehicles—*blimps* to us old guys. I described an exciting new airship as looking ". . . like a beach ball being carried on the back of a manta ray." My editor thought the description was too localized and kids in the midwest wouldn't know what a manta ray was. We finally decided to say it looked ". . . like a baseball with a handle attached."

Paleontology is going through changes due to recent discoveries. Good old brontosaurus has become apatasaurus, and some scientists have recently formed the opinion that many species may have been warm-blooded and herded in family units. Current opinions may disagree with what was once considered fact.

The elementary level, which covers fourth, fifth and sixth grades, is the largest of all the markets for children's writers. Beyond sheer volume, your readers are loyal and appreciative. They write fan letters and buy or read all the books a favorite writer produces. That loyalty is the reason so many publishers want series books for this age. A few publishers won't even look at books that can't be made into a series, and presenting the possibility of a series in a book proposal may be a big plus with any publisher.

Fiction stories should have lots of action, and a carefully crafted modern plot is absolutely necessary at this point. Many manuscripts are rejected simply because the plots are weak or outdated. Take the time to find out what hobbies and sports are currently popular, what issues children have to deal with and what their dreams are; it will go a long way in helping sell your book.

Science fiction is often a great way of explaining science concepts or imparting facts. As with any science fiction writing, your "hard science" facts must be correct.

Nonfiction comes into its own in fourth, fifth and sixth grades. Magazines and books specialize in science, mathematics, world events and much more. When you write for these markets, keep track of your source material in case you need to supply a bibliography or support a fact. Do not submit a bibliography with a manuscript written for a periodical unless you are asked to do so or you know the publisher requires it. *The Children's Writer's and Illustrator's Market* listings sometimes note if one is necessary. When writing a nonfiction book, reference material should be cited.

Writing Samples. The following excerpt demonstrates the fourth grader's new interest in nonfiction and world events.

Towns are like families. The people who work give money to run the town. That year, more than half the people in South Renovo were out of work. That means they had over 50 percent unemployment. So the town didn't have much money to spend. It was so bad even the local YMCA had to shut down.

It also meant Debra Burrows, the park director, had no money for summer projects. What she did have was over one hundred kids with nothing to do. She must have felt like Old Mother Hubbard. There were only two things left in the playground cupboard. They had two gallons of white glue and some paper. So the kids decided to see how long a paper chain they could make.

Later in the same story is this paragraph, capitalizing on the interest of readers learning about measurements:

. . . Some kids had odometers on their bikes. They used them to measure one-tenth of a mile along the playground fence. The kids then measured their work in picnic tables (six feet). When they finished a picnic table length, they laid it along the fence. Eighty-eight picnic tables made one fence length. The kids made about one fence length, or one-tenth of a mile, each day.

FOURTH GRADE WORD LIST

abandon	afterward	ankle	assist	banyan
accident	agate	annual	assistance	bareback
according	agriculture	antler	assistant	bargain
accuse	alabaster	anxiety	astonish	barley
accustom	alas	anxious	astound	baron
acid	aloe	appetite	astronaut	barrel
acorn	aloud	approve	astronomy	barren
acquaint	altar	arch	atmosphere	bashful
acquire	alter	arise	backbone	basin
ad	ambition	armor	background	beak
adapt	amen	arouse	backpack	beard
adept	amend	arrowhead	backward	beech
admit	amethyst	artichoke	backwoods	beet
adobe	amid	ascend	bacon	behave
adore	amuse	ashamed	ballast	behavior
advertise	anchor	aspen	ballet	bellow
affect	anchovy	assault	baneberry	beloved
affection	angel	assemble	banquet	bench

Bible	brow	celebrate	commute	cowardly
birch	brownstone	celery	compass	cowboy
biscuit	buckeye	cement	compete	crack
bison	buddy	challenge	complain	cracker
blackmail	budge	champion	composition	cradle
blacksmith	bulge	channel	compound	crayfish
blank	bulk	chap	comrade	crazy
bleach	bullet	chapel	conceal	creak
bleat	bumble	charity	conceive	creek
blizzard	bunk	chef	concrete	crest
bloodshed	bureau	chemical	condemn	criminal
bloodthirsty	bushel	chemistry	conference	crunch
bloom	butcher	chess	confess	crush
blossom	buttonhole	chestnut	conflict	cube
blot	buzzard	childhood	confuse	cure
blur	cabbage	chili	congress	daily
blush	cabinet	chocolate	conquer	deserve
boast	cafe	Christ	conscience	detective
bobbin	cameo	Christian	consequence	device
bodyguard	canal	cigar	constant (ly)	diamond
bolt	candidate	cigarette	constitute	diet
bonbon	cannibal	circuit	consult	differ
boulevard	cannon	circular	consume	discontinue
boundary	canoe	civilization	contact	distance
boundless	canyon	clang	contest	distant
boyfriend	capable	clank	continent	district
boyhood	cape	clasp	contrary	divide
breakers	caper	climate	contrast	divorce
breakwater	carbon	cling	contribute	dumpling
breed	career	cloak	convenient	dwarf
breeze	caretaker	cluster	convert	dwell
brick	carload	clutch	convey	dwelling
bride	carnation	clutter	convince	earl
bridesmaid	carpenter	coach	copper	earnest
brilliant	carpet	coarse	cord	echo
broadsword	carton	cock	corporal	economy
broccoli	carve	collar	corporation	effective
broil	cask	college	costume	elbow
bronze	casserole	colonial	cottage	elevation
brooch	catholic	column	couch	elsewhere
brood	cauliflower	commit	courage	embrace
broth	ceiling	commodore	courtesy	emotion

emperor	female	funeral	grocery	illustration
empire	fetch	furious	grove	image
empress	fever	furnace	growl	immense
enable	fiddle	furnish	guilt (y)	immortal
enclose	fierce	fury	gulf	impose
encounter	film	fuse	hail	imprint
encourage	fingernail	gallant	halt	income
endeavor	flap	gallop	hamburger	indicate
endure	flatter	garment	handkerchief	ingredient
energy	flavor	gasp	harmonize	inlet
engineer	flipper	generation	harmony	inn
enormous	flourish	generous	harness	insect
entertain	flush	genius	harp	inspire
enthusiasm	foam	gesture	harvest (ing)	instruct
envy	foe	gill	hatch	intelligent
ere	folly	girlfriend	haul	interfere
erect	fond	glare	heap	intestine
errand	forbid (den)	glide	hedge	issue
error	forecast	glimpse	heed	jaguar
erupt	forehead	glitter	height	jail
especially	formal	globe	heir	jaw
estate	formation	glove	hesitate	jellybean
eternal	fortunate	glum	highway	jest
evergreen	fossil	gnash	hillside	joint
exceed	foul	goal	hind	jolly
exchange	fowl	gobble	hood	jungle
excite	fraction	goblin	hook	junior
exhaust	framework	goggle	horizon	jury
exhibit	frank	goggles	horrid	keen
expedition	freeze (ing)	golf	horrify	kettle
experience	freight	gown	horror	knapsack
explore	frequent	grab	host	knead
expose	freshwater	graduate	hostile	kneel
extend	frock	grasp	howl	knit
eyeglasses	frost	grateful	hull	knot
Fahrenheit	froze	gravel	humble	knuckle
fairy	fuel	gravy	humor	laboratory
fasten	fugitive	greed (y)	hut	lace
fatal	fulfill	grim	hyena	ladle
federal	function	grind	identify	lame
fee	fund	grip	idle	lance
feeble	fundamental	grizzly	ignorant	lane

lash	marble	mums	outcome	piano
lasso	marvel	murmur	outcry	pier
lava	marvelous	muscle	outline	pierce
layer	mash	muse	overlook	pike
lazy	mast	museum	overseas	pillow
leech	mate	mushroom	oxygen	pimento
Lent	mayonnaise	musician	oyster	pinch
lest	mayor	mustang	package	pineapple
lettuce	medicine	mustard	palm	pioneer
liberal	melody	mutt	paprika	planet
lieutenant	mercy	mutter	papyrus	plaster
lightweight	merit	myrtle	paradise	platform
limb	mermaid	mystic	parcel	plot
limber	microscope	myth	pardon	plow
lime	migrant	naked	parlor	plum
limestone	mild	narcissus	parsley	plunge
linen	mingle	nasturtium	parsnip	plural
linger	minister	nay	particular	polish
loaf	minnow	Nazareth	passenger	polite
loan	mirror	nebula	pastel	political
locality	mischief	neglect	pastor	politics
lodge	miserable	nephew	patch	pomegranate
logger	misery	nettle	patent	poodle
logo	mistress	nevertheless	patient	poplar
luggage	mixture	nibble	patriot	portion
lump	mob	nightingale	peak	potato
lung	mock	nucleus	pear	practical
luster	moderate	numerous	pearl	prairie
luxury	modest	nutmeg	peasant	praise
lynx	moist	oarlock	pebble	preach
madam	monk	o'clock	peculiar	precious
magnificent	Monsieur	odd	peep	preserve
maiden	moonbeam	offend	pepper	pressure
maim	moonlight	offensive	peppermint	prey
maintain	Mormon	olive	percent	priest
majesty	mortal	opera	perch	principle
male	mosquito	orbit	perform	probably
mallard	motor	orchid	periodic	proceed
manage	mourn	ore	perish	process
manager	muffin	organ	persimmon	procession
mankind	mulberry	organize	petrify	proclaim
mantle	mumble	ornament	pheasant	product

production	recipe	rifle	serious	sovereign
professor	recover	ripple	severe	spear
profit	redwood	risk	shabby	speck
program	reed	rival	shaft	spike
progress	reflect	roam	shallow	spine
project	regard	roast	shelter	splendid
prompt	region	robe	shepherd	splendor
pronounce	register	rote	sheriff	split
proof	reign	rough	shield	spoil
prophet	rejoice	rouse	shift	spur
proportion	relate	route	shower	spy
propose	relation	russet	showroom	squire
prospect	relative	rye	shriek	squirt
protect (ion)	relax	sacred	shrub	stable
protest	relief	sacrifice	shrug	staff
provision	relieve	saddle	shudder	stagger
publication	religion	saffron	shutter	stain
publicity	remark	sage	sift	stalk
publicize	remedy	sagebrush	signal	stallion
publish	rend	salute	similar	startle
pudding	renew	sardine	simmer	statue
puma	repair	sassafras	sincere	steed
pump	repeat	sausage	sire	steer
punch	represent	saute	situation	stern
punish	reptile	scamper	skeleton	sting
pupil	republic	scarce	slay	stocking
purse	request	scarlet	slender	stomp
puzzle	rescue	scoop	slight	stout
quake	resemble	scorn	slither	stovepipe
qualify	resist	scramble	slumber	strain
quality	respecting	scrape	sly	stretch
quantity	responsible	scratch	snatch	structure
quarrel	restless	sculptor	sneak	stuck
queer	retire	sculpture	sniff	stumble
quiver	retreat	scuttle	snooze	stun
rabbi	reveal	secretary	soap	stupid
rage	reverence	section	sober	submit
rapid	reverend	seep	sole	sulphur
rare	review	seldom	solve	sumac
realm	reward	select	sore	summon
reap	rhubarb	senate	sorrow	superior
rebuke	ribbon	series	source	support

surf	theme	trim	vent	whence
suspicion	thence	trout	venture	whereas
swamp	thicket	trunk	verse	wherefore
swarm	thistle	tumble	vessel	whereupon
swear	thorough	twig	veterinarian	whip
sweep	thrash	twinkle	vice	whippoorwill
swift	thrill	ugh	victim	whirl
Swiss	throne	ugly	victory	whisk
switch	thrust	underground	violin	whistle
swoop	thyme	universal	virtue	wicked
sword	tingle	universe	visible	widow
sycamore	tiptoe	university	vision	width
sympathy	tobacco	upright	volcano	wilderness
syrup	toenail	upward	vow	wilt
tablecloth	toil	urge	voyage	wobble
tablespoon	tomato	utter	wade	woe
tackle	towhead	vain	waist	worship
tailor	traitor	vale	warp	wrath
tame	tramp	valuable	warrior	wreath
taro	tread	various	watercress	wreck
telegram	treason	vary	weapon	ye
telescope	treasure	vast	weary	yield
temper	treaty	veal	weave	yon
tempt	tremendous	vein	wedge	yonder
thatch	trial	velvet	weep	zone

Fifth Grade

Social Changes. Fifth graders begin to embark on the stage of growth that changes their focus from home to peers. This is fully realized by sixth and seventh grades, but it starts here. Friends' opinions can have as much influence now as a parent's.

One of the exciting things that happens in fifth and sixth grades is that children often get to put together "real" television broadcasts. Even the smallest schools can now produce packages (a complete program on tape meant to function as a self-contained, finished unit) of news programs, original plays or other material to run free of charge on public-access cable television channels.

In the Classroom. Current events generally become part of classroom learning and discussion in fifth grade. In most areas, fifth- or sixth-grade students have to memorize the states and their capitals. The children have a general idea of what each state is like, including their major agricultural and economic products.

Most animals can be recognized at this level; echidnas and platypuses join more familiar animals as good subjects for stories and articles. Many cities, countries and sites are introduced by fifth grade. If you choose to write about an unusual country, you should be sure to place it geographically; tell your reader Belize is in Central America and Ghana is on the west coast of Africa.

Prehistory is usually studied in fifth grade. Early man, cave paintings, fire and the development of civilization are often covered. Science teachers would like to make sure the children know that people did not keep dinosaurs as pets and that they actually know the eras these different species walked the earth.

Ecology and environmentalism are major issues in children's magazines, textbooks and general literature. These topics will remain important areas in children's publishing for many years to come.

Nonfiction subjects that are often introduced in fourth grade in a rather casual way, such as hard science and current events, now become very important both in the classroom and out.

Publishing. Become familiar with the magazines for this level. There are a large number of magazines covering everything from unusual animals and robots to ongoing peace and war negotiations to killer bees. Make a visit to your local elementary school and see what magazines they carry.

For the teacher or writer, producing material for a television program (or the program itself) can engage their students and readers in tremendously exciting projects in acting, reading, writing and researching that have relevance to the children's lives. It also provides an excellent and growing market for those who want to write plays for children or work in other dramatic forms. It is just as easy to write for this medium correctly (and teach children to write for it correctly) as it is to produce something in a haphazard manner. Actually, most of the rules for broadcast writing are meant to make the material easier to use during production.

Another alternate market is working with children in the electronic media. That could include computer programs or radio broadcasting, but, because of the low cost and ease of accessiblity, most of the time it means television.

One of the ways to make news stories and other academic subjects relevant and interesting is a process called localization; that is, find a local angle for the story. To do that, you might interview a family from a different country or cover a local ethnic festival. Localization is highly desirable in the classroom, in broadcast writing and writing for local periodicals, but you must be careful not to assume that a broader audience will recognize, or be interested in, local references. National magazines and books aimed at a national market are leery of any type of localization.

This is also a good place to become aware of your options that go beyond the "normal" forms of publishing. Many of these alternate markets are grouped under "electronic rights" in your book publishing contract. Unimportant until recently, they include the possibility of your work being included in computer databases or sent by fax. Some publishers are beginning to only sell material via electronic marketing. To find these publishers, look under the syndicates listing in *Writer's Market*.

Writing Samples. The following excerpt illustrates the technique of sneaking in a history lesson while actually telling a nonfiction story.

> The tales of lost missions in Mexico are told wherever treasure hunters get together. The stories usually start off telling about gold and jewels hidden in the missions. They often end up being about the curses that are supposed to protect the treasure.
>
> Most of these legends are, at best, flights of fancy. They grew out of daydreams and years of searching. Yet, the missions themselves are probably real. More than that, there is some proof the curses are real, too.

Later in the same piece, a geography lesson is incorporated:

> Mountains run down Mexico's west coast and few people live there. Even in the south, where there is lots of water, there are only a few place names on the map. Most of the "towns" shown are really only ranches where you can get some rest.

FIFTH GRADE WORD LIST

abacus	amaze	barge	broadcloth	choir
abide	amazon	barometer	brocade	chord
abode	ambassador	baton	bruise	chorus
abolish	amber	battery	Buddhist	chow
abolition	ambergris	bawl	budget	chowder
abroad	ample	bayonet	bumblebee	chute
abrupt	anarchy	bayou	bundle	clambake
absence	ancestor	bazaar	burden	clamp
absent	annoy	B.C.	burnoose	clan
absorb	ape (copy)	bedraggled	burrow	clash
abundant	appreciate	beer	buzz	classic
ache	Arab	belly	cafeteria	clatter
achieve	archaeology	berate	calculate	cleat
acknowledge	archer	beseech	canine	clog
acrobat	arena	bestow	canter	clot
A.D.	array	betray	caramel	coil
adder	aspect	billion	carcass	collapse
addict	asphalt	bishop	careless	cologne
adjust	assign	blemish	cargo	combat
admiral	associate	blend	carp	comedian
admire	association	blimp	carriage	comedy
adolescent	assort	blister	casual	comet
agent	assume	blond	catalog	comic
agitate	astrology	boar	cathedral	comment
agony	athlete	bobolink	caution	commentator
aide	atom	bodily	cautious	commercial
airtight	attach	bog	cavity	commissar
albatross	attitude	bomb	celebrity	committee
alcohol	attract	boomerang	cellophane	commodity
alert	austere	boon	cellular	commonwealth
algae	avenge	booth	ceremony	commotion
alien	await	borax	chagrin	communicate
alight	award	boulder	chalk	communism
Allah	awhile	brace	chamber	compact
allergic	babe	bracelet	chamberlain	compassion
allergy	badge	brahman	chandelier	compassionate
allowance	ballad	breeches	chant	competition
alternate	bane	bribe	cherish	compliment
altitude	banister	brim	chickadee	comprehend
amateur	barbecue	broadcast	chip	compromise

conceited	debris	disbelief	emerge	fatigue
concentrate	decay	discourage	emergency	fern
confront	deceive	discuss	emphasize	ferret
conserve	declare	disease	employ	fertile
console	decode	disguise	encircle	fertilizer
conspicuous	defeat	disgust	encode	festive
constellation	defend	dishearten	encyclopedia	festivity
consul	degree	disintegrate	enforce	fetish
contain	deity	dispense	engage	fez
contemporary	dejected	dispose	engrave	fiction
contempt	delay	disposition	enlarge	fiery
contend	delegate	distinctive	enterprise	fife
contrite	delegation	distress	entitle	filch
conversation	delicate	domicile	envelope	filter
convict	delicatessen	dominant	equipment	fingerprint
cooperate	deliver	dominate	escort	firecracker
copal	demand	dormitory	essay	fishline
cornmeal	demure	dough	esteem	fizz
correspond	deny	downhearted	estimate	flagpole
corridor	depart	drain	ethics	flamingo
cough	deposit	drake	eve	flank
council	depress	drama	eventually	flannel
counter	depth	drape	evidence	flea
countless	design	droop	evident	flee
cram	desire	drum	examine	flicker
crate	desperate	dune	excess	flint
crease	despise	dungeon	execute	flounder
credit	destiny	dusk	executive	flute
cremate	destruction	dynamic	exile	focus
crimson	destructive	eager	expand	folklore
critical	detail	earthenware	expert	ford
criticize	determine	earthquake	export	forego
Cro-magnon	develop	eclipse	express	foreign
crouch	devote	ecology	extinct	forge
cruel	devotee	elaborate	extraordinary	fort
cuddle	devour	elder (ly)	extreme	forthright
curtain	dial	electronic	fable	fortress
customer	dialect	elegant	fabric	foundation
damage	difficult	eliminate	facility	foxglove
damp	dinar	embarrass	factor	fragrant
dangle	diplomat	emblem	fang	frantic
dazzle	disappoint	embroider	fascinate	fresco

fret	grease	imp	interpret	legal
friar	grief	impatient	interview	legend
fried	gripe	imperial	intimate	legislation
frightened	groom	imply	introduce	leisure
fringe	groove	import	invade (ing)	license
frizz	grub	impress	invest	lilac
fro	grudge	impression	investigate	limp
frontier	grudgingly	impulse	iris	linden
fumble	grumble	incense	Islam	link
fungus	gust	incident	itch	liquor
future	gymnasium	incline (d)	item	literature
gallery	half-mast	indifferent	jackal	locomotive
gamble	hardship	indignant	jackdaw	locust
gape	hardy	induce	jagged	loft
garb	harsh	indulge	jasper	lofty
garrison	haunch	industry	jealous	longitude
gaze	hearth	infant	jeer	loom
gazelle	hearty	inferior	jersey	loop
gelatin	heave	infinite	jewel (ry)	lope
genial	hemp	influence	jovial	lotus
genuine	herb	inform	justification	loyal
geographic	hermit	informal	juvenile	lull
geography	heroic	information	kindle	lurch
geologist	herring	inherit	kingfisher	lure
geology	hindquarter	initiate	knave	lurk
gigantic	Hindu	injure	Koran	mackerel
ginger	hinge	injury	lagoon	magician
gland	hoarse	inland	lair	magnolia
glee (ful)	hoax	inner	landslide	magpie
gnarled	holy	innocent	lanky	mainland
gnat	homespun	innumerable	lantern	mammal
goldenrod	honeysuckle	inscribe	lark	mammoth
goldfinch	hoop	insist	larkspur	mandarin
good-natured	hornet	inspect	Latin	mango
gooseberry	hothouse	instance	latitude	manifest
gorge	hover	instinct	launch	mansion
gorgeous	hurl	institute	laurel	manure
gossip	hymn	insult	lawyer	margin
gourd	identity	insure	lecture	marigold
grapefruit	ignore	intent	ledge	marine
gravity	imitate	interior	lee	marrow
graze	immature	international	leek	marsh

marshal	morsel	outer	pistol	profession
mason	mosque	outer space	pivot	profile
massive	motive	overflow	plague	prolong
mastiff	mush	overtake	plait	promenade
material	musical	overwhelm	plank	prominent
mathematical	musk	ozone	plantation	promote
mathematics	musket	packet	plaque	promotion
mature	muskrat	pagoda	plea	pronghorn
mean (average)	mutton	paleontologist	plead	prop
meatloaf	mutual	pallet	pleat	prosper
mechanic	napkin	pane	pledge	protein
mediate	naught	pantry	plod	prow
medium	naughty	parakeet	plug	pulse
menace	navigate	parallel	plumber	pursue
mental	Neanderthal	paranormal	plunder	pursuit
mention	noisy	particle	policy	pyramid
meteor	nominate	partner	poll	quaint
midge	nonetheless	pasty	Pope	quay
milestone	nonfiction	patron	porridge	quote
mimosa	nonsense	pave	porter	ragged
mineral	normal	pavilion	portrait	rally
minor	nostril	peddler	pounce	ranch
minstrel	notable	penalty	poverty	rascal
mint	notch	penetrate	prank	rave
minuet	notion	peril	precaution	ravine
miracle	novel	permanent	precise	react
mirth	novice	persist	prehistoric	reality
miser	numeral	personality	prehistory	receipt
misfortune	oath	persuade	preoccupy	reception
mislead	oatmeal	petal	pretext	recite
mission	obstacle	pewter	prevail	reckless
moan	obstinate	philosophy	previous (ly)	reckon
mode	obtain	phonograph	prick	recommend
modify	obvious	photograph	prim	recreation
mold	onyx	phrase	primary	reef
molecule	opal	physical	prime	reel
monarch	operator	picnic	primitive	refer
monastery	opponent	pilgrim	prior	reform
mongoose	orchard	pillar	privilege	refuge
monstrous	orient	pilot	pro	refute
moor	orphan	pimple	procure	regiment
mope	osprey	pirate	profess	registration

regret	romance	shimmer	spar	sullen
regulate	roust	shipment	sparkle	sultan
reject	rubbish	shipwreck	sparrow	summit
release	rugged	shove	spearhead	superintendent
relic	ruin	shred	species	supernatural
rely	rumor	shrill	specific	superstition
remote	rural	shrine	specimen	suppress
renaissance	saber	shrink	spectacle	supreme
renown	saber-toothed	shuttle	spectator	surge
replace	sable	siege	spiritual	surgeon
reproduce	sally	sieve	splotch	surrender
reputation	sample	site	spout	survey
research	sapling	sketch	sprint	survive
resent	sauce	skull	spurt	suspect
reside	savage	skyline	squat	suspend
residence	scar	slab	squeeze	sustain
resident	scheme	slam	stab	swagger
resign	scholar	slaughter	stalagmite	sweetmeat
resin	scissors	sled	stall	swine
resolution	scold	sleeve	stampede	symbol
resolve	scorpion	slice	stanza	tank
resort	screech	slim	starve	Taoist
resource	scroll	slipper	stereoscope	taper
respond	scuff	slit	stoop	target
restaurant	seam	slob	strait	tariff
restore	selfish	sloth	strand	tarry
restrain	sensation	slug	strap	tart
resume	sensitive	slugger	streak	taunt
retain	sensitivity	slump	stride	tavern
retort	sentiment	smite	strife	television
revenge	sentinel	smog	strive	temperature
reverse	sentry	snarl	stroll	temporary
revolt	sergeant	sneeze	strut	temptation
revolution	sermon	snorkel	stubborn	tenant
revolve	serpent	snort	studio	tendency
revolver	shaggy	snout	submarine	tense
rhythm	shaman	snuggle	submerge	terrace
ridge	shatter	soak	substance	terrier
rigid	shear	solemn	substantial	terrific
robust	sheer	solitary	substitute	theory
roe	shellfish	solution	suitor	threat
rogue	sherbet	sooth	sulky	three-fourths

threshold	torture	trousers	vex	wharf
throb	tote	trudge	vexation	wheeze
throng	tough	turban	vibrant	whiff
thrush	tourist	turbulent	vibrate	whimper
thyself	tournament	turf	viewpoint	whine
tilt	tradition	turmoil	vigor	wholesome
timber	traffic	turquoise	vigorous	wholly
timid	tragedy	turret	Viking	widespread
tinge	trample	tusk	villain	wigwam
tinker	transfer	tyrant	violent	willing
tinkle	transform	udder	vital	wince
tint	translate	undoubtedly	volunteer	wither
tissue	transparent	unidentified	waddle	wont
toast	transport	unit	waft	worrisome
token	traverse	unite	wail	wouldst
tolerate	treatment	unity	ward	wren
tomb	trench	uproar	ware	wriggle
tomfoolery	tribute	vacuum	warehouse	wring
toolbox	trickery	vague	warrant	wrist
topic	trifle	vanity	wary	wrought
torch	triumph	vase	waver	yawn
torment	tropical	vault	weevil	yeoman
torrent	trot	venison	welfare	zinc

Sixth Grade

Social Changes. Most sixth graders are preteens or teenagers whose egos are dependent on being seen as that and not as children. Some have their own sources of income, groups of friends and favorite rock bands. Even though your reader may seem to have taken a giant step toward growing up, you should stay away from any positive portrayal of drugs, tobacco, alcohol, street language, explicit sex, graphic crime or violence. Drunkenness should not be portrayed as humorous.

Sixth graders are often very aware of their appearance and, subsequently, how characters in stories look. Description is not only acceptable, it's desired.

In the Classroom. If they haven't already done so, students must now memorize the states, their capitals and their major economic contributions.

Difficult subjects such as death and divorce are often dealt with at this level. Sixth grade also includes sex and health education. As a result, both in-school and leisure reading materials are often problem oriented.

Publishing. Easy-reading books (also called Hi-Lo for high interest, low reading level) begin to appear at this level. Most children now have a fairly sophisticated reading vocabulary and the low achiever has begun to slip between the cracks. The easy-reading book is one way schools and other programs are trying to prevent that from happening. These books are written to cover readers from twelve-years-old through young adults, but they use a controlled vocabulary and sentence length appropriate to the lower vocabulary levels. These books are short and run from 400 to 1,200 words in length. They use a lot of action and dialogue and often use sports, romance, mystery and ethnic-urban problems as subjects for their stories.

Besides being a part of the elementary eight- to twelve-year-old market, the sixth grader is often a real part of the "high school" market. This group officially targets the thirteen- to seventeen-year-old but many readers are somewhat younger. This group uses an adult vocabulary (as long as it is not too sophisticated) and sentence structure. Most books range from 25,000 to 55,000 words and longer lengths are permissible. Popular fiction subjects include romance, suspense, mild horror, the supernatural and humor.

More magazines are aimed at the elementary/junior high group than any other. Eighty percent of the magazine stories are nonfiction and include age-related problems, dress, dating, interviews, fads and special interests. Periodical stories usually range from 1,000 to 3,500 words.

By sixth grade it becomes important to the reader to know exactly how a character, especially a leading character, looks. The just-preteen reader identifies with the leading characters in the books she reads and her concerns about her own appearance are directly transferred to those characters.

Writing Samples. The following example shows the increased description present in stories for this age group. Not only do readers now have longer attention spans, they *want* descriptive details and like to know how characters look.

Elizabeth thought that it was impossible not to admire him. Yet, if you looked at his features one at a time, there was little special about him. He was slim for his 5 feet 10 inches. Besides his eyes, his gold hair and beard were his best features. Elizabeth smiled to herself. She remembered how Bob had grown that beard. . . .

The following excerpt from a nonfiction piece uses the longer sentence length and, again, more description than books for younger readers.

One of the reasons we are not sure if these creatures are real is because their habitats are desolate mountain ranges. In Asia, the Abominable Snowman is supposed to live in the areas that are permanently covered with snow. Its shaggy white coat is the perfect camouflage for its surroundings. In North America, Bigfoot's dark shaggy hair serves the same purpose and, if it is real, it stays well hidden in the shadows and foliage.

SIXTH GRADE WORD LIST

abbey	acute	alto	arid	bachelor
abbot	adhere	alum	aristocrat	balcony
abbreviate	adhesive	aluminum	arrogant	bald
abdomen	adjective	a.m.	artificial	ballot
abduct	adjoin	ambulance	assert	barrier
abhor	adjourn	ambush	assertive	befriend
ablaze	administer	ammonia	asteroid	behalf
abominable	adorn	ammunition	asthma	belle
abstain	adrift	amplify	astride	beverage
abstract	aggress	anguish	attain	beware
absurd	aggressive	animate	attire	bias
abuse	agile	anoint	audible	billiards
accent	alias	anticipate	autobiography	binoculars
access	alibi	antique	autograph	biography
accessory	alkaline	anvil	automatic	biosphere
accommodate	allege	apologize	aviation	blink
accumulate	alley	apology	awe	blotch
accurate	allied	apparatus	awkward	bluff
acquit	alloy	ardent	babble	blunt

bondage	cartridge	comprise	credible	distribute
bonnet	cauldron	concede	credulous	disturb
bonus	cavalry	concession	creed	draught
bounce	cayuse	concord	crepe	dread
bouquet	celestial	condense	crescent	dubious
bout	cemetery	confederate	crevice	duplicate
boycott	census	confide	crotch	durable
bract	cereal	confident	cultivate	dynamite
brandish	certificate	confidential	culture	eaves
bravado	certify	conform	cunning	ecstasy
bravo	chancellor	confound	curfew	eddy
brew	characteristic	congratulate	custom	ejaculate
brier	charcoal	congregation	cutlass	elastic
brig	chariot	conscious	cylinder	emigrant
brigantine	chauffeur	conscript	daft	eminent
brink	chime	conscription	damsel	emphatic
brisk	chivalry	constable	dangerous	enamel
bristle	chronicle	consternation	decapitate	enchant
bronco	chum	contagious	decline	encrust
brutal	cinch	contaminate	dedicate	endanger
brute	circumstantial	contemplate	deduce	endow
buckle	cite	contrive	defy	enlist
buckskin	clamor	controversy	deliberate	enliven
buffet	clause	convent	demigod	enrage (d)
buggy	clergyman	convention	demonstrate	enrich
bugle	client	conventional	depose	environment
bung	clumsy	cope	depression	episode
burlap	coax	cordial	derelict	equator
bust	cocaine	core	descend	equivalent
bustle	coffin	cork	desolate	era
calamity	cog	corps	detest	err
calcium	collision	corrupt	dethrone	essential
calico	combustion	cosmetics	devastate	et cetera
camouflage	commence	courtier	diminutive	etc.
campus	commend	covert	din	evolution
cancel	compartment	covet	dire	exaggerate
cancer	compensation	cow (intimidate)	disaster	excel
canopy	competent	cowpuncher	discard	exclude
canvas	complex	craftsmanship	discipline	exclusive
capacity	complicate	crag	dispute	exert
caption	comply	cramp	distaste	exhilarate
caravan	compress	crave	distinguish	expel

expire	formula	gypsy	impetus	lard
exploit	forsake	habitable	implement	latch
exquisite	fortnight	habitat	imprison	laundry
exterminate	fragile	hackle	incapable	lavish
extravagant	fragment	hark	inconvenient	leak
faculty	frail	haughty	incredible	lease
famine	fraud	hazard	incredulous	legion
fantastic	friction	headache	indispensable	legitimate
fathom	frigid	heartache	index	levee
fauna	frolic	heathen	indoor	levy
fend	furrow	helm	infect	liable
ferry	gait	hemisphere	inflect	limpid
fervor	gallows	hemlock	ingenious	listless
feud	garage	hereafter	inhabit	liter
fidelity	garbage	hew	initial	literal
fixture	gargle	hideous	initiative	logic
flail	garland	hinder	insane	loincloth
flair	garnish	hither	inscription	lounge
flare	gaunt	hoarfrost	insert	lowland
flax	germ	hoary	install	lunatic
fleece	ghastly	hoist	intend	lunge
fleet	gild	homage	intense (ive)	lush
flexible	gin	horde	intention	lust
fling	gingerly	horizontal	internal	lyre
flirt	girdle	hose	interval	ma'am
flop	glaze	hue	intricate	magistrate
flora	glen	hunch	intrude	malice
flotation	glimmer	hunker	invisible	malignant
flotsum	glisten	hydrogen	involve	malinger
fluid	gnome	hysteria	inward	manuscript
fluorescent	gospel	hysterical	irk	mar
fluster	graham	identical	irregular	marquis
foliage	grammar	idiot	irritate	martyr
fore	grapeshot	idol (ize)	jaunty	massacre
forefather	grapple	ignite	jibe	mattress
foreman	grope	illuminate	jostle	maturity
foresight	gruel	illusion	joust	maxim
foretell	guarantee	illustrious	khaki	maximum
forfeit	guidepost	immaculate	kilo	mead
forlorn	gully	immigrant	laden	mechanical
former	gutter	immobile	lament	mechanism
formidable	guttural	impart	lapse	medal

meddle	obscure	pestilence	proprietor	reconcile
meditate	occupation	petroleum	province	recount
melancholy	omen	petticoat	provoke	recourse
mellow	ominous	petty	prowess	recruit
menu	omit	Pharaoh	prudent	recur
merchandise	oppress	phase	pry	redeem
mercury	oracle	phenomenon	psalm	redouble
mesa	orchestra	physics	psychic	refine
metropolitan	ordain	piecemeal	psychology	reflex
microphone	organic	pious	pulp	refrain
mimic	organism	pipeline	quarry	refresh
mince	outlandish	piteous	quench	regain
miniature	outrage	plateau	query	regal
minimum	outright	platter	quill	rehearse
minority	outward	plight	quilt	reheat
miraculous	outwit	plume	quoit	relay
mobil	pageant	plump	radiant	relish
mobilize	pamphlet	ply	radiate	reluctant
mock-up	panel	p.m.	radical	remnant
momentum	pang	poach	radioactive	remonstrate
monopoly	papier-mache	poise	radius	remorse
mortgage	paragraph	pomp	raft	renounce
motivate	paralysis	ponder	rafter	repel
motto	paralyze	pore	raid	repent
municipal	parish	pork	ramble	replenish
muster	parson	postpone	ramp	repose
mute	partial	poultry	rampart	reproach
mutiny	partition	precede	random	repulse
muzzle	passion	precipice	ransom	requisition
myriad	passport	predict	rapture	respiration
narrate	pastime	preface	rash	respite
naturalist	pathetic	prejudice	ratify	restrict
negative	patter	preliminary	ratio	retrieve
neutral	peal	premise	ravage	revenue
nitrogen	pellet	prescribe	ravenous	revive
nook	peninsula	preside	ravish	rhyme
nourish	pension	presume	razor	ridicule
nuclear	perceive	privateer	reassure	ridiculous
nuisance	perpetual	prod	reclaim	riot
nymph	perplex	profound	recline	rite
obligation	persecute	prohibit	recollect	ritual
oblige	perspire	propel	recompense	role

rotate	shawl	stalwart	tact	tumult
routine	sheaf	stamen	tactics	tunic
rove	shelf	stammer	taint	tussle
ruby	shirk	staple	tankard	tutor
ruffle	shrewd	starch	tapestry	twain
Sabbath	shroud	stature	tarpaulin	twang
saga	shun	stimulate	tawny	typical
salesperson	sickle	stitch	tedious	tyranny
saloon	signature	stockade	tenement	ultimate
salvation	significant	stow	terminate	unanimous
sanction	signify	strangle	tether	unbidden
sane	simulate	strategy	text	uncanny
sapphire	sinew	strenuous	texture	unique
sash	skim	stress	thermometer	unison
satellite	slant	stricken	thresh	unruly
satin	slash	strict	thrift	uphold
satyr	sledge	stubble	thrive	upholster
saunter	slouch	stud	toll	upholstery
savior	smack	stunt	topple	uranium
savor	smother	subdue	tornado	urgent
savory	smuggle	sublime	totter	usher
scabbard	snare	subsequent	towel	utensil
scandal	sneer	subside	trait	utilize
scant	snore	subtle	tranquil	vacant
scarf	snuff	suburb	transit	valiant
schedule	snug	succession	transmit	valve
scoff	soar	suckling	transom	vamoose
scope	socket	suffice	treacherous	vanquish
scorch	sod	suffocate	treble	veer
scour	sodden	sundry	tremor	vehicle
scourge	sombrero	superb	trespass	vengeance
scow	sonnet	supervise	tribunal	verdict
scrub	spade	supple	trigger	verge
scull	span	surly	trinket	version
scurvy	spasm	surmise	tripod	vertical
senior	spectrum	surmount	trophy	veteran
sensible	speculate	surpass	tropic	vicinity
serene	sphere	surplus	troth	vicious
serf	spire	swarthy	trough	vile
serge	splinter	syllable	truant	vinegar
session	sprawl	symphony	truce	virgin
shale	squadron	symptom	tumor	virtually

vivid	warble	whiskey	wrench	yelp
vocabulary	wardrobe	whoop	wrest	yoke
void	wasteland	wield	wrestle	yore
wallet	wayfarer	wile	wretched	zeal
wallow	weld	withal	writ	zealous
waltz	whim	wizard	writhe	zephyr
wan	whir	woo	yearn	zest

Thesaurus

The thesaurus is used like any other thesaurus — as a tool for substituting words. I've tried to include words from a range of grades; however, sometimes this is not possible. You'll find that at times you'll have to substitute phrases and clauses because there is no word that's accurate.

Some of the words previously listed in the book are not included in the thesaurus either because they don't have any synonyms or there are no synonyms understood at sixth grade and below. For example, the word nitrogen has no synonyms, so if you don't think your audience will understand it, define it or introduce it to them in the text.

a K: one K
abandon 4th:
    A. desert 1st, discard 6th, forsake 6th, give up K, leave 1st, quit 1st, reject 5th, surrender 5th, yield 4th
    B. freedom 3rd, liberty 3rd, license 5th, recklessness 5th
abbey 6th: convent 6th, monastery 5th
abbot 6th: monk 4th, priest 4th
abbreviate 6th: abstract 6th, condense 6th, contract 3rd, cut K, cut down K, lessen 1st, reduce 3rd, shorten 2nd, shrink 5th
abdomen 6th: belly 5th, gut 1st, stomach 2nd, tummy K
abduct 6th: kidnap 2nd, seize 3rd, steal 3rd
abhor 6th: condemn 4th, despise 5th, detest 6th, hate 2nd, scorn 4th
abide 5th:
    A. dwell 4th, live K, reside 5th
    B. endure 4th, survive 5th, tolerate 5th
    C. accept 3rd, cling 4th, continue 2nd, remain 2nd
ablaze 6th:
    A. aglow 2nd, alight 5th, gleaming 1st
    B. afire 2nd, aflame 2nd, burning 3rd, on fire K
able 3rd:
    A. capable 4th, competent 6th, qualified 4th
    B. clever 3rd, expert 5th, intelligent 4th, smart 1st
aboard 2nd:
    A. beside 1st
    B. inside K, on K
abode 5th: dwelling 4th, home K, house K, place 1st, residence 5th
abolish 5th: blot out 4th, cancel 6th, destroy 2nd, exterminate 6th

abolition 5th: cancellation 6th, destruction 6th

abominable 6th:

    A. bad K, inferior 5th, poor K, sorry 2nd

    B. cursed 3rd, detestable 6th, hateful 3rd, horrible 4th, horrid 4th, offensive 4th

about K:

    A. around 1st, near 1st

    B. concerning 3rd, regard 4th, respecting 4th

above K: higher 1st, over K

abroad 5th: about K, away K, out K, out of the country K, overseas 1st

abrupt 5th: fast 1st, hasty 2nd, hurried 1st, quick 1st, sharp 1st, sheer 5th, speedy 3rd, steep 2nd, sudden 1st, unexpected 2nd

absence 5th: lack 1st, need 1st, want K

absent 5th: gone 1st, lacking 1st, missing K, not here K, wanting K

absolute 3rd:

    A. clear 2nd, complete 3rd, entire 3rd, genuine 5th, outright 6th, perfect 3rd, real 1st, solid 3rd

    B. ideal 3rd, pure 3rd, simple 2nd, true K, whole 1st

absorb 5th: consume 4th, draw in K, gather 1st, soak up 5th, swallow up 1st, take in K

abstain 6th: decline 6th, deny 5th, forego 5th, give up K, quit 1st, refrain 6th, reject 5th

abstract 6th:

    A. brief 3rd, part 1st, sketch 5th

    B. divide 4th, remove 2nd, separate 3rd, take away K

    C. difficult 5th, general 2nd, ideal 3rd, universal 4th, vague 5th

absurd 6th: comic 5th, dumb 1st, fantastic 6th, foolish 2nd, funny 1st, idiotic 6th, illogical 6th, ridiculous 6th, silly 1st, unreasonable 2nd

abundant 5th: ample 5th, full K, generous 4th, lush 2nd, more than enough 1st, plentiful 2nd

abuse 6th:

    A. exploitation 6th, mistreatment 3rd

    B. damage 5th, harm 3rd, hurt K, injure 5th, mistreat 3rd, misuse 3rd, mock 4th, put down K, ridicule 6th, spoil 4th, wrong 1st

accent 6th:

    A. emphasize 5th, mark 1st, stress 6th

    B. emphasis 5th, pitch 2nd, rhythm 5th, tone of voice 3rd, voice 1st

accept 3rd: adopt 3rd, assume 5th, believe 1st, commence 6th, embrace 4th, get K, receive 2nd, take K

access 6th: admit 4th, approach 3rd, door K, entrance 3rd, entry 3rd, gate 1st, nearing 1st, route 4th, way K

accessory 6th:
>A. aide 5th, helper 1st
>B. decoration 3rd, jewelry 5th, ornament 4th, trim 4th

accident 4th: casualty 5th, chance 2nd, disaster 6th, injury 5th, misadventure 3rd, misfortune 3rd, mistake 1st, twist of fate 3rd

accommodate 6th:
>A. adjust 5th, fit K, suit 1st
>B. aid 2nd, assist 4th, help K

accompany 3rd: attend 3rd, combine 3rd, conduct 3rd, connect 3rd, escort 5th, go with K, join 3rd, link 5th

accomplish 2nd: achieve 5th, close K, complete 3rd

accord 4th:
>A. award 5th, bestow 5th, grant 2nd
>B. admit 4th, agree 2nd, allow 2nd, consent 3rd, permit 3rd

account 3rd:
>A. article 2nd, report 1st, story K, tale 3rd
>B. cause 2nd, motive 5th, reason 1st, sake 3rd
>C. regard 4th, value 2nd, worth 3rd

accumulate 6th: assemble 4th, collect 3rd, gather 1st, keep K, multiply 2nd

accurate 6th:
>A. careful 1st, particular 4th
>B. correct 3rd, exact 2nd, faultless 3rd, precise 5th, right K, true K, without error 4th

accuse 4th: blame 2nd, charge 2nd, fault 3rd

accustom 4th:
>A. adapt 4th, adjust to 5th
>B. acquaint 4th, harden 2nd, season 2nd

ace 2nd:
>A. achieve 5th, best K, get it K, win K
>B. card 1st, eleven 1st, expert 5th, one K, shark 1st, top K

ache 5th:
>A. sadness 1st, sorrow 4th, suffer 2nd
>B. hurt K, pain 2nd, pang 6th

achieve 5th: accomplish 2nd, ace 2nd, complete 3rd, conquer 4th, do K, effect 3rd, finish 1st, fulfill 4th, get K, manage 4th, perform 4th, win K

acid 4th: bitter 3rd, harsh 5th, sour 2nd, tart 5th

acknowledge 5th: accept 3rd, admit 4th, allow 2nd, answer 1st, concede 6th, declare 5th, grant 2nd, profess 4th, reveal 4th

acquaint 4th: accustom 4th, advise 3rd, educate 3rd, inform 5th, instruct 4th, introduce 5th, mention 5th, teach 1st

acquire 4th: assume 5th, attain 6th, buy K, gain 2nd, get K, obtain 5th, purchase 3rd, secure 3rd, take 1st, win K

acquit 6th: clear 2nd, excuse 3rd, find not guilty 4th, forgive 2nd, free K, pardon 4th, release 5th

acrobat 5th: gymnast 5th, tumbler 4th

across 1st: astride 6th, crosswise 1st, opposite to 3rd, over 1st, span 6th

act K:
A. behave 4th, do K, operate 3rd, perform 4th
B. imitate 5th, pretend 2nd
C. action 1st, deed 1st, dramatize 5th, function 4th, play K, task 3rd, work K

action 1st:
A. act K, behavior 4th, conduct 3rd, deed 1st
B. cause 2nd, fulfillment 4th, motion 3rd, movement 2nd, operation 3rd, process 4th, work K

active 3rd: alert 5th, alive 3rd, busy 1st, energetic 4th, moving 1st, productive 3rd, wide-awake 3rd

actor 2nd: agent 5th, doer K, player K

actual 3rd: certain 1st, nonfiction 5th, present K, real 1st, true K

acute 6th: aware 3rd, critical 5th, cutting 1st, intense 6th, keen 4th, pointed 1st, serious 4th, severe 4th, sharp 1st

ad 4th: advertisement 4th, announcement 3rd, promotion 5th, publication 4th, publicity 4th

adapt 4th: accustom 4th, adjust 5th, alter 4th, change 2nd, conform 6th, fit K, harmonize 4th, modify 5th, qualify 4th, regulate 5th, suit 1st

add K: addition 3rd, attach 5th, calculate 5th, combine 3rd, connect 3rd, enlarge 5th, fasten 4th, figure 4th, plus 1st, sum 1st, total 2nd

addict 5th:
A. devotee 5th, one who surrenders to 5th
B. accustom 4th, have a habit 3rd, surrender to 5th

addition 3rd: add K, calculation 5th, extra 1st, mathematics 5th, plus 1st, sum 1st, total 2nd

additionally 3rd: also K, besides 1st, furthermore 3rd

address K:
A. home K, house K, location 3rd
B. aim 3rd, direct 1st, point 1st
C. appeal 3rd, greet 3rd, speak to 1st, speech 2nd, talk to K

adept 4th: able 3rd, capable 4th, expert 5th, good K, skilled 2nd

adhere 6th: attach 5th, cling 4th, combine 3rd, fasten 4th, glue 1st, hold to 1st, join 3rd, link 5th, paste 1st, stick K, tape 1st, unite 5th

adhesive 6th: glue 1st, paste 1st, sticky K, tape 1st

adjoin 6th: attach 5th, connect 3rd, contact 4th, join 3rd, link 5th, meet K, next to K

adjourn 6th: close K, end K, interrupt 3rd, leave 1st, postpone 6th, quit 1st, stop K

adjust 5th: accommodate 6th, accustom 4th, adapt 4th, alter 4th, change 2nd, correct 3rd, fit K, fix 1st, modify 5th, move K, regulate 5th, suit 2nd, vary 4th

adjustment 5th: allowance 5th, change 2nd, concession 6th

administer 6th:
  A. dispense 5th, give K
  B. conduct 3rd, control 2nd, direct 1st, furnish 4th, manage 4th, operate 3rd, oversee 1st, run K, supervise 6th

admire 5th: adore 4th, appreciate 5th, desire 5th, esteem 5th, prize 3rd, regard 4th, respect 2nd, value 2nd

admit 4th:
  A. allow 2nd, let in K, permit 3rd
  B. acknowledge 5th, agree 2nd, concede 6th, confess 4th, reveal 4th

adolescent 5th:
  A. immature 5th, inexperienced 4th
  B. juvenile 5th, teen 2nd, teenager 3rd, youth 2nd

adopt 3rd: acquire 4th, assume 5th, choose 3rd, embrace 4th, receive 1st, take in K

adore 4th: admire 5th, cherish 5th, honor 1st, idolize 6th, love K, prize 3rd, respect 2nd, worship 4th

adorn 6th: beautify 1st, decorate 3rd, dress up K, ornament 4th, trim 4th

adrift 6th:
  A. aimless 3rd, uncertain 1st, unstable 4th
  B. at sea 1st, drifting 2nd, floating 2nd

adult 1st:
  A. grown-up 1st
  B. aged 1st, developed 5th, mature 5th, ripe 1st

advance 2nd: aid 2nd, assist 4th, develop 5th, further 2nd, help K, lift 1st, progress 4th, promote 5th, propel 6th, speed 3rd

advantage 3rd:
  A. edge 1st
  B. beneficial 3rd, benefit 3rd, improvement 3rd, power 1st, useful 2nd

adventure 3rd: exploit 6th, feat 1st, risk 4th, thrill 4th, trip 1st, undertaking 1st, venture 4th

advertise 4th: announce 3rd, promote 5th, publicize 4th

advertisement 4th: ad 4th, announcement 3rd, promotion 5th

advice 3rd: caution 5th, counsel 5th, intelligence 4th, opinion 3rd, suggestion 2nd, teaching 1st, warning 3rd

advise 3rd: acquaint 4th, caution 5th, counsel 5th, guide 1st, persuade 5th, recommend 5th, suggest 2nd, urge 4th

affair 2nd:
  A. circumstance 6th, event 3rd, incident 5th, occasion 3rd, party K
  B. business 2nd, concern 3rd, matter 2nd

affect 4th:
  A. act K, fake 1st, pretend 2nd, simulate 6th
  B. alter 4th, change 2nd, drive 1st, impress 5th, influence 5th, move K,
      stir 3rd, sway 3rd, touch 1st, transform 5th
affection 4th: devotion 5th, emotion 4th, feeling K, fondness 4th, leaning 3rd,
  love K, passion 6th, warmth 2nd
afford 3rd:
  A. allow 2nd, bear K, manage 4th
  B. accord 4th, bestow 5th, confer 4th, furnish 3rd, give K, grant 2nd, offer 2nd
afire 2nd: aflame 2nd, on fire K
aflame 2nd: afire 2nd, burning 3rd, on fire K
afloat 2nd:
  A. in the air K, on air K
  B. adrift 6th, at sea 1st, drifting 2nd, floating 2nd, on board 1st
afraid 1st: anxious 4th, fearful 1st, frightened 5th, scared 1st, shy 1st, timid 5th
after K: back 1st, behind 1st, below 1st, following 1st, later 1st, next K,
  rear 3rd, then K
afternoon 1st: evening 1st, p.m. 6th
afterward 4th: later 1st, subsequently 6th, when it was over K
again K: another time 1st, in addition 3rd, once more 1st,
  repeatedly 4th
against 1st:
  A. beside 1st, touching 1st
  B. contrary 4th, disagree 2nd, opposed to 3rd
age 1st:
  A. era 6th, period 2nd
  B. develop 5th, grow old K, mature 6th, ripen 1st, season 2nd, years 1st
aged 1st: adult 1st, mature 5th, old K, seasoned 2nd
agent 5th: actor 2nd, executive 5th, instrument 3rd, medium 5th, operator 5th,
  vehicle 6th, worker 1st
aggress 6th: assault 4th, attack 3rd, invade 5th, provoke 6th
aggressive 6th: assertive 6th, attacking 3rd, forceful 2nd, invading 5th,
  offensive 4th, pushy 1st
agile 6th: flexible 6th, limber 4th, supple 6th, swift 4th
agitate 5th: disturb 6th, excite 4th, move K, rock K, shake 1st, shock 1st,
  stir 3rd, sway 3rd, upset 3rd
ago 1st: before 1st, earlier 1st, gone 1st, past 1st, previous 5th
agony 5th:
  A. struggle 1st
  B. ache 5th, anguish 6th, distress 5th, grief 5th, hurt K, misery 4th, pain 2nd,
      suffering 2nd, torment 5th, trial 4th

agree 2nd: accord 4th, acknowledge 5th, conform 6th, consent 3rd, correspond 5th, harmonize 4th

agriculture 4th: cultivation 6th, farming 1st, gardening K, harvesting 4th

ahead 1st:
    A. forward 3rd
    B. before K, first 1st, in front 1st

aid 2nd:
    A. gift K, relief 4th
    B. assist 4th, back 1st
    C. assistance 4th, backing 1st, help K, support 4th

aide 5th: assistant 4th, helper 1st

aim 3rd:
    A. address K, direct 1st, focus 5th, point 1st
    B. design 5th, end K, goal 4th, intent 5th, level 3rd, object 1st, objective 2nd

air K:
    A. express 5th, proclaim 4th, reveal 4th, say K, tell K, utter 4th, vent 4th, voice 1st
    B. feeling K
    C. atmosphere 4th, oxygen 4th, ozone 5th

airfield 2nd: airport 1st, landing strip 3rd

airplane 1st: aircraft 1st, airship 1st, jet K, plane 1st

airport 1st: airfield 2nd, field 2nd, landing strip 3rd

airship 1st: aircraft 1st, airplane 1st, jet K

airtight 5th: closed K, sealed 1st, self-contained 5th

alarm 3rd:
    A. bell K, horn 3rd, whistle 4th
    B. alert 5th, amaze 5th, astound 4th, frighten 5th, horrify 4th, scare 1st, shock 1st, startle 4th, surprise 1st, terrify 3rd, upset 3rd, warn 3rd

alas 4th: oh my 1st, pity 3rd, too bad 1st, woe 4th

album 1st: book K, chronicle 6th, record 2nd, register 4th, scrapbook 3rd

alcohol 5th: ale 2nd, beer 1st, liquor 5th, spirits 2nd, wine 1st

ale 2nd: beer 1st, malt 2nd

alert 5th:
    A. active 3rd, awake 3rd, aware 3rd, lively 2nd, wide-awake 3rd
    B. alarm 3rd, awaken 3rd, call attention to 2nd, notify 3rd, warn 3rd

alias 6th: also known as 1st, false name 3rd, name K, pen name 1st

alibi 6th: defense 5th, excuse 3rd, explanation 2nd, justification 5th, pretext 5th, reason 2nd

alien 5th:
    A. foreigner 5th, immigrant 6th, outsider 1st, stranger 1st
    B. different 1st, foreign 5th, hostile 4th, outside 1st, strange 1st, unknown 2nd

alight 5th:
   A. descend 6th, dismount 3rd, get off K
   B. bright 1st, lit K, shining 3rd
   C. land K, perch 5th, roost 2nd

alike 1st: comparable 3rd, equivalent 6th, identical 6th, matching 3rd, same K, similar 4th

alive 3rd:
   A. breathing 1st, existing 3rd, live 1st, living 1st
   B. active 3rd, alert 5th, animated 6th, dynamic 5th, vital 5th

allege 6th: assert 6th, claim 2nd, declare 5th, imply 5th, insist 5th, proclaim 4th, profess 5th, say K, state 1st

allergy 5th: reaction 5th, sensitivity 5th, weakness 3rd

alley 6th: back street 1st, lane 4th, path 1st, road K, walkway 3rd

allied 6th: associated 5th, cooperative 5th, joined 3rd, parallel 5th, related 4th, similar 4th, together 1st

allow 2nd:
   A. acknowledge 5th, admit 4th, concede 6th
   B. endure 4th, go along 1st, let K, permit 3rd, stand K, tolerate 5th, yield 4th
   C. accord 4th, give 4th, grant 2nd

allowance 5th:
   A. amount 2nd, money K, portion 4th, share 2nd, wages 3rd
   B. adjustment 5th, agreement 2nd, change 2nd, concession 6th, consent 3rd

alloy 6th: combination 3rd, compound 4th, mixture 4th

ally 6th:
   A. join 3rd, side with 1st
   B. associate 5th, friend 1st, partner 5th

almost K: approaching 3rd, barely 3rd, just about 1st, nearing 1st, nearly 1st

alone K: apart 3rd, individual 3rd, lone 2nd, lonely 2nd, only K, remote 5th, separate 3rd, single 3rd, sole 4th, solitary 5th, unique 6th

along 1st: beside 1st, in accordance 5th, in the direction 1st, next to K, throughout 2nd, with K

aloud 4th: audible 6th, clearly 2nd, out loud 1st, plainly 2nd, spoken 2nd

alphabet 2nd: code 3rd, letters 1st, signs 1st, symbols 5th

already 1st: before K, by now 1st, previously 5th, so soon K, yet 1st

also K: additionally 3rd, and K, as well K, besides 1st, furthermore 3rd, moreover 3rd, together with 1st, too 1st

altar 4th: platform 4th, table K, temple 3rd

alter 4th: adapt 4th, adjust 5th, amend 4th, change 2nd, correct 3rd, mix 1st, modify 5th, transform 5th, vary 4th

alternate 5th: change 2nd, change off 2nd, other 1st, periodic 4th, rotate 6th, substitute 5th, switch 4th

although 2nd: but K, however 3rd, though 2nd

altitude 5th:
 A. elevation 4th, height 4th, upward 4th
 B. peak 4th, point 1st, top K
always K: constantly 4th, ever K, every time 1st, forever 3rd, regularly 3rd
a.m. 6th: morning 1st
am K: are K, be K, exist 3rd
amateur 5th: beginner 2nd, learner 1st, novice 5th, unpaid 2nd
amaze 5th: astonish 4th, astound 4th, bewilder 3rd, confound 6th, perplex 6th, shock 1st, stun 4th, wow 1st
ambassador 5th: delegate 5th, diplomat 4th, minister 4th
ambition 4th:
 A. aim K, dream K, goal 4th
 B. desire 5th, drive 1st, hope K, need 1st, wish K
ambulance 6th: emergency vehicle 6th
ambush 6th: assault 4th, attack 3rd, entrap 3rd, snare 6th, surprise 1st
amen 4th: so be it K, truly 1st, yes K
amend 4th: adapt 4th, adjust 5th, alter 4th, change 2nd, correct 3rd, modify 5th, reform 5th
amid 4th: among 1st, center 2nd, during 1st, in K, mixed 1st
amiss 3rd: astray 3rd, bad K, faulty 4th, off K, wrong 1st
ammunition 6th: arms 1st, bullets 4th, guns K, rifles 4th, shells 1st, weapons 4th
among 1st: amid 4th, between 1st, in K, mixed 1st, surrounded 3rd, within 1st
amount 2nd:
 A. measure 2nd, part 1st, portion 4th
 B. count K, number K, sum 1st, total 2nd, whole 1st
ample 5th: big K, enough 1st, generous 4th, huge 1st, liberal 4th, many K, much 1st, plenty 1st, sufficient 3rd, unlimited 3rd
amplify 6th: broaden 3rd, develop 5th, enlarge 5th, exaggerate 6th, expand 5th, extend 4th, increase 3rd, overdo 1st
amuse 4th: charm 3rd, entertain 4th, interest 1st, please K
anarchy 5th: disorder 3rd, mess 1st, riot 6th, without discipline 6th
ancestor 5th: forefathers 6th, parent 3rd, relative 4th
anchor 4th:
 A. prop 5th, weight 1st
 B. attach 5th, fix 1st, grasp 4th, hold 1st, moor 5th, secure 3rd
ancient 3rd: antique 6th, elderly 5th, old K
and K: also K, too 1st
anew 3rd: again 1st, newly 1st, once more K, renew 4th
angel 4th: fairy 4th, good K, heavenly 2nd, spirit 2nd
anger 1st:
 A. annoy 5th, bother 2nd, vex 5th

B. annoyance 5th, indignance 5th, rage 4th, vexation 5th

angle 3rd:
  A. catch 1st, fish K
  B. corner 2nd, curve 3rd
  C. aspect 5th, attitude 5th, side K, slant 6th, viewpoint 5th

angry 1st: annoyed 5th, cross 1st, enraged 6th, frantic 5th, mad K, vexed 5th, violent 5th

anguish 6th: ache 5th, agony 5th, distress 5th, grief 5th, heartache 6th, hurt K, misery 4th, pain 2nd, regret 5th, sorrow 4th, suffering 2nd, torment 5th, torture 5th

animal K:
  A. bodily 5th, brutal 6th, physical 5th
  B. beast 3rd, creature 3rd, mammal 5th

animate 6th: alive 3rd, create 3rd, enliven 6th, moving 1st

animated 6th: active 3rd, alert 5th, alive 3rd, busy 1st, dynamic 5th, energetic 4th, live 1st, lively 1st, moving 1st

announce 3rd: advertise 4th, broadcast 5th, communicate 5th, declare 5th, inform 5th, post 1st, proclaim 4th, promote 5th, publish 4th, state 1st, tell K

announcement 3rd: ad 4th, bulletin 3rd, promotion 5th, publicize 4th, statement 2nd

annoy 5th: anger 1st, badger 2nd, bother 2nd, fret 5th, pester 2nd, trouble 1st, vex 5th, worry 1st

annual 4th: yearly 2nd

anoint 6th: bless 3rd, choose 3rd, oil K

another 1st:
  A. different 1st, other 1st
  B. an extra 1st, one more K

answer K:
  A. acknowledgment 5th, retort 5th
  B. acknowledge 5th, defend 5th, refute 5th, respond 5th

anticipate 6th: await 5th, expect 2nd, forecast 4th, foretell 6th, hope K, predict 6th, prevent 3rd, stop K

antique 6th: ancient 3rd, elderly 5th, old K

antler 4th: horn 3rd, rack 1st

anxiety 4th: anguish 6th, care K, concern 3rd, doubt 5th, dread 6th, fear 1st, trouble 1st, worry 1st

anxious 4th: nervous 1st, restless 4th, suffering 2nd, worried 1st

any K: all K, every K, one K, some K, whatever 1st

anybody 1st: anyone 1st

anyone 1st: anybody 1st, everybody 3rd, everyone 1st, whoever 1st

anything 1st: everything 1st, whatever 1st

anyway 1st: however 3rd, nevertheless 4th, so K

apart 3rd: aside 3rd, away 1st, disjointed 4th, distant 4th, far 1st, private 3rd, secret 1st, separate 3rd, singly 3rd

apartment 1st: abode 5th, chamber 5th, dwelling 4th, room K

ape 5th: copy 3rd, imitate 5th, mock 4th

apologize 6th: beg pardon 4th, confess 4th, regret 5th

apology 6th: alibi 6th, amend 4th, excuse 3rd, explanation 2nd, make amends 4th, reason 2nd

apparatus 6th: a fixture 6th, construction 3rd, device 4th, equipment 5th, instrument 3rd, machinery 1st, mechanism 6th, tool 1st

apparent 3rd: clear 2nd, evident 2nd, noticeable 3rd, obvious 5th, plain 2nd, visible 4th

appeal 3rd:
A. plea 5th, prayer 3rd, request 4th
B. address K, ask K, beg 1st, plead 5th

appear 2nd:
A. look K, seem 1st
B. arrive 2nd, emerge 5th, rise 1st

appearance 2nd:
A. arrival 2nd, coming K, emergence 5th
B. attitude 5th, look K

appetite 4th: craving 6th, desire 5th, hunger 2nd, longing 1st, lust 6th, passion 6th, taste 1st

apply 2nd:
A. employ 5th, use K
B. add K, lay on 1st, stick K
C. ask K, beg 1st, request 4th, seek 1st

appoint 3rd: choose 3rd, commission 2nd, determine 5th, elect 3rd, name K, set K

appreciate 5th:
A. comprehend 5th, detect 4th, realize 2nd, recognize 3rd, understand 1st
B. admire 5th, cherish 5th, like K, prize 3rd, respect 2nd, treasure 4th, value 2nd

approach 3rd:
A. address 3rd, greet 3rd
B. begin K, start 1st
C. advance 2nd, near 1st

approve 4th:
A. allow 2nd, authorize 3rd, certify 6th, commend 6th
B. admire 5th, like K, value 2nd

apron 3rd: cover 1st, skirt 3rd

apt 5th:
A. adept 4th, clever 3rd

B. fitting 2nd, inclined 5th, likely 1st, proper 3rd

aquarium 2nd: pond 1st, pool 1st, tank 5th

arc 4th: arch 4th, bend K, bow 1st, curve 3rd

arch 4th:

    A. arc 4th, bend K, bow 1st, curve 3rd

    B. clever 3rd, cunning 6th, sly 4th

arctic 3rd: cold K, freezing 4th, frigid 6th, frozen 4th, polar 3rd

ardent 6th: eager 5th, enthusiastic 4th, intense 6th, passionate 6th, severe 4th, zealous 6th

are K: am K, exist 3rd, to be K

area 3rd: belt 2nd, district 4th, locality 4th, part 1st, range 3rd, region 4th, section 4th, space 1st, territory 3rd, vicinity 6th, zone 4th

arena 5th: field 2nd, stage 3rd

argue 3rd: discuss 5th, dispute 6th, explain 2nd, object 1st

arid 6th: bald 6th, bare 3rd, barren 5th, dry 1st, scorched 6th

arise 4th: appear 2nd, ascend 4th, elevate 2nd, emerge 5th, lift 1st, rise 1st, soar 6th, start 1st

aristocrat 6th: gentleman 3rd, noble 3rd, nobleman 3rd

arithmetic 3rd: math 5th, mathematics 5th

ark 2nd: boat 1st, ship 1st

arm K:

    A. branch 2nd, limb 4th

    B. ammunition 6th, equip 5th, weapon 4th

armload 2nd: bunch 3rd, enough K, full K, lots K, plenty 1st

armor 4th: cover 1st, defend 5th, protection 4th, shield 4th

arms 1st: ammunition 6th, guns K, weapons 4th

army 1st:

    A. legion 6th, military 3rd, soldiers 3rd

    B. bunch 3rd, horde 6th, host 4th, mob 4th, swarm 4th

around 1st: about K, all over K, encircle 5th, near 1st, outside 1st, surrounding 3rd

arouse 4th: alarm 3rd, alert 5th, awaken 3rd, compel 3rd, get up K, motivate 6th, provoke 6th, roust 5th

arrange 3rd:

    A. accommodate 6th, decide 1st, plan 1st, settle 2nd

    B. align 5th, array 5th, class 1st, group 1st, line up K, organize 4th, order 1st, sort 2nd

array 5th:

    A. attire 6th, dress K

    B. align 5th, arrange 3rd, battery 5, line up K, order 1st, place K

arrest 3rd: capture 3rd, catch 1st, halt 4th, imprison 6th, jail 4th, seize 3rd, stop K, take K

arrive 2nd: appear 2nd, come K, happen 1st, land K, occur 3rd

arrogant 6th: haughty 6th, proud 2nd, self-important 2nd, vain 4th

arrow 2nd: arm K, focus 5th, point 1st, pointer 1st, signal 4th, spear 4th

art K: ability 3rd, craft 2nd, cunning 6th, skill 2nd

article 2nd: account 3rd, clause 6th, detail 5th, item 5th, object 1st, piece 1st, story K, thing K, unit 5th

artificial 6th: fake 1st, false 3rd, imitation 5th, man-made 1st, manufactured 3rd, mock 4th, unreal 1st

as K: because K, similarly 4th, since 1st, so K

ascend 4th: arise 4th, climb 1st, elevate 2nd, float 1st, go up K, incline 5th, lift 1st, mount 2nd, raise 1st, rise 1st, soar 6th

ash 3rd: coal 2nd

ashamed 4th: embarrassed 5th, humbled 4th, shy 1st, uneasy 1st

ashore 2nd: beached 1st, grounded 1st, on land K, on shore 1st

aside 3rd:
A. apart 3rd, away K
B. beside 1st, by K, next to K, parallel 5th

ask K: demand 5th, examine 5th, expect 2nd, inquire 3rd, question 1st, request 4th

asleep 3rd: idle 4th, nap K, napping 1st, resting 1st, sleeping 1st, snoozing 4th

aspect 5th: angle 3rd, appearance 2nd, look K, point of view 2nd, quality 4th, slant 6th

asphalt 5th: blacktop 1st

assault 4th: attack 3rd, batter 1st, beat 1st, pound 2nd, raid 6th

assemble 4th: collect 3rd, compose 4th, gather 1st, put together 1st, summon 4th

assert 6th: allege 6th, claim 2nd, declare 5th, profess 5th, push 1st, state 1st

assertive 6th: aggressive 6th, pushy 1st, strong 1st

assign 5th: appoint 3rd, award 5th, give K, grant 2nd, name K, set K

assist 4th: accommodate 6th, aid 2nd, help K, support 4th

assistance 4th: aid 2nd, backing 1st, help K, relief 4th, support 4th

assistant 4th: aid 2nd, clerk 2nd, helper K, maid 3rd

associate 5th:
A. companion 3rd, friend 1st, partner 5th
B. connect 3rd, join 3rd, link 5th, mix 1st, relate 4th

association 5th:
A. companionship 3rd, friendship 2nd, union 3rd
B. club 1st, group 1st, society 3rd

assort 5th: class 1st, grade 2nd, list 2nd, organize 4th, separate 3rd, sort 1st

assume 5th:
A. acquire 4th, adopt 3rd, take on K
B. gather 1st, guess 1st, presume 6th, suppose 2nd, theory 5th, think 1st

assure 3rd: assert 6th, insure 5th, secure 3rd, support 4th

astonish 4th: amaze 5th, astound 4th, surprise 1. *See* astound.

astound 4th: amaze 5th, astonish 4th, bewilder 3rd, confound 6th, perplex 6th, stun 4th

astray 3rd: amiss 3rd, false 3rd, mistaken 1st, off K, wrong 1st

astride 6th: across 1st

astronaut 4th: pilot 5th, star man K

at K: in K, near 1st, on K, upon 1st, within 1st

athlete 5th: acrobat 5th, sportsman 1st, sportswoman 1st

atmosphere 4th:
A. condition 3rd, feel K, feeling K, setting 2nd
B. air 1st, ozone 5th

atom 5th: bit 1st, molecule 5th, particle 5th

atop 3rd: high K, on top K, summit 5th

attach 5th: add K, adhere 6th, adjoin 6th, fasten 4th, fix 1st, join 3rd, link 5th, pin K, stick K, stop K

attack 3rd: aggress 6th, ambush 6th, assault 4th, battle 2nd, charge 2nd, fight K, raid 6th

attain 6th: accomplish 2nd, achieve 5th, acquire 4th, fulfill 4th, gain 2nd, get K, realize 2nd, secure 3rd, win K

attempt 2nd: begin K, initiate 5th, start 1st, strive 5th, tackle 4th, try K

attend 3rd:
A. go to K, visit 1st
B. mind 1st, nurse K, watch 1st

attention 2nd: alertness 5th, awareness 3rd, focus 5th, note 1st, notice 3rd, observe 3rd, regard 4th

attire 6th:
A. adorn 6th, array 5th, dress up K
B. clothes 1st, dress K, garb 5th

attitude 5th: angle 3rd, appearance 2nd, bearing 2nd, feeling K, position 2nd, slant 6th, thought 1st, view 2nd

attract 5th: charm 3rd, draw K, engage 5th, fascinate 5th, invite 3rd, lure 5th, pull K

audible 6th: aloud 6th, heard K, out loud 1st

austere 5th: bare 3rd, formal 4th, grim 4th, harsh 5th, plain 2nd, severe 4th, stern 4th, stiff 3rd, strict 6th

author 3rd: composer 4th, creator 3rd, maker 1st, writer 1st

authority 3rd:
A. adept 4th, expert 5th, knowledgeable 3rd, master 1st
B. control 2nd, force 1st, power 1st, rule K

authorize 3rd:
A. establish 3rd, institute 5th

B. allow 2nd, let K, permit 3rd

autobiography 6th: confessions 6th, diary 3rd, history 2nd, journal 2nd, memory 3rd

autograph 6th: name K, signature 6th

automatic 6th: habit 3rd, mechanical 6th, reflex 6th, self-acting 3rd, set K, trained 1st

automobile 3rd: car K

autumn 3rd: fall K, harvest 4th

avenge 5th: punish 4th, repay K, revenge 5th

avenue 3rd: approach 3rd, boulevard 4th, lane 4th, road K, street 1st, way K

average 3rd: center 2nd, common 2nd, mean 5th, middle 2nd, normal 5th, ordinary 3rd, typical 6th, usual 3rd

aviation 6th: flight 2nd, flying K

avoid 3rd: escape 2nd, shun 6th, skirt 3rd

await 5th: abide 5th, expect 2nd, stay 2nd, wait for K

awake 3rd: alert 5th, alive 3rd, aware 3rd, conscious 6th, up K, watchful 2nd

awaken 3rd: arouse 4th, roust 5th, waken 1st, wake up 1st

award 5th:
   A. bonus 6th, medal 6th, prize 3rd, trophy 6th
   B. allow 2nd, bestow 5th, give K, grant 2nd, present K

aware 3rd:
   A. familiar 3rd, informed 5th, know 1st
   B. alive 3rd, awake 3rd, conscious 6th

away K: abroad 5th, absent 5th, far 1st, gone 1st, not here K, there 1st

awe 6th: astonishment 4th, bewilderment 3rd, fear 1st, respect 2nd, reverence 6th, surprise 1st, wonder 1st

awful 3rd: bad K, dreaded 6th, fearful 2nd, horrible 4th, terrible 3rd

awkward 6th: coarse 4th, clumsy 6th, rough 4th, rude 2nd, uneasy 1st

ax K:
   A. pick 1st
   B. chop 2nd, cut K, hack 6th, split 4th

babble 6th: chatter 1st, gab 1st, gossip 5th, talk K

babe 5th: baby K, girl K, infant 5th, tot 2nd

baby K:
   A. humor 4th, indulge 5th, pet 1st, spoil 4th
   B. babe 5th, child K, infant 5th, newborn 1st

bachelor 6th: man K, single 3rd

back K:
   A. behind 1st, other side 1st, reverse 5th
   B. spine 4th
   C. aid 2nd, assist 4th, help K, support 4th

backbone 4th:
    A. back 1st, spine 4th
    B. character 2nd, courage 4th, guts 1st, resolve 5th, spirit 2nd
background 4th:
    A. conditions 3rd, experience 4th
    B. distance 1st, environment 6th, horizon 4th, setting 2nd, surroundings 3rd
backing 1st: aid 2nd, assistance 4th, encouragement 4th, help K, relief 4th,
    support 4th
backpack 4th: bag 1st, knapsack 4th
backward 4th: awkward 6th, inside out 1st, reverse 5th, wrong 1st
backwoods 4th: country 1st, forest 2nd, frontier 5th, outback 1st, wild 2nd,
    wilderness 4th, woods 1st
bacon 4th:
    A. ham K, pork 6th
    B. earnings 2nd, money K, wages 3rd
bad K:
    A. broken 1st, false 3rd, faulty 2nd, soiled 2nd, wrong 1st
    B. not good K, poor K
    C. dreadful 6th, evil 3rd, harmful 3rd, ill 1st, rotten 1st
badge 5th: button 1st, crest 4th, identification 4th, mark 1st, patch 4th,
    sign 1st
badger 2nd: annoy 5th, bait 5th, bother 2nd, disturb 6th, pester 2nd,
    provoke 6th, trouble 1st, vex 5th
bag 1st:
    A. backpack 4th, purse 4th, sack 1st, suitcase 1st
    B. capture 3rd, catch 1st, pack 1st, snare 6th, trap 1st
bait 3rd: badger 2nd, charm 3rd, heckle 3rd, interest 1st, lure 5th, tease 3rd,
    trap 1st
bake 1st: boil 3rd, burn 3rd, cook 1st, dry 1st, hot K, roast 4th, scorch 6th
balance 3rd:
    A. arrange 3rd, order 1st, organize 4th, total 2nd
    B. difference 1st, extra 1st, rest 1st
    C. calm 3rd, poise 6th, stability 4th, steadiness 3rd
balcony 6th: porch 3rd, railing 2nd
bald 6th: bare 3rd, hairless K, naked 4th, nude 6th, obvious 5th, open K,
    plain 2nd
ball K:
    A. dance 1st, party K
    B. blast 2nd, fun K
    C. globe 4th, orb 4th, sphere 6th
ballad 5th: poem 3rd, song K
ballast 4th: balance 3rd, level 3rd, steady 3rd, weight 1st

ballet 4th: dance 1st

balloon 1st:
    A. fatten 1st, fill out 1st, grow K, rise 1st, swell 3rd
    B. ball K, bubble 2nd

ballot 6th: ticket 1st, vote 2nd

ban K: bar 3rd, condemn 4th, disallow 2nd, forbid 4th, prevent 3rd, prohibit 6th, reject 5th, stop K

band 1st:
    A. bond 3rd, collect 3rd, gather 1st, group 1st, tie 1st, troop 3rd, unite 5th
    B. belt 2nd, cord 4th, ribbon 4th

bandit 3rd: criminal 4th, gangster 1st, pirate 5th, robber K, thief 3rd

bane 5th: curse 3rd, pain 2nd, poison 3rd, problem 1st, trouble 1st, wrong 1st

bang 3rd:
    A. hit K, pound 2nd, slam 5th, smash 3rd
    B. boom 1st, crash 2nd, explode 3rd, thud 3rd

banister 5th: pole K, post 1st, rail 2nd

bank 1st:
    A. bar 3rd, incline 5th, reef 5th, shore 1st, slope 3rd
    B. collect 3rd, gather 1st, heap 4th, mass 3rd, pile 1st
    C. depend 3rd, rely 5th, save 1st, trust 1st

banner 3rd: flag 3rd, ribbon 4th, streamer 1st

banquet 4th: dinner 1st, feast 1st, meal 3rd, meeting 1st, party K

bar 3rd:
    A. pole K, rod 1st, shaft 4th, stick K
    B. saloon 6th, tavern 5th
    C. ban K, block 1st, dam K, forbid 4th, prohibit 6th

barbecue 5th:
    A. banquet 4th, feast 1st, party K
    B. bake 1st, cook 1st, roast 4th, toast 5th

barber 2nd:
    A. haircutter 1st
    B. cut K, shave 1st, trim 4th

bare 3rd:
    A. reveal 4th, show 1st, strip 3rd, uncover 1st
    B. arid 6th, bald 6th, naked 4th, plain 2nd, simple 1st, unadorned 6th

bargain 4th:
    A. arrange 3rd, deal 2nd, settle 2nd
    B. agreement 2nd, contract 3rd, deal 2nd, understanding 1st

barge 5th:
    A. force 1st, interrupt 3rd, intrude 6th, push 1st
    B. boat 1st, float 1st

bark 3rd:
    A. covering 1st, shell 1st, skin 2nd
    B. howl 4th, yap 1st
barn K: stable 4th, stall 5th
baron 4th: aristocrat 6th, gentleman 3rd, nobility 3rd, royalty 3rd
barrel 4th: cask 4th, keg 1st, tank 5th
barren 4th: arid 6th, bald 6th, bare 3rd, dead 1st, dry 1st, empty 3rd,
    naked 4th, scarce 1st
barrier 6th: bar 3rd, block 1st, wall K
base 1st: bottom 1st, foot K, home K, low K, stand K, support 4th
basement 3rd: cellar 1st
bashful 4th: backward 4th, modest 4th, shy K, timid 5th
basic 2nd: base 1st, fundamental 4th, main 3rd, primary 5th
basin 4th: bowl 1st, depression 6th, pan K, sink 3rd
basis 2nd: base 1st, cause 2nd, foundation 5th, ground 1st, law 1st,
    support 4th
basket 1st: box K, case 2nd, pouch 1st
bat K:
    A. blow 1st, hit K, smack 6th
    B. baton 5th, club 1st, stick K
batch 2nd: array 5th, bunch 3rd, bundle 5th, group 1st, mess 1st, set K
bath 1st: dip 1st, shower 4th, wash 1st
bathe 1st: clean K, rinse 3rd, shower 4th, wash 1st
bathroom 1st: restroom K, toilet 2nd, washroom 1st
bathtub 1st: basin 5th, tub 1st
baton 5th: bat K, rod 1st, stick K, wand 3rd
batter 1st:
    A. dough 5th, paste 1st
    B. beat 1st, fighter K, hitter 1st, pound 2nd, smack 6th
battery 5th: array 5th, group 1st, set K, stand 1st
battle 2nd: action 1st, argument 3rd, combat 5th, discussion 5th,
    fight K, war 1st
bawl 5th: bellow 4th, cry K, exclaim 3rd, howl 4th, roar 1st, shout 1st
bay K:
    A. bark 3rd, cry K, howl 4th, scream 1st, yell K
    B. inlet 4th, harbor 2nd
bayonet 5th: blade 2nd, knife 1st
bazaar 5th: fair 1st, market 2nd
be K:
    A. last K, remain 1st, stay 1st
    B. am K, exist 3rd, happen 1st, live 1st, occur 3rd
beach K: bank 1st, coast 2nd, land K, shore 1st, strand 1st

beached 1st: ashore 2nd, stranded 5th

bead K: bubble 2nd, dot K, drop K, jewel 5th, pearl 4th

beak 4th: bill 1st, nose 1st

beam 3rd:
A. board 1st, plank 5th, stick K
B. flash 2nd, gleam 1st, ray 1st, streak 5th

bear K:
A. birth 1st, bring K, carry K, drop K, give K, lay 1st, produce 2nd, transfer 5th
B. force 1st, press 1st, push 1st
C. endure 4th, hold 1st, stand K, support 4th, yield 4th

beard 4th: hair K

beast 3rd: animal K, creature 3rd, hog K, mammal 5th, pig K

beat 1st:
A. accent 6th, pulse 5th, rhythm 5th, tone 3rd
B. assault 4th, hit K, pound 2nd, punch 4th, strike 2nd, swat 3rd, whip 4th
C. conquer 4th, defeat 5th, win K

beautiful 1st: attractive 5th, fair 1st, great K, handsome 3rd, lovely 1st, pretty 1st

beautify 2nd: adorn 6th, decorate 3rd, polish 4th

because K: as K, due 2nd, for K, since 2nd, so K

become 1st: change 2nd, grow into 1st, happen 1st, occur 3rd, transform 5th

bed K:
A. retire 4th, sleep K
B. bunk 4th, cot 1st, couch 4th, cradle 4th, crib 2nd

bedraggled 5th: dirty 1st, messy 1st, soil 2nd, worn 3rd

beef 5th: cattle 3rd, meat 1st

been K: was K, were 1st

beep K: honk 1st, squeek 5th

beer 5th: alcohol 5th, ale 2nd, malt 2nd

before K: ahead 1st, earlier 1st, forward 3rd, in advance 2nd, previous 5th, sooner K

befriend 6th: accept 3rd, familiarize 3rd, like K, make friends 1st, protect 4th, take in K

beg 1st: ask K, beseech 5th, persuade 5th, seek 1st

begin K: initiate 5th, start 1st

beginner 2nd: amateur 5th, novice 5th, student 3rd

behalf 6th: for K, represent 4th

behave 4th: act K, conduct 3rd, conform 6th, function 4th, perform 4th

behavior 4th: action 1st, bearing K, conduct 3rd, habits 3rd

behind 1st:
A. back 4th, support 4th

B. after 1st, afterwards 4th, following 1st, later 1st

behold 3rd: eye K, look at K, notice 1st, observe 3rd, see K, stare 3rd, view 2nd, watch 1st

being 1st:

    A. animal K, beast 3rd, body 1st, creature 3rd, thing K

    B. animation 6th, existence 3rd, individual 3rd, personality 5th

believe 1st:

    A. accept 3rd, credit 5th, have faith 3rd, know 1st, think 1st

    B. assert 6th, certainty 2nd, claim 2, maintain 2nd

bell K: alarm 3rd, chime 6th, curve 3rd, mark 1st, ring 1st, signal 4th

belle 6th: beautiful 1st, girl K

bellow 4th: howl 4th, roar 1st, shout 1st, yell K

belly 5th: abdomen 6th, gut 1st, stomach 2nd, tummy K

belong 1st:

    A. hold 1st, own 1st, possess 3rd

    B. apply 2nd, member of 1st, relate 4th

beloved 4th: admired 5th, adored 4th, cherished 5th, dear 1st, favorite 3rd, loved 1st

below 1st: beneath 1st, lower 1st, under K, underground 4th

belt 2nd:

    A. hit K, punch 4th, strike 2nd

    B. area 3rd, region 4th, zone 4th

    C. band 1st, cinch 6th, encircle 5th, fasten 4th, sash 6th, tie 1st

bench 4th: seat 1st, stall 5th

bend 1st:

    A. mold 5th, shape 1st, twist 1st

    B. arch 4th, bow 1st, circle K, curve 3rd, hook 4th

beneath 1st: below 1st, down K, under K, underneath 4th

beneficial 3rd: helpful 1st, valuable 4th

benefit 3rd: advantage 3rd, aid 2nd, help K, improve 3, profit 4th, service 1st

bent K:

    A. aptitude 3rd, gift 1st, talent 2nd

    B. curved 3rd, twisted 1st

berate 5th: chew out 1st, criticize 5th, curse 3rd, put down K, scold 5th

beseech 5th: ask K, beg 1st

beside 1st: against 1st, bordering 1st, close K, nearby 1st, next to K, other than 1st, parallel 5th

besides 1st: additionally 3rd, also K, furthermore 3rd, too 1st

best K: ace 2nd, choice 3rd, excellent 1st, finest 1st, prime 5th, superb 6th, superior 4th, top K

bestow 5th: afford 3rd, confer 4th, favor 1st, give K, grant 2nd, hand K, pass K

bet 1st: gamble 5th, risk 4th, stake 1st

betray 5th: deceive 5th, double cross 3rd, give away K, mislead 5th, reveal 4th, sell out 1st

better K:
    A. advance 2nd, improve 3rd, raise 1st
    B. good K, preferable 4th, superior 4th

between 1st: amid 4th, among 1st, in the middle 2nd, joining 3rd, linking 5th

beverage 6th: drink 1st, liquid 3rd, refreshment 6th

beware 6th: be careful 1st, caution 5th, mind 1st, watch out 1st

bewilder 3rd: confound 6th, confuse 4th, mystify 4th, puzzle 4th

beyond 1st: farther 3rd, outside 1st, over K, past 1st

bias 6th: point of view 2nd, prejudice 6th, slant 6th, view 2nd

bib 1st: apron 3rd, drape 5th, napkin 5th

bicycle 2nd: bike 1st

bid 1st: offer 2nd, propose 4th, suggest 2nd

big K: giant 2nd, grand 2nd, great K, heavy 1st, huge 1st, large K, vast 4th

bike 1st: bicycle 2nd

bill 1st:
    A. act K, law 1st, notice 1st
    B. acount 3rd, check 1st, record 2nd
    C. beak 4th

billboard 3rd: ad 4th, advertisement 4th, sign 1st

billiards 6th: pool 1st

bin 1st: basket 1st, box K, case 2nd, can K, container 5th, drawer 1st

bind 2nd: attach 5th, connect 3rd, fasten 4th, hold 1st, link 5th, strap 5th, tie 1st

binoculars 6th: scope 6th, sights 1st, telescope 4th

biography 6th: history 2nd, life story 1st

biscuit 4th: bun 2nd, cookie K, cracker 4th, sweet K

bishop 5th: churchman 1st, clergyman 6th, holy man 5th

bit 1st: atom 5th, detail 5th, dot K, fraction 4th, piece 1st, speck 4th, trace 3rd

bite 1st: gnaw 1st, nip 1st

bitter 3rd:
    A. mocking 4th, scornful 4th, unhappy K
    B. acid 4th, sour 2nd, tart 5th, unsweet K

black K:
    A. African 5th
    B. dark K, evil 3rd, night 1st, sinful 1st

blackboard 3rd: slate 1st

blackmail 4th:
    A. force 1st, make K
    B. bribe 5th, ransom 6th, steal 3rd

blacktop 1st: asphalt 5th

blade 2nd: edge 1st, knife 1st, sword 4th

blame 2nd:
  A. responsibility 4th
  B. accuse 4th, criticize 5th, fault 3rd
blank 4th: bare 3rd, clean K, empty 3rd, nothing 1st, plain 2nd, vacant 6th, void 6th
blanket 3rd:
  A. conceal 4th, enclose 1st
  B. comforter 3rd, cover 1st, quilt 4th
blast 2nd:
  A. bellow 4th, honk 1st, horn 3rd
  B. force 1st, injure 5th, ruin 5th
blaze 1st:
  A. bright 1st, flash 2nd, gleam 1st, glow 1st
  B. burn 3rd, fire K, flame 3rd
bleach 4th: fade 1st, pale 3rd, whiten 1st
bleat 4th: cry K, yelp 6th
blemish 5th:
  A. damage 5th, injure 5th
  B. defect 5th, flaw 2nd, mark 1st, pimple 5th, spot 1st, stain 4th
blend 5th: combine 3rd, compound 4th, mix 1st
bless 3rd: anoint 6th, make sacred 4th, pray 3rd, thank 1st, wish well K
blimp 5th: airship 1st, balloon 1st
blind 3rd:
  A. ignorant 4th, unaware 3rd
  B. sightless 1st
blink 6th: flicker 5th, wink 2nd
blister 5th: boil 3rd, bulge 4th, burn 3rd, pimple 5th, swelling 3rd
blizzard 4th: snow storm 2nd, wind 1st
block 1st:
  A. brick 4th, cube 4th, piece 1st
  B. bar 3rd, dam K, restrain 5th, stop K
blond 5th: fair 1st, pale 3rd, yellow K
blood 1st: family K, life 1st, red K
bloodshed 4th: battle 2nd, death 3rd, massacre 6th, murder 3rd, war 1st
bloodthirsty 4th: brutal 6th, fierce 4th, savage 5th
bloom 4th: blossom 4th, flower K, grow 1st, thrive 6th
blossom 4th:
  A. grow K
  B. bloom 4th, flower K
blot 4th:
  A. dry 1st, soak up 5th
  B. blemish 5th, brand 2nd, mar 6th, mark 1st, smear 3rd, stain 4th

blotch 6th: blemish 5th, mark 1st, spot 1st, stain 4th

blouse 1st: shirt 1st, top K

blow 1st:
   A. blast 2nd, sound 1st
   B. hit K, punch 4th, slap 2nd
   C. breeze 4th, sail 1st
   D. enlarge 5th, expand 5th

blue K:
   A. sky K
   B. rare 4th, sad K, unhappy 1st

bluff 6th:
   A. fool 2nd, tease 3rd, trick 1st
   B. blunt 6th, cliff 2nd, hill K, open K, plain 2nd

blunt 6th:
   A. dull 1st, rounded K
   B. open K, plain 2nd, rude 2nd, short 1st

blur 4th:
   A. soil 2nd, stain 4th
   B. out of focus 5th, unclear 2nd

blush 4th: color K, glow 1st, redden K

board 1st:
   A. beam 3rd, panel 6th, plank 5th, wood 1st
   B. close K, nail down 2nd
   C. accommodate 6th, feed 1st, house K, lodge 4th

boast 4th: brag 3rd, crow 2nd, pride 2nd

boat 1st: ark 2nd, canoe 4th, ship 1st

bobbin 4th: spool 2nd

body 1st:
   A. being 1st, creature 3rd, person 1st
   B. bunch 3rd, group 1st, mass 3rd
   C. build 1st, figure 1st, frame 3rd, skeleton 4th

bodyguard 4th: guard 1st, protector 4th

bog 5th: marsh 5th, swamp 4th

boil 3rd:
   A. bubble 2nd, pimple 5th, sore 4th
   B. anger 1st, simmer 4th, steam 2nd, stew 2nd

bold 2nd: adventurous 3rd, brave 1st, confident 6th, courageous 4th, daring 2nd, fearless 1st

bolt 4th:
   A. block 1st, latch 6th, lock 1st, tie 1st
   B. jump K, run K, start 1st

bomb 5th:
  A. explosive 3rd, mine 1st
  B. assault 4th, attack 3rd, explode 3rd
bonbon 4th: candy K, surprise 1st, sweet K, treat 2nd
bond 3rd:
  A. agreement 2nd, guarantee 6th, security 3rd
  B. connection 3rd, link 5th, restraint 5th, tie 1st
bondage 6th: restraint 5th, slavery 3rd
bonfire 3rd: fire K
bonnet 6th: hat K
bonus 6th: award 5th, extra 1st, gift K, present K, prize 3rd, reward 4th
boob 2nd: clumsy 6th, idiot 6th, stupid 4th
book K: literature 5th, magazine 3rd, publication 4th
bookkeeper 3rd: accountant 3rd, clerk 2nd, recorder 2nd
boom 1st: bang 3rd, blast 2nd, clap 2nd, explosion 3rd, roar 1st, rumble 3rd
boomerang 5th:
  A. stick K
  B. return 2nd, reverse 5th
boon 5th: advantage 3rd, benefit 3rd, extra 1st, favor 2nd, gift K, present K, tip 1st
boot 1st:
  A. fire K, terminate 6th
  B. kick 1st
  C. foot cover 1st, shoe K
booth 5th: closet 2nd, counter 5th, room K, stall 5th, stand K
border 1st: boundary 4th, brim 5th, edge 1st, line K, margin 5th, rim 1st
bore 2nd:
  A. drill 2nd, penetrate 5th, punch 4th
  B. annoy 5th, burden 5th, tire 2nd, wear out 1st
borrow 2nd: ask K, beg 1st, take K, use K
boss K:
  A. control 2nd, direct 1st, lead 1st
  B. chief 1st, employer 5th, head K, manager 4th, supervisor 6th
both K: each K, including 3rd, two K
bother 2nd: annoy 5th, bait 5th, irk 6th, pester 2nd, trouble 1st, vex 5th
bottle 3rd: container 5th, glass 1st, package 4th
bottom 1st: base 1st, foot K, ground 1st, rest 1st, support 4th
bought 2nd: acquired 4th, purchased 3rd
boulder 5th: rock K, stone 2nd
boulevard 4th: avenue 3rd, road K, street 1st, strip 3rd, way K
bounce 6th: drop K, fire K, hop K, jump K, leap 3rd, spring K

bound 2nd:
>   A. connected 3rd, fastened 4th, held 1st, restrained 5th, tied 1st
>   B. hop K, jump K, leap 3rd
>   C. meant 1st, ought 1st

boundary 4th: border 1st, edge 1st, frame 3rd, frontier 5th, limit 3rd, line K, outline 4th

boundless 4th: eternal 4th, infinite 5th, unending 2nd, unlimited 3rd, vast 4th

bouquet 6th:
>   A. fragrance 5th, incense 5th, odor 3rd, perfume 3rd, scent 3rd, smell 3rd
>   B. arrangement 3rd, bunch 3rd, cluster 4th, flowers 1st

bout 6th:
>   A. shift 4th, spell 2nd, turn 1st
>   B. fight K, match 3rd, meet K

bow 1st:
>   A. defer 6th, submit 4th, yield 4th
>   B. kneel 4th
>   C. bend K, curve 3rd, flex 6th

bowl 1st:
>   A. strike 2nd, throw 1st
>   B. crater 3rd, depression 6th
>   C. basin 4th, dish 1st, sink 3rd, tub 1st

box K:
>   A. carton 4th, case 2nd, package 4th
>   B. cuff 1st, hit K, punch 4th
>   C. enclose 4th, pack 1st, seal K

boxer 1st: fighter 1st

boy K: child K, lad K, male 4th, youth 2nd

boycott 6th: avoid 3rd, block 1st, ignore 5th, prevent 3rd, shun 6th

boyfriend 4th: chum 6th, friend 1st, lover 1st, mate 4th, pal K

boyhood 4th: childhood 4th, youth 4th

brace 5th:
>   A. couple 3rd, pair 1st
>   B. band 1st, prop 5th, support 4th

bracelet 5th: band 1st, circle K, encircle 1st

brag 3rd: boast 4th, crow 2nd

braid 2nd: curl 2nd, knit 4th, weave 4th, wind 1st

brain 3rd: intelligence 4th, mind 1st, reason 1st

brake 1st: limit 3rd, slow 1st, stop K

branch 2nd: limb 4th, twig 4th

brand 2nd:
>   A. label 3rd, mark 1st, stamp 3rd, tag K
>   B. class 1st, kind K, make K

brandish 6th: display 4th, flourish 4th, shake 1st, show 1st, swing 1st, wave K

brass 2nd:
  A. metal 3rd
  B. bravery 1st, nerve 1st, strength 2nd

brat 3rd: child K, imp 5th, kid K

bravado 6th: boasting 4th, bragging 3rd

brave 1st:
  A. challenge 4th, dare 2nd, defy 6th, encounter 4th, meet K, oppose 3rd
  B. courageous 4th, unafraid 1st

bread 2nd:
  A. money K
  B. dough 5th, living 1st, loaf 4th

break 1st:
  A. gap K, opening 1st, space 1st, split 4th
  B. bust 6th, crack 4th, destroy 2nd, shatter 5th

breakwater 4th: barrier 6th, reef 5th, wall K

breast 3rd: chest 2nd, front 1st

breath 1st: air K, breeze 4th, wind 1st

breathe 1st:
  A. share 2nd, tell K, whisper 1st
  B. gasp 4th, puff 2nd

breeches 5th: pants 1st, trousers 5th

breed 4th: cultivate 6th, generate 4th, grow K, mate 4th, produce 2nd, raise 1st, reproduce 5th

breeze 4th: air current 3rd, wind 1st

brew 6th:
  A. ale 2nd, beer 5th
  B. plan 1st, think 1st, spin 1st
  C. cook up 1st, mix 1st, soak 1st, stew 2nd

bribe 5th: pay K, ransom 6th, tip 1st

brick 4th: block 1st

bride 4th: mate 4th, partner 5th, wife 1st

bridge 1st: connect 3rd, cross 1st, join 3rd, link 5th, span 6th

brief 3rd:
  A. communicate 5th, inform 5th, tell K
  B. compact 5th, fast 1st, quick 1st, short 1st, sudden 1st, swift 4th

brier 6th: bush 2nd, root 3rd, wood 1st

brig 6th: jail 4th, prison 3rd

bright 1st:
  A. intelligent 4th, smart 1st
  B. brilliant 4th, clear 2nd, light K, quick 1st, shining 1st

brilliant 4th: bright 1st, gleaming 1st, glittering 4th

brim 5th: border 1st, brink 6th, edge 1st, margin 5th, rim 1st

bring K: bear K, carry K, deliver 5th, get K, fetch 4th, take K, transport 5th

brink 6th: border 1st, boundary 4th, edge 1st, margin 5th, rim 1st

brisk 6th: abrupt 5th, active 3rd, agile 6th, fast 1st, quick 1st, sharp 1st

bristle 6th:
  A. hair K
  B. parade 2nd, strut 5th, swagger 5th

broad 3rd: deep 1st, entire 3rd, extended 4th, full K, large K, vast 4th, whole 1st, wide 1st

broadcast 5th: advertise 4th, announce 3rd, circulate 4th, distribute 6th, proclaim 4th, publish 4th

broil 4th: barbecue 5th, cook 1st, fight K, flame 3rd, heat 1st, toast 5th

bronco 6th: horse K

bronze 4th: cover 1st, gild 6th, plate 1st

brooch 4th: pin K

brood 4th:
  A. fret 5th, fuss 1st, mourn 4th, sorrow 4th, stew 2nd, sulk 5th, worry 1st
  B. band 1st, children K, group 1st, litter 2nd, nest 1st, pups K, young 1st

brook 2nd:
  A. creek 4th, stream 3rd
  B. allow 2nd, bear K, endure 4th, stand K, suffer 2nd, tolerate 5th

broth 4th: liquid 3rd, soup 1st

brother 1st: associate 5th, relative 4th

brow 4th: brink 6th, edge 1st, overhang 4th, peak 4th, rim 1st, top K

brown K:
  A. cook 1st, fry 1st
  B. beige 3rd, chestnut 4th, chocolate 4th, tan K

brownie 2nd:
  A. elf 1st, fairy 4th
  B. cake 1st

bruise 5th:
  A. blemish 5th, mark 1st
  B. beat 1st, hurt K, pound 2nd, sore 4th, wound 3rd

brush 2nd:
  A. broom 2nd
  B. graze 5th, rub 1st, skim 6th, touch 1st

brutal 6th: cold K, rough 4th, rude 2nd

brute 6th: animal K, beast 3rd, creature 3rd, monster 1st

bubble 2nd: ball K, balloon 1st, bead K, burp 3rd, drop K .

buck 1st:
  A. challenge 4th, go against 1st, oppose 3rd
  B. bound 2nd, hop K, jump K, leap 3rd

C. deer K, stag 1st

D. youth 2nd

bucket 3rd: barrel 4th, can K, cask 4th, drum 5th, keg 1st, pail 2nd, pan K, tub 1st

buckle 6th:

A. bend K, bow 1st, bulge 4th, flex 6th, fold 1st

B. clasp 4th, clip 2nd, fasten 4th, hook 4th

buckskin 6th: hide 1st, leather 1st

bud 1st: bloom 4th, flower K, shoot 3rd

buddy 4th: chum 6th, friend 1st, mate 4th, pal K

budge 4th: go K, move K, push 1st, shift 4th, stir 3rd

budget 5th: cost 4th, expense 3rd, plan 1st, program 4th

buffet 6th:

A. cafeteria 5th, dinner 1st, restaurant 5th

B. beat 1st, blow 1st, hit K, pound 2nd, rap 1st, slap 2nd, strike 2nd

bug K:

A. insect 4th

B. annoy 5th, badger 2nd, bother 2nd, problem 1st

buggy 6th: coach 4th, wagon 2nd

bugle 6th: brass 2nd, horn 3rd

build 1st:

A. body 1st, figure 4th, form 1st, frame 3rd, shape 1st

B. construct 3rd, create 3rd, develop 5th, erect 4th, establish 3rd, found K, increase 3rd, make K, start 1st

building 1st: house K, lodge 4th, structure 4th

bulb 2nd:

A. light K

B. root 3rd

C. swelling 3rd

bulge 4th:

A. extend 4th, project 4th, rise 1st, stick out K, swell 3rd

B. bump 2nd, lump 4th, swelling 3rd

bulk 4th:

A. greater part K, most 1st

B. mass 3rd, volume 3rd, weight 1st

bull K:

A. bunk 4th, nonsense 5th

B. steer 5th

bullet(s) 4th: lead 1st, rocket K, shell 1st, shot 1st

bulletin 3rd: announcement 3rd, journal 2nd, newsletter 1st, newspaper 3rd, notice 1st, publication 4th, review 4th

bull's-eye 1st: center 2nd, exactly 2nd, target 5th

bully 1st:

    A. attack 3rd, bulldoze 1st, menace 5th, pick on 1st, rule K

    B. brat 3rd, tough guy 5th

bumble 4th: fumble 5th, hesitate 4th, stumble 4th

bump 2nd:

    A. lump 4th

    B. bang 3rd, bulge 4th, hit K, hump 3rd, jar K, knock 3rd, meet K, rise 1st

bun 2nd: biscuit 4th, roll 1st

bunch 3rd:

    A. collect 3rd, gather 1st, tie up 1st

    B. batch 2nd, bouquet 6th, bundle 5th, clump 3rd, cluster 4th, collection 3rd, group 1st, pack 1st, set K

bundle 5th:

    A. collect 3rd, gather 1st

    B. batch 2nd, box K, bunch 3rd, cluster 4th, pack 1st

bung 6th: cork 6th

bunk 4th:

    A. junk 3rd, nonsense 5th, rot 1st, rubbish 5th

    B. bed K, cot 1st, couch 4th, sleep K

bunny K: hare 5th, rabbit K

bunt 2nd: hit K, push 1st, tap K

burden 5th: charge 2nd, cross 1st, duty 1st, load 2nd, responsibility 4th, tax K, weight 1st

bureau 4th:

    A. department 2nd, division 4th, section 4th

    B. cabinet 4th, chest 2nd, dresser 2nd

burglar 1st: criminal 4th, robber K, thief 3rd

burlap 6th: homespun 5th, sacking 1st

burn 3rd:

    A. fire K, flame 3rd

    B. long 1st, thirst 2nd

    C. hurt K, sore 4th

burning 3rd: afire 2nd, aflame 2nd, baking 1st, broiling 4th, on fire K, roasting 4th

burnoose 5th: hat K, scarf 6th

burrow 5th:

    A. dig 1st, mine 1st, scoop 4th, shovel 1st

    B. cave 1st, den 1st, hole K, lair 5th, recess 2nd

burst 3rd: blow 1st, break 1st, explode 3rd, shatter 5th, smash 3rd

bury 3rd: conceal 4th, cover 1st, hide 1st

bus K:
    A. vehicle 6th, wagon 2nd
    B. move K, transport 5th
bush 2nd: brier 6th, plant K, shrub 4th
business 2nd: company 2nd, employment 5th, job K, occupation 6th, profession 5th, trade 2nd, work K
bust 6th:
    A. head 1st, sculpture 4th
    B. break 1st, destroy 2nd, explode 3rd, shatter 5th
bustle 6th: hurry 1st, motion 3rd, movement 2nd, rush 2nd
busy 1st: active 3rd, intent 5th, involved 6th, occupied 3rd
busybody 3rd: gossip 5th, informer 5th, nosy 1st, talker K
but K: although 2nd, however 3rd, yet 1st
butcher 4th:
    A. grocer 4th
    B. cut up K, destroy 2nd, kill 1st, massacre 6th, slaughter 5th, slay 4th
butter 2nd: spread 2nd
button 1st: clasp 4th, close K, fasten 4th, hook 4th
buy K: acquire 4th, get K, obtain 5th, pay for K, purchase 3rd
by K: along 1st, near 1st, over K, through 1st, with K
cab K: carriage 5th, taxi 1st
cabin 1st: cottage 4th, house K
cabinet 4th: box K, chest 2nd, closet 2nd
cable 1st: cord 4th, line K, rope 1st
cafe 4th: restaurant 5th
cafeteria 5th: buffet 6th, restaurant 5th
cage 1st:
    A. enclose 4th, restrain 5th
    B. box K, jail 4th, pen 1st
cake K:
    A. bun 2nd, cookie K, treat 2nd
    B. compact 5th, harden 1st, thicken 2nd
calamity 6th: accident 4th, agony 5th, disaster 6th, torture 5th, trouble 1st
calculate 5th: add K, compute 1st, count 5th, determine 5th, figure 1st, sum 1st
calendar 1st: day book K, log K, record 2nd
calico 6th: cloth 1st, cotton 2nd, print 1st
call K:
    A. ask K, invite 3rd, shout 1st, summon 4th, telephone 2nd, yell K
    B. name K, order 1st, pronounce 4th
    C. stay 1st, visit 1st
calm 3rd: peaceful 4th, quiet K, serene 6th, still 1st, tranquil 6th

cameo 4th:
   A. carving 4th, pin K
   B. appearance 2nd, walk-on K
camouflage 6th: conceal 4th, cover 1st, disguise 5th, hide 1st, mask 2nd
camp 1st:
   A. site 5th, tent 5th
   B. settle 2nd, sleep K, stop K
campaign 3rd:
   A. operation 3rd, plan 1st
   B. canvas 6th, run K
campus 6th: grounds 1st, school K, site 5th
can K:
   A. able 3rd, capable 4th
   B. container 5th, jar K, tin 1st
canal 4th: channel 4th, path 1st, pipe 1st, tube 3rd, waterway 1st
cancel 6th: ban K, call off K, deny 5th, end K, halt 4th, stop K
cancer 6th: growth K, malignant 6th, tumor 6th
candidate 4th: nominee 5th, politician 4th, runner K, seeker 1st
candle 2nd: flame 3rd, light K
candy K: chocolate 4th, sweets K
cane 3rd: pole 1st, stick K, support 4th
canine 5th: dog K, tooth 1st
cannibal 4th: man-eater K, monster 1st
cannon 4th: gun K, law 1st, order 1st, rule 2nd
cannot 1st: can't 1st, not able 3rd, unable 2nd
canoe 4th: boat 1st
canopy 6th: cover 1st, drape 5th, shade 2nd, top 1st
can't 1st: not able 3rd, unable 3rd
canter 5th: jog 2nd, ride K, trot 5th
canvas 6th: base 1st, burlap 6th, sail 1st, tarpaulin 6th
canyon 4th: divide 4th, gorge 5th, ravine 5th, split 4th, valley 2nd
cap K:
   A. bonnet 6th, hat K
   B. cover 1st, lid 1st, top K
capable 4th: able 3rd, adept 4th, can K, clever 3rd, competent 6th, skilled 2nd
capacity 6th:
   A. extent 4th, size 1st, volume 3rd
   B. ability 3rd, gift K, skill 2nd, talent 2nd
cape 4th:
   A. cloak 4th, cover 1st, wrap 3rd
   B. peninsula 6th, point 1st, tip 1st

caper 4th: dance 1st, hop K, joke 1st, play K, plot 4th, prank 5th, skip 2nd, theft 3rd, trick 1st

capital 2nd:
   A. investment 5th, money K
   B. center 2nd, chief 1st, funds 4th, leading 1st, main 3rd, primary 5th, support 4th, top K

capitalize 3rd: exploit 6th, realize 2nd, take advantage of 3rd, use K

captain 2nd: chief 1st, direct 1st, headmaster 1st, lead 1st, officer 1st

caption 6th: explanation 2nd, heading 1st, legend 5th, tag K, title 3rd

capture 3rd: carry off K, catch 1st, snare 6th, snatch 4th, take K, trap 1st

car K: automobile 3rd, cab K, vehicle 6th

caramel 5th: candy K, sweet K

caravan 6th: group 1st, line K, train K

carcass 5th: body K, frame 3rd, shell 1st

card 1st: identification 4th, postcard 1st

cardinal 3rd:
   A. red K
   B. churchman K
   C. chief 1st, highest K, main 3rd, prime 5th

care K: attention 2nd, charge 2nd, concern 3rd, love K, protection 4th, worry 1st

career 4th: employment 5th, job K, living 1st, occupation 6th, trade 1st, work K

carefree 3rd: cheerful 3rd, gay 1st, happy K, worry free 1st

careful 1st: accurate 6th, alert 5th, detailed 5th, exacting 2nd, strict 6th, thorough 4th

careless 5th: casual 5th, messy 1st, rude 2nd, thoughtless 1st

caretaker 4th: housekeeper 3rd, keeper 1st, manager 4th

cargo 5th: carload 4th, contents 3rd, freight 4th, load 2nd

carload 4th: cargo 5th, contents 3rd, load 2nd

carnival 2nd: ball K, celebration 5th, circus 1st, fair 1st, festival 5th, party K

carol 3rd:
   A. poem 3rd, song K, tune 1st
   B. sing 1st

carp 5th: blame 2nd, complain 4th, criticize 5th, gripe 5th

carpenter 4th: builder 1st, contractor 3rd

carpet 4th: cover 1st, flooring 2nd, rug 1st

carriage 5th: body 1st, buggy 6th, car K, coach 4th, frame 3rd, wagon 2nd

carry K: bear K, cart K, deliver 5th, give K, lift 1st, move K, push 1st, support 4th, tote 5th, transport 5th

cart 1st:
   A. truck 1st, wagon 2nd

B. carry 1st, lift 1st, move K, tote 5th

carton 4th: box K, case 2nd, container 5th, package 4th

cartoon 2nd:
- **A.** animation 6th, movie 1st
- **B.** drawing 1st, picture K, sketch 5th

cartridge 6th: bullet 4th, case 2nd, holder 1st, insert 6th, shell 1st

carve 4th: chip 5th, cut K, engrave 5th, fashion 3rd, sculpture 4th, shape 1st

case 2nd:
- **A.** action 1st, event 3rd, example 2nd, illustration 4th, lawsuit 5th, statement 1st, suit 1st
- **B.** box K, carrier 2nd, carton 4th, cover 1st, protector 4th

cash 2nd: change 2nd, coins 3rd, money K

cask 4th: barrel 4th, case 2nd, keg 1st

casserole 4th:
- **A.** dish 1st
- **B.** food K, mixture 4th

cast 2nd:
- **A.** pitch 2nd, throw 1st, toss 2nd
- **B.** arrange 3rd, mold 5th, shape 1st
- **C.** discard 6th, junk 3rd, scrap 3rd
- **D.** assembly 4th, company 2nd, group 1st

castle 3rd: mansion 5th, palace 1st

casual 5th:
- **A.** accidental 4th, chance 2nd
- **B.** cool 1st, relaxed 4th

catalog 5th:
- **A.** book K, bulletin 3rd
- **B.** count K, list 2nd, number K, sort 1st

catalogue 5th: same as catalog

catch 1st:
- **A.** come down with 2nd, get K, obtain 5th
- **B.** grasp 4th, understand 1st
- **C.** capture 3rd, gain 2nd, grab 4th, snare 6th, trap 1st

cathedral 5th: church K, temple 3rd

catholic 4th: universal 4th, world-wide 1st

cattle 3rd: animals K, beef 2nd, cows K, herd 2nd

cauldron 6th: kettle 4th, pot K

cause 2nd:
- **A.** beginning 1st, reason 2nd, start 1st
- **B.** author 3rd, compel 3rd, create 3rd, make K, produce 2nd

caution 5th:
- **A.** alertness 5th, care 1st, concern 3rd, thought 1st

B. advise 3rd, alert 5th, tell K, warn 3rd

cautious 5th: alert 5th, careful 1st, wary 5th

cavalry 6th: army 1st, horse troop 3rd, riders K, soldiers 3rd

cave 1st:

A. give in K

B. cavity 5th, chamber 5th, hole K, hollow 3rd

cavity 5th: cave 1st, hole K, hollow 3rd

cease 3rd: close K, end K, finish 1st, quit 1st, stop K

ceiling 4th: cover 1st, lid 1st, roof 1st

celebrate 4th:

A. honor 1st, keep K, observe 3rd

B. party K, play K

celebration 5th: holiday K, party K, ritual 6th

celebrity 5th: fame 3rd, glory 3rd, honor 2nd

celestial 6th:

A. sky 1st, stars 5th

B. heavenly 1st, holy 5th

cell 1st: booth 5th, chamber 5th, closet 2nd, cocoon 2nd, compartment 6th, room K, stall 5th

cellar 1st: basement, 3rd, below stairs 2nd

cement 4th:

A. concrete 4th, plaster 4th

B. adhere 6th, bond 3rd, glue 1st, join 3rd, paste 1st

cemetery 6th: field 2nd, plot 4th

census 6th: count 1st, figures 1st, study 2nd

cent 1st: coin 3rd, penny 1st

center 2nd: core 6th, focus 5th, middle 2nd

central 3rd:

A. main 3rd, principal 3rd

B. core 6th, focus 5th, middle 2nd

century 2nd:

A. one hundred years 1st

B. age 1st, period 2nd

cereal 6th: breakfast 1st, grain 3rd, meal 3rd

ceremony 5th: observance 3rd, rite 6th, ritual 6th, service 1st

certain 1st:

A. particular 4th, single 3rd, special 2nd

B. confident 6th, positive 2nd, sure K

certainly 1st: surely 1st, positively 2nd

certificate 6th: award 5th, bill 1st, note 1st, paper 6th

certify 6th: authorize 3rd, support 4th, uphold 6th

chagrin 5th:
   A. embarrassment 5th, irritation 6th
   B. annoy 5th, embarrass 5th, shame 3rd, vex 5th
chain 3rd:
   A. bond 3rd, control 2nd, fasten 4th, links 5th, restraint 5th, tie 1st
   B. course 3rd, series 4th, train K
chair 1st:
   A. bench 4th, seat 1st, stool 2nd
   B. govern 1st, lead 1st
chalk 5th: crayon K, marker 1st, pencil 1st
challenge 4th:
   A. problem 1st, puzzle 4th
   B. disagree 2nd, dispute 6th, question 1st
   C. call K, dare 2nd
chamber 5th: apartment 1st, cell 1st, room 1st
champion 4th: back K, conqueror 4th, defend 5th, hero 1st, leader 1st,
   victor 4th, winner 1st
chance 2nd:
   A. accident 4th, fortune 3rd, luck 1st
   B. dare 2nd, risk 4th, try K
   C. opportunity 3rd, turn 1st
chancellor 6th: head K, leader 1st
chandelier 5th: lamp 1st, light K
change 2nd:
   A. adjustment 5th, growth 1st
   B. coins 3rd, money K
   C. adapt 4th, adjust 5th, alter 4th, amend 4th, differ 4th, fix 1st, modify 5th
channel 4th: bed K, canal 4th, course 3rd, passage 3rd, path 1st, road K,
   tube 3rd, way K
chant 5th:
   A. carol 3rd, intone 3rd, say K, sing 1st
   B. hymn 5th, song K, tune 1st
chap 4th: lad K, mate 4th, man K
chapel 4th: church K, house of worship 4th, temple 3rd
chapter 3rd: division 4th, part 1st, portion 4th, section 4th
character 2nd:
   A. essence 6th, personality 5th, quality 4th
   B. code 3rd, figure 1st, label 3rd, mark 1st, symbol 5th
   C. being 1st, individual 3rd, person 1st, role 1st, someone 1st
characteristic 6th: aspect 5th, bent K, feature 3rd, leaning 3rd, quality 4th,
   style 3rd, symptom 6th, tone 3rd, trait 6th

charge 2nd:
  A. care K, control 2nd, protection 4th, rule K, supervision 6th
  B. attack 3rd, direct 1st, run K, rush 2nd, storm 2nd
  C. accuse 4th, blame 2nd
  D. ask K, ask a price K, command 2nd, cost K, credit 5th, expect 2nd,
      impose 4th, price K

chariot 6th: carriage 5th, coach 4th

charity 4th: benefit 3rd, courtesy 4th, favor 1st, gift 1st, kindness K, love K,
  service 1st

charm 3rd:
  A. appeal 3rd, attractiveness 5th, beauty 1st, grace 3rd
  B. bewitch 1st, delight 3rd, enchant 6th

chart 1st: guide 1st, map 1st, outline 4th, plot 4th

chase 1st: follow 1st, hunt 2nd, pursue 5th, run after K, track 1st, trail 2nd

chat 1st: babble 6th, converse 5th, gossip 5th, talk K

chatter 1st: babble 6th, chat 1st, gab 1st, gossip 5th, talk K

chauffeur 6th: driver 1st

cheap 3rd:
  A. bargain 4th, inexpensive 3rd, low K
  B. junky 3rd, poor K, shabby 4th, tacky 1st

cheat 3rd: deceive 5th, exploit 6th, fake 1st, fraud 6th, hoax 5th, steal 3rd,
  trick 1st

check 1st:
  A. look into 1st, notice 1st, study 1st, test 3rd
  B. arrest 3rd, control 2nd, curb 3rd, interrupt 3rd, stay 1st, stop K

cheek 2nd:
  A. face K
  B. gall 4th, nerve 1st

cheer 3rd:
  A. enthusiasm 4th, fun K, gaiety 1st, good spirits 2nd
  B. chant 5th, clap 2nd, cry K, encourage 4th, shout 1st, yell K

chef 4th: cook 1st

cherish 5th: adore 4th, love K, prize 3rd, treasure 4th, worship 4th

chest 2nd:
  A. breast 3rd, front 1st
  B. bureau 4th, cabinet 4th, carton 4th, crate 5th

chew 1st:
  A. bite 1st, eat K, gnaw 1st, nibble 4th
  B. study 2nd, think 1st

chicken K: chick 2nd, fowl 4th, hen K

chief 1st:
    A. first 1st, head K, important 1st, main 3rd, necessary 1st, primary 5th, principal 3rd, supreme 5th, vital 5th
    B. boss K, key K, leader 1st

child K: adolescent 5th, kid K, minor 5th, youth 2nd

childhood 4th: adolescence 5th, growing up K, youth 2nd

chili 4th: stew 2nd

chill 3rd: arctic 3rd, brisk 6th, cold K, cool 1st, freezing 4th, frigid 6th, icy 1st

chime 6th: alarm 3rd, bell K, clang 4th, ring 1st

chip 5th:
    A. bit 1st, piece 1st
    B. break 1st, carve 4th, chop 2nd

chirp 2nd: chime 6th, peep 4th, tweet 4th

chivalry 6th: bravery 1st, courage 4th, daring 2nd, fairness 1st, gallantry 4th, goodness K, manners 2nd

choice 3rd:
    A. decision 2nd, desire 5th, opinion 3rd, preference 3rd, selection 4th, will K
    B. elegant 5th, favorite 3rd, fine 1st, good K, rare 4th
    C. solution 5th, vote 2nd, way out K

choir 5th: chorus 5th, singers 1st

choke 1st: clog 5th, close K, cover 1st, gag 1st, smother 6th, strangle 6th

choose 3rd: appoint 3rd, elect 3rd, favor 2nd, nominate 5th, pick 1st, prefer 3rd, select 4th, sort 1st, take K

chop 2nd: ax K, chip 5th, cut K, divide 4th, hew 6th, mince 6th, slice 5th

chorus 5th: choir 5th, singers 1st

chow 5th: eat K, food K

chowder 5th: broth 4th, soup 1st

chrome 2nd: metal 3rd, plate K, silver 1st

chronicle 6th: account 3rd, article 2nd, diary 3rd, history 2nd, journal 2nd, log K, record 2nd, report 1st, story K

chubby 2nd: fat 1st, plump 6th, portly 5th

chum 6th: buddy 4th, companion 3rd, friend 1st, mate 4th, pal K, partner 5th

church K: chapel 4th, place of worship 4th, temple 3rd

churn 3rd: beat 1st, blend 5th, mix up 1st, stir 3rd, turn 1st, whip 4th

chute 5th: channel 4th, course 3rd, passage 4th, path 1st, slide 2nd

cider 2nd: apple juice K

cinch 6th:
    A. belt 2nd, grasp 4th, hold 1st, tighten 2nd
    B. certain 1st, easy 1st, sure K

circle K:
    A. ball K, disk 2nd, sphere 6th, wheel 1st
    B. associates 5th, friends 1st

C. encompass 4th, group 1st, spin 1st, surround 3rd, turn 1st

circuit 4th: connection 3rd, journey 3rd, path 1st, round K, route 4th, surround 3rd, tour 3rd, way K

circular 4th:

    A. circle K, curved 3rd, global 4th, indirect 2nd, round K, spherical 6th

    B. advertisement 4th, booklet 2nd, bulletin 3rd, pamphlet 6th, sheet 1st

circumstance 6th:

    A. event 3rd, happening 1st, incident 5th, occurrence 3rd

    B. detail 5th, fact 1st, factor 5th, feature 3rd, item 5th, point 1st, surroundings 3rd

circus 1st: carnival 2nd, fair 1st, show 1st

cite 6th: call K, invite 3rd, name K, number K, quote 5th, recount 6th, repeat 4th, summon 4th, tell K

citizen 3rd: national 2nd, native 1st, resident 5th, subject 3rd

city K: area 3rd, metropolis 6th, town K

civil 3rd: gentle 3rd, mannerly 2nd, polite 4th, thoughtful 2nd

civilization 4th: community 2nd, culture 6th, society 3rd

claim 2nd:

    A. allegation 6th, assertion 6th

    B. deed 1st, title 3rd

    C. allege 6th, assert 6th, declare 5th, demand 5th, maintain 4th, state 1st

clamor 6th: bellow 4th, noise 1st, racket 2nd, roar 1st, uproar 5th

clamp 5th: clasp 4th, grasp 4th, hold 1st, lock 1st, vise 4th

clan 5th: family K, group 1st, house K, tribe 3rd

clang 4th: bang 3rd, chime 6th, clank 4th, ring 1st

clank 4th: *See* clang.

clap 2nd:

    A. cheer 3rd

    B. blow 1st, hit K, knock 3rd, slap 2nd

clash 5th:

    A. bang 3rd, clang 4th, noise 1st

    B. battle 2nd, collision 6th, conflict 4th, fight K, war 1st

clasp 4th: catch 1st, fasten 4th, grab 4th, hold 1st, hook 4th

class 1st:

    A. course 3rd, study 1st, lesson 3rd

    B. division 4th, grade 2nd, group 1st, level 3rd, rank 3rd, realm 4th, society 3rd, type 1st

classic 5th: remarkable 4th, superior 4th, top K

clatter 5th: bang 3rd, clamor 6th, crash 2nd, din 6th, noise 1st, racket 2nd, rattle 2nd

clause 6th:

    A. condition 3rd, provision 4th, requirement 2nd, terms 3rd

B. article 2nd, paragraph 6th, sentence 1st, verse 4th

claw 1st:
   A. hoof 1st, paw 1st, talon 6th
   B. divide 4th, hook 1st, scratch 4th, spur 4th, tear 2nd

clay 1st: earth 1st, ground 1st, mud 1st, soil 2nd

clean K:
   A. neat K, nice 1st, pure 3rd, spotless 1st
   B. cleanse 2nd, dress K, launder 6th, polish 4th, wash 1st

clear 2nd:
   A. apparent 3rd, distinct 5th, plain 2nd, readable 3rd
   B. cut K, make vacant 6th, remove 2nd, rid 1st
   C. clean K, fair 1st, light K, shiny 3rd, sunny 1st
   D. bare 3rd, barren 4th, open K, transparent 5th, void 6th

clergyman 6th: pastor 4th, priest 4th, reverend 4th

clerk 2nd: accountant 3rd, assistant 4th, cashier 3rd, official 3rd, secretary 4th

clever 3rd: brilliant 4th, gifted 1st, handy 1st, intelligent 4th, knowing 1st, resourceful 5th, skilled 2nd, sly 4th, smart 1st, talented 2nd, witty 1st

click 2nd: beat 1st, clack 2nd, snap 2nd, tap K, tick 1st

client 6th: buyer 1st, customer 5th, follower 1st, patron 5th, shopper 1st, user 1st

cliff 2nd: bank 1st, bluff 6th, edge 1st, ridge 5th, slope 3rd

climate 4th:
   A. atmosphere 4th, feel K, mood 3rd, spirit 2nd
   B. condition 3rd, environment 6th, temperature 5th, weather 1st

climb 1st: advance 2nd, ascend 4th, go up K, mount 2nd, rise 1st, scale 3rd, soar 6th

cling 4th: adhere 6th, bond 3rd, hold 1st, hug 1st, stick K

clinic 1st: hospital 3rd, ward 5th

clip 2nd:
   A. cut K, shave 1st, shorten 1st, snip 4th, trim 4th
   B. clasp 4th, fastener 4th, hook 4th, latch 6th
   C. part 1st, piece 1st, sample 5th, scrap 3rd
   D. attach 5th, catch 1st, connect 1st, fasten 4th, pin K

cloak 4th:
   A. cape 4th, coat 1st, wrap 3rd
   B. cover 1st, hide 1st, mask 2nd, secret 1st

clock 1st: measure 2nd, timer 1st, watch 1st

clog 5th: block 1st, clot 5th, congest 4th, dam K, hinder 6th, jam K, obstruct 5th, stop up K

close K:
   A. bolt 4th, fasten 4th, seal K, secure 3rd, shut 1st
   B. bind 2nd, connect 3rd, join 3rd, tie 1st

C. like K, similar 4th

D. bordering 1st, friendly 1st, intimate 5th, near 1st, neighboring 2nd, small 1st, stuffy 1st, tight 1st

closet 2nd: box K, cabinet 4th, cell 1st, cupboard 2nd, hide 1st, locker 3rd, room K

clot 5th: clog 5th, gel 5th, lump 4th, mass 3rd, thicken 2nd

clothes 1st: array 5th, attire 6th, dress K, garments 4th

cloud 1st:

A. fog 1st, mist 1st, vapor 3rd

B. bewilder 3rd, confuse 4th, cover 1st, darken 1st, depress 5th, dim 1st

clown 1st:

A. fool 2nd, joker 1st

B. entertain 4th, perform 4th, play K, show off 1st

club 1st:

A. bat K, baton 5th, stick K

B. association 5th, group 1st, organization 4th, society 3rd

clue 2nd:

A. feeling K, idea 1st

B. hint 1st, sign 1st, suggestion 2nd

clump 3rd: batch 2nd, bunch 3rd, bundle 5th, cluster 4th, join 3rd, knot 4th, pack 1st, unite 5th

clumsy 6th: awkward 6th, halting 4th, rough 4th, slow 1st

cluster 4th:

A. batch 2nd, bunch 3rd, bundle 5th, clump 3rd, collection 3rd, knot 4th, pack 1st

B. collect 3rd, gather 1st, group 1st, unite 5th

clutch 4th:

A. clasp 4th, grab 4th, hold 1st, possess 3rd, seize 3rd, snatch 4th

B. brood 4th, nest 1st

clutter 4th: disorder 2nd, mess 1st, trash 2nd

coach 4th:

A. direct 1st, educate 3rd, guide 1st, instruct 4th, support 4th, teach 1st, train K

B. buggy 6th, car K, carriage 5th, vehicle 6th

coarse 4th: bumpy 2nd, crude 5th, gross 3rd, rough 4th, rugged 5th, sandy 1st

coast 2nd:

A. beach K, shore 1st, shoreline 1st

B. drift 2nd, float 1st, glide 4th, sail 1st, slide 2nd

coat 1st:

A. cloak 4th, cover 1st, jacket 3rd, wrap 3rd

B. fur K, hide 1st, wool 3rd

C. cover 1st, paint 2nd

coax 6th: beg 1st, charm 3rd, encourage 4th, urge 4th

cock 4th: bend K, incline 5th, ready 1st, tilt 5th, tip 1st, turn 1st, twist 1st

cocoa 1st: chocolate 4th, beverage 6th

cocoon 2nd: cell 1st, chamber 5th

code 3rd:
    A. creed 6th, ethics 5th, law 1st, philosophy 5th
    B. hide 1st, mark 1st, symbolize 5th

coffin 6th: box K

cog 6th: wheel 1st

coil 5th: circle K, curl 2nd, roll 1st, rotate 6th, spring K, wind 1st, wrap 3rd

coin 3rd:
    A. cash 2nd, money K
    B. create 3rd, invent 2nd, make K, mint 5th

cold K:
    A. arctic 3rd, chilly 3rd, cool 1st, freezing 4th, frigid 6th, frosty 4th, icy 1st
    B. abrupt 5th, hostile 4th, unfriendly 1st

collapse 5th: break 1st, cave in 1st, downfall 2nd, explode 3rd, fail 2nd, faint 3rd, fall K, fold 1st, ruin 5th

collar 4th:
    A. neckpiece 1st
    B. arrest 3rd, corner 2nd, grab 4th, grasp 4th, seize 3rd

collect 3rd: accumulate 6th, assemble 4th, bunch 3rd, gather 1st, harvest 4th, pack 1st, save 1st, take in K

college 4th: institute 5th, school K, university 4th

collision 6th: bump 2nd, clash 5th, crash 2nd, hit K, impact 6th, meeting K, wreck 4th

cologne 5th: perfume 3rd, scent 3rd

colony 3rd: community 2nd, settlement 2nd, society 3rd

color K:
    A. hue 6th, shade 2nd, tint 5th, tone 3rd
    B. badge 5th, banner 3rd, flag 3rd

colorful 2nd: entertaining 4th, intense 6th, interesting 3rd, lively 1st, vivid 6th

column 4th:
    A. pillar 5th, pole 1st, post 1st, support 4th
    B. editorial 3rd, news story 1st
    C. line K, list 2nd, row K

comb 2nd:
    A. arrange 3rd, brush 2nd, fix 1st, straighten 3rd
    B. inspect 5th, rake 1st, search 1st, separate 3rd

combat 5th: assault 4th, attack 3rd, battle 2nd, beat 1st, contest 4th, encounter 4th, fight K, meet K, oppose 3rd, war 1st

combine 3rd:
   A. blend 5th, fuse 4th, mix 1st
   B. accompany 3rd, band 1st, compound 4th, group 1st, join 3rd, pool 1st,
      unite 5th
combustion 6th: burning 3rd, explosion 3rd, flame 3rd, ignite 6th
come K:
   A. appear 2nd, approach 3rd, arrive 2nd, near 1st
   B. happen 1st, evolve 6th, occur 3rd
comedian 5th: clown 1st, comic 5th, joker 1st
comedy 5th: funny 1st, humor 4th, jest 4th, joke 1st, wit 1st
comfort 3rd:
   A. calm 3rd, ease 3rd, peace 1st
   B. cheer 3rd, console 5th, snuggle 5th, strengthen 2nd
comfortable 3rd: easy K, happy K, peaceful 1st, secure 3rd, snug 6th, warm 1st
comic 5th: absurd 6th, amusing 4th, funny 1st, humorous 4th, laughable 2nd,
   silly 1st
command 2nd:
   A. commission 2nd, demand 5th, direct 1st, force 1st, order 1st
   B. control 2nd, govern 1st, manage 4th, regulate 5th, rule 2nd
   C. ability 3rd, skill 2nd
commence 6th: begin K, commit 4th, lead 1st, organize 4th, origin 4th,
   start 1st
commend 6th: approve 4th, celebrate 4th, compliment 5th, praise 4th,
   recognize 3rd, recommend 5th
comment 5th: explain 2nd, observe 3rd, note 1st, remark 1st, statement 1st
commercial 5th:
   A. ad 4th, advertisement 4th, bulletin 3rd
   B. merchant 3rd, of business 2nd, of trade 4th, public 1st
commission 2nd:
   A. appoint 3rd, authorize 3rd, charge 2nd, command 2nd, license 5th,
      name K, order 1st
   B. allowance 5th, cut K, part 1st, percentage 4th, piece 1st, share 2nd
   C. board 1st
commit 4th:
   A. do K, perform 4th, practice 1st
   B. assure 3rd, dedicate 6th, entrust 3rd, pledge 5th, promise 1st, swear 4th
committee 5th: association 5th, board 1st, commission 2nd, council 5th
commodity 5th: article 2nd, item 5th, merchandise 6th, thing K
common 2nd:
   A. average 3rd, everyday 2nd, general 2nd, normal 5th
   B. both K, joint 4th, shared 2nd

commotion 5th: confusion 4th, disorder 3rd, disturbance 6th, turmoil 5th, uproar 5th, upset 3rd

communicate 5th: contact 4th, converse 5th, inform 5th, make known 1st, mention 5th, say K, speak 1st, talk K, tell K, utter 4th

community 2nd: colony 3rd, group 1st, neighborhood 2nd, public 1st, settlement 2nd, society 3rd, town K, village 2nd

commute 4th:
A. drive K, travel 1st, trip 1st
B. alter 4th, change 2nd, exchange 4th, modify 5th, transform 5th

compact 5th: close K, condensed 6th, crowded 2nd, firm 2nd, hard 1st, small 1st, tight 1st

companion 3rd: associate 5th, buddy 4th, chum 6th, escort 5th, friend 1st, mate 4th, pal K, partner 5th

company 2nd:
A. association 5th, companionship 3rd
B. business 2nd, corporation 4th, group 1st
C. guest 3rd, party K, visitor 1st

comparable 3rd: alike 1st, near 1st, resembling 4th, similar 4th

compare 3rd: associate 5th, contrast 4th, equate 3rd, explain 2nd, liken 1st, match 3rd, parallel 5th, relate 4th, sort 2nd

compartment 6th: box K, cabinet 4th, cell 1st, department 2nd, locker 3rd, nook 6th, place 1st, space 1st, stall 5th

compass 4th:
A. achieve 5th, acquire 4th, gain 2nd, obtain 5th
B. circle K, hem 1st, ring 1st, surround 3rd

compassion 5th: care K, pity 4th, sympathy 4th, tenderness 3rd, understanding 1st

compassionate 5th: caring 1st, gentle 3rd, loving 1st, sympathetic 4th, tender 3rd, understanding 1st, warm 1st

compel 3rd: cause 2nd, command 2nd, control 2nd, drive 1st, force 1st, influence 5th, make K, order 1st, require 1st

compensation 6th:
A. earnings 2nd, income 4th, pay K, payment 1st, salary 3rd, wages 3rd
B. amends 4th, fee 4th, fine 1st, penalty 5th, return 2nd

compete 4th: battle 2nd, challenge 4th, contest 4th, counter 5th, dispute 6th, fight K, meet K, oppose 3rd, strive 5th, struggle 1st

competent 6th: able 3rd, capable 4th, effective 4th, fit K, qualified 4th, skillful 2nd

competition 5th: battle 2nd, challenge 4th, contest 4th, game K, match 3rd, meet K, rivalry 4th, tournament 5th

complain 4th: criticize 5th, disapprove 4th, fault 3rd, gripe 5th, grumble 5th, object 1st, protest 4th

complete 3rd:
  A. all K, entire 3rd, every K, perfect 3rd, whole 1st
  B. achieve 5th, close K, end K, finish 1st, terminate 6th
complex 6th:
  A. complicated 6th, compound 4th, difficult 5th, intricate 6th, involved 6th
  B. structure 4th, system 2nd
complicate 6th: confuse 4th, involve 6th, mix 1st, puzzle 4th, snare 5th
compliment 5th:
  A. commend 6th, flatter 4th, honor 1st
  B. courtesy 4th, flattery 4th, praise 4th, tribute 5th
comply 6th: agree 2nd, consent 3rd, go along 1st, mind 1st, obey 3rd,
  submit 4th, yield 4th
composition 4th:
  A. article 2nd, essay 5th, paper K, theme 4th
  B. blend 5th, compound 4th, creation 3rd, union 3rd
compound 4th:
  A. add K, blend 5th, combine 3rd, mix 1st
  B. combination 3rd, mixture 4th
  C. complex 6th, intricate 6th, many K, multiple 2nd
comprehend 5th: conceive 4th, decode 5th, get K, grasp 4th, know 1st,
  perceive 6th, see K, understand 1st
compress 6th: bind 2nd, compact 5th, condense 6th, contract 3rd, cram 5th,
  crowd 2nd, deflate 6th, force 1st, pinch 4th, press 1st, shrink 5th,
  squeeze 5th, tighten 1st
comprise 6th: compound 4th, contain 5th, cover 1st, include 3rd, involve 6th,
  make up 1st, span 6th
compromise 5th: adjust 5th, agree 2nd, arrange 3rd, concession 6th, give in K,
  settle 2nd, trade 2nd, yield 4th
comrade 4th: associate 5th, buddy 4th, chum 6th, companion 3rd, friend 1st,
  mate 4th, partner 5th
con 3rd:
  A. against 1st
  B. negative 6th, no K
  C. cheat 3rd, deceive 5th, mislead 5th, plot 4th, sting 4th, trick 1st
conceal 4th: bury 3rd, camouflage 6th, cover 1st, disguise 5th, harbor 2nd,
  hide 1st, mask 2nd, obscure 6th, screen 1st, shelter 4th, shield 4th, veil 3rd
concede 6th: acknowledge 5th, admit 4th, allow 2nd, comply 6th, confess 4th,
  give up K, grant 2nd, let K, recognize 3rd, release 5th, yield 4th
conceited 5th: arrogant 6th, not humble 4th, proud 2nd, self-important 3rd,
  stuck-up 4th, vain 4th
conceive 4th: create 3rd, fancy 3rd, form 1st, imagine 2nd, invent 2nd, plan 1st,
  plot 4th, realize 2nd, think up 1st

concentrate 5th:
    A. aborsb 5th, give attention 2nd, ponder 6th, think 1st
    B. center 2nd, compact 5th, condense 6th, focus 5th

concern 3rd:
    A. apply 2nd, have to do with K, relate to 4th
    B. care K, doubt 5th, regard 4th, thought 1st, trouble 1st, worry 1st
    C. affair 2nd, business 2nd

concerning 3rd: about K, in regard 4th, relating to 4th

concession 6th:
    A. allowance 5th, apology 6th, surrender 5th
    B. favor 2nd, gift K, grant 2nd
    C. business 2nd, lease 6th

conclude 3rd:
    A. cease 3rd, close K, complete 3rd, end K, finish 1st, halt 4th, stop K,
       terminate 6th
    B. decide 1st, determine 5th, gather 1st, guess 1st, think 1st

concord 6th: accord 4th, agreement 2nd, friendship 1st, harmony 4th, peace 2nd

concrete 4th: certain 1st, particular 4th, real 1st, single 3rd, solid 3rd,
    specific 5th, substantial 5th

condemn 4th: blame 2nd, charge 2nd, convict 5th, criticize 5th, curse 3rd,
    find guilty 4th, judge 1st, sentence 1st

condense 6th: compact 5th, concentrate 5th, contract 3rd, shorten 1st,
    shrink 5th. *See also* compress.

condition 3rd:
    A. qualify 4th, requirement 2nd, term 3rd
    B. disease 5th, illness 1st
    C. fix 1st, shape 1st, situation 4th, state 1st, status 6th

conduct 3rd:
    A. actions 1st, behavior 4th, ethics 5th
    B. direct 1st, operate 3rd, run K
    C. accompany 3rd, escort 5th, guide 1st, lead 1st, take K

confederate 6th: associate 5th, helper 1st, partner 5th

conference 4th: assembly 4th, convention 6th, council 5th, interview 5th,
    meeting 1st, session 6th

confess 4th: acknowledge 5th, admit 4th, concede 6th, grant 2nd, own 1st,
    reveal 4th, tell K

confide 6th:
    A. reveal 4th, tell K
    B. believe 1st, depend on 3rd, trust 1st

confident 6th: assured 3rd, certain 1st, cheerful 3rd, convinced 4th, poised 6th,
    positive 2nd, secure 3rd, sure K

confidential 6th: close K, intimate 5th, personal 3rd, private 3rd, secret 1st

conflict 4th: battle 2nd, clash 5th, competition 5th, contest 4th, disagreement 2nd, fight K, match 3rd, rivalry 4th, struggle 1st, war 1st

conform 6th: accept 3rd, adapt 4th, adjust 5th, correspond 5th, fit K, match 3rd, square 2nd

confound 6th: amaze 5th, astonish 4th, bewilder 3rd, confuse 4th, mystify 4th, perplex 6th, puzzle 4th, surprise 1st

confront 5th: challenge 4th, defy 6th, encounter 4th, face K, meet K, tackle 4th

confuse 4th: bewilder 3rd, cloud 1st, complicate 6th, disorder 3rd, mix 1st, mystify 4th, puzzle 4th, scramble 4th

congratulate 6th: celebrate 4th, cheer 3rd, great K, praise 4th, support 4th

congregation 6th: assembly 4th, community 2nd, conference 4th, followers 1st, gathering 1st, members 2nd

connect 3rd: add K, adjoin 6th, associate 5th, attach 5th, bind 2nd, bridge 1st, fasten 4th, join 3rd, link 5th, relate 4th, tie 1st, unite 5th

conquer 4th: achieve 5th, beat 1st, best 1st, crush 4th, defeat 5th, dominate 5th, master K, overcome 2nd, triumph 5th, vanquish 6th, win K

conscience 4th: ethics 5th, honesty 3rd, justice 3rd, morality 3rd, virtue 4th

conscious 6th:
A. deliberate 6th, intentional 5th, known 1st, planned 1st, realized 2nd
B. alert 5th, awake 3rd, aware 3rd, know 1st, thinking 1st

conscript 6th: call K, elect 3rd, impress 5th, name K, obtain 5th, recruit 6th, register 4th, select 4th

consent 3rd: accept 3rd, agree 2nd, allow 2nd, approve 4th, authorize 3rd, comply 6th, grant 2nd, let K, license 5th, permit 3rd

consequence 4th:
A. fame 3rd, importance 1st, significance 6th, value 2nd
B. effect 3rd, outcome 4th, reaction 5th, result 2nd

conserve 5th: economize 4th, guard 1st, maintain 4th, preserve 4th, protect 4th, save 1st, shield 4th

consider 2nd:
A. ponder 6th, review 4th, study 2nd, think about 1st, wonder 1st
B. heed 4th, judge 1st, mind 1st, note 1st

consist 3rd:
A. ingredients 4th, involve 5th, make up K
B. agree 2nd, conform 6th, fit K

console 5th:
A. calm 3rd, cheer 3rd, comfort 3rd, relieve 4th, support 4th
B. cabinet 4th, furniture 3rd

conspicuous 5th: noticeable 2nd, obvious 5th, outstanding 2nd, prominent 5th

constable 6th: officer 1st, marshal 5th, policeman 1st, sheriff 4th

constant 4th:
A. devoted 5th, faithful 3rd, loyal 5th, true K

B. continuous 2nd, even 1st, lasting 1st, regular 3rd, same K, set K,
   steady 3rd, uniform 1st

constantly 4th: always 1st, forever 3rd

constellation 5th: group 1st

consternation 6th: alarm 3rd, astonishment 4th, bewilderment 3rd,
   confusion 4th, dread 6th, fear 1st, horror 4th, panic 1, terror 3rd

constitute 4th:
   A. are K, compose 4th, form 1st, is K, make up 1st, to be K
   B. compound 4th, create 3rd, establish 3rd, institute 5th

construct 3rd: build 1st, compose 4th, erect 4th, frame 3rd, make K,
   process 4th, shape 1st

consul 5th: ambassador 5th, delegate 5th, diplomat 5th, representative 4th

consult 4th: advise 3rd, ask K, communicate 5th, confer 4th, consider 2nd

consume 4th:
   A. fascinate 4th, hold 1st
   B. absorb 5th, destroy 2nd, eat K, use K, waste 1st

contact 4th: call K, collide 6th, communicate 5th, connection 3rd, meet K,
   reach 1st, touch 1st

contagious 6th: catching 1st, infectious 6th, spreading 2nd

contain(ed) 5th: control 2nd, curb 3rd, enclose 4th, have K, hold 1st,
   include 3rd, incorporate 4th, restrain 5th

contaminate 6th: poison 3rd, pollute 3rd, soil 2nd, spoil 4th, taint 6th

contemplate 6th:
   A. aim 3rd, design 5th, intend 6th, plan 1st, purpose 4th
   B. consider 2nd, meditate 4th, ponder 6th, reflect 4th, study 2nd, think 1st,
      watch 1st

contemporary 5th: at the same time 1st, current 3rd, living 1st, modern 2nd,
   present day K

contempt 5th: disgust 5th, dislike 1st, distaste 6th, hate 2nd, mock 4th,
   scorn 4th

contend 5th:
   A. assert 6th, believe 1st, hold 1st, maintain 4th, say K
   B. battle 2nd, compete 4th, fight K, oppose 3rd, quarrel 4th

content 3rd:
   A. cheerful 3rd, happy K, pleased 1st, satisfied 3rd
   B. filling 1st, insides 1st, volume 3rd
   C. cheer 3rd, comfort 3rd, meaning 1st, satisfy 3rd, substance 5th

contest 4th:
   A. disagree 2nd, dispute 6th, oppose 3rd
   B. battle 2nd, conflict 4th, competition 5th, event 3rd, fight K, game K,
      match 3rd, meet K, struggle 1st, tournament 5th, war 1st

continent 4th: controlled 2nd, pure 3rd, restrained 6th

continue 2nd: carry on K, endure 4th, keep on K, last K, persist 5th, proceed 4th, remain 2nd, stay 1st

contract 3rd:
    A. agreement 2nd, bargain 4th, pledge 5th, treaty 4th, understanding 1st
    B. condense 6th, decline 6th, shrink 5th, wither 5th

contrary 4th: contradict 4th, different 1st, headstrong 2nd, hostile 4th, opposite 3rd, unruly 6th

contrast 4th: compare 3rd, conflict 4th, differ 4th, oppose 3rd, parallel 5th, stand apart 3rd, vary 4th

contribute 4th: bestow 5th, fund 4th, give K, grant 2nd, pledge 5th

contrite 5th: grief-ridden 5th, regretful 5th, remorseful 6th, repentant 6th, sorry 4th

contrive 6th: construct 3rd, design 5th, frame 3rd, imagine 2nd, invent 2nd, plan 1st, scheme 5th

control 2nd: administer 6th, conduct 3rd, direct 1st, dominate 5th, govern 1st, guide 1st, lead 1st, manage 4th, power 1st, rule K, supervise 6th

controversy 6th: argument 3rd, contention 5th, disagreement 2nd, dispute 6th, quarrel 4th

convenient 4th: close K, easy 1st, handy 2nd, helpful 2nd, near 1st, practical 4th, ready 1st, simple 2nd, usable 3rd

convent 6th: abbey 6th

convention 6th:
    A. custom 6th, tradition 5th
    B. gathering 1st, meeting 1st
    C. contract 3rd, deal 2nd

conventional 6th: common 2nd, correct 3rd, customary 6th, formal 4th, normal 5th, ordinary 3rd, proper 3rd, traditional 5th

conversation 5th: chat 1st, dialogue 5th, discussion 5th, talk K

convert 4th:
    A. adjust 5th, change 2nd, exchange 4th, persuade 5th, switch 4th, trade 2nd
    B. believer 1st, follower 1st

convey 4th: carry K, deed 1st, move K, send K, shift 4th, take K, transmit 6th, transport 5th

convict 5th:
    A. condemn 4th, prove guilty 4th, sentence 1st
    B. criminal 4th, offender 4th, prisoner 3rd, villain 5th

convince 4th: assure 3rd, compel 3rd, demonstrate 6th, persuade 5th, prove 1st, reason 1st, sway 3rd

cook 1st: bake 1st, boil 3rd, broil 4th, heat 1st, roast 4th, saute 4th, warm 1st

cool 1st:
    A. calm 3rd, collected 3rd, serene 6th, tranquil 6th
    B. chilly 3rd, cold K, frigid 6th, icy 1st

cooperate 5th: agree 2nd, agreeable 2nd, cooperative 5th, help K, helpful K, unite 5th, work with K

cop K: officer 1st, police 1st

cope 6th: accept 3rd, contend 2nd, deal with 2nd, live through 1st, manage 4th

copper 4th: penny 1st

copy 3rd: ape K, carbon 4th, duplicate 6th, imitate 5th, mock 4th

cord 4th: line K, rope 1st, string 1st, twine 3rd

cordial 6th: friendly 1st, gracious 3rd, pleasant 3rd, sincere 4th, sympathetic 4th, warm 1st

core 6th: center 2nd, heart K, middle 2nd, nucleus 4th

cork 6th: cap K, lid 1st, stopper 1st, top K

corner 2nd:
  A. angle 3rd, bend 1st, edge 1st
  B. area 3rd, part 1st, region 4th
  C. control 2nd, difficulty 5th, jam K, mess 1st, monopoly 6th, plight 6th, trap 1st, trouble 1st

corny 2nd: feeble 4th, foolish 2nd, humor 4th, silly 1st

corporal 4th: actual 3rd, animal K, flesh 3rd, material 5th, physical 5th, real 1st, true K

corporation 4th: association 5th, business 5th, company 2nd, firm 2nd, institution 5th

corps 6th: association 5th, band 1st, crew 2nd, group 1st

correct 3rd:
  A. adjust 5th, alter 4th, amend 4th, better K, improve 3rd, modify 5th, remedy 4th
  B. accurate 6th, exact 2nd, precise 5th, right K

correspond 5th:
  A. agree 2nd, comply 6th, conform 6th, jibe 6th
  B. communicate 5th, write K

corridor 5th: alley 6th, hall 1st, lane 4th, passage 4th, path 1st

corrupt 6th:
  A. dishonest 3rd, evil 3rd, false 3rd
  B. pollute 3rd, ruin 5th, soil 2nd, warp 4th, wreck 4th

cosmetics 6th: makeup 1st

cost K:
  A. harm 3rd, hurt K, injure 5th
  B. charge 2nd, price K, value 2nd, worth 3rd

costume 4th: clothing 1st, disguise 5th, dress K, mask 3rd, uniform 1st

cot 1st: bed K

cottage 4th: cabin 1st, house K

cotton 2nd: fabric 5th, soft K

couch 4th:
> A. seat 1st
> B. put K, site 5th

cough 5th: choke 1st, gag 1st, gasp 4th

could K: able 3rd. *Also see* can.

couldn't 1st: unable 3rd

council 5th: administration 6th, assembly 4th, board 1st, commission 2nd, committee 5th, congress 4th

counsel 5th: advise 3rd, direct 1st, guide 1st

count K: add K, compute 1st, number K

counter 5th: against 1st, contrary 4th, opposed 3rd, opposite 3rd

countless 5th: abundant 5th, infinite 5th, legion 6th, many K, numerous 4th

country 1st:
> A. farm land K, suburban 6th
> B. nation 2nd

couple 3rd:
> A. pair 1st, two K
> B. put together 1st, yoke 6th

courage 4th: boldness 2nd, bravery 1st, daring 2nd, heart K, heroism 5th, pluck 1st, spirit 2nd, strength 2nd

course 3rd:
> A. passage 4th, path 1st, route 4th, way K
> B. class 1st, plan 1st, program 4th, subject 3rd
> C. bearing 1st, direction 1st, heading 1st, trend 2nd

court 3rd: attract 5th, bid 1st, charm 3rd, invite 3rd

courtesy 4th: civil 3rd, gallant 4th, kindness K, manners 2nd

courtier 6th: gallant 4th, gentleman 3rd, noble 3rd

courtroom 3rd: arena 5th, chambers 5th

cover 1st:
> A. camouflage 6th, hide 1st, protect 4th, shield 4th
> B. contain 5th, include 3rd, take K
> C. blanket 3rd, cap K, case 2nd, coat 1st, lid 1st, shroud 6th, surface 3rd, top K, veil 3rd, wrap 3rd

covert 6th: camouflage 6th, concealed 4th, covered 1st, disguised 5th, hidden 1st, secret 1st, unseen 1st

covet 6th: crave 6th, desire 5th, envy 4th, lust 6th, resent 5th, want K, yearn for 6th

cow K: bully 1st, embarrass 5th, frighten 2nd

cowardly 4th: afraid 1st, fearful 1st, frightened 2nd, scared 1st, timid 5th

crab K: complain 4th, snap 2nd, sulk 5th

crack 4th: break 1st, burst 3rd, crevice 6th, hit K, rend 4th, shatter 5th, snap 2nd, split 4th

cracker 4th: biscuit 4th, chip 5th

crackle 3rd: snap 2nd

cradle 4th: bed K, crib 2nd, hold 1st, rock K, snuggle 5th

craft 2nd: art K, boat 1st, cunning 6th, skill 2nd, talent 2nd, trade 2nd, vessel 4th

craftsmanship 6th: ability 3rd, skill 2nd, workmanship 3rd

crag 6th: cliff 2nd

cram 5th: fill K, force 1st, pack 1st, push 1st, ram K, stuff 1st

cramp 6th:
  A. clamp 5th, grab 4th
  B. pain 2nd, pang 6th, spasm 6th

crash 2nd: accident 4th, bang 3rd, collision 6th, destroy 2nd, failure 2nd, finish 1st, hit K, ruin 5th, shatter 5th, smash 3rd, wreck 4th

crate 5th: box K, carton 4th, case 2nd, container 5th

crater 3rd: depression 5th, hole K, opening K

crave 6th: covet 6th, demand 5th, desire 5th, hunger 2nd, long for 1st, lust 6th, need 1st, require 1st, want K, yearn 6th

crawl 1st: creep 1st, trail 2nd

crazy 4th: absurd 6th, insane 6th, mad K, silly 1st

creak 4th: squeak 2nd

cream 1st:
  A. grease 5th, oil K
  B. beat 1st, defeat 5th, mash 4th
  C. best K, nobility 3rd, royalty 3rd

crease 5th: edge 1st, fold 1st, pleat 5th, ridge 5th

create 3rd: cause 2nd, construct 3rd, design 5th, develop 5th, device 4th, engineer 4th, establish 3rd, institute 5th, invent 2, make K, produce 2nd

creature 3rd: animal K, being 1st, individual 3rd, monster 1st

credible 6th: assured 3rd, believable 1st, certain 1st, conceivable 4th, convincing 4th, dependable 3rd, reliable 5th, true K, trusty 1st

credit 5th:
  A. believe 1st, have faith in 3rd, trust 1st
  B. assign 5th, belief 1st, charge 2nd, reputation 5th

credulous 6th: believing 2nd, foolish 2nd, trusting 1st

creed 6th: belief 1st, faith 3rd, religion 4th

creek 4th: river K, stream 3rd

creep 1st: crawl 1st, prowl 2nd, slither 4th, sneak 4th

creeping 1st: crawling 1st, sneaking 4th

cremate 5th: burn 3rd

crepe 6th:
  A. pancake 1st
  B. fabric 5th, fiber 3rd

crescent 6th: circle K, curve 3rd, moon 1st

crest 4th: edge 1st, peak 4th, rise 1st, top K

crevice 6th: break 1st, crack 4th, gap K, split 4th

crew 2nd: bunch 3rd, gang 1st, herd 2nd, party K, race 1st, row 4th, staff 4th, team 1st

crib 2nd: bed K, cradle 4th

crime 2nd: harm 3rd, hurt K, offense 4th, sin 1st, vice 4th, wrong 1st

criminal 4th: convict 5th, illegal 1st, offender 4th, prohibited 6th

crimson 5th: red K, ruby 6th, scarlet 4th

critical 5th:
   A. difficult 5th, negative 6th, severe 4th
   B. acute 6th, essential 6th, important 1st

criticize 5th: accuse 4th, blame 2nd, charge 2nd, complain 4th, condemn 4th, crab K, fault 3rd, reproach 6th, scold 5th

crop 2nd:
   A. bounty 5th, harvest 4th, produce 2nd, yield 4th
   B. clip 2nd, cut K, shorten 1st, snip 4th, trim 4th

cross 1st:
   A. angry 1st, furious 1st, mad K, upset 3rd
   B. betray 5th, cheat 3rd, deceive 5th, deny 5th
   C. bridge 1st, meet K, span 6th, transport 5th, travel 1st, traverse 5th

crosswise 1st: across 1st, side to side K

crotch 6th: angle 3rd, bend K, fork 1st

crouch 5th: bend K, crawl 1st, hunch 6th, stoop 5th

crow 2nd: boast 4th, brag 3rd, show off 1st

crowd 2nd:
   A. bunch 3rd, gathering 1st, group 1st, mass 3rd, mob 4th, pack 1st, throng 5th
   B. crush 4th, jam K, press 1st, push 1st, shove 5th, squeeze 5th, swarm 4th

crown 1st: cap K, point 1st, summit 5th, top K

cruel 5th: brutal 6th, fierce 4th, hard K, harsh 5th, mean 1st, savage 5th, severe 4th, stern 4th, strict 6th, tough 5th, unkind 2nd

crunch 4th: chew 1st, crush 4th, gnaw 1st, grind 4th, mash 4th, smash 3rd

crush 4th: bruise 5th, defeat 5th, grind 4th, mash 4th, pound 2nd, powder 3rd, press 1st, push 1st, put down K, smash 3rd, squash 2nd, stomp 4th, squeeze 5th

cry K: address K, announce 3rd, howl 4th, moan 5th, sob 1st, weep 4th, whimper 5th, whine 5th, yell K

crystal 3rd: clear 2nd, glass 1st, rock K, transparent 5th

cub K:
   A. bear K, pup K, puppy K
   B. baby K, boy K, child K, lad K

cube 4th: block 1st, box K, square 2nd

cuddle 5th: cradle 4th, hold 1st, hug 1st, love K, pet 1st, snuggle 5th, squeeze 5th, touch 1st

cue 2nd: clue 2nd, guide 1st, hint 1st, indicator 4th, key K, lead 1st, mark 1st, prompt 4th, remind 3rd, sign 1st, signal 4th, tip 1st

cuff 1st:
   A. band 1st, edge 1st
   B. box K, hit K, punch 4th, slap 2nd, strike 2nd

cultivate 6th: breed 4th, develop 5th, further 2nd, grow 1st, improve 3rd, nurse K, promote 5th, rear 3rd, teach 1st, train K

cultivation 6th:
   A. agriculture 4, farming 1st, gardening K
   B. development 5th, improvement 3rd, teaching 1st

culture 6th:
   A. customs 6th, habits 3rd, society 3rd, tradition 5th, ways K
   B. background 4th, breeding 4th, civilization 4th, cultivation 6th, education 3rd, polish 4th, taste 1st

cunning 6th:
   A. clever 3rd, crafty 4th, foxy 1st, sly 4th, smart 1st, tricky 1st
   B. craft 2nd, skill 2nd

cup K:
   A. bowl 1st, can K, glass 1st, mug 1st
   B. bend K, depression 6th

curb 3rd:
   A. block 1st, check 1st, control 2nd, limit 3rd, restrain 5th, restrict 6th, stop K
   B. border 1st, boundary 4th, edge 1st, margin 5th, ridge 5th, rim 1st

cure 4th: correct 3rd, fix 1st, repair 4th

curfew 6th: bedtime K, deadline 2nd

curious 3rd: interested 1st, questioning 1st, wondering 1st

curl 2nd: bend K, coil 5th, curve 3rd, hook 4th, turn 1st, twist 1st, wind 1st

current 3rd:
   A. drift 2nd, flow 1st, pull K, river K, stream 3rd, tide 1st
   B. actual 3rd, contemporary 5th, immediate 3rd, popular 3rd, present K, universal 4th

curse 3rd:
   A. evil 3rd, plague 5th, scourge 6th
   B. abuse 6th, condemn 4th, punish 4th, swear 4th

cursed 3rd: condemned 4th, hateful 2nd, ruined 5th, terrible 1st

curtain 5th:
   A. cover 1st, hide 1st, shield 4th
   B. blind 3rd, drape 5th, screen 1st, shade 2nd, shutter 4th, wall K

curve 3rd: arc 4th, arch 4th, bend K, bow 1st, coil 5th, curl 2nd, orbit 4th, turn 1, twist 1st

custom 6th: form 1st, habit 3rd, law 1st, manners 2nd, practice 1st, rite 6th, ritual 6th, tradition 5th, use K, way K

customer 5th: buyer 1st, client 6th, patron 5th, shopper 2nd

cut K:
    A. hurt K, injure 5th, wound 3rd
    B. carve 4th, rip K, scratch 4th, slash 6th, slice 5th, slit 5th, tear 2nd
    C. piece 1st, portion 4th, section 4th
    D. canal 4th, channel 4th, division 4th, furrow 6th, groove 5th, hew 6th, trim 4th

cute 1st: funny 1st, precious 4th, pretty 1st, sweet K

cutlass 6th: blade 2nd, saber 5th, sword 4th

cutting 1st:
    A. acute 6th, keen 4th, sharp 1st
    B. bit 1st, part 1st, particle 5th, piece 1st

dab 1st: bead K, bit 1st, dot K, drop 1st, fragment 6th, pat K, pinch 4th, poke 1st, speck 4th, spot 1st

dad K: daddy K, father K, papa 1st, pop K

daft 6th: confused 4th, crazy 4th, dazed 5th, foolish 2nd, insane 6th, mad K, silly 1st, simple 1st

daily 4th: common 2nd, customary 6th, everyday 1st, normal 5th, ordinary 3rd, regular 3rd, routine 6th, usual 3rd

dam K: bar 3rd, block 1st, clog 5th, halt 4th, hinder 6th, hold 1st, jam K, obstruct 5th, prevent 3rd, stop K

damage 5th:
    A. destruction 5th, disaster 6th, loss K
    B. abuse 6th, destroy 5th, harm 3rd, hurt K, impair 6th, injure 5th, loss K, ruin 5th

damp 5th: foggy 1st, juicy 1st, misty 1st, moist 4th, watery 1st, wet K

damsel 6th: girl K, lady 1st, lass 1st, maiden 4th, miss K

dance 1st:
    A. ball K, ballet 4th, prom 5th
    B. bounce 6th, hop K, rock K, spin 1st, swing 1st, whirl 4th

dandy 1st: fine 1st, great K, swell 3rd

danger 1st: chance 2nd, hazard 6th, menace 5th, peril 5th, risk 4th, threat 5th

dangerous 6th: hazardous 6th, perilous 5th, risky 4th, threatening 5th, uncertain 1st, unsafe 1st

dangle 5th: drop K, hang 2nd, suspend 5th, swing 1st, trail 2nd

dare 2nd:
    A. challenge 4th, defy 6th, face K
    B. bear K, brave 1st, endure 4th, meet K, provoke 6th, risk 4th

dark K: black K, dim 1st, dull 1st, gloomy 3rd, obscure 6th, shady 2nd, shadowy 3rd

dart 1st:
  A. arrow 2nd, spear 4th
  B. fly K, rush 2nd, sail 1st, shoot 3rd, speed 3rd

date 1st:
  A. appointment 3rd, engagement 5th, meeting 1st, reservation 3rd
  B. day K, period 2nd, season 2nd, time 1st

daughter 1st: child K, female 4th, girl K

day K:
  A. light K
  B. date 1st, time 1st

daydream 2nd: dream K, idea 1st, imagine 2nd, thought 1st, wish K

daylight 1st: light K, morning 1st, sun K, sunshine 1st

dazzle 5th:
  A. shine 1st, sparkle 5th
  B. amaze 5th, astonish 4th, blind 3rd, confound 6th, confuse 4th, stun 4th

dead 1st: gone 1st, not alive 3rd, still 1st

deal 2nd:
  A. assign 5th, deliver 5th, give K, share 2nd
  B. agreement 2nd, bargain 4th, contract 3rd

dear 1st:
  A. costly 1st, expensive 3rd, priceless 1st, valuable 4th
  B. admired 5th, beloved 4th, favorite 3rd, loved 1st, precious 4th

debris 5th: junk 3rd, mess 1st, rubbish 5th, ruins 5th, trash 2nd, waste 1st

decapitate 6th: behead 2nd, chop off 2nd

decay 5th: decline 6th, fail 2nd, rot 1st, spoil 4th, waste 1st

deceive 5th: cheat 3rd, con 3rd, fool 2nd, lie to 2nd, mislead 5th, trick 1st

decide 1st: consider 2nd, determine 5th, judge 1st, make up your mind 1st, resolve 5th, settle 2nd, weigh 1st

deck 1st:
  A. floor K, porch 3rd
  B. adorn 6th, decorate 3rd, grace 3rd, ornament 4th

declare 5th: announce 3rd, assert 6th, claim 2nd, express 5th, inform 5th, proclaim 4th, profess 5th, publish 4th, say K, state 1st

decline 6th:
  A. deny 5th, reject 5th, resist 4th, turn down 1st
  B. descend 6th, go down K, slant 6th, slope 3rd

decode 5th: read K, understand 1st

decorate 3rd: adorn 6th, beautify 2nd, ornament 4th

decoration 3rd: ornament 4th, trim 4th

dedicate 6th: bless 3rd, devote 5th, focus 5th, give K, offer 2nd, surrender 5th

deduce 6th: conclude 3rd, gather 1st, infer 5th, think 1st, understand 1st

deed 1st:

    A. achievement 5th, act K, action 1st, assign 5th, exploit 6th, feat 1st, job K, task 3rd, transfer 5th, work K

    B. title 3rd

deep 1st:

    A. absorbed 5th, fascinated 5th, involved 6th, lost in K

    B. difficult 5th, hidden 1st, instinctive 5th, mysterious 1st, unclear 2nd

    C. intent 5th, obscure 6th, profound 6th, serious 4th, sincere 4th

defeat 5th: beat 1st, best K, conquer 4th, crush 4th, destroy 2nd, dominate 5th, master 1st, overthrow 6th, ruin 5th, stop K, vanquish 6th

defend 5th:

    A. argue 3rd, justify 3rd, maintain 4th

    B. guard 1st, police 1st, protect 4th, shelter 4th, shield 4th, support 5th

defy 6th: brave 1st, challenge 4th, dare 2nd, disobey 3rd, face K, ignore 5th

degree 5th:

    A. class 1st, grade 2nd, level 3rd, rank 3rd, status 6th

    B. amount 2nd, measure 2nd, size 1st, strength 1st

deity 5th: god 1st

dejected 5th: blue K, depressed 5th, gloomy 3rd, melancholy 6th, sad K, unhappy K, weary 4th

delay 5th: hold 1st, linger 4th, slow 1st, suspend 5th, wait K

delegate 5th:

    A. assign 5th, charge 2nd, enable 4th

    B. representative 4th

delegation 5th:

    A. assignment 5th, mission 5th

    B. board 1st, body 1st, commission 2nd, group 1st

deliberate 6th:

    A. consider 2nd, intend 5th, plan 1st

    B. designed 5th, intentional 5th, planned 1st, willful 5th

delicate 5th: dainty 5th, elegant 5th, frail 6th, gentle 3rd, rare 4th, slight K, small K, smooth 2nd, soft K, thin 1st, weak 3rd

delicatessen 5th: cafe 4th, restaurant 5th

deliver 5th:

    A. bring K, give K, send 1st

    B. address K, announce 3rd, say K, speak 1st

    C. free K, hand K, release 5th, save 1st

demand 5th: ask 5th, claim 2nd, insist 5th, need 1st, order 1st, request 4th, require 2nd

demonstrate 6th: exhibit 4th, explain 2nd, prove 1st, show 1st

demure 5th: bashful 4th, meek 2nd, quiet K, shy 1st

den 1st:
- A. library 3rd, study 2nd
- B. bar 3rd, tavern 5th
- C. burrow 5th, cave 1st, lair 5th

dent 1st: crease 5th, depression 6th, dip 1st

deny 5th: contradict 4th, decline 6th, disprove 3rd, object 1st, refuse 2nd, reject 5th, resist 4th

depart 5th: exit 3rd, flee 5th, go K, leave 1st, move 1st

department 2nd: branch 2nd, division 4th, office 1st, section 4th, unit 5th

depend 3rd: lean 3rd, rely 5th, trust 1st

depose 6th: dethrone 4th, kick out 1st, unseat 2nd

deposit 5th: leave 1st, place 1st, sediment 4th, set K

depress 5th:
- A. dent 1st, lower K
- B. deject 5th, discourage 5th, downcast 5th, drain 5th, oppress 6th, tire 2nd, weary 4th

depression 6th:
- A. blue 1st, despair 6th, discouraged 5th, gloom 3rd, low K, sadness 2nd
- B. cavity 5th, hollow 3rd

depth 5th: deepness 1st, middle 2nd, range 3rd, scope 6th, span 6th, substance 5th, width 4th

derelict 6th:
- A. beggar 2nd, tramp 4th
- B. abandoned 4th, careless 5th, deserted 1st, desolate 6th, discarded 6th, left 1st, negligent 4th, reckless 5th, rejected 5th

descend 6th: alight 5th, decline 6th, dismount 3rd, fall K, go down K, land K, lower 1st

desert 1st:
- A. abandon 4th, betray 5th, due 2nd, forsake 6th, ignore 5th, leave 1st, quit 1st, reject 5th
- B. badlands 3rd, wasteland 6th

deserve 4th: merit 4th, reward 4th, worthy 3rd

design 5th: aim 3rd, arrange 3rd, develop 5th, draw K, form 1st, goal 4th, intend 6th, mean 1st, plan 1st, plot 4th, sketch 5th

desire 5th: ambition 4th, covet 6th, crave 6th, hope K, long 1st, want K, wish K

desk 2nd: table K

desolate 6th: alone K, bare 3rd, deserted 3rd, forlorn 6th, lone 2nd, lonely 2nd, ruined 5th, solitary 5th

desperate 5th:
- A. bold 2nd, daring 2nd, rash 6th, reckless 5th
- B. critical 5th, urgent 6th

C. dire 6th, hopeless 2nd

despise 5th: detest 6th, hate 2nd, look down on 1st, mock 4th, scorn 4th

destiny 5th: chance 2nd, end K, fate 3rd, fortune 3rd, future 5th, lot K, luck 1st

destroy 2nd: abolish 5th, crush 4th, damage 5th, destruct 2nd, erase 2nd, exterminate 6th, kill 1st, ruin 5th, slaughter 5th, smash 3rd, spoil 4th, wreck 4th

destruction 5th: damage 5th, ruin 5th, wreckage 4th

destructive 5th: evil 3rd, harmful 3rd, killing 1st, negative 6th, ruinous 5th

detail 5th:

    A. fact 1st, item 5th, part 1st, particular 4th, point 1st

    B. detect 4th, exact 2nd, find K, list 2nd, locate 3rd, note 1st, notice 2nd

detective 4th: investigator 5th

determine 5th: conclude 3rd, decide 1st, establish 3rd, find K, fix 1st, learn 1st, resolve 5th, rule K, settle 2nd, solve 4th

detest 6th: despise 5th, dislike K, hate 2nd, scorn 4th

dethrone 6th: overthrow 6th, unseat 1st

devastate 6th: destroy 2nd, overwhelm 5th, ravage 6th, ruin 5th, spoil 4th, waste 1st, wreck 4th

develop 5th: advance 2nd, age 1st, bloom 4th, grow K, increase 3rd, mature 5th, progress 4th, ripen 1st

device 4th: equipment 5th, instrument 3rd, machine 1st, tool 1st

devote 5th: bless 3rd, commit 4th, concentrate 5th, dedicate 6th, give K, offer 2nd, pledge 5th, promise 1st

devotee 5th: addict 5th, believer 1st, follower 1st

devour 5th: consume 4th, destroy 2nd, eat K, finish 1st, ravage 6th, swallow 1st

dew 1st: moisture 3rd

dial 5th:

    A. adjust 5th, call K, select 4th, spin 1st, tune 1st

    B. circle K, disk 2nd, indicator 4th

dialect 5th: accent 6th, language 2nd, speech 2nd, tongue 3rd

diary 3rd: account 3rd, history 2nd, journal 2nd, log 1st, notes 1st, record 2nd

die 2nd: cease 3rd, end K, expire 6th, fade K, pass away K, perish 4th, stop K, weaken 3rd

diet 4th:

    A. fast 1st, reduce 3rd, slim 5th, trim 4th

    B. food K, meals 3rd

differ 4th:

    A. disagree 3rd, oppose 3rd

    B. change 2nd, contrast 4th, unlike 2nd, vary 4th

different 1st:

    A. contrary 4th, distinct 5th, separate 3rd

    B. extraordinary 5th, strange 1st, unusual 3rd

difficult 5th: annoying 5th, awkward 6th, challenging 4th, complex 6th, demanding 5th, hard 1st, not easy K, puzzling 4th, tough 5th, trying 1st, unpleasant 3rd

dig 1st:
    A. enjoy 2nd, like K, understand 1st
    B. burrow 5th, mine 1st, scoop 4th, shovel 1st
    C. archeology site 5th

dim 1st: cloudy 1st, dark K, faint 3rd, foggy 1st, pale 3rd, shadowy 3rd, unclear 2nd, weak 3rd

diminutive 6th: little K, short 1st, small K, tiny 2nd

din 6th: blast 2nd, clamor 6th, noise 1st, racket 1st, uproar 5th

dine 1st: banquet 4th, dinner 1st, eat K, feast 1st

dinner 1st: feast 1st, meal 3rd, supper 2nd

dip 1st:
    A. ladle 6th, lower 1st, plunge 4th, scoop 4th
    B. bathe 1st, soak 5th, submerge 5th

diplomat 5th: ambassador 5th, counselor 5th, go-between 1st

dire 6th: acute 6th, awful 3rd, critical 5th, disastrous 6th, dreadful 6th, evil 3rd, fearful 1st, frightful 2nd, grave 3rd, horrible 4th, ominous 6th, terrible 1st, tragic 5th, urgent 6th

direct 1st: address K, aim 3rd, boss K, control 2nd, manage 4th, supervise 6th

direction 1st:
    A. charge 2nd, control 2nd, instruction 4th
    B. bearing 2nd, control 2nd, course 3rd, lead 1st, location 3rd, movement 2nd, position 2nd, way K

dirt 1st: mud K, sand 1st, stain 4th

disabled 3rd: broken 1st, hurt K, injured 5th, ruined 5th, weakened 3rd

disagree 2nd: argue 3rd, contrast 4th, disagree 2nd, oppose 3rd, vary 4th

disappoint 5th: depress 5th, fail 2nd, let down K, sadden 2nd

disaster 6th: calamity 6th, misadventure 4th, tragedy 5th. *See* accident.

disbelief 5th: challenge 4th, distrust 3rd, doubt 5th, rejection 5th

discard 6th: cast 2nd, dispose of 5th, junk 3rd, reject 5th, rid 1st, scrap 3rd, throw 1st, toss 2nd, trash 2nd

discipline 6th: coach 4th, control 2nd, correct 3rd, direct 1st, drill 2nd, educate 3rd, guide 1st, harden K, instruct 4th, punish 4th, rule K, school K, teach 1st, train K

discontinue 4th: abandon 4th, cease 3rd, end K, quit 1st, stop K

discourage 5th:
    A. caution 5th, hinder 6th, warn 3rd
    B. dishearten 5th, sadden 2nd

discover 1st: determine 5th, find K, locate 3rd, notice 1st, recognize 3rd, uncover 1st

discuss 5th: chat 1st, confer 4th, converse 5th, go over K, speak 1st, talk K

disease 5th: complaint 4th, condition 3rd, illness 2nd, sickness 2nd

disguise 5th:
    A. camouflage 6th, deceive 5th, hide 1st
    B. cloak 4th, costume 4th, mask 2nd

disgust 5th: aversion 4th, offend 4th, revolt 5th, shock 1st, sicken 2nd

dish 1st: container 5th, dip 1st, ladle 6th, plate K, platter 6th, serve 1st

dishearten 5th: discourage 5th, deject 5th, depress 5th, dull 1st

disintegrate 5th: decay 5th, fall apart 3rd, rot 1st, spoil 4th

dispense 5th: administer 6th, distribute 6th, divide 4th, give out K, share 2nd

display 3rd: arrange 3rd, exhibit 4th, present 3rd, show 1st, stage 3rd

dispose 5th:
    A. cast 2nd, junk 3rd, rid 1st, scrap 3rd, throw away 1st, toss 2nd, trash 2nd
    B. arrange 3rd, assort 5th, order 1st, range 3rd
    C. affect 4th, bend K, bias 6th

disposition 5th: humor 4th, mood 3rd, nature 1st, spirit 2nd, temper 4th

dispute 6th: argue 3rd, disagree 3rd, discuss 5th, fight K, oppose 3rd, quarrel 4th

distance 1st:
    A. length 2nd, measure 2nd, range 3rd, reach 1st, remove 2nd, scope 6th, space 1st, stretch 4th
    B. reserve 3rd, restraint 5th
    C. future 5th, horizon 4th

distant 4th:
    A. apart 3rd, far 1st, remote 5th, removed 2nd, separate 3rd
    B. cold K, composed 4th, faint 3rd, unemotional 4th, unfriendly 2nd

distaste 6th: contempt 5th, disgust 5th, dislike 2nd, horror 4th, repulsion 6th

distinctive 5th: individual 3rd, one of a kind K, separate 3rd, special 2nd, unique 6th, unusual 3rd

distinguish 6th: brand 2nd, group 1st, individualize 4th, mark 1st, rate 1st, separate 3rd, set apart 3rd, sort out 2nd

distress 5th: agony 5th, grief 5th, hardship 5th, misery 4th, sadness 1st, sorrow 4th, suffering 2nd, worry 1st

distribute 6th: bestow 5th, deal 2nd, deliver 5th, give K, hand out K

district 4th: area 3rd, community 2nd, division 4th, neighborhood 2nd, region 4th

disturb 6th: bother 2nd, disorder 2nd, disorganize 4th, interrupt 3rd, move K, shift 4th, trouble 1st, unsettle 2nd, upset 3rd

dive 1st: descend 6th, drop K, fall K, jump K, leap 3rd, plunge 4th

divide 4th: cut K, distribute 6th, part 1st, separate 3rd, sort 1st, split 4th

divorce 4th: divide 4th, part 1st, separate 3rd, split 4th

do K: accomplish 2nd, achieve 5th, act K, execute 5th, fix 1st, happen 1st, make K, manage 4th, perform 4th, satisfy 3rd, work K

dock 1st:
A. moor 5th, park 1st
B. pier 4th, wharf 5th

doctor 1st:
A. healer 3rd, physician 5th, surgeon 5th
B. fix 1st, heal 3rd, repair 4th, treat 2nd

doing 1st: achieving 5th, action 1st, deed 1st, feat 1st, working K

doll K: figure 1st, girl K

domicile 5th: abode 5th, dwelling 4th, home K, house K, location 3rd, place 1st, shelter 4th

dominant 5th:
A. main 3rd, major 3rd, paramount 5th, primary 5th, uppermost 4th
B. aggressive 6th, boss K, commanding 2nd, controlling 2nd, ruling 2nd

dominate 5th: boss K, command 2nd, control 2nd, rule K

done 1st: complete 3rd, finished 1st, over K, through 1st

door K: entrance 3rd, entry 3rd, gate 1st, opening K

doorway 2nd: entrance 3rd, entry 3rd, gate 1st, opening K

dope 1st:
A. dumb 1st, dummy 1st, foolish 2nd, stupid 4th
B. drugs 1st

dormitory 5th: apartment 1st, bedroom 3rd

dose 1st: measure 2nd, portion 4th, quantity 4th

dot K: dab 1st, drop K, point 1st, speck 4th, spot 1st

double 3rd:
A. by two K, pair 1st, twice 3rd
B. duplicate 6th

doubt 1st:
A. question 1st, suspect 5th
B. concern 3rd, fear 1st, suspicion 4th

doubtful 1st: questionable 3rd, suspect 5th, suspicious 4th, uncertain 2nd, undecided 1st

dough 5th:
A. money K
B. batter 1st, paste 1st

down K:
A. bleak 4th, blue K, gloomy 3rd, idle 4th, ill 1st, sad K, sick K, unhappy 1st
B. below 1st, beneath 1st, low K, under K

downhearted 5th: blue K, depressed 6th, gloomy 3rd, sad K, unhappy 1st

drag 3rd:
A. carry K, draw K, haul 4th, pull K, tow 1st

B. lag 1st, limp along 5th, trail 2nd

drain 5th: clear 2nd, draw off 1st, empty 3rd, exhaust 4th, reduce 3rd, sap 1st, take K

drama 5th: play K, skit 3rd, theater 3rd, tragedy 5th

dramatize 5th: act K, stage 3rd

drape 5th: cloak 4th, cover 1st, curtain 5th, hang 2nd, hide 1st

draught 6th: drink 1st, measure 2nd

draw K:

    A. deadlock 3rd, tie 1st

    B. cartoon 2nd, outline 4th, sketch 5th, trace 3rd

    C. attract 5th, lure 5th, pull K

dread 6th: alarm 3rd, fear 1st, horror 4th, panic 1st, worry 1st

dream K: daydream 2nd, fantasy 6th, idealize 3rd, plan 1st, think 1st, vision 4th

dress K:

    A. clothe 1st, deck 1st, put on K

    B. attire 6th, clothing 1st, costume 4th, garment 4th, outfit 2nd

dresser 2nd: cabinet 4th, chest 2nd, closet 2nd

drift 2nd:

    A. current 3rd, flow 1st, progress 4th, run K, tend K

    B. adrift 6th, aim 3rd, drifting 2nd, goal 4th, intent 5th, meaning 1st

drill 2nd:

    A. exercise 1st, practice 1st, test 3rd

    B. coach 4th, teach 1st, train K

    C. bore 2nd, grind 4th, pierce 4th, punch 4th

drink 1st: consume 4th, draw K, gulp 1st, sip 1st, swallow 1st

drip 2nd: drop K, leak 6th, mist 1st, seep 4th

drive K:

    A. ride K, take K, taxi 1st

    B. energy 4th, power 1st, spirit 2nd

    C. aim 3rd, control 2nd, move K, push 1st, urge 4th

droop 5th: curve 3rd, drop K, fade 1st, fall K, hang 2nd, sag 1st, sink 3rd, wilt 4th, wither 5th

drop K:

    A. descend 6th, dive 1st, fall K, lower 1st, plunge 4th, sink 3rd, tumble 4th

    B. abandon 4th, desert 1st, leave 1st, unload 2nd

    C. bead K, bubble 2nd

drove 1st: cattle 3rd, group 1st, herd 2nd, pack 1st. *See* drive.

drown 1st: descend 6th, flood 2nd, sink 3rd, submerge 5th, swamp 4th

drug 1st:

    A. chemical 4th, dope 1st, medicine 4th, narcotic 4th

    B. blunt 6th, dull 1st, poison 3rd

drum 5th:
    A. barrel 4th, keg 1st, tom-tom 1st
    B. beat 1st, pound 2nd, tap K

dry 1st: arid 6th, baked 1st, bare 3rd, hard K, powdery 3rd

dubious 6th: doubtful 5th, questionable 2nd, uncertain 2nd, unsure K, vague 5th

duck K:
    A. avoid 3rd, dodge 3rd, hide 1st
    B. dip 1st, dive 1st, dunk 3rd, submerge 5th

due 2nd: earned 2nd, fit K, in for K, merited 4th, needed 1st, owed 3rd, payable K, required 2nd, rightful 2nd

dull 1st:
    A. blunt 6th
    B. boring 2nd, lazy 4th, monotonous 5th, slow 1st, stupid 4th, tiring 2nd

dumb 1st: quiet K, silent 3rd, speechless 2nd

dummy 1st: doll K, figure 1st, model 3rd

dump 2nd: discard 6th, reject 5th, throw out 1st, toss 2nd, trash 2nd, unload 2nd

dune 5th: hill K, pile 1st, sand 1st

dungeon 5th: cell 1st, cellar 1st, chamber 5th, prison 3rd

duplicate 6th:
    A. copy 3rd, double 3rd, reproduce 5th
    B. doubled 3rd, reproduction 5th, similar 4th

durable 6th: enduring 4th, lasting 1st, permanent 5th, stable 4th, steady 3rd, strong K

during 1st: at the same time 1st, meanwhile 3rd, through 1st, throughout 2nd, while 1st

dusk 5th: afternoon 1st, dark K, dim 1st, end of day K, evening 1st, obscure 6th, sunset 1st

dust 2nd: dirt 1st, earth 1st, loam 4th, sand 1st

duty 1st:
    A. assignment 5th, job K, profession 5th, task 3rd, work K
    B. care K, charge 2nd, obligation 6th, responsibility 4th

dwarf 4th:
    A. midget 4th
    B. overpower 3rd, reduce 3rd, stunt 6th

dwell 4th: live 1st, lodge 4th, remain 1st, reside 5th, settle 2nd, stay 1st

dwelling 4th: abode 5th, domicile 5th, home K, house K, residence 5th

dye 2nd:
    A. change color 2nd, decorate 3rd
    B. color K, shade 2nd, tint 5th, tone 3rd

dynamic 5th: active 3rd, alive 3rd, brisk 6th, forceful 2nd, powerful 2nd, vital 5th

dynamite 6th:
  A. terrific 5th, wonderful 1st
  B. explosive 3rd, great K, powerful 2nd, strong K

each K: all K, any K, every K, individual 3rd, separate 3rd

eager 5th: alert 5th, animated 6th, anxious 4th, bright 1st, enthusiastic 4th, excited 4th, hopeful K, in a hurry 1st, inspired 4th, lively 5th, wishful K

earl 4th: gentleman 3rd, noble 3rd

early 1st:
  A. ancient 3rd, antique 6th, original 3rd, previous 5th
  B. ahead 1st, before K, immediate 3rd, soon K, too soon K

earn 2nd: deserve 4th, gain 2nd, get K, make K, merit 4th, obtain 5th, rate 1st, win K

earnest 4th: concentrated 5th, dedicated 6th, determined 5th, devoted 5th, grave 3rd, intense 6th, passionate 6th, serious 4th, sincere 3rd, sober 4th, solemn 5th

earth 1st:
  A. globe 4th, planet 4th, sphere 6th, world 1st
  B. one world 1st, people K, the whole world 1st, world 1st
  C. clay 1st, dirt 1st, ground 1st, land K, loam 4th, mud 1st

earthenware 5th: clay 1st, pottery 4th

earthquake 5th: earth tremor 6th, shock 1st

ease 3rd:
  A. capability 4th, skill 2nd
  B. aid 2nd, calm 3rd, clear 2nd, help K, lessen 1st, lighten K, reduce 3rd, relax 4th, relieve 4th, rest 1st, smooth 3rd
  C. calm 3rd, comfort 3rd, content 3rd, effortless 2nd, grace 3rd, leisure 5th, peace 1st, rest 1st, smooth 2nd

easy K: breeze 4th, cinch 6th, clear 2nd, comfortable 3rd, free K, gentle 3rd, loose 3rd, no problem 1st, no sweat 3rd, obvious 5th, restful 2nd, simple 2nd, uncomplicated 6th

eat K: bite 1st, chew 1st, consume 4th, crunch 4th, devour 5th, dine 1st, feast 1st, gobble up 4th, gulp down 1st, nibble 4th, snack 2nd, swallow 1st, wolf K

eaves 6th: edges 1st, gutter 6th, rims 1st, roof 1st

echo 4th:
  A. copy 1st, mimic 6th, mock 4th, repeat 4th, restate 2nd, return 1st
  B. fake 1st, imitation 5th, mirror 4th

eclipse 5th: cloud 1st, conceal 4th, cover 1st, darken 1st, dim 1st, hide 1st, mask 2nd, screen 1st, shadow 3rd

economy 4th: business 2nd, finance 4th

ecstasy 6th: delight 3rd, excitement 4th, happiness K, joy 1st, paradise 4th, pleasure 2nd, rapture 6th, thrill 4th

eddy 6th: circle K, current 3rd, rotate 6th, spin 1st, whirl 4th, whirlpool 4th

edge 1st: advantage 3rd, border 1st, boundary 4th, brink 6th, end K, frame 3rd, head start 1st, limit 3rd, rim 1st

edit 3rd: adapt 4th, change 2nd, revise 6th, rewrite 2nd

educate 3rd: acquaint 4th, coach 4th, inform 5th, instruct 4th, prepare 1st, train K

education 3rd: development 5th, direction 1st, information 5th, instruction 4th, schooling 1st, teaching 1st, training 1st

effect 3rd:
A. accomplish 2nd, achieve 5th, follow 1st
B. consequence 4th, feeling K, impression 5th, product 4th, result 2nd

effective 4th: in order 1st, useful 2nd, working 1st

effort 2nd: achievement 5th, act K, action 1st, activity 3rd, energy 4th, exertion 6th, muscle 4th, try K, work K

egg K:
A. seed 1st
B. provoke 6th, push 1st, urge 4th

either 2nd: one or the other 1st

ejaculate 6th: call out K, expel 6th, fire K

elaborate 5th:
A. complete 3rd, complicated 6th, decorated 3rd, detailed 5th, elegant 5th
B. amplify 6th, develop 5th, enlarge 5th, expand 5th, explain 2nd, improve 3rd, increase 3rd, polish 4th, refine 6th

elastic 6th: flexible 6th, springy 1st, stretchy 4th

elbow 4th:
A. bend K, crazy bone 4th, corner 2nd, fold 1st, funny bone 1st
B. bulldoze 1st, bump 2nd, hit K, push 1st, shove 5th

elder 5th: older 1st

elderly 5th: ancient 3rd, mature 5th, old K

elect 3rd:
A. exclusive 6th, special 2nd
B. choose 3rd, pick 1st, select 4th, vote 2nd

electric 3rd: exciting 4th, moving K, rousing 4th, stirring 3rd, thrilling 4th

electronic 5th: battery powered 5th, electric powered 3rd, mechanical 6th

elegant 5th: choice 3rd, elaborate 5th, excellent 1st, exquisite 6th, fine 1st, lovely 1st, noble 3rd, rare 4th, simple 2nd

element 3rd: detail 5th, feature 3rd, fragment 6th, ingredient 4th, item 5th, member 1st, part 1st, piece 1st, portion 4th, section 4th, unit 5th

elevate 2nd: arise 4th, ascent 4th, enrich 6th, improve 3rd, lift 1st, rise 1st

elevation 4th: altitude 5th, height 4th, hill K, mountain 2nd, peak 4th, tallness K

elevator 2nd: lift 1st

elf 1st: brownie 2nd, fairy 4th, goblin 4th, gnome 6th

eliminate 5th: abolish 5th, do away with K, drop K, erase 2nd, exclude 6th, get rid of 1st, put an end to K

else 1st: or K, other 1st

elsewhere 4th: another place 1st, not here K, there 1st

embarrass 5th: distress 5th, fluster 6th, make uncomfortable 3rd, shame 3rd

embarrassed 5th:
  A. ashamed 4th, ill at ease 3rd, timid 5th
  B. bother 2nd, upset 3rd

emblem 5th: badge 5th, banner 3rd, crest 4th, flag 3rd, mark 1st, representation 4th, seal K, sign 1st, symbol 5th

embrace 4th: accept 3rd, adopt 3rd, cuddle 5th, hug 1st, nuzzle 1st, snuggle 5th, squeeze 5th, welcome 1st

embroider 5th: add to K, decorate 3rd, elaborate 5th, needlework 3rd, sew 2nd

emerge 5th: appear 2nd, arise 4th, begin K, develop 5th, happen 1st, loom 5th, show 1st, start 1st

emergency 5th: accident 4th, bind 2nd, crisis 5th, difficulty 5th, mess 1st, trouble 1st

emigrant 6th: alien 5th, foreigner 5th

eminent 6th: celebrated 4th, elevated 2nd, famous 2nd, honorable 1st, honored 1st, noble 3rd, noted 1st, outstanding 2nd, renowned 6th, respected 2nd

emotion 4th: affection 4th, feeling K, love K, passion 6th

emperor 4th: king 1st, ruler 2nd

emphasize 5th: accent 6th, stress 6th

emphatic 6th: bold 2nd, clear 2nd, critical 5th, earnest 4th, important 1st, intense 6th, plain 2nd, strong K, urgent 6th

empire 4th: kingdom 3rd, nation 2nd

employ 5th: apply 2nd, hire 3rd, out to work K, sign 1st, use K

empress 4th: queen K

empty 3rd: abandoned 4th, blank 4th, hollow 3rd, lacking 1st, unreal 1st, vacant 6th, void 6th

enable 4th: aid 2nd, allow 2nd, assist 4th, energize 4th, equip 5th, establish 3rd, help K, let K, qualify 4th, strengthen 1st

enamel 6th:
  A. coat 1st, decorate 3rd, finish 1st, metalize 4th, paint 2nd, plate 1st
  B. coating 1st, glaze 6th, polish 4th

enchant 6th: bewitch 3rd, captivate 3rd, catch 1st, charm 3rd, fascinate 5th, win K

encircle 5th: circle K, embrace 4th, encompass 4th, enclose 4th, ring 1st, surround 3rd

enclose 4th: cage 1st, close K, contain 5th, encircle 5th, fence 1st, imprison 6th, include 3rd, insert 6th, pen 1st, wall K

encode 5th: hide 1st, puzzle 4th, symbolize 5th

encounter 4th:
A. greeting 3rd, joining 3rd, meeting K, struggle 1st
B. brush 2nd, bump 2nd, confront 5th, face K, join 3rd, meet K

encourage 4th: animate 6th, assure 3rd, cheer 3rd, excite 4th, fire up K, influence 5th, inspire 4th, motivate 6th, reassure 6th, root 3rd, support 4th, urge 4th

encrust 6th: bread 2nd, cover 1st

end K:
A. aim 3rd, close K, completion 3rd, conclusion 3rd, effect 3rd, ending K, extreme 5th, finish 1st, goal 4th, limit 3rd, outcome 4th, purpose 1st, reason 1st, result 2nd
B. abandon 4th, complete 3rd, conclude 3rd, destroy 2nd, die 2nd, finish 1st, limit 3rd, quit 1st, settle 2nd, stop K, term 3rd, terminate 6th

endanger 6th: chance 2nd, dare 2nd, risk 4th

endeavor 4th:
A. attempt 2nd, labor 2nd, striving 5th, struggle 1st, work K
B. attempt 2nd, effort 2nd, strive 5th, struggle 1st, try K, work K

endow 6th: award 5th, bestow 5th, confer 4th, contribute 4th, enrich 6th, equip 5th, give K, grant 2nd, invest 5th, present K, provide 3rd, supply 1st

endure 4th: allow 2nd, bear K, continue 2nd, encounter 4th, hold 1st, last K, meet K, permit 3rd, persist 5th, remain 2nd, stand K, stay 1st, suffer 2nd, survive 5th, wait K

enemy 2nd: attacker 3rd, foe 4th, hostile 4th, opponent 5th, rival 4th

energy 4th: action 3rd, bounce 6th, calorie 3rd, enthusiasm 4th, fire K, force 1st, glow 1st, heat 1st, muscle 4th, passion 6th, power 1st, push 1st, spirit 2nd, strength 2nd

enforce 5th: boss K, bully 1st, cause 2nd, compel 3rd, control 2nd, demand 5th, direct 1st, force 1st, fulfill 4th, implement 6th, maintain 4th, make K, perform 4th, pressure 4th, realize 2nd, require 1st, sanction 6th

engage 5th: agree 2nd, attract 5th, battle 2nd, catch 1st, charm 3rd, commit 4th, contest 4th, contract 3rd, draw K, encounter 4th, entertain 4th, fascinate 5th, hold 1st, interest 1st, meet K, occupy 3rd, pledge 5th, promise 1st, pull K, win K

engine 3rd: machine 1st, motor 4th

engineer 4th: accomplish 2nd, achieve 5th, arrange 3rd, conduct 3rd, design 5th, direct 1st, do K, guide 1st, handle 2nd, lead 1st, make K, manage 4th, perform 4th, plan 1st, produce 2nd, run K, steer 5th

engrave 5th: brand 2nd, carve 4th, cut K, fix 1st, imprint 4th, line K, lodge 4th, mark 1st, print 1st, stamp 2nd

enjoy 2nd: appreciate 5th, like K, love K, relish 6th

enlarge 5th: add K, develop 5th, double 3rd, expand 5th, extend 4th, grow K, heighten 4th, increase 3rd, lengthen 2nd, magnify 3rd, mature 5th, multiply 2nd, spread 2nd, stretch 4th, swell 3rd, thicken 2nd, widen 1st

enlist 6th: compel 3rd, employ 5th, engage 5th, hire 3rd, join 3rd, obtain 5th, pull in K, recruit 6th, secure 3rd, volunteer 5th

enliven 6th: animate 6th, brighten 1st, cheer 3rd, energize 4th, excite 4th, fire up K, inspire 4th, refresh 6th, renew 4th, restore 5th, revive 6th, rouse 4th, stir 3rd, thrill 4th, vitalize 5th, waken 1st

enormous 4th: gigantic 3rd, huge 1st, immense 4th, mammoth 5th, massive 5th, monstrous 5th, vast 4th

enough 1st: abundant 5th, ample 5th, plenty 1st, sufficient 3rd

enrage 6th: anger 1st, fire up K, incense 5th, madden 2nd, provoke 6th

enraged 6th: angry 1st, cross 1st, fuming 3rd, mad K, violent 5th

enrich 6th: better K, brighten 1st, contribute 4th, decorate 3rd, develop 5th, endow 6th, improve 3rd, make rich K, polish 4th, refine 6th, sharpen 1st

enter 1st: admit 4th, begin K, board 1st, go in K, insert 6th, introduce 5th, intrude 6th, invade 5th, penetrate 5th, pierce 4th, start 1st

enterprise 5th: adventure 3rd, attempt 2nd, business 2nd, cause 2nd, company 2nd, corporation 4th, courage 4th, effort 2nd, energy 4th, feat 1st, force 1st, plan 1st, power 1st, project 4th, push 1st, store K, struggle 1st, task 3rd, work K

entertain 4th: absorb 5th, amuse 4th, charm 3rd, clown 1st, engage 5th, enliven 6th, feed 1st, house K, interest 1st, joke 1st, occupy 3rd, please K, shelter 4th, welcome 1st

enthusiasm 4th: abandon 4th, animation 6th, confidence 6th, delight 3rd, determination 5th, ecstasy 6th, emotion 4th, energy 4th, excitement 4th, fire K, hope K, life 1st, passion 6th, spirit 2nd, vigor 5th, zeal 6th

entire 3rd: absolute 3rd, all K, clear 2nd, complete 3rd, extended 4th, full K, pure 3rd, sheer 5th, total 2nd, whole 1st

entitle 5th: address K, call K, enable 4th, label 3rd, let K, license 5th, owe 2nd, qualify 4th, term 3rd

entrance 3rd:

A. attract 5th, charm 3rd, dazzle 5th, delight 3rd, enchant 6th, interest 1st, please K

B. access 6th, admission 4th, approach 3rd, beginning 2nd, door K, drive K, entry 2nd, gate 1st, hall 1st, invasion 5th, lane 4th, opening K, path 1st, penetration 5th, porch 3rd, ramp 6th, road K, route 4th, start 1st, way K

entrap 3rd: bait 3rd, catch 1st, fool 2nd, net 3rd, reveal 4th, trap 1st, trick 1st

envelope 5th: case 2nd, cloak 4th, container 5th, cover 1st, mask 2nd, wrap 3rd

environment 6th: atmosphere 4th, background 4th, conditions 3rd, habitat 6th, mood 3rd, setting 2nd, surroundings 3rd

envy 4th:
A. jealousy 5th, resentment 5th, rivalry 4th
B. covet 6th, crave 6th, desire 5th, resent 5th, want K, wish for K

episode 6th: action 1st, adventure 3rd, chapter 3rd, division 4th, event 3rd, experience 4th, happening 1st, scene 1st, story K

equal 2nd:
A. match 3rd, partner 5th, peer 1st, rival 4th, similar 4th, steady 3rd
B. alike 1st, equivalent 6th, identical 6th, like K, same K

equator 6th: center 2nd

equip 5th: arm K, prepare 1st, provide 3rd, stock 1st, store K, supply 1st, weapon 4th

equipment 5th: furniture 3rd, gear 1st, machinery 2nd, material 5th, supplies 1st, tools 1st, untensils 6th

equivalent 6th: alike 1st, equal 2nd, identical 6th, like K, match 3rd, same K

era 6th: age 1st, day K, period 2nd, reign 4th, rule K, time 1st

erase 2nd: abolish 5th, cancel 6th, eliminate 5th, remove 2nd, rub out 1st

ere 4th: before K

erect 4th:
A. elevated 2nd, standing 1st, straight 3rd, tall K
B. assemble 4th, build 1st, construct 3rd, create 3rd, elevate 2nd, form 1st, make K, raise 1st

err 6th: mistake 1st

errand 4th: assignment 5th, duty 1st, job K, task 3rd, trip 1st, work K

error 4th: err 6th, flaw 2nd, mistake 1st

erupt 4th: blow up 1st, ejaculate 6th, explode 3rd

escape 1st:
A. daydream 2nd, exit 3rd, flight 2nd, freedom 3rd, opening K, release 5th, vacation 2nd
B. flee 5th, fly K, run K

escort 5th:
A. assistant 4th, guide 1st, leader 1st, protector 4th
B. accompany 3rd, conduct 3rd, direct 1st, guide 2nd, lead 1st

especially 4th: exceptional 3rd, mainly 3rd, mostly 1st, particularly 4th, special 2nd, unusually 3rd

essay 5th: article 2nd, attempt 2nd, effort 2nd, paper K, struggle 1st, theme 4th, try K, work K

essential 6th: absolute 3rd, basic 5th, fundamental 4th, important 1st, main 3rd, necessary 1st

establish 3rd: build 1st, create 3rd, fix 1st, form 1st, found K, install 6th, make K, organize 4th, set K, settle 2nd, start 1st

estate 4th: home K, land K, mansion 5th, property 3rd, residence 5th, will K

esteem 5th:

    A. approval 4th, favor 1st, love K, regard 4th, respect 2nd

    B. admire 5th, appreciate 5th, honor K, regard 4th, respect 2nd, treasure 4th, value 2nd

estimate 5th: figure 2nd, guess 1st, judge 1st, value 2nd

et cetera 6th: and K, so on K

eternal 4th: constant 4th, endless 1st, fixed 1st, immortal 4th, infinite 5th, perpetual 6th, permanent 5th

eve 5th: beginning 1st, evening 1st, night before 1st

even 1st: balanced 3rd, constant 4th, equal 2nd, flat 2nd, horizontal 6th, level 3rd, like 4th, same K, similar 4th, smooth 2nd, stable 4th, steady 3rd, straight 3rd, uniform 1st

evening 1st: eve 5th, night 1st, p.m. 6th, sundown K, sunset 1st

event 3rd: act K, action 1st, deed 1st, episode 6th, experience 4th, happening 1st, incident 5th, outcome 4th, result 2nd

eventually 5th: finally 3rd, last K, ultimately 6th

ever K: always K, constantly 4th, eternally 4th, forever 3rd

every K: all K, any 1st, each K

everybody 3rd: all K, everyone 1st

everyone 1st: all K, everybody 1st

everything 1st: all K

evidence 5th: demonstrate 6th, facts 1st, ground 1st, information 5th, proof 1st, show 1st, support 4th

evident 5th: apparent 3rd, clear 2nd, exposed 4th, obvious 5th, plain 2nd

evil 3rd:

    A. mischief 4th, misery 5th, sin 1st, wickedness 4th

    B. bad K, dark K, foul 4th, horrible 1st, mean 1st, villainous 5th, wicked 4th

evolution 6th: creation 3rd, change 2nd, development 5th, growth K

exact 2nd:

    A. command 2nd, demand 5th, require 2nd

    B. accurate 6th, careful K, correct 3rd, flawless 2nd, precise 5th, right K

exaggerate 6th: boast 4th, brag 3rd, elaborate 5th, enrich 6th, stretch 4th

examine 5th: inspect 5th, investigate 5th, observe 3rd, question 1st, research 5th

example 2nd: case 2nd, ideal 3rd, illustration 4th, model 3rd, pattern 3rd, sample 5th, specimen 5th, standard 3rd

exceed 4th: dominate 5th, eclipse 5th, excel 6th, pass K, surpass 6th

excel 6th: eclipse 5th, exceed 4th, pass K, surpass 6th

excellent 1st: great K, ideal 3rd, perfect 3rd, outstanding 2nd, superior 4th, terrific 5th, wonderful 1st

except 1st: but K, excluding 6th, however 3rd, minus 1st, not K

excess 5th: beyond 1st, overflow 5th, surplus 6th, too much 1st

exchange 4th: trade 2nd

excite 4th: agitate 5th, animate 6th, arouse 4th, awaken 3rd, egg on K, encourage 4th, energize 4th, inspire 4th, provoke 6th, rally 5th, revive 6th, rouse 4th, spark 3rd, stir 3rd

exclaim 3rd: cry K, shout 1st

exclude 6th: bar 3rd, eliminate 5th, forbid 4th, forget 1st, eliminate 5th, prevent 3rd, reject 5th, remove 2nd, rule out K, shut out 1st

exclusive 6th: choosy 3rd, elect 3rd, elegant 5th, fancy 3rd, individual 3rd, particular 4th, select 4th, single 3rd, special 2nd

excuse 3rd: acquit 6th, alibi 6th, apology 6th, claim 2nd, explanation 2nd, forgive 2nd, pardon 4th, reason 2nd

execute 5th: achieve 5th, cause 2nd, complete 3rd, engineer 4th, finish 1st, manage 4th, perform 4th, produce 2nd

executive 5th: boss K, director 1st, head K, leader 1st, manager 4th, president 1st, principal 3rd

exercise 1st:
A. movement 2nd, sports 1st, work K
B. drill 2nd, employ 5th, practice 1st, use K, utilize 6th, work out K

exert 6th: attempt 2nd, employ 5th, labor 2nd, struggle 1st, sweat 3rd, trouble 1st, use K, work K

exhaust 4th: drain 5th, fatigue 5th, tire 2nd, weary 4th

exhibit 4th:
A. display 3rd, show 1st
B. demonstrate 6th, display 3rd, expose 4th, parade 2nd, reveal 4th, show 1st

exhilarate 6th: animate 6th, brighten 1st, cheer 3rd, encourage 4th, delight 3rd, energize 4th, enliven 6th, inspire 4th, revive 6th, thrill 4th

exile 5th: ban K, expel 6th, separate 3rd

exist 3rd: be K, breathe 1st, endure 4th, live 1st, remain 1st, survive 5th

exit 3rd:
A. escape 1st, flee 5th, fly K
B. departure 5th, door K, gate 1st, leave 1st, opening K, quit 1st, way out K

expand 5th: amplify 6th, enlarge 5th, fatten 1st, increase 3rd, multiply 2nd, spread 2nd, stretch 4th, swell 3rd

expect 2nd: await 5th, hope K, look K

expel 6th: exile 5th, throw out 1st

expense 3rd: amount 2nd, charge 2nd, cost 1st, fee 4th, price K, rate 1st

experience 4th:
A. adventure 3rd, happening 1st, life 1st
B. endure 4th, episode 6th, live 1st, try K, undergo 2nd, understand 1st

experiment 3rd: explore 4th, question 1st, sample 5th, try 1st

expert 5th: artist 2nd, authority 3rd, genius 4th, knowledgeable 3rd, master 1st

expire 6th: complete 3rd, conclude 3rd, die 2nd, end K, fail 2nd, finish 1st, pass K, run out K, stop K, terminate 6th

explain 2nd: excuse 3rd, discuss 5th, interpret 5th, justify 3rd, teach 1st

explode 3rd: blow up 1st, dynamite 6th

exploit 6th:
A. use K
B. achievement 5th, act K, deed 1st, feat 1st

explore 4th: examine 5th, experiment 3rd, inspect 5th, search 1st

export 5th: send K, ship 1st

expose 4th: display 3rd, exhibit 4th, find K, parade 2nd, reveal 4th, show 1st, uncover 1st

express 5th: air K, announce 3rd, say K, speak 1st, specific 5th, tell K, utter 4th, voice 1st

exquisite 6th: delicate 5th, elegant 5th, intense 6th, perfect 3rd, rare 4th

extend 4th: draw out K, enlarge 5th, expand 5th, lengthen 2nd, spread 2nd, stretch 4th

exterminate 6th: abolish 5th, erase 2nd, kill 1st, remove 2nd

extinct 5th: dead 1st, exterminated 6th, gone 1st, lost K, nonexistent 4th, past 1st, vanished 3rd

extra 1st: more K, plus 1st, surplus 6th

extraordinary 5th: choice 3rd, rare 4th, special 2nd, strange 1st, surprising 1st

extravagant 6th: absurd 6th, excessive 5th, extreme 5th, lavish 6th, silly 1st

extreme 5th: excessive 5th, greatest K, least 1st, most 1st, smallest K, total 2nd

eye K: see K, study 2nd, watch 1st

fable 5th: fiction 5th, myth 4th, story K, tale 3rd

fabric 5th: material 5th

face K:
A. expression 5th, features 3rd, front 1st
B. confront 5th, encounter 4th, meet K

facility 5th: ease 3rd, factory 1st, plant K

fact 1st: certainty 1st, information 5th, reality 5th, truth 1st

factor 5th: agent 5th, component 4th, element 3rd, ingredient 4th, instrument 3rd, part 1st

factory 1st: facility 5th, plant K, shop 1st

faculty 6th:
A. ability 3rd, gift K, power 1st, talent 2nd
B. instructor 4th, teacher 1st

fad K: craze 4th, fashion 3rd, rage 4th, style 3rd, trend 2nd

fade 1st: lessen 1st, thin 2nd, vanish 3rd, wither 5th

fail 2nd: fault 3rd, lose K

faint 3rd:
    A. fall K, pass out K
    B. light K, weak 3rd
fair 1st:
    A. carnival 2nd, exhibit 4th, market 1st, show 1st
    B. average 3rd, beautiful 1st, blond 5th, common 2nd, just 1st, light K,
        medium 5th, ordinary 3rd, pretty 1st
fairy 4th: angel 4th, brownie 2nd, elf 1st, gnome 6th
faith 3rd: belief 1st, church K, conviction 4th, creed 6th, loyalty 5th,
    religion 4th, trust 1st
fake 1st:
    A. cheat 3rd, fraud 6th
    B. lie 1st, make up 1st, pretend 2nd, trick 1st
fall K:
    A. autumn 3rd
    B. drop 1st, sink 3rd
false 3rd: deceit 5th, mistaken 1st, not true K, untrue 1st, wrong 1st
falter 3rd: hesitate 4th, pause 3rd, shake 1st, stumble 4th, waver 5th
fame 3rd: celebrity 5th, glory 3rd, honor 1st, renown 6th
familiar 3rd: close K, common 2nd, intimate 5th, well-known 1st
family K: clan 5th, relatives 4th
famine 6th: hunger 2nd, starvation 5th
famous 2nd: celebrated 5th, renowned 6th, well-known 1st
fan K: follower 1st
fancy 3rd:
    A. decorated 3rd, elaborate 5th, elegant 5th
    B. dream K, enjoy 2nd, like K, love K
    C. fantasy 6th, whim 6th
fang 5th: tooth 1st
fantastic 6th: absurd 6th, extravagant 6th, extreme 5th, fanciful 4th, odd 4th,
    strange 1st
far 1st: away K, distant 4th, faraway 3rd, remote 5th
fare 3rd:
    A. cost K, fee 4th, price K
    B. banquet 4th, food K, menu 6th
farm K: cultivate 6th, grow K, till 1st
farmer K: peasant 4th
farming 1st: agriculture 4th, cultivation 6th, tilling 1st
farther 3rd: beyond 1st, further 2nd, past 1st
fascinate 5th: attract 5th, captivate 3rd, charm 3rd, enchant 6th, engage 5th
fashion 3rd:
    A. fad K, manner 2nd, method 2nd, rage 4th, trend 2nd

B. create 3rd, form K, make K, manufacture 3rd

fast 1st: rapid 4th, speedy 3rd, swift 4th

fasten 4th: add K, attach 5th, bind 2nd, connect 3rd, fix 1st, join 3rd, link 5th, secure 3rd, tie 1st

fat 1st: chubby 2nd, plump 6th, stout 4th

fatal 4th: deadly 2nd

fate 3rd: certainty 1st, destiny 5th, fortune 3rd

father K: dad K, daddy K, papa 1st

fathom 6th: grasp 4th, plumb 5th, sound 1st, understand 1st

fatigue 5th: drained 5th, exhaustion 4th, tiredness 2nd, weariness 4th

fault 3rd: error 4th, flaw 2nd, mistake 1st, vice 4th

faultless 3rd: ideal 3rd, perfect 3rd, pure 3rd

fauna 6th: animal K, nature 2nd

favor 1st:

    A. gift K, good deed 1st, kindness K, present 2nd

    B. aid 2nd, assist 4th, encourage 4th, help K, like K, support 4th

favorite 3rd: popular 3rd, preferred 3rd, selected 4th

fear 1st: alarm 3rd, dread 6th, fright 2nd, horror 4th, panic 1st

fearful 1st: afraid 1st, frightened 5th, scared 5th, shy 1st, timid 5th

feast 1st:

    A. dine 1st, eat K

    B. banquet 4th, carnival 2nd, celebration 4th, meal 3rd

feat 1st: achievement 5th, act K, adventure 3rd, deed 1st, exploit 6th

feather 2nd: pad K, secure 3rd, soften 2nd

feature 3rd: characteristic 6th, detail 5th, mark 1st, property 3rd, quality 4th, trait 6th

federal 4th: government 1st, national 2nd

fee 4th: bill 1st, charge 2nd, cost K, fare 3rd, pay K, price K, salary 3rd, wage 3rd

feeble 4th: delicate 5th, fragile 6th, frail 6th, weak 3rd

feed 1st: dine 1st, fill 1st, gratify 4th, graze 5th, nourish 6th

feel K: handle 2nd, pet 1st, touch 1st

feeling K: affection 4th, emotion 4th, hint 1st, impression 5th, passion 6th, pity 3rd, reaction 5th, sensation 5th, sympathy 4th, touch 1st

fellow 1st: brother 1st, equal 2nd, friend 1st, male 4th, man K, member 2nd, peer 1st, sister 1st

female 4th: girl K, lady 1st, woman K

fence 1st:

    A. cage 1st, pen 1st

    B. cage 1st, enclose 4th, surround 3rd, wall 1st

fend 6th: bar 3rd, defend 5th, fight K, prevent 3rd

ferret 5th: hunt 2nd, search 1st, seek 1st

ferry 6th:
    A. boat 1st, ship 1st
    B. carry 1st, transfer 5th
fertile 5th: fruitful 2nd, productive 4th, rich K, seeded 1st
fervor 6th: delight 3rd, enthusiasm 4th, excitement 4th, passion 6th, zeal 6th
festive 5th: decorated 3rd, happy K, joyous 1st, merry 3rd
festivity 5th: celebration 4th, party K
fetch 4th: capture 3rd, catch 1st, get K, grab 4th, retrieve 6th
fetish 5th: charm 3rd
feud 6th: argument 3rd, disagreement 2nd, fight K, quarrel 4th
fever 4th:
    A. fire K, heat 1st, temperature 5th
    B. excitement 4th
few K: little K, not many K, scarce 4th, small K, three K
fez 5th: cap K, hat K
fib 1st:
    A. misrepresent 4th, withhold 1st
    B. falsehood 4th, lie 2nd, story K, untruth 2nd, tale 3rd
fiber 3rd: component 4th, fabric 5th, material 5th, substance 5th, thread 2nd,
    weave 4th
fiction 5th: fable 5th, false 3rd, myth 4th, not real 1st, story K, tale 3rd
fiddle 4th:
    A. play K, toy with K
    B. bow 1st, violin 4th
fidelity 6th: allegiance 6th, devotion 5th, faith 3rd, loyalty 5th, steadiness 3rd
field 2nd: area 3rd, domain 5th, park 1st, range 3rd, space 1st, territory 3rd
fierce 4th: cruel 5th, grim 4th, harsh 5th, intense 6th, savage 5th, violent 5th,
    wild 2nd
fiery 5th:
    A. blazing 1st, flaming 3rd, glowing 1st, heated 1st
    B. eager 5th, fierce 4th, peppery 4th, spirited 2nd
fife 5th: flute 5th, pipe 1st
fight K: attack 3rd, battle 2nd, combat 5th, conflict 4th, confront 5th,
    contest 4th, dispute 6th, match 3rd, war 1st
figure 2nd:
    A. design 5th, form 1st, image 4th, outline 4th, picture K, sculpture 4th,
        shape 1st
    B. add K, amount 2nd, body 1st, calculate 5th, cost 2nd, sum 1st, total 2nd
filch 5th: lift 1st, rob 1st, steal 3rd, take K, thieve 3rd
file 1st: alphabetize 2nd, line up K, organize 4th, rank 3rd, row K, sort 2nd
fill K: crowd 2nd, feed 1st, furnish 4th, occupy 3rd, provide 3rd, supply 1st
film 4th: base 1st, coat 1st, cover 1st, layer 4th, thin 2nd

filter 5th: clean, drain 5th, screen 1st, strain 4th

final 3rd: closing 1st, end K, last K

finance 1st:
    A. aid 2nd, fund 4th, pay for K
    B. banking 1st, cash 2nd, economics 4th, loan 4th, money K

find K: discover 1st, get K, locate 3rd, notice 1st

finding 1st: award 5th, conclusion 3rd, decision 1st

fine 1st: charge 2nd, delicate 5th, good K, penalize 5th, pure 3rd, quality 4th, small K, tiny 2nd

finger 1st: identify 4th, point out 1st

finish 1st: accomplish 2nd, achieve 5th, attain 6th, close K, complete 3rd, do K, end K

fire K:
    A. energy 4th, power 1st
    B. blaze 1st, burn 3rd, flame 3rd, light K, spark 3rd

fireman K: fire fighter 1st

fireworks 2nd: explosion 3rd, fire K, storm 2nd

firm 2nd:
    A. hard K, solid 3rd, steady 3rd, stiff 3rd
    B. business 2nd, company 2nd

first 1st: beginning 2nd, best K, earliest 1st, main 3rd, primary 5th, start K, top K

fish K: angle 3rd, cast 2nd, hunt for 2nd, look for K, search for 1st

fist 2nd: grab 4th, grasp 4th, grip 4th, hand K, hit K, ram K, seize 3rd

fit K:
    A. correct 3rd, proper 3rd
    B. adapt 4th, adjust 5th, apt 5th, attack 3rd, change 2nd, healthy 1st, prepare 1st, ready 1st, spasm 6th, strong K, suit 2nd

fitness 3rd: good shape 1st, health K, hearty 5th, vigor 5th

fitting 2nd: appropriate 4th, correct 3rd, proper 3rd, right K

fix 1st: adjust 5th, alter 4th, attach 5th, cement 4th, establish 3rd, fasten 4th, mend 1st, plight 6th, secure 3rd, set K

fixture 6th: device 4th, instrument 3rd

fizz 5th: buzz 5th, hiss 3rd, swish 2nd

flag 3rd: banner 3rd, colors K, signal 4th, streamer 3rd

flail 6th: beat 1st, fight K, flounder 5th, thrash 4th, whip 4th

flair 6th: ability 3rd, brilliance 4th, class 1st, gift K, learning 3rd, skill 2nd, style 3rd, talent 2nd

flake 1st: bit 1st, chip 5th, peel 2nd, skin 1st

flame 3rd: blaze 1st, brilliance 4th, fire K, glare 4th, gleam 1st, glow 1st, spark 3rd

flank 5th: border 1st, bound 2nd, curb 3rd, edge 1, side K, wall K

flap 4th: edge 1st, fold 1st

flare 6th:
  A. direct 1st, guide 1st, signal 4th
  B. blaze 1st, burst 3rd, dart 1st, flame 3rd, flash 2nd, explode 3rd, glow 1st

flash 2nd: blaze 1st, flame 3rd, flare 6th, glare 4th, gleam 1st, glitter 4th, spark 3rd

flat 2nd: even 1st, level 3rd, smooth 2nd

flatter 4th: compliment 5th, fawn 5th, glorify 3rd, praise 4th

flavor 4th: taste 1st

flaw 2nd: blemish 5th, fault 3rd, mark 1st, scar 5th, spot 1st, stain 4th

flee 5th: escape 2nd, fly K, leave 1st, run K, take off 1st

fleece 6th: covering 1st, hide 1st, skin 1st, wool 3rd

fleet 6th: fast 1st, quick 1st, rapid 4th, speedy 3rd, swift 4th

flesh 3rd: animal K, body 1st, physical 5th, skin 1st

flexible 6th: agile 6th, bendable 1st, elastic 6th, limber 4th, plastic 3rd, pliable 6th, springy 2nd

flicker 5th: flame 3rd, flare 6th, flash 2nd, gleam 1st, glimmer 6th, glitter 4th, sparkle 5th, twinkle 4th, waver 5th

flight 2nd:
  A. departure 5th, trip 1st
  B. gliding 4th, sailing 1st, soaring 6th

fling 6th: cast 2nd, hurl 5th, shoot 3rd, throw 1st, toss 2nd

flint 5th: rock K, stone 2nd

flip 2nd:
  A. easy K, light K, pert 1st, tactless 6th
  B. fling 6th, revolve 5th, toss 2nd, turn 1st, twist 1st

flipper 4th: fin 1st, paddle 1st, turner 1st

flirt 6th: pet 1st, play K, tease 3rd, toy K

float 1st: drift 2nd, glide 4th, hover 5th, rest on 1st, sail 1st, swim K

flock 2nd: assembly 4th, bunch 3rd, congregation 6th, crowd 2nd, group 1st, herd 2nd, swarm 4th

flood 2nd: cover 1st, drown 1st, excess 5th, flow 1st, overflow 5th, stream 1st, tide 1st, waves K

floor K: base 1st, bottom 1st, deck 1st, platform 4th

flop 6th: drop K, fall down K, flounder 5th, limp 5th

flora 6th: foliage 6th, greenery 3rd, plants K

flotsum 6th: debris 5th, pieces 1st

flounder 5th: flail 6th, flop 6th, plunge 4th, struggle 1st, stumble 4th, trash 2nd, trip 1st, tumble 4th

flourish 4th:
  A. display 3rd, shake 1st, show 1st, wave 1st
  B. brandish 6th, grow K, succeed 2nd, thrive 6th

flow 1st: arise 4th, current 3rd, issue 4th, run K, start 1st, stream 3rd, tide 1st

flower K:

    A. flourish 4th, grow K, prosper 5th

    B. bloom 4th, blossom 4th, bud 1st, flora 6th

fluid 6th: juice K, liquid 3rd, water K

fluorescent 6th: glowing 1st, shining 1st

flush 4th:

    A. wash 1st

    B. bloom 4th, blush 4th, color K, red K, rosy 1st

fluster 6th: agitate 5th, bother 2nd, confound 6th, confuse 4th, disturb 6th, excite 4th, upset 3rd

flute 5th: fife 5th, pipe 1st

fly K: bolt 4th, dart 1st, drift 2nd, float 1st, hang 2nd, hover 5th, sail 1st, soar 6th

foam 4th: bubbles 2nd, fizz 5th

focus 5th:

    A. aim 3rd, direct 1st, point 1st

    B. center 2nd, core 6th, heart K

foe 4th: enemy 2nd, opponent 5th, rival 4th

fog 1st:

    A. cloud 1st, mist 1st, overcast 2nd, smog 5th, vapor 3rd

    B. darken 2nd, dim 1st, obscure 6th

fold 1st: bend K, crease 5th, double K, flap 4th, tuck 1st, turn 1st

foliage 6th: flora 6th, greenery 3rd, leaves 1st, plants K

folk 3rd: family K, parents 3rd, people K, relatives 4th

folklore 5th: fairy tales 4th, history 2nd, stories 1st

follow 1st:

    A. accept 3rd, adopt 3rd, mind 1st, obey 3rd

    B. chase 1st, go after 1st, pursue 5th, replace 5th, succeed 2nd, trail 2nd

following 1st: admirers 5th, after 1st, behind 1st, devotees 5th, fans K, later 1st, next K, succeeding 2nd

folly 4th: foolish 2nd, humor 4th, idiocy 6th, joke 1st, madness 3rd, mistake 1st, nonsense 5th, stupidity 4th

fond 4th: affectionate 4th, loving 1st, sweet on K

food K: bread 2nd, diet 4th, meals 3rd

fool 2nd:

    A. deceive 5th, trick 1st

    B. clown 1st, dummy 1st, idiot 6th, silly 1st

foolish 2nd: careless 5th, crazy 4th, dumb 1st, ill-advised 3rd, silly 1st, simple 1st, unwise 1st

foot K: base 1st, bottom 1st, foundation 5th, prop 5th, support 4th

footstep 3rd: footprint 1st, mark 1st, step 1st, stride 5th

for K: as K, because K, belonging to 1st, concerning 3rd, during 1st, fit to K, to K

forbid 4th: ban K, deny 5th, eliminate 5th, not allow 2nd, outlaw 1st, prevent 3rd, prohibit 6th, reject 5th, stop K

force 1st:
    A. command 2nd, compel 3rd, insist 5th, order 1st, pressure 4th, push 1st, require 2nd, shock 1st, strain 4th
    B. energy 4th, might 1st, power 1st, strength 1st, violence 5th

forceful 2nd: aggressive 6th, intense 6th, powerful 2nd, pushy 1st, strong K

ford 5th: cross 1st

fore 6th: ahead 1st, before K, first 1st, front 1st

forecast 4th:
    A. prediction 6th
    B. anticipate 6th, foretell 6th, guess 1st, predict 6th

forefather 6th: ancestor 5th, creator 3rd, parent 3rd

forego 5th: avoid 3rd, give up K, quit 1st, refrain 6th

forehead 4th: brow 4th, front 1st

foreign 5th: alien 5th, odd 4th, outside 1st, peculiar 4th, strange 1st, unfamiliar 3rd

foreigner 5th: alien 5th, immigrant 6th, outsider 1st, stranger 1st

foreman 6th: boss K, director 1st, manager 4th, overseer 1st, supervisor 6th

foresight 6th:
    A. understanding 5th, vision 4th
    B. care K, caution 5th, prudence 6th, readiness 1st

forest 1st: brush 2nd, grove 4th, woods 1st

foretell 6th: forecast 4th, indicate 4th, predict 6th, prophesy 5th, see K

forever 3rd: always K, constantly 4th, endlessly 3rd, ever K, without end 1st

forfeit 6th: give up K, lose 3rd

forge 5th:
    A. copy 3rd, counterfeit 6th, duplicate 6th, imitate 5th, reproduce 5th
    B. beat 1st, fabricate 6th, fashion 3rd, form 1st, make K, manufacture 3rd, pound 2nd

forget 1st: ignore 5th, never mind 1st, not remember 1st, overlook 4th, skip 2nd

forgive 2nd: acquit 6th, clear 2nd, erase 2nd, excuse 3rd, overlook 4th, pardon 4th

fork 1st:
    A. tool 1st, utensil 6th
    B. give K, lift 1st
    C. branch 2nd, divide 4th, separate 3rd, split 4th

forlorn 6th: alone K, depressed 5th, gloomy 3rd, grim 4th, hopeless 2nd, lonely 2nd, lonesome 3rd, miserable 4th, sad K, solitary 5th, unhappy K

form 1st:
    A. ceremony 5th, method 2nd, process 4th, rite 6th, ritual 6th, system 2nd
    B. forge 5th, make K
    C. figure 4th, frame 3rd, outline 4th, shape 1st

formal 4th:
    A. ceremonial 5th, dress up K, fancy 3rd
    B. conventional 6th, exact 2nd, fixed 1st, standard 3rd, stiff 3rd

formation 4th:
    A. design 5th, figure 2nd, outline 4th, pattern 3rd, shape 1st
    B. beginning 2nd, creation 3rd, start 1st, system 2nd

former 6th: before K, earlier 2nd, first 1st, gone 1st, late K, old K, past 1st, previous 5th, prior 5th

formidable 6th: alarming 3rd, awe-inspiring 4th, difficult 5th, frightening 2nd, horrifying 4th, huge 1st, imposing 4th, scary 1st, strong K, wild 2nd

formula 6th: method 2nd, pattern 3rd, recipe 4th, rules K, system 2nd

forsake 6th: abandon 4th, deny 5th, desert 1st, leave 1st, quit 1st, reject 5th

fort 5th: camp 1st, castle 3rd, fortress 5th, stronghold 3rd

forth 2nd: away K, forward 3rd, onward 3rd, out K

forthright 5th: blunt 6th, direct 1st, frank 4th, honest 3rd, honorable 3rd, just 1st, open K, outspoken K, straight 3rd

fortnight 6th: two weeks K

fortress 5th: castle 3rd, fort 5th, shelter 4th

fortunate 4th: advantageous 4th, beneficial 3rd, favorable 4th, good K, happy K, lucky K

fortune 3rd:
    A. income 4th, money K, wealth 3rd
    B. accident 4th, chance 2nd, destiny 5th, fate 3rd, luck 1st

forward 1st:
    A. flip 2nd, pushy 1st, rude 2nd
    B. advanced 2nd, ahead 1st, early 1st
    C. ahead 1st, before K, in front 1st, onward 3rd, toward 1st

fossil 4th: bones 1st, remains 1st, skeleton 4th

foul 4th:
    A. mistake 1st, out of bounds 2nd
    B. contaminate 6th, mess up 1st, pollute 3rd, soil 2nd, stain 4th
    C. dirty 1st, offensive 4th, soiled 2nd, stained 4th, unclean K

found K: build 1st, create 3rd, set up K, start 1st

foundation 5th:
    A. basis 2nd, cause 2nd, reason 1st
    B. base 1st, bottom 1st, ground 1st
    C. association 5th

fountain 3rd: jet K, source 4th, spray 2nd, spring K

fowl 4th: bird K, chicken K, hen K, poultry 6th

fraction 4th: bit 1st, fragment 6th, part 1st, piece 1st, section 4th, slice 5th

fragile 6th: delicate 5th, fine 1st, frail 6th, slight 4th, weak 3rd

fragment 6th: bit 1st, chip 5th, fraction 4th, part 1st, piece 1st, remnant 6th, section 4th, slice 5th, splinter 6th

fragrance 5th: bouquet 6th, incense 5th, odor 3rd, perfume 3rd, scent 3rd, smell 3rd

fragrant 5th: perfumed 3rd, scented 3rd, spicy 3rd, sweet-smelling 3rd

frail 6th: delicate 5th, fine 1st, fragile 6th, infirm 2nd, sickly K, slender 4th, slight 4th, thin 1st, unwell K, weak 3rd

frame 3rd:

    A. body 1st, structure 4th, support 4th

    B. assemble 4th, build 1st, construct 3rd, contrive 6th, create 3rd, devise 4th, edge 1st, erect 4th, fabricate 6th, invent 2nd, make K, raise 1st, set up K, surround 3rd

framework 4th: frame 3rd, skeleton 4th, structure 4th

frank 4th: blunt 6th, candid 4th, clear 2nd, forthright 5th, free K, genuine 5th, honest 3rd, open K, plain 2nd, sincere 4th

frantic 5th: crazy 4th, furious 4th, hysterical 6th, insane 6th, mad K, raving 5th, upset 3rd, wild 2nd

fraud 6th: cheat 3rd, deception 5th, fake 1st, hoax 5th, trickery 5th

freckles 1st: dots K, spots 1st

free K: acquit 6th, clear 2nd, frank 4th, idle 4th, independent 3rd, liberate 4th, loose 3rd, open K, release 5th, unbound 4th, untied 1st

freedom 3rd: independence 3rd, leisure 5th, liberation 4th, liberty 3rd, license 5th, range 3rd, release 5th, scope 6th

freely K: candidly 4th, frankly 4th, generously 4th, openly 1st

freeze 4th: chill 3rd, cool 1st, frost 4th, glacial 3rd, ice 1st, refrigerate 2nd

freezing 4th: arctic 5th, cold 1st, frigid 6th, icy K

freight 4th: burden 5th, cargo 5th, haul 4th, load 2nd, luggage 4th, weight 1st

frequent 4th: common 2nd, constant 4th, normal 5th, often 1st, regular 3rd, repeated 4th, usual 3rd

fresco 5th: painting 2nd

fresh 2nd: alert 5th, different 1st, energetic 4th, hearty 5th, modern 2nd, new K, novel 5th, original 3rd, recent 3rd, unusual 3rd, vital 5th

freshwater 4th: lake 1st, river K, stream 3rd

fret 5th: agitate 5th, agitation 3rd, agonize 5th, annoyance 5th, complain 4th, friction 6th, irritation 6th, worry 1st, writhe 6th

friar 5th: brother 1st, father K, monk 4th

friction 6th: argument 3rd, clash 5th, dispute 6th, fight K, rub 1st

fried 5th: cooked 1st, sautéed 4th

friend 1st: ally 6th, associate 5th, buddy 4th, companion 3rd, comrade 4th, mate 4th, pal K, partner 5th, peer 1st

friendship 2nd: accordance 4th, affection 4th, agreement 2nd, fondness 4th, harmony 4th

fright 2nd:
A. horrify 4th, shock 1st, startle 4th
B. alarm 3rd, anxiety 4th, dread 6th, fear 1st, horror 2nd, panic 1st, terror 3rd

frighten (ed) 5th: afraid 1st, alarmed 3rd, fearful 1st, horrified 4th, scared 1st, shocked 1st, terrified 3rd

frigid 6th: arctic 3rd, cold K, cool 1st, formal 4th, frosty 4th, glacial 3rd, icy 2nd, prim 5th, remote 5th

fringe 5th: border 1st, decoration 3rd, edge 1st, end K, rim 1st, verge 6th

frock 4th: clothes 1st, dress K

frolic 6th: fun K, gaiety 1st, merriment 3rd, mirth 5th, play K, prank 5th, sport 1st

front 1st: entrance 2nd, exterior 5th, face K, fore part 6th

frontier 5th: borderland 1st, boundary 4th, fringe 5th, limit 3rd

frost 4th: chill 3rd, coldness K, cool 1st, freeze 4th, frigidity 6th, ice 1st

frown 2nd: glare 4th, grimace 4th, scowl 6th

fruit 2nd: crop 2nd, harvest 4th, outcome 4th, result 2nd, reward 4th, yield 4th

fry 1st: brown K, burn 3rd, sauté 4th, toast 5th

fuel 4th:
A. coal 2nd, gas 1st, gasoline 1st, oil K
B. energy 4th, feed 1st, nourish 6th

fugitive 4th: brief 5th, deserter 1st, escapee 1st, passing 2nd, runaway 1st, short-lived 1st, transient 6th

fulfill 4th: accomplish 2nd, achieve 5th, complete 3rd, execute 5th, finish 1st, implement 6th, obey 3rd, observe 3rd, perfect 3rd, realize 2nd

fulfillment 4th: achievement 5th, action 1st, performance 4th, realization 2nd

full K: abundant 5th, armload 2nd, complete 3rd, enough 1st, limit 3rd, maximum 6th, plenty 1st, solid 3rd, total 2nd, whole 1st

fumble 5th: flounder 5th, miss K, slip 3rd, stumble 4th

fume 3rd:
A. fret 5th, rage 4th, stew 2nd
B. smell 3rd, smoke 1st, stink 2nd, vapor 3rd

fun K: cheer 3rd, delight 3rd, jest 4th, mirth 5th, play K, pleasure 2nd, recreation 5th, sport 1st

function 4th: duty 1st, job K, operate 3rd, perform 4th, purpose 1st, role 6th, use K

fund 4th:
A. finance 1st, pay K, support 4th

B. account 3rd, accumulation 6th, grant 2nd, investment 5th, savings 1st, supply 1st

fundamental 4th: base 1st, basic 2nd, bottom 1st, essential 6th, initial 6th, necessary 1st, original 3rd, primary 5th

funeral 4th: burial 3rd, ceremony 5th, farewell 3rd, rite 6th

fungus 5th: mold 5th, mushroom 4th

funnel 3rd: channel 4th, direct 1st, pour 3rd

funny 1st: amusing 4th, clever 3rd, comic 5th, humorous 4th, jolly 4th, laughable 3rd, odd 4th, queer 4th, strange 1st, weird 1st

fur K: coat 1st, covering 1st, hair K

furious 4th: angry 1st, crazed 4th, heated 1st, mad K, raging 4th, storming 2nd, violent 5th, wild 2nd

furnace 4th: fireplace 2nd, heater 2nd, oven 1st

furnish 4th: equip 5th, give K, provide 3rd, supply 1st

furrow 6th: channel 4th, groove 5th, row K, rut 1st, trench 5th, truck 1st

further 2nd:

  A. abroad 5th, away K, farther 3rd

  B. besides 1st, likewise 1st, moreover 3rd, then K

  C. advance 2nd, aid 2nd, assist 4th, forward 3rd, help K, nourish 6th, promote 5th, push 1st

fury 4th: anger 1st, fit K, furor 4th, passion 6th, rage 4th, violence 5th

fuse 4th: blend 5th, combine 3rd, dissolve 4th, melt 2nd, unite 5th, wed K, weld 6th

fuss 1st: ado 2nd, agitation 5th, annoy 5th, argument 3rd, bother 2nd, complain 4th, fight K, fret 5th, to-do 2nd

future 5th: coming K, down K, expected 2nd, next K, outlook 4th, probable 4th, prospect 4th, the road 1st, tomorrow 1st

gab 1st: chatter 1st, gossip 5th, talk K

gag 1st:

  A. jest 4th, joke 1st

  B. hold back 1st, restrain 5th, suppress 5th, tie 1st, trick 1st

gain 2nd:

  A. benefit 3rd, interest 1st, profit 4th, reward 4th, use K

  B. achieve 5th, acquire 4th, advance 2nd, carry K, gather 1st, get K, improve 3rd, make K, obtain 5th, reap 4th, win K

gait 6th: pace 3rd, step 1st, stride 5th, walk K

gale 2nd: air current 3rd, disturbance 6th, wind 1st

gallant 4th: bold 2nd, brave 1st, chivalrous 6th, civil 3rd, courteous 4th, courtly 3rd, gentle 3rd, polite 4th, unafraid 1st

gallery 5th: corridor 5th, hall 1st, museum 4th, passage 4th

gallop 4th: canter 5th, hurry 1st, run K, rush 2nd, trot 5th

gamble 5th:
    A. chance 2nd, hazard 6th, try K
    B. bet 1st, risk 6th, wager 3rd

game K: challenge 4th, contest 4th, match 3rd, recreation 5th, sport 1st

gang 1st: association 5th, crowd 2nd, gathering 1st, group 1st, team 1st

gap K:
    A. blank 2nd, emptiness 3rd, void 6th
    B. break 1st, canyon 4th, cavity 5th, crack K, hole K, separation 3rd, space 1st, split 4th

gape 5th: gaze 5th, show astonishment 4th, stare 3rd

garage 6th: shelter 4th, storage 2nd

garb 5th: attire 6th, clothes 1st, costume 4th, dress K

garbage 6th: leavings 1st, rejects 5th, remains 1st, waste 2nd

garden K:
    A. cultivate 6th, farm K, plant K
    B. plants K, plot 4th, yard K

gargle 6th: rinse 3rd

garland 6th: crown 1st, flowers K, loop 5th, wreath 4th

garment 4th: attire 6th, clothes 1st, cover 1st, dress K, garb 5th, shirt 1st

garnish 6th: adorn 6th, beautify 2nd, deck 1st, decorate 3rd, dress up K, ornament 4th, top K

garrison 5th:
    A. fort 5th, post 1st
    B. guard 1st, preserve 4th, protect 5th
    C. division 4th, unit 5th

gas 1st: fuel 4th, steam 2nd, vapor 3rd

gasp 4th: breath 1st, gulp 1st, short breath 1st

gate 1st: access 6th, door K, entry 2nd, opening K, portal 5th

gather 1st: accumulate 6th, assemble 4th, collect 3rd, take in K

gaunt 6th: lean 3rd, skinny 1st, thin 1st

gay 1st: animated 6th, bright 1st, cheerful 3rd, cheery 3rd, gleeful 5th, happy K, joyful 1st, joyous 1st, lively 2nd, merry 3rd, up K

gaze 5th: look at 1st, notice 1st, stare 3rd

gear 1st: apparatus 6th, equipment 5th, machinery 2nd, materials 5th, tools 1st

general 2nd: common 2nd, most 1st, overall 3rd, universal 4th

generation 4th: age 1st

generous 4th: ample 5th, lavish 6th, liberal 4th, open K

genial 5th: cordial 6th, friendly 1st, good natured 1st, pleasant 3rd, sociable 2nd

genius 4th: brilliance 4th, brains 3rd, gift K, intelligence 4th, sharpness 1st, talent 2nd, wisdom 1st

gentle 3rd: considerate 2nd, delicate 5th, kind K, mild 4th, peaceful 1st, soft K, tender 3rd, thoughtful 2nd

gentleman 3rd: aristocrat 6th, man K, noble 3rd

genuine 5th: pure 3rd, real 1st, simple 1st, sincere 4th, true K

germ 6th: bug K, dirt 1st, disease 5th

gesture 4th: motion 3rd, move K, signal 4th, wave K

get K: ace 2nd, acquire 4th, attain 6th, carry K, collect 2nd, come by K, earn 2nd, gain 2nd, gather 1st, obtain 5th, receive 1st

ghastly 6th: awful 3rd, dreadful 6th, frightening 2nd, frightful 2nd, horrible 4th, horrid 4th, scary 1st, sickening K, terrible 1st, ugly 4th

ghost K: image 4th, specter 6th, spirit 2nd

giant 2nd: big K, enormous 4th, fat 1st, grand 2nd, great K, huge 1st, large K, vast 4th

gift K:
A. ability 3rd, flair 6th, genius 4th, intelligence 4th, talent 2nd
B. favor 1st, offering 2nd, present K, prize 3rd, tip 1st

gigantic 5th: *See* giant.

gild 6th: adorn 6th, coat 1st, cover 1st, decorate 3rd, paint 2nd, plate K

gin 6th: bait 3rd, lure 5th, net 3rd, trap 1st

gingerly 6th: attentively 2nd, carefully 5th, guardedly 1st, shyly K, timidly 5th

girdle 6th: belt 2nd, circle K, enclose 4th, ring 1st, surround 3rd, wrap 3rd

girl K: child K, female 4th, lass 1st, maid 3rd, miss K, woman K, young lady 1st

girlfriend 4th: buddy 4th, chum 6th, friend 1st

give K: bestow 5th, confer 4th, contribute 4th, impart 6th, leave 1st, offer 2nd, present K, transfer 5th

glad K: cheerful 3rd, delighted 3rd, gay 1st, happy K, jolly 4th, joyful 2nd, merry 3rd, pleased K

glance 3rd:
A. bounce off 6th, skim 6th, touch 1st
B. brush 2nd, glimpse 4th, look K, observe 3rd, peak 4th, notice 1st, see K, view 2nd

glare 4th:
A. dark look 1st, frown K, gaze 5th, stare 3rd
B. blaze 1st, flame 3rd, flare 6th, gleam 1st, light K, shine 1st

glass 1st:
A. cup K, tumbler 3rd
B. mirror 4th, pane 5th, window 1st

glasses 1st: eyeglasses 4th, lenses 1st, spectacles 6th

glaze 6th: color K, gloss 6th, luster 4th, paint 2nd, polish 4th, sheen 6th

gleam 1st: flash 2nd, glint 6th, glitter 4th, glimmer 6th, shine 1st, spark 3rd, sparkle 5th, twinkle 4th

glee 5th: cheer 3rd, delight 3rd, happiness K, joy 1st, mirth 5th, pleasure 2nd

gleeful 5th: joyous 1st, overjoyed 1st, sunny 6th. *See* glee.

glen 6th: gap K, valley 2nd

glide 4th: coast 2nd, drift 2nd, float 1st, graze 5th, move K, roll 1st, slide 2nd, slip 3rd

glimmer 6th: beam 3rd, glare 4th, gleam 1st, glitter 4th, shine 1st, spark 3rd

glimpse 4th: glance 3rd, look K, peek 2nd, see K

glisten 6th: flare 6th, flash 2nd, glance 3rd, gleam 1st, glimmer 6th, glint 6th, glitter 4th, shine 1st, sparkle 5th, twinkle 4th

glitter 4th: *See* glisten.

globe 4th: ball K, earth 1st, sphere 6th, world 1st

gloom 3rd: darkness K, depression 6th, low spirits 2nd, melancholy 6th, misery 4th, sadness 2nd, shadow 3rd

glory 3rd: credit 5th, fame 3rd, honor 1st, success 2nd, victory 4th

glove 4th: clothe 2nd, cover 1st, fit K

glow 1st: brightness 1st, brilliance 4th, flare 6th, glare 4th, light K, radiance 6th, shine 1st

glue 1st:
  A. adhesive 6th
  B. adhere 6th, cement 4th, paste 1st, seal K, stick K

glum 4th: depressed 5th, down K, gloomy 3rd, silent 3rd, sulky 5th, sullen 5th

gnarled 5th: bent K, bumpy 2nd, knotted 4th, twisted 1st

gnash 4th: bite 1st, gnaw 1st, grind 4th, scrape 3rd

gnaw 1st: bite 1st, chew 1st, grind 4th

gnome 6th: brownie 2nd, dwarf 4th, elf 1st, fairy 4th

go K: act K, advance 2nd, depart 5th, follow 1st, leave 1st, move K, operate 3rd, pass K, perform 4th, reach 1st, run K, shift 4th, vanish 3rd, work K

goal 4th: aim 3rd, end K, ideal 3rd, object 1st, purpose 1st, target 5th

gobble 4th: cram 5th, eat K, stuff 1st

goblin 4th: brownie 2nd, elf 1st, fairy 4th, gnome 6th

goggle 4th: glare 4th, look K, look hard 1st, see K, stare 3rd, view 2nd

goggles 4th: glasses 1st, spectacles 6th

gold K:
  A. metal 3rd, yellow K
  B. fortune 3rd, money K, riches K, wealth 3rd

good K: capable 4th, competent 6th, correct 3rd, genuine 5th, honest 3rd, just 1st, moral 3rd, noble 3rd, positive 2nd, real 1st, right K, virtue 4th

good-bye 1st: farewell 3rd, see you 1st

good-natured 5th: agreeable 2nd, cheerful 3rd, easygoing 1st, gentle 3rd, good K, kind K, obliging 6th, polite 4th

gorge 5th:
  A. canyon 6th, gulf 4th
  B. cram 5th, fill K, gobble up 4th, stuff 1st

gorgeous 5th: attractive 5th, beautiful 1st, dazzling 5th, grand 2nd, great K, perfect 3rd, pleasant 3rd, splendid 4th, super 1st

gospel 6th:
  A. certainty 1st, fact 1st, truth 1st
  B. belief 1st, word K

gossip 5th: chatter 1st, earful 1st, report 1st, rumor 5th, small talk 1st, talk K

govern 2nd: boss K, command 2nd, control 2nd, order 1st, rule K

government 1st: authority 3rd, in charge 2nd, leadership 1st, management 4th, rulers K

gown 4th: attire 6th, cape 4th, dress K, frock 4th, garb 5th, garment 4th, mantle 4th, robe 4th

grab 4th: capture 3rd, catch 1st, clutch 4th, grasp 4th, seize 3rd, take 4th

grace 3rd: beauty 1st, charm 3rd, elegance 5th, manners 1st, polish 4th

grade 2nd:
  A. angle 3rd, bank 1st, hill K, slant 6th
  B. class 1st, degree 5th, mark 1st, measure 2nd, merit 4th, rank 3rd, rating 1st, scale 3rd, score 1st, value 2nd, worth 3rd

gradual 3rd: by degree 5th, even 1st, orderly 1st, regular 2nd, slowly 1st, steady 3rd

graduate 4th:
  A. achieve 5th, pass K, succeed 2nd
  B. make the grade 2nd, one who passed 1st, one who succeeded 2nd
  C. grade 2nd, mark off 1st, order 1st, range 3rd

grain 3rd: bit 1st, cereal 6th, particle 5th, piece 1st, scrap 3rd, seed 1st, speck 4th, wheat 1st

grammar 6th: basics 5th, laws 1st, principles 4th, rules 1st, speech 2nd, system 2nd, talk K

grand 2nd: big K, great K, imposing 4th, impressive 5th, large K, lofty 5th, magnificent 4th, noted 1st, splendid 4th, stately 2nd, superb 6th

grandfather 1st: forefather 6th, granddad 1st, grandpa 1st, relative 4th

grandmother 1st: grandma 1st, granny 1st, relative 4th

grant 2nd:
  A. contribution 4th, favor 1st, gift K, offering 2nd
  B. admit 4th, agree 2nd, concede 6th, consent 3rd
  C. allow 2nd, award 5th, bestow 5th, furnish 4th, give 1st, offer 2nd, present K, provide 3rd, supply 1st

grapple 6th: battle 2nd, fight K, grasp 4th, press 1st, scuffle 5th, secure 3rd, seize 3rd, squeeze 5th, struggle 1st, take hold 1st, wrestle 6th

grasp 4th:
  A. comprehend 5th, get K, realize 2nd, understand 1st
  B. catch 1st, clutch 4th, grab 4th, hold 1st, secure 3rd, seize 3rd, take K

grass K: green K, lawn 2nd, sod 6th

grateful 4th: appreciate 5th, obliged 6th, thankful 2nd

grave 3rd:
    A. grim 4th, sober 4th, solemn 5th, thoughtful 1st, unsmiling 1st
    B. burial ground 3rd, tomb 5th
    C. important 1st, serious 4th, vital 5th

gravel 4th: sand 1st, stones 2nd

gravity 5th:
    A. force 1st, pull K, weight 1st
    B. grimness 4th, importance 1st, seriousness 4th

gray 1st: cloudy 1st, colorless 1st, dark K, gloomy 3rd, overcast 2nd, pale 3rd, smoky 1st

graze 5th: brush 2nd, feed 1st, pasture 5th, scrape 4th, touch 1st

grease 5th: butter 2nd, fat 1st, oil K

great K: big K, gigantic 5th, huge 1st, important 1st, large K, magnificent 4th, wonderful 1st. *See also* grand.

greed 4th: hunger 2nd, itch 5th, longing 1st

green K: immature 5th, new K, unskilled 2nd, young 1st

greenery 3rd: foliage 6th, flora 6th, leaves 2nd, plants 1st

greet 3rd: address K, hail 4th, hello K, wave to K, welcome 1st

grief 5th: ache 5th, agony 5th, anguish 6th, distress 5th, heartache 6th, hurt K, misery 4th, pain 2nd, sorrow 4th, suffering 2nd, woe 4th

grim 4th: bad K, dark K, depressing 5th, evil 3rd, firm 2nd, forbidding 4th, hard K, harsh 5th, merciless 4th, severe 4th, stern 4th

grin 1st: laugh 1st, smile 1st

grind 4th:
    A. toil 4th, work K
    B. crush 4th, grate 4th, scrape 4th, smash 3rd

grip 4th: clutch 4th, grasp 4th, hold 1st, possess 3rd, seize 3rd

gripe 5th:
    A. distress 5th, trouble 1st, worry 1st
    B. complain 4th, find fault 3rd, object 1st

grizzly 4th: awful 3rd, chilling 3rd, ghastly 6th, grim 4th, horrible 1st, horrid 4th, ugly 4th

groan 3rd: complain 4th, moan 5th, mourn 4th, sigh 3rd, sob 1st

groom 5th:
    A. brush 2nd, clean K, maintain 4th
    B. husband 1st

groove 5th: crack 4th, line K, rim 1st

grope 6th: clasp 4th, clutch 4th, feel K, grab 4th, grasp 4th, seize 3rd

gross 3rd:
    A. all K, complete 3rd, entire 3rd, whole 1st
    B. disgusting 5th, plain 2nd, raw 1st, rude 2nd

C. extreme 5th, glaring 4th, large K, obvious 5th, outright 1st, total 2nd

ground 1st: base 1st, clay 1st, earth 1st, fix 1st, foundation 5th, install 6th, root 3rd, set K, settle 2nd, soil 2nd

group 1st: array 5th, band 1st, batch 2nd, class 1st, classify 1st, club 1st, company 2nd, crew 2nd, file 1st, organization 4th, pack 1st, rank 3rd, set K, tribe 3rd

grove 4th: forest 2nd, orchard 5th, woods 1st

grow K: breed 4th, enlarge 5th, expand 5th, get bigger 1st, increase 3rd, mature 5th, raise 1st

growl 4th: bark 3rd, complain 4th, howl 4th, moan 5th, roar 1st, snarl 5th, threaten 3rd

grown-up 1st: adult 1st, big K, grown 1st, mature 5th

grub 5th: dig K, explore 4th, mine 1st, spade 6th, worm 5th

grudge 5th: covet 6th, envy 4th, jealousy 5th, malice 6th, offense 4th, resent 5th, resentment 5th, spite 3rd

gruel 6th: oatmeal 5th, porridge 5th

gruff 1st: bluff 6th, blunt 6th, grumpy 5th, harsh 5th, hoarse 5th, rude 2nd, sour 6th, sullen 5th

grumble 5th: complain 4th, fuss 1st, growl 4th, roar 1st, snarl 5th

guarantee 6th: bond 3rd, certify 6th, contract 3rd, oath 5th, promise 1st, secure 3rd, warrant 5th

guard 1st: cover 1st, defend 5th, defender 5th, guide 1st, keep watch 1st, make safe K, patrol 1st, protect 4th, save 1st, secure 3rd, shield 4th, supervise 6th

guess 1st: believe 1st, figure 2nd, reckon 3rd, surmise 6th, theory 5th, think 1st

guest 3rd: caller 1st, company 2nd, visitor 1st

guide 1st: advise 3rd, counsel 5th, escort 5th, guard 1st, instruct 4th, lead 1st, model 3rd, navigate 5th, pattern 3rd, pilot 5th, rule K, steer 5th, teach 1st

guilt 4th: blame 2nd, contrition 5th, fault 3rd, regret 5th, remorse 6th, sorrow 4th

guilty 4th: contrite 5th, criminal 4th, sinful 1st, unholy 5th, wrong 1st

gulf 4th: break 1st, canyon 6th, hole K, inlet 4th, opening K, sea 1st, space 1st

gully 6th: canyon 4th, valley 2nd

gulp 1st: devour 5th, guzzle 1st, swallow 1st

gum K: adhesive 6th, glue 1st

gun K: cannon 4th, pistol 5th, revolver 5th, rifle 4th, shotgun 1st

gust 5th: blast 2nd, blow 1st, breath 1st, breeze 4th, burst 3rd, puff 2nd

gut 1st: abdomen 6th, belly 5th, stomach 2nd

guts 1st: bravery 3rd, courage 4th, nerve 1st, spirit 2nd

gutter 6th: ditch 2nd, drain 5th, eaves 6th, rut 1st, sewer 2nd, spout 5th

guttural 6th: gruff 1st, hoarse 5th, thick 2nd, throaty 2nd

guy 1st: boy K, buddy 4th, chap 4th, fellow 1st, male 4th, man K, mate 4th

gym 1st: arena 5th, court 3rd, gymnasium 5th

gymnasium 5th: arena 5th, court 3rd, gym 1st

gymnast 5th: acrobat 5th, tumbler 4th

gypsy 6th: drifter 2nd, migrant 4th, tramp 4th, wanderer 3rd

habit 3rd:
  A. addiction 5th, weakness 3rd
  B. bent 1st, disposition 5th, pattern 3rd, practice 1st, routine 6th, rut 1st, way K
  C. attire 6th, costume 4th, custom 6th, dress K, uniform 1st

habitable 6th: livable 3rd, occupiable 3rd, warm 1st

habitat 6th: area 3rd, environment 6th, ground 1st, locality 4th, range 3rd, region 4th, suroundings 3rd, territory 3rd, vicinity 6th

hail 4th: address K, call K, cry out 1st, greet 3rd, hello K, meet K, receive 1st, salute 4th, shout 1st, signal 4th, welcome 1st, yell K

hair K: bristle 6th, coat 1st, fiber 3rd, fur K, mane 1st, thread 2nd

hale 2nd:
  A. drag 3rd, pull K, tow 1st
  B. fit K, healthy 1st, hearty 5th, mighty 1st, robust 5th, strong K, sturdy 3rd, vigorous 5th, well K

half 1st: hemisphere 6th, part 1st

hall 1st: corridor 5th, entry 3rd, passage 4th, way K

halt 4th: arrest 3rd, cease 3rd, close K, end K, falter 3rd, hinder 6th, quit 1st, restrain 5th, stall 5th, stop K

hammer 2nd: beat 1st, club 1st, hit K, pound 2nd, slap 2nd, strike 2nd

hand K: aid 2nd, assist 4th, deliver 5th, employee 5th, furnish 4th, give K, help K, helper 1st, pass K, present K, produce 2nd, workman 1st

handkerchief 4th: napkin 5th, tissue 5th

handle 2nd: carry K, feel K, finger 1st, grip 4th, heave 5th, hold 1st, lift 1st, pat K, shaft 4th, stroke 1st, touch 1st

handsome 3rd:
  A. free K, generous 4th, liberal 4th, unselfish 5th
  B. attactive 5th, beautiful 1st, fair 1st, good-looking 2nd, lovely 1st, pretty 1st

hang 2nd: dangle 5th, suspend 5th, swing 1st

happen 1st: become 1st, chance 2nd, come about 1st, occur 3rd, result 2nd, turn up 1st

happy K: cheerful 3rd, delighted 3rd, fortunate 4th, glad 1st, jolly 4th, joyful 2nd, jovial 5th, light-hearted 2nd, lucky K, merry 3rd, pleased 1st

harbor 2nd:
  A. house K, lodge 4th, port 1st, refuge 5th, shelter 4th
  B. cloak 4th, conceal 4th, cover 1st, guard 1st, hide 1st, protect 4th

hard K:
  A. difficult 5th, tough 5th
  B. compact 5th, firm 4th, solid 3rd, strong K
harden 2nd: cement 4th, set K, solidify 4th, toughen 5th
hardship 5th: burden 5th, difficulty 5th, harm 3rd, hurt K, need 1st, neglect 4th, plight 6th, ruin 5th, stress 6th
hardy 5th: fit K, healthy 1st, hearty 5th, mighty 1st, robust 5th, strong K, sturdy 3rd, vigorous 5th, well 1st
hark 6th: hear K, listen 1st, notice 1st, pay attention 2nd
harm 3rd: abuse 6th, damage 5th, hurt K, ill 1st, injure 5th, injury 5th, pain 2nd, spoil 4th, torment 5th, woe 4th, wound 3rd
harmonize 4th: adapt 4th, agree 2nd, compose 4th
harmony 4th: agreement 3rd, balance 3rd, order 1st, unity 5th
harness 4th:
  A. reins 1st, yoke 6th
  B. control 2nd, hold 1st, tie 1st
harp 4th: complain 4th, persist in 5th, repeat 4th
harsh 5th: coarse 4th, rough 4th
harvest 4th: collect 3rd, cultivate 6th, gather 1st, reap 4th
harvesting 4th: cultivating 6th, farming 1st
haste 2nd: eagerness 5th, enthusiasm 4th, hurry 1st, impatience 5th, quickness 2nd, rapidity 4th, rush 2nd, speed 3rd
hasty 2nd: brisk 6th, careless 5th, fast 1st, quick 1st, rapid 4th, rash 6th, speedy 3rd, sudden 1st, swift 4th, urgent 6th
hat K: bonnet 6th, cap K, crown 1st
hatch 4th:
  A. door K, escape 1st, opening 1st
  B. breed 4th, conceive 4th, devise 4th, plan 1st, scheme 5th
hate 2nd: despise 5th, detest 6th, dislike 2nd
hateful 3rd: cursed 4th, evil 3rd, hideous 6th, horrible 1st, mean 1st, repulsive 6th, wicked 4th
haughty 6th: arrogant 6th, lordly 2nd, proud 2nd, self-important 2nd, vain 4th
haul 4th: convey 4th, drag 5th, draw K, heave 5th, lift 1st, lug 1st, move K, pull K, tow 1st, transport 5th
haunch 5th: hip 1st, side K, thigh 3rd
haunt 2nd: burden 5th, linger 4th, possess 3rd, trouble 1st, visit 1st, worry 1st
have K: own K, possess 3rd
hay K: feed 1st, straw 2nd
hazard 6th: accident 4th, danger 1st, dare 2nd, endanger 6th, gamble 5th, offer 2nd, risk 4th, threat 5th, venture 4th
head K:
  A. crown 1st, face K, front 1st

B. boss K, chief 1st, leader 1st, manager 4th, master 1st, president 1st, principal 3rd, supervisor 6th

headache 6th: pain 2nd

headquarters 3rd: base 1st, office 1st, station 1st

heal 3rd: cure 4th, doctor 1st, improve 3rd, make well 2nd, mend 1st, recover 4th, remedy 4th, renew 4th, repair 4th, restore 5th

health K: fitness 3rd, power 1st, strength 1st, vitality 5th, well-being 2nd,

heap 4th:
A. bulk 4th, mass 3rd, pile 1st
B. accumulate 6th, gather 1st, mound 2nd, reserve 3rd, stack 6th, stock 6th, supply 1st

hear K: attend 3rd, hark 6th, heed 4th, learn of 2nd, listen to 2nd, notice 1st, regard 4th

heart K:
A. center 2nd, core 6th, focus 5th, middle 2nd
B. emotion 4th, feeling K, kindness 1st, love K, passion 6th, spirit 2nd, soul 3rd

heartache 6th: agony 5th, anguish 6th, grief 5th, hurt K, misery 4th, pain 2nd, sadness 1st, sorrow 4th, suffering 2nd, torment 5th, woe 4th

hearth 5th: fireplace 2nd, home K

hearty 5th: ardent 6th, cordial 6th, earnest 4th, friendly 2nd, healthy 1st, sincere 4th, sound 1st, vigorous 5th, warm 1st

heat 1st: bake 1st, cook 1st, fever 4th, furor 5th, passion 6th, roast 4th, warm 1st, warmth 2nd

heathen 6th: primitive 5th, savage 5th

heave 5th: cast 2nd, fling 6th, haul 4th, hurl 5th, launch 5th, lift 1st, raise 1st, throw 1st, toss 2nd, tug 1st

heaven 1st: delight 3rd, ecstacy 6th, paradise 4th, rapture 6th

heavenly 2nd: blessed 4th, delightful 3rd, glorious 4th, good K, holy 5th, ideal 3rd, sainted 3rd

heavy 1st: ample 5th, big K, bulky 4th, huge 1st, immense 4th, large K, massive 5th, weighty 2nd

hectic 3rd: burning 3rd, busy 1st, excited 4th, feverish 4th, furious 4th, stormy 3rd, wild 2nd

hedge 4th: border 1st, cheat 3rd, cover 1st, edge 1st, fence 1st, halt 4th, hesitate 4th, hold back 1st, limit 3rd, restrain 5th

heed 4th: care K, caution 5th, consider 2nd, consideration 3rd, guard 1st, note 1st, obey 3rd, observe 3rd, pay attention to 2nd, remember 1st, respect 2nd, think 1st

heel 3rd: back K, bottom 1st, dog K, end K, foot K, hoof 1st, hound 2nd, last K, remnant 6th, trail 2nd

height 4th: altitude 5th, ceiling 4th, elevation 4th, extreme 5th, high point 2nd, length 2nd, limit 3rd, loftiness 5th, tallness 1st

heir 4th: assign 5th, child K, ward 5th

hello K: greetings 3rd, hi K, salutations 4th

helm 6th: control 2nd, head K, reins 1st, throne 4th, wheel 1st

help K: advance 2nd, aid 1st, assist 4th, benefit 3rd, contribute 4th, employee 5th, hand K, maintain 4th, relief 4th, save 1st, servant 3rd, service 1st, support 4th, use K

helper 1st: aid 1st, ally 6th, assistant 5th, attendant 4th, patron 5th, supporter 5th

hem 1st: circle K, close in, edge 1st, hedge in 4th, limit 3rd, margin 5th, rim 1st, ring 1st, skirt 3rd, surround 3rd

hemisphere 6th: half 1st, part 1st

hen K: chicken K, fowl 4th

hence 3rd: from now on 2nd, so K, then K, thence 4th, therefore 2nd, thus 1st

herald 3rd: air K, announce 3rd, omen 6th, pioneer 4th, proclaim 4th, scout 1st, signal 4th, symptom 6th

herb 5th: spice 3rd

herd 2nd:
A. bunch 3rd, flock 2nd, group 1st, pack 1st
B. collect 3rd, crowd 2nd, gather 1st

here K: present K, now K

hereafter 6th: after this K, finally 3rd, forever 3rd, from now on K, heaven 1st, hence 3rd, in the future 5th, later 1st, paradise 4th

hermit 5th: holy man 5th, monk 4th

hero 1st: champion 4th, ideal 3rd, idol 6th, model 3rd, star K, victor 4th

heroic 5th: adventurous 3rd, bold 2nd, brave 1st, courageous 4th, daring 3rd, gallant 4th, grand 2nd, great K, noble 3rd, valiant 6th

hesitate 4th: delay 5th, falter 1st, hang back 3rd, hedge 4th, pause 3rd, put off 2nd, stall 5th, waver 5th

hew 6th: axe K, carve 4th, chop 2nd, clip 5th, cut K, hit K, sculpt 4th, slash 6th, trim 4th

hi K: greetings 3rd, hello K, hey K, salutations 4th

hidden 1st: concealed 4th, covered 1st, covert 6th, masked 3rd, obscure 6th, secret 1st, unclear 3rd

hide 1st:
A. coat 1st, fur K, skin 1st
B. conceal 4th, disguise 5th, harbor 2nd, retire 4th, screen 1st, veil 3rd, withdraw 2nd

hideous 6th: awful 3rd, disgusting 5th, foul 4th, hateful 3rd, horrid 4th, monstrous 5th, offensive 4th, repellant 6th, repulsive 6th, terrible 1st, ugly 4th, vile 6th

high K: costly 1st, elevated 2nd, expensive 3rd, lofty 5th, noble 3rd, prominent 5th, raised 1st, remote 5th, steep 2nd, tall K, towering 4th

highway 4th: avenue 3rd, boulevard 4th, drive K, freeway 2nd, road K, street 1st, strip 3rd

hike 3rd: climb 1st, march 1st, plod 5th, stroll 5th, tramp 4th, trudge 5th, walk K

hill K: bluff 6th, climb 1st, elevation 4th, heap 4th, incline 5th, mound 2nd, pile 1st, ramp 6th, slope 3rd

hind 4th: after K, back K, end K, final 3rd, rear 3rd

hinder 6th: bar 3rd, block 1st, dam K, delay 5th, halt 4th, interfere 4th, limit 3rd, obstruct 5th, prevent 3rd, stop K

hindquarter 5th: back 1st

hinge 5th: center 2nd, depend 3rd, hang 2nd, joint 4th, pivot 5th, rest 1st, rotate 6th, turn 1st

hint 1st: clue 2nd, cue 2nd, idea 1st, omen 6th, signal 4th, suggestion 2nd, warning 3rd

hip 1st: aware 3rd, bottom 1st, bright 1st, clever 3rd, cool 1st, current 3rd, flank 5th, side K, smart 1st

hire 3rd:
    A. earnings 3rd, fee 4th, salary 3rd, wage 3rd
    B. employ 5th, engage 5th, lease 6th, rent K, pay K, use K

hiss 3rd: buzz 5th, mock 4th, scorn 4th, taunt 5th, whisper 1st

history 2nd: background 4th, biography 6th, chronicle 6th, legend 5th, past 1st, record 2nd, story K, tale 3rd

hit K: beat 1st, box 1st, bump 2nd, club 1st, collide with 6th, pound 2nd, punch 4th, slap 2nd, slug 5th, smack 6th, spank 2nd, strike 2nd, tap K

hither 6th: far 1st, there 1st

hive 2nd: house K

hoard 6th: accumulate 6th, amass 3rd, heap 4th, hide 1st, pile 1st, reserve 3rd, save 1st, store K

hoarse 5th: cracked 1st, dry 1st, gruff 1st, loud 1st, rough 4th

hoary 6th: aged 2nd, ancient 3rd, bearded 4th, crusty 4th, elderly 5th, grizzly 4th, old K

hoax 5th:
    A. deception 6th, fake 1st, fraud 6th, imitation 5th
    B. cheat 3rd, deceive 5th, fool 2nd, joke 1st, trick 1st

hobby 3rd: amusement 4th, collection 3rd, entertainment 4th, pastime 3rd, recreation 5th, sport 1st

hoe 2nd: cultivate 6th, dig 1st, farm K, garden K, rake 1st, till 1st

hog K:
    A. pig K
    B. amass 3rd, be selfish 5th, keep K

hoist 6th: elevate 2nd, erect 4th, heave 5th, lift 1st, raise 1st

hold 1st: bear K, carry K, clasp 4th, clutch 4th, contain 5th, embrace 4th, grip 4th, hug 1st, keep K, maintain 4th, reserve 3rd, restrict 6th, seize 3rd, support 4th

hole K: cavity 5th, dent 1st, dip 1st, gap K, hollow 3rd, opening 1st, rut 1st, space 1st, vent 4th, void 6th

holiday K: celebration 5th, ceremony 5th, festival 5th, observance 5th, vacation 2nd

hollow 3rd:
  A. senseless 2nd, useless 2nd, worthless 3rd
  B. depression 5th, pocket 1st, sunk 3rd
  C. empty 3rd, vacant 6th

holy 5th: blessed 3rd, celestial 6th, divine 5th, heavenly 2nd, moral 3rd, pious 6th, pure 3rd, religious 4th, saintly 4th

homage 6th: admiration 5th, awe 6th, esteem 5th, honor 1st, respect 2nd, reverence 4th, tribute 5th, worship 4th

home K: abode 5th, address K, domicile 5th, dwelling 4th, habitat 6th, habitation 6th, hearth 5th, house K, location 3rd, quarters 2nd, residence 5th, shelter 4th

homespun 5th: homemade 1st, homey 1st, modest 4th, plain 2nd, simple 2nd

homework 1st: lessons 3rd, studies 2nd

honest 3rd: fair 1st, frank 4th, honorable 3rd, just 1st, moral 3rd, sincere 4th, trustworthy 3rd, truthful 2nd, worthy 3rd

honor 1st: admire 5th, celebrate 4th, esteem 5th, fame 3rd, glorify 4th, glory 3rd, hail 4th, respect 2nd, salute 4th, tribute 5th, worship 4th

hood 4th: bonnet 6th, cap K, hat K, scarf 6th, veil 3rd

hoof 1st: foot K, paw 1st

hook 4th: angle 3rd, bend K, bow 1st, catch 1st, curve 3rd, sickle 6th, snare 6th, trap 1, turn 1st

hoop 5th: band 1st, circle K, ring 1st, wheel 1st

hoot 1st: bawl 5th, cry K, howl 4th, roar 1st, shout 1st

hop K: bound 2nd, jump K, leap 3rd, skip 2nd, spring K, vault 5th

hope K: await 5th, believe 1st, desire 5th, dream K, expect 3rd, foresee 6th, long 1st, longing 2nd, suppose 2nd, trust 1st, want K, wish K, yearn 6th

horde 6th: band 1st, herd 2nd, host 4th, lot K, mass 3rd, mob 4th, pack 1st, throng 5th, tribe 3rd

horizon 4th: distance 4th, prospect 4th, range 3rd, scope 6th, skyline 5th, view 1st

horizontal 6th: flat 2nd, level 3rd, plane 1st, sideways 1st

horrible 1st: *See* horrid.

horrid 4th: awful 3rd: dreadful 6th, horrible 1st, terrible 1st

horrify 4th: alarm 3rd, frighten 5th, scare 1st, startle 4th, terrify 3rd

horror 4th: dread 6th, fear 1st, terror 3rd

hose 6th:

    A. sock 1st, stocking 4th, tights 1st

    B. channel 4th, pipe 1st, spray 2nd, tube 3rd, water 1st

hospital 3rd: clinic 1st, medical center 5th

host 4th: army 1st, band 1st, herd 2nd, horde 6th, legion 6th, mob 4th, pack 1st, throng 5th

hostile 4th: angry 1st, contrary 4th, fighting 1st, mad K, malicious 6th, mean 1st, unfriendly 3rd, unkind 1st

hot K: angry 1st, baking 2nd, blazing 2nd, burning 3rd, eager 5th, earnest 4th, fiery 5th, furious 5th, keen 4th, scorching 6th, spicy 4th, strong K, tart 5th, warm 1st

hotel 3rd: inn 4th, lodging 4th, motel 3rd, tavern 5th

hothouse 5th: greenhouse 1st, pavilion 5th

hound 2nd:

    A. dog K, pup K

    B. badger 2nd, bait 3rd, force 1st, heel 3rd, hunt 2nd, pursue 5th, stalk 4th, tail 1st

hour 1st: time 1st

house K: abode 5th, address K, domicile 5th, dwelling 4th, habitat 6th, habitation 6th, home K, lodge 4th, quarters 2nd, residence 5th, shelter 4th

housekeeper 3rd: cleaner 1st, help K, maid 3rd, servant 3rd

hover 5th: float 1st, fly K, hang 2nd, linger 4th, suspend 5th, wait near 2nd

how K: how come 1st, whereby 4th, wherefore 4th, why K

however 1st: although 2nd, anyway 1st, but K, even though 2nd, in any case 2nd, nevertheless 4th, regardless 4th

howl 4th: bark 3rd, growl 4th, roar 1st, shout 1st, wail 5th, yell K, yelp 6th

hue 6th: color K, shade 2nd, tint 5th, tone 3rd

hug 1st: clasp 4th, clutch 4th, cuddle 5th, embrace 4th, grip 4th, hold 1st, snuggle 5th, squeeze 5th

huge 1st: big K, enormous 4th, grant 2nd, infinite 5th, large K, massive 5th, tremendous 4th, unlimited 4th

hull 4th: body 1st, case 2nd, frame 3rd, outside 1st, shell 1st, skeleton 4th, structure 4th

hum 1st: buzz 5th, murmur 4th, sing 1st, vibrate 5th, vibration 5th

human 3rd: being 1st, individual 3rd, mortal 4th, person 1st, soul 3rd

humble 4th:

    A. put down 2nd, shame 3rd

    B. base 1st, belittle 4th, common 2nd, dishonor 3rd, lower 1st, lowly 1st, mean 1st, meek 2nd, mild 4th, modest 4th, plain 2nd, simple 1st

humor 4th: comedy 5th, heart K, jest 4th, joke 1st, mood 3rd, nature 1st, soul 3rd, spirit 2nd, wit 1st

hump 3rd: bulge 4th, bump 2nd, hunch 6th, lump 4th, mass 3rd, swelling 3rd

hunch 6th:

    A. bet 1st, feeling 1st

    B. bend K, squat 5th, stoop 5th

hunger 2nd: appetite 4th, craving 6th, desire 5th, longing 1st, urge 4th, want K

hungry 2nd: craving 6th, longing 1st, starving 5th, yearning 6th

hunker 6th: crouch 5th, stoop 5th

hunt 2nd: chase 1st, comb 2nd, follow 1st, look for 1st, pursue 5th, search 1st, seek 1st, stalk 4th, track 1st

hurl 5th: cast 2nd, fling 6th, heave 5th, launch 5th, pitch 2nd, send K, shoot 3rd, throw 1st, toss 2nd

hurried 1st: careless 5th, feverish 4th, hasty 2nd, rushed 3rd, urgent 6th

hurry 1st: drive on 1st, fly K, hasten 2nd, provoke 6th, rush 2nd, speed 3rd, sprint 5th, stimulate 6th

hurt K:

    A. ache 5th, ill 1st, pain 2nd, woe 4th

    B. abuse 6th, damage 5th, harm 3rd, injure 5th, injury 5th, ruin 5th, wound 3rd

husband 1st: groom 5th, mate 4th, partner 5th

hush 3rd: lull 5th, quiet K, rest 1st, silence 4th, solitude 5th, still 1st

hut 4th: cabin 1st, cottage 4th, house K

hymn 5th: carol 3rd, chant 5th, melody 4th, psalm 6th, song K, tune 1st

hysteria 6th: craze 4th, eruption 4th, explosion 4th, fit K, madness 3rd

hysterical 6th: crazed 4th, emotional 4th, funny 1st, mad 2nd, raving 6th

I K: me K

ice K: frost 4th, frozen 4th

icebox 1st: refrigerator 2nd

idea 1st: belief 1st, concept 4th, feeling K, notion 5th, opinion 3rd, thought 1st, viewpoint 5th

ideal 3rd:

    A. example 2nd, model 3rd, original 3rd, pattern 3rd

    B. aim 3rd, goal 4th, objective 2nd

    C. abstract 6th, perfect 3rd, truth 1st

identical 6th: alike 1st, duplicate 6th, equal 2nd, equivalent 6th, same 1st

identify 4th: call K, know 1st, label 3rd, point out 1st, prove 1st, recognize 3rd, select 4th, term 3rd

identity 5th: itself 2nd, myself 1st, name K, oneself 3rd, person 1st, self 3rd, uniqueness 6th

idiot 6th: fool 2nd, silly 1st, simple 2nd, stupid 4th

idle 4th:

    A. do nothing 1st, laze 4th, loaf 4th

    B. inactive 3rd, lazy 4th, not working 1st, unoccupied 3rd

idol 6th: dream K, god 1st, hero 1st, vision 4th

idolize 6th: adore 4th, magnify 3rd, worship 4th

if K: although 2nd, provided 3rd, though 1st, whether 1st

ignite 6th: burn 3rd, fire K, light K, set on fire K

ignorant 4th: blind 3rd, in the dark 2nd, unaware 3rd, uneducated 3rd, unknowing 2nd, unschooled 1st

ignore 5th: disregard 4th, neglect 4th, overlook 4th, push aside 3rd

ill 1st:
  A. bad K, evil 3rd, sinful 2nd, wicked 4th
  B. poorly 1st, sick 1st, sickly 1st, unwell 1st

illegal 1st: forbidden 4th, lawless 2nd, unlawful 3rd

illuminate 6th:
  A. educate 3rd, explain 2nd, guide 1st, inform 5th, tell K
  B. light K, light up 1st, shine 1st

illusion 6th: false idea 3rd, fancy 3rd, fantasy 6th, imagination 2nd, vision 4th

illustration 4th:
  A. example 2nd, explanation 2nd, sample 5th
  B. drawing 1st, photograph 5th, sketch 5th

illustrious 6th: celebrated 5th, famous 2nd, popular 3rd, renowned 5th

image 4th: likeness 2nd, photograph 5th, picture K, portrait 5th, statue 4th

imagine 2nd: conceive 4th, dream up 1st, envision 4th, fancy 3rd, picture K, think 1st

imitate 5th: ape 5th, copy 3rd, mimic 6th, mock 4th, simulate 6th

immaculate 6th: clean 1st, fresh 2nd, perfect 3rd, pure 3rd, spotless 1st

immature 5th: childish 1st, new K, not ripe 1st

immediate 3rd: abrupt 5th, direct 1st, nearest 2nd, now K, prompt 4th, sudden 1st

immense 4th: big K, broad 3rd, enormous 4th, giant 2nd, great K, huge 1st, large K, vast 4th, wide 1st

immigrant 6th: alien 5th, foreigner 5th, stranger 1st

immobile 6th: constant 4th, firm 2nd, fixed 1st, stationary 3rd, steady 3rd, unmoving 3rd

immortal 4th: constant 4th, everlasting 5th, never-ending 1st, undying 4th, without end 1st

imp 5th: demon 4th, devil 1st, dwarf 4th, elf 1st, gnome 6th, spirit 2nd

impart 6th: communicate 5th, give K, pass on K, reveal 4th, tell 1st

impatient 5th: jumpy 1st, nervous 1st, restless 4th, rude 2nd, short 1st, uneasy 2nd, unquiet 1st

imperial 5th: kingly 1st, queenly 1st, regal 6th, royal 3rd, ruling 1st

impetus 6th: drive K, energy 4th, force 1st, momentum 6th, push 1st, speed 3rd

implement 6th:
  A. instrument 3rd, tool 1st, utensil 6th
  B. enforce 5th, execute 5th, follow 1st
imply 5th: assume 5th, hint 1st, include 3rd, involve 6th, mean 1st, suggest 2nd, suppose 2nd
import 5th:
  A. bring in K, carry K, introduce 5th
  B. concern 3rd, meaning 1st, sense 1st, value 2nd, worth 3rd
important 1st: large K, main 3rd, major 3rd, matters 1st, needed 1st, significant 6th
impose 4th: ask K, demand 5th, direct 1st, order 1st, put on K, require 1st
impossible 3rd: absurd 6th, can't 1st, out of the question 2nd, unable 3rd
impress 5th:
  A. affect 4th, influence 5th, move K, reach 1st, touch 1st
  B. imprint 4th, print 1st, push 1st, stamp 2nd, strike 2nd
impression 5th:
  A. imprint 4th, mark 1st, print 1st
  B. concept 4th, idea 1st, image 4th, opinion 3rd, sense 1st, thought 1st, view 2nd
imprint 4th: impression 5th, print 1st, stamp 2nd
imprison 6th: cage 1st, capture 3rd, catch 1st, close in 1st, jail 4th, put in prison 3rd
improve 3rd: better 1st, clean K, develop 5th, fix 1st, help K, put right K, repair 4th
impulse 5th: desire 5th, liking 1st, motive 5th, passion 6th, spur 4th, stimulus 6th
in K: at K, inside 1st, on K
incapable 6th: helpless 1st, incompetent 6th, powerless 2nd, unable 3rd, weak 3rd
incense 5th: anger 1st, enrage 6th, fire up 2nd, irritate 6th, provoke 6th
inch 1st: creep 1st, move slowly 1st
incident 5th: episode 6th, event 3rd, happening 1st, matter 1st, occurrence 3rd
incline 5th:
  A. grade 2nd, slant 6th
  B. prefer 3rd, tend K
inclined 5th: apt 5th, eager 5th, likely 1st
include 3rd: cover 1st, embrace 4th, involve 6th, take in 1st
income 4th: fee 4th, pay K, salary 3rd, wages 3rd
inconvenient 6th: awkward 6th, ill timed 2nd, out of the way K
increase 3rd: enlarge 5th, expand 5th, gain 2nd, multiply 4th, raise 1st
incredible 6th: absurd 6th, crazy 4th, doubtful 5th, strange 1st, unbelievable 3rd, unreal 2nd

incredulous 6th: doubtful 5th, unbelieving 2nd, uncertain 1st

indeed 1st: certainly 1st, in fact 1st, surely K, truly K, yes K

independent 3rd:

    A. alone 1st, lone 2nd, separate 3rd, unconnected 3rd

    B. confident 6th, direct 1st, free K, self-reliant 5th, self-sufficient 3rd

index 6th:

    A. label 3rd, mark 1st, sort 2nd

    B. guide 1st, key K

indicate 4th:

    A. point 1st, point out 1st, show 1st, signal 4th

    B. express 5th, hint 1st, imply 5th, mean 1st, state 1st, suggest 2nd, tell K

indifferent 5th: detached 5th, disinterested 3rd, distant 4th, uncaring 1st, unconcerned 3rd, unemotional 4th

indignant 5th: angry 1st, annoyed 5th, irritated 6th, mad K

indispensable 6th: basic 5th, important 1st, necessary 1st, significant 6th

individual 3rd:

    A. being 1st, creature 3rd, person 1st

    B. characteristic 6th, distinct 5th, one K, separate 3rd, single 3rd, sole 4th, special 2nd, specific 5th, unique 6th

indoor 6th: enclosed 4th, in K, inside 1st, sheltered 4th

induce 5th: convince 4th, motivate 6th, persuade 5th, prompt 4th, provoke 6th, spur 4th

indulge 5th: baby K, fulfill 4th, humor 4th, oblige 6th, satisfy 3rd, spoil 4th

industry 5th: business 2nd, commerce 5th, employment 5th, labor 1st, trade 2nd, work K

infant 5th: babe 5th, baby K, newborn 2nd

infect 6th:

    A. affect 4th, influence 5th, inspire 4th

    B. contaminate 6th, poison 3rd, spoil 4th, taint 6th

inferior 5th: below 1st, dependent 3rd, lesser 2nd, lower 1st, poorer 1st, secondary 2nd, second class 2nd, under K

infinite 5th: boundless 4th, constant 4th, continuous 2nd, eternal 4th, innumerable 5th, limitless 3rd, never ending 1st, nonstop 1st, ongoing 1st, unlimited 3rd, vast 4th

inflect 6th: arch 4th, bend K, curve 3rd, loop 5th, turn 1st

influence 5th:

    A. affect 4th, change 2nd, direct 1st, impress 5th, manage 4th, sway 3rd

    B. authority 3rd, effect 3rd, force 1st, power 1st, strength 1st

inform 5th: acquaint 4th, animate 6th, announce 3rd, communiate 5th, educate 3rd, inspire 4th, teach 1st, tell K

informal 5th: casual 5th, common 2nd, easygoing 1st, every day K, off hand K, plain 2nd

information 5th: advice 3rd, facts 1st, knowledge 2nd, report 1st

ingenious 6th: clever 3rd, creative 3rd, cunning 6th, inventive 3rd, skillful 2nd, smart 1st

ingredient 4th: component 4th, element 3rd, factor 5th, item 5th, member 1st, unit 5th

inhabit 6th: abide 5th, dwell 4th, live 1st, live in 1st, occupy 3rd, reside 5th

inherit 5th: get K, receive 2nd

initial 6th: beginning 2nd, first 1st, primary 5th

initiate 5th:
  A. educate 3rd, instruct 4th, teach 1st
  B. begin 1st, establish 3rd, found 2nd, install 6th, open K, start 1st

initiative 6th:
  A. beginning 2nd, first step 1st, lead 1st
  B. ambition 4th, desire 5th, drive K

injure 5th: abuse 6th, bruise 5th, damage 5th, harm 3rd, hurt 1st, wound 3rd, wrong 1st

injury 5th: bruise 5th, hurt 1st, ill 1st, pain 2nd, wound 3rd

inland 5th: interior 5th, internal 6th, offshore 1st

inlet 4th: bay K, nook 6th

inn 4th: hotel 3rd, tavern 5th

inner 5th: inside 1st, interior 5th, internal 6th, inward 6th, within 3rd

innocent 5th:
  A. blameless 2nd, guiltless 4th, pure 3rd
  B. harmless 3rd

innumerable 5th: countless 5th, infinite 5th, many K, unlimited 3rd

inquire 3rd: ask K, examine 5th, question 1st, search 1st

insane 6th: crazy 4th, lunatic 6th, mad K, unbalanced 3rd

inscribe 5th: address K, autograph 6th, mark 1st, print 1st, sign 1st, write K

inscription 6th: address K, caption 6th, legend 5th, message 1st, name K, note 1st

insect 4th: bug 1st, fly K

insert 6th: add in K, introduce 5th, place 1st, put in K

inside 1st: inner 5th, interior 5th, internal 6th

insist 5th: assure 3rd, compel 3rd, demand 5th, press 1st, stress 6th, urge 4th

inspect 5th: examine 5th, observe 3rd, scan 6th, study 1st

inspire 4th: cheer 3rd, encourage 4th, enliven 6th, fire K, impress 5th

install 6th: establish 3rd, initiate 5th, put in K, set up 1st

instance 5th: case 2nd, example 2nd, illustration 4th, sample 5th

instant 3rd:
  A. immediate 3rd, prompt 4th, quick 1st, urgent 6th
  B. flash 2nd, minute 1st, moment 1st, second 1st

instead 1st: in place of 1st, rather 1st

instinct 5th: impulse 5th, leaning 3rd, reaction 5th, tendency 5th

institute 5th:
    A. establish 3rd, found 2nd, organize 4th
    B. association 5th, clinic 1st, school K

instruct 4th:
    A. command 2nd, direct 1st, order 1st
    B. acquaint 4th, educate 3rd, school K, teach 1st, train K

instrument 3rd: agent 5th, channel 4th, device 4th, machine 1st, method 2nd, tool 1st

insult 5th: abuse 6th, offend 4th, put down 1st, shame 3rd

insure 5th: assure 3rd, guarantee 6th, make sure 1st, protect 4th, secure 3rd

intelligence 4th: brain 3rd, cleverness 3rd, mind 1st, mentality 5th, reason 1st, sense 1st

intelligent 4th: alert 5th, aware 3rd, bright 1st, brilliant 4th, clever 3rd, mental 5th, quick 1st, sharp 1st, smart 1st

intend 6th:
    A. aim 3rd, mean 1st, purpose 1st, scheme 5th
    B. design 5th, plan 1st

intense 6th: fierce 4th, harsh 5th, passionate 6th, stressed 6th, strong K, violent 5th

intensive 6th: *See* intense.

intent 5th:
    A. aim 3rd, design 5th, end K, intention 6th, objective 2nd, purpose 2nd
    B. absorbed 5th, firm 2nd, fixed 1st, rapt 6th

intention 6th: aim 3rd, goal 4th, objective 2nd, purpose 2nd

interest 1st:
    A. absorb 5th, amuse 4th, engage 5th, excite 4th, stimulate 6th
    B. business 2nd, care K, concern 3rd

interfere 4th: block 1st, butt in 1st, hinder 6th, intrude 6th, meddle 6th, obstruct 5th

interior 5th: hidden 1st, inner 5th, inside 1st, internal 6th, inward 6th, personal 3rd, secret 1st, within 3rd

internal 6th: inborn 2nd, native 1st, natural 2nd, true K. *See* interior.

international 5th: general 2nd, global 4th, universal 4th, worldly 2nd

interpret 5th: comment 5th, demonstrate 6th, explain 2nd, illustrate 5th, show 1st, spell out 1st, translate 5th

interrupt 3rd: arrest 3rd, cease 3rd, check 1st, end K, halt 4th, interfere 4th, postpone 6th, stop K, suspend 5th

interval 6th: break 1st, era 6th, gap K, interruption 3rd, lull 5th, pause 3rd, period 2nd

interview 5th:
    A. consult 4th, examine 5th, question 1st

B. conference 4th, discussion 5th, meeting 1st

intestine 4th: guts 1st, organs 4th, stomach 2nd

intimate 5th:

    A. buddy 4th, companion 3rd, comrad 4th, friend 1st

    B. comfortable 3rd, small K, warm 1st

    C. buddy-buddy 4th, close K, dear 1st, friendly 2nd

intricate 6th: complex 6th, complicated 6th, involved 6th, obscure 6th, puzzling 4th, tangled 3rd

introduce 5th:

    A. begin K, found 2nd, invent 2nd, originate 3rd

    B. acquaint 4th, make known 2nd, meet K, present K

intrude 6th: bother 2nd, impose 4th, interfere 4th, invade 5th, push in 1st

invade 5th: agress 6th, attack 3rd, enter 2nd, intrude 6th, trespass 6th

invent 2nd: begin K, coin 3rd, conceive 4th, create 3rd, design 5th, devise 4th, make K, originate 3rd

invest 5th: fund 4th, give 1st, grant 2nd, install 6th, support 4th

investigate 5th: examine 5th, inquire 3rd, question 1st, research 5th, search 1st

invisible 6th: ghostly 1st, imaginary 2nd, unseen 2nd

invite 3rd: appeal 3rd, ask K, bid 1st, call 1st, plead 3rd, request 4th

involve 6th: affect 4th, confuse 4th, contain 5th, embrace 4th, engage 5th, include 3rd, mean 1st, puzzle 4th

inward 6th: inborn 3rd, inner 5th, inside 1st, interior 5th, internal 6th, within 3rd

irk 6th: agitate 5th, anger 1st, annoy 5th, bother 2nd, irritate 6th, provoke 6th, vex 5th

iron 2nd: press 1st, smooth 2nd, straighten 3rd

irregular 6th: different 1st, not normal 5th, odd 4th, peculiar 4th, strange 1st, unusual 3rd

irritate 6th: *See* irk.

issue 4th:

    A. child K, heir 4th

    B. declare 5th, originate 4th, proclaim 4th, put out 1st, send K

    C. conclusion 3rd, controversy 6th, effect 3rd, outcome 4th, point 1st, proceed 4th, result 2nd, subject 3rd

itch 5th:

    A. crave 6th, desire 5th, want K, wish K, yearn 6th

    B. annoy 5th, irritate 6th, sting 4th

item 5th: article 2nd, aspect 5th, detail 5th, feature 3rd, ingredient 4th, point 1st

ivory 3rd: beige 3rd, bone 1st, cream 1st, tan K, tooth 1st, tusk 5th

jab 1st: hit K, poke 1st, punch 4th, push 1st, slap 2nd, smack 6th, stick K, strike 2nd

jack 1st:
    A. banner 3rd, flag 3rd, streamer 3rd
    B. hoist 6th, lift 1st, raise 1st

jacket 3rd: cloak 4th, clothing 1st, coat 1st, cover 1st, sweater 3rd

jagged 5th: irregular 6th, sharp 1st, zigzag 3rd

jail 4th:
    A. imprison 6th, intern 6th
    B. cell 1st, dungeon 5th, fortress 5th, prison 3rd

jam K:
    A. gelatin 5th, jelly 1st, preserves 4th
    B. block 1st, cram 5th, crowd 2nd, fix 1st, pack 1st, press 1st, problem 1st, push 1st, squeeze 5th

jar K:
    A. clash 5th, shock 1st, strike 2nd
    B. container 5th, glass 1st, pot K

jaunty 6th: alive 3rd, bouncy 6th, gay 1st, happy K, showy 1st, stylish 3rd

jaw 4th:
    A. criticize 5th, scold 5th, talk K
    B. chin 1st, chops 2nd, mouth 1st

jealous 5th: covetous 6th, distrustful 2nd, doubtful 1st, envious 4th, suspicious 4th

jeans 1st: pants 1st

jeep 1st: military car 3rd, vehicle 6th

jeer 5th: ridicule 6th, scoff 6th, sneer 6th, tease 3rd

jell 1st: set K, stick K

jelly 1st: gelatin 5th, jam K, preserves 4th

jersey 5th: shirt 1st

jest 4th:
    A. fool 2nd, mock 4th, tease 3rd
    B. gag 1st, joke 1st, prank 5th

jet K:
    A. airplane 1st, plane 1st
    B. fly 1st, hurry 1st, speed 3rd

jewel 5th: ornament 4th, precious 4th, stone 2nd, treasure 4th

jewelry 5th: jewels 5th, ornament 4th, treasures 4th

jibe 6th: agree 2nd, conform 6th, fit K, harmonize 4th, match 3rd

jingle 2nd:
    A. chime 6th, ring 1st, sing 1st
    B. advertisement 4th, poem 3rd, rhyme 6th, song K, verse 4th

job K: activity 3rd, duty 1st, employment 5th, function 4th, labor 1st, occupation 6th, project 4th, role 6th, task 3rd, trade 1st, work K

jog 2nd:
  A. brisk walk 6th, run K, trot 5th
  B. bump 2nd, poke 1st, prod 6th, push 1st, shake 1st

join 3rd: add K, adhere 6th, adjoin 6th, associate 5th, attach 5th, combine 3rd, connect 3rd, embrace 4th, link 5th, tie 1st, unite 5th

joined 3rd: allied 6th, combined 3rd, together 1st

joint 4th:
  A. hinge 5th, seam 5th
  B. combination 3rd, connection 3rd, link 5th

joke 1st: gag 1st, humor 5th, jest 4th, prank 5th

jolly 4th: bright 1st, cheery 3rd, gay 1st, glad K, happy K

jostle 6th:
  A. hurry 1st, rush 2nd
  B. bump 2nd, knock 3rd, push 1st, shake 1st

jot 1st:
  A. note 1st, write K
  B. atom 5th, bit 1st, scant 6th, smallness 1st, tiny 2nd

journal 2nd: book K, diary 3rd, log K, magazine 3rd, newspaper 1st, record 2nd, review 4th

journey 3rd: adventure 3rd, expedition 4th, tour 3rd, travel 1st, trip 1st, voyage 4th

joust 6th: fence 1st, fight K, strive 5th, wrestle 6th

jovial 5th: cheerful 3rd, gay 1st, happy K, high spirits 2nd, jolly 4th, merry 3rd, witty 2nd

joy 1st: cheer 3rd, delight 3rd, ecstasy 6th, gladness 1st, happiness 2nd, merriment 3rd, pleasure 2nd

judge 1st:
  A. critic 5th, officer 1st, protector 4th
  B. choose 3rd, condemn 4th, decide 1st, decision maker 3rd, expert 5th, merit 4th, try 4th, weigh 1st

jug 1st: container 5th, jar K, pot K

juice K: extract 4th, fluid 6th, liquid 3rd, sap 1st, syrup 4th

jump K: bounce 6th, bound 2nd, hop K, leap 3rd, pounce 5th, skip 2nd, spring K, vault 5th

jungle 4th:
  A. confusion 4th, disarray 5th, mess 1st
  B. rain forest 2nd, thicket 4th, woods 1st

junior 4th: child K, heir 4th, juvenile 5th, lesser 2nd, minor 5th, newer 1st, undergraduate 4th, younger 2nd

junk 3rd:
    A. garbage 5th, trash 2nd
    B. discard 6th, scrap 3rd, throw away 1st
jury 4th:
    A. court 3rd, panel 6th
    B. choose 3rd, decide 1st, judge 1st
just 1st: correct 3rd, earned 2nd, fair 1st, honest 3rd, honorable 3rd, legal 5th, legitimate 6th, right K, true K, virtuous 4th
justice 3rd: fairness 2nd, ideal 3rd, lawfulness 2nd, legality 5th, right K
justification 5th: alibi 6th, excuse 3rd, reason 2nd
juvenile 5th: minor 5th, junior 4th, teen 2nd, under age 1st, youngster 2nd, youth 2nd
kaiser 5th: emperor 4th, king 1st, ruler 3rd
kangaroo 1st:
    A. unjust 2nd
    B. jump K
keen 4th:
    A. sorrow 4th, wail 5th, weep 4th
    B. acute 6th, eager 5th, intense 6th, larger 5th, sharp 1st, smart 1st
keep K:
    A. castle 3rd, fort 5th
    B. accumulate 6th, celebrate 4th, conserve 5th, hold 1st, obey 3rd, observe 3rd, possess 3rd, preserve 4th, save 1st, support 4th
keeper 1st: guard 1st, guardian 3rd, manager 4th, owner 1st
keg 1st: barrel 4th
kettle 4th: pot K
key K:
    A. important 1st, main 3rd, principal 3rd
    B. access 6th, opener 1st
    C. input 1st, type 1st
keyboard 1st: piano 4th, typewriter 1st
khaki 6th: brown K, tan K
kick 1st:
    A. object 1st, oppose 3rd, protest 4th
    B. blow 1st, boot 1st, hit K, move K, tap K
kid K:
    A. goat K
    B. joke 1st, mock 4th, rib 1st, tease 3rd
    C. boy K, child K, girl K, youth 2nd
kill 1st: execute 5th, murder 3rd, slay 4th
kin 1st: ally 6th, family K, relative 4th

kind K:
  A. mode 5th, sort 1st, type 1st
  B. charitable 4th, gentle 3rd, tolerant 5th, warm 1st
kindle 5th: burn 3rd, fire K, ignite 6th, light K
king K: crown 1st, emperor 4th, kaiser 5th, noble 3rd, ruler 3rd
kingdom 3rd: country 1st, estate 4th, land K
kiss K: embrace 4th, greet 3rd
kit 1st: gear 1st, set K, supplies 1st, tools 1st
kite K: fly 1st, glide 4th, sail 1st, soar 6th
kitten K: cat K, kitty 1st
knapsack 4th: backpack 4th, bag 1st, tote bag 5th
knave 5th: chessman 4th, noble 3rd, rascal 5th, villain 5th
knead 4th: fold 1st, pound 2nd, push 1st, shape 1st, work K
kneel 4th: bow 1st
knife 1st: blade 2nd, cut K, pierce 4th, stab 5th, stick K, sword 4th
knight 2nd: noble 3rd, prince 1st, soldier 3rd
knit 4th: plait 5th, weave 4th
knock 3rd: bang 3rd, pound 2nd, rap 1st, strike 2nd, tap K
knot 4th: loop 5th, problem 1st, tie 1st
know 1st: comprehend 5th, realize 2nd, recognize 3rd, understand 1st
know-how 2nd: ability 3rd, competence 6th, intelligence 4th, knowledge 2nd,
    skill 2nd
knowledge 2nd: information 5th, learning 1st, scholarship 5th,
    understanding 3rd
known 1st: learned 2nd, recognized 3rd, understood 2nd
knuckle 4th: hit K, punch 4th
lab 1st: laboratory 4th, study 1st, workshop 2nd
label 3rd: brand 2nd, mark 1st, stamp 2nd, tag 1st
labor 1st: effort 2nd, job K, toil 4th, trouble 1st, work K
laboratory 4th: lab 1st, study 1st, workshop 2nd
lace 4th: secure 3rd, string 2nd, thread 2nd, tie 1st
lack 1st: absence 5th, need 1st, want K
lad K: boy K, youth 2nd
ladder 2nd: stairs 2nd, stairway 3rd
laden 6th: filled 1st, full K, loaded 2nd, packed 2nd, weighted 2nd
ladle 4th: dish 1st, scoop 4th, spoon 1st
lady 1st: female 4th, woman K
lag 1st: delay 5th, linger 4th, slow 1st, wait 1st
lagoon 5th: bay K, inlet 4th, lake 1st, pond 1st, swamp 4th
lair 5th: cave 1st, den 1st
lake 1st: lagoon 5th, pond 1st, pool 1st
lamb K: gentle 3rd, meek 2nd, mild 4th

lame 4th: disabled 3rd, hurt K, injured 5th, sore 4th

lament 6th: cry 1st, grieve 5th, mourn 4th, sorrow 4th, weep 4th

lamp 1st: bulb 2nd, illumination 6th, light K

lance 4th: spear 4th

land K:
> A. dirt 1st, earth 1st, ground 1st, perch 5th, plot 4th, roost 5th, sod 6th, yard 1st
>
> B. achieve 5th, alight 5th, gain 2nd, reach 1st

landing 1st: arrival 3rd

landslide 5th: mudslide 2nd

lane 4th: alley 6th, drive 1st, path 1st, road K, street 1st, way K

language 2nd: dialect 5th, speech 2nd, vocabulary 6th, words K

lanky 5th: lean 3rd, long 1st, tall K, thin 1st

lantern 5th: lamp 1st, light K

lap K: seat 1st

lapse 6th: break 1st, error 4th, fall K, mistake 1st, pause 3rd, slip 3rd

lard 6th: butter 2nd, fat 1st

large K: big K, giant 2nd, great K, huge 1st, mammoth 5th, vast 4th

lark 5th: adventure 3rd, fun K, game K

lash 4th: beat 1st, bind 2nd, tie 1st, whip 4th

lass 1st: girl K, young woman 1st

lasso 4th:
> A. rope 1st
>
> B. catch 1st, grab 4th

last K:
> A. endure 4th, persist 5th, remain 2nd, stay 1st, survive 5th
>
> B. end K, final 3rd, latest 1st

latch 6th: buckle 6th, clasp 4th, close K, lock 1st

late K: behind 1st, contemporary 5th, dead 1st, delayed 5th, modern 2nd, old K, overdue 3rd, recent 3rd

later 1st: after 1st, afterward 4th, behind 1st, next K

latter 3rd: end K, last K, later 1st, second 1st

laugh 1st: joke 1st

launch 5th: begin K, float 1st, push 1st, send off 1st, start 1st

laundry 6th: clothes 1st, dirty clothes 1st, wash 1st

laurel 5th: award 5th, honor 1st, prize 3rd, reward 4th

lavish 6th: abundant 5th, bountiful 5th, extravagant 6th, generous 4th, lush 6th, luxuriant 4th

law 1st: regulation 5th, rule 2nd

lawn 2nd: grass 1st, landscape 5th, sod 6th, yard 1st

lawyer 5th: advocate 5th, counsel 5th

lay 1st:
    A. aim 3rd, direct 1st, point 1st
    B. leave 1st, place 1st, put K, rest 1st, set K
layer 4th: coat 1st, level 3rd, wrapping 3rd
lazy 4th: idle 4th, inactive 3rd, listless 6th
lead 1st: guide 1st, pilot 5th, steer 5th
league 3rd: association 5th, federation 5th, partnership 5th
leak 6th: drain 5th, drip 2nd, hold K
lean 3rd:
    A. skinny 1st, thin 2nd
    B. angular 4th, incline 5th, recline 6th, slant 6th, slope 3rd, tilt 5th
leaning 3rd: bias 6th, tendency 5th
leap 3rd: hop K, jump K, spring 1st
learn 1st: comprehend 5th, master 1st, realize 2nd
lease 6th: hire 3rd, rent K
least 1st: last K, littlest 1st, smallest 1st
leather 1st: hide 1st
leave 1st: abandon 4th, allow 2nd, assign 5th, depart 5th, desert 1st, go K,
    let K, permit 3rd, quit 1st, will K, yield 4th
lecture 5th: address K, speech 1st, talk K
ledge 5th: bluff 6th, edge 3rd, shelf 6th
lee 5th: calm 3rd, protection 4th, safety 2nd, shelter 4th
leech 4th: sponge 5th, suck 1st, take 1st
leek 5th: onion 2nd
leg K: lap K, limb 4th
legal 5th: allowable 5th, lawful 2nd, right K
legend 5th: adventure 3rd, caption 6th, myth 4th, saga 6th, story K, tale 3rd
legion 6th: army 1st, military 3rd
legislation 5th: laws 1st
legitimate 6th: honest 3rd, lawful 2nd, legal 5th, proper 3rd, right K
leisure 5th: comfort 3rd, ease 3rd, freedom 3rd, holiday K, liberty 3rd, rest 1st,
    vacation 2nd
lend K: give K, loan 4th, provide 3rd
length 2nd: distance 4th, extent 4th, measure 2nd, size 1st
lens 1st: glass 1st
less 1st: fewer 1st, smaller 1st
lesson 3rd: assignment 5th, homework 1st, knowledge 2nd, learning 1st,
    lecture 5th, studies 2nd, teaching 1st
lest 4th: unless 2nd
let K:
    A. charter 2nd, hire 3rd, lease 6th, rent K
    B. allow 2nd, permit 3rd, sanction 6th

letter 1st: message 1st, note 1st, report 2nd

letters 1st: alphabet 2nd

levee 6th: bank 1st, dam K, dock 1st, pier 4th, wharf 5th

level 3rd:

    A. aim 3rd, direct 1st, point 1st

    B. even 1st, flat 2nd, plane 1st, smooth 2nd

liable 6th: answerable 4th, exposed 4th, open K, responsible 4th

liberal 4th: abundant 5th, ample 5th, generous 4th, tolerant 5th

liberty 3rd: freedom 3rd, independence 3rd, license 5th

license 5th:

    A. allow 2nd, permit 3rd

    B. allowance 5th, commission 2nd, freedom 3rd, liberty 3rd

lick 1st:

    A. taste 1st

    B. beat 1st, conquer 4th, defeat 5th

lid 1st: cover 1st, seal K, top K

lie 1st: falsehood 4th, fib 1st, untruth 3rd

life 1st: animation 6th, biography 6th, nature 1st, soul 3rd, spirit 2nd

lift 1st: arise 4th, elevate 2nd, raise 1st

light K:

    A. ignite 6th, illuminate 6th

    B. easy 1st, simple 2nd

    C. fair 2nd, lightweight 4th, pale 3rd, small K, tiny 2nd, weightless 2nd

    D. fire K, glow 1st, lamp 1st, lantern 5th

lighthouse 2nd: guide 1st, signal 4th, warning 3rd

like K:

    A. equal 2nd, same 1st, similar 4th

    B. enjoy 2nd, fancy 3rd, love K, prefer 3rd

likely 1st: apt 5th, inclined 5th, liable 6th

limb 4th: arm K, branch 2nd, leg K, part 1st

limber 4th: agile 6th, flexible 6th, supple 6th

limit 3rd:

    A. bound 2nd, check 1st, restrict 6th

    B. border 1st, curb 3rd, edge 1st, end K, margin 5th

limp 5th: floppy 6th, loose 3rd, soft K, weak 3rd

limpid 6th: clear 2nd, pure 3rd, transparent 5th

line K:

    A. chain 3rd, file 1st, row K, series 4th, strip 3rd, stripe 1st

    B. arrange 3rd, draw K

linen 4th: cloth 1st, fabric 5th, sheets 1st, towels 6th

linger 4th: remain 1st, stay 1st, wait K

link 5th: adhere 6th, associate 5th, connect 3rd, join 3rd, tie 1st

lip 1st: mouth 1st

liquid 3rd: drink 1st, fluid 6th

liquor 5th: alcohol 5th, spirits 2nd

list 2nd:
    A. schedule 6th, table 1st
    B. catalog 5th, record 2nd, roll 1st

listen 1st: attend 3rd, hear 1st, pay attention 3rd

listless 6th: idle 4th, inactive 4th, lazy 4th

literal 6th: exact 2nd

literature 5th: book K, writing 1st

litter 2nd:
    A. clutter 4th, junk 3rd, mess 1st, trash 2nd
    B. dump 2nd, pollute 3rd, scatter 3rd

little K: miniature 6th, small K, tiny 2nd

live 1st: alive 3rd, be K, breathe 1st, endure 4th, exist 3rd

livestock 3rd: cattle 3rd, cows K, herds 2nd

living 1st: active 3rd, alive 3rd, energetic 4th, strong K

load 2nd: burden 5th, cargo 5th, charge 2nd, contents 3rd, duty 1st, freight 4th, responsibility 4th, weight 1st

loaf 4th: idle 4th, linger 4th, lounge 6th, relax 4th, rest 1st

loan 4th:
    A. advance 2nd, credit 5th
    B. lease 6th, lend K

local 3rd: close by 1st, domestic 5th, folk 3rd, native 1st, near 1st, nearby 2nd, regional 4th

locality 4th: area 3rd, district 4th, neighborhood 2nd, place 1st, region 4th

locate 3rd: catch 1st, detect 4th, discover 1st, establish 3rd, find K, lay 1st, place 1st, position 2nd, put K, set K, situate 4th, spot 1st, uncover 2nd

location 3rd: address K, area 3rd, district 4th, place 1st, position 2nd, region 4th

lock 1st: bolt 4th, clamp 5th, clasp 4th, corner 2nd, hook 4th, latch 4th, restrain 5th, trap 1st

locomotive 5th: engine 3rd, mobile 6th, moving 1st

lodge 4th: association 5th, brotherhood 4th, cabin 1st, club 1st, community 2nd, hotel 3rd, hut 4th, inn 4th, resort 5th, shelter 4th

loft 5th: attic 2nd, balcony 6th

lofty 5th: ambitious 4th, elevated 2nd, excellent 1st, grand 2nd, heavenly 1st, high K, prominent 5th, soaring 6th, splendid 4th, tall K

log K:
    A. chart 1st, journal 2nd, record 2nd, report 2nd
    B. beam 3rd, board 1st, branch 2nd, plank 5th, pole K, trunk 4th

logger 4th: lumberman 1st, woodsman 3rd

logic 6th: judgment 4th, reason 2nd, sense 1st, thought 1st, wisdom 2nd

logo 4th: seal K, stamp 2nd, symbol 5th

lone 2nd: alone 1st, apart 3rd, exclusive 6th, free K, independent 3rd, individual 3rd, one K, separate 3rd, single 3rd, solitary 5th, unique 6th

lonely 2nd: lonesome 2nd, separate 3rd, solitary 5th

long 1st:

    A. covet 6th, crave 6th, desire 5th, lust 6th, want K, yearn 6th

    B. extended 4th, lengthy 3rd, tedious 6th

longing 1st: desire 5th, hope K, lust 6th, want K, wish K

look K:

    A. appear 2nd, gaze 5th, glance 3rd, inspect 5th, observe 3rd, peek 2nd, see K, seem 1st, watch 1st

    B. appearance 3rd, aspect 5th, front 1st, sight 1st, view 2nd

loom 5th:

    A. weave 4th

    B. appear 2nd, arise 4th, emerge 5th, hover 5th, spin 1st, threaten 5th

loop 5th: band 1st, bow 1st, circle K, coil 5th, curl 2nd, hoop 5th, ring 1st

loose 3rd: casual 5th, easy 1st, feeble 4th, floppy 6th, limp 5th, reckless 5th, relaxed 4th, vague 5th, wild 2nd, untied 5th

lope 5th: bound 2nd, hop K, hurry 1st, jaunt 6th, jump K, sprint 5th

lord 2nd: chief 1st, king K, leader 2nd, master 1st, noble 3rd, president 1st, ruler 2nd

lose K: drop 1st, fail 2nd, forget 1st, give up 1st, misplace 3rd, sacrifice 4th, surrender 5th

loss K: casualty 5th, cost 1st, damage 5th, hurt K, injury 5th, penalty 5th, ruin 5th

lost K: absent 5th, confused 4th, dead 1st, extinct 5th, forgotten 2nd, gone 1st, missing 1st

lot K:

    A. land K, mass 3rd, plot 4th, property 3rd

    B. batch 2nd, bunch 3rd, chance 2nd, destiny 5th, division 4th, fate 3rd, fortune 3rd, luck 1st, much 1st, part K, piece 1st

lots 5th: enough 1st, full K, plenty 1st

loud 1st: conspicuous 5th, flashy 2nd, glaring 4th, noisy 5th, shrill 5th, vocal 2nd

lounge 6th:

    A. loaf 4th, recline 6th, relax 4th, repose 6th, rest 1st

    B. bar 3rd, couch 4th, den 1st, idle 4th, inn 4th, pub 1st, saloon 6th, tavern 5th

love K:

    A. adore 4th, cherish 5th, desire 5th, honor 1st, idolize 6th, like K, prize 3rd, treasure 4th, value 2nd, worship 4th

B. affection 4th, care K, devotion 5th, emotion 4th, friendship 2nd, passion 6th, romance 5th, sympathy 4th

lovely 1st: attractive 5th, beautiful 1st, delicate 5th, elegant 5th, pretty 1st

low K:

A. sad K

B. base 1st, beneath 1st, cheap 3rd, down K, economical 4th, humble 4th, inferior 5th, inexpensive 4th, short 1st, under K

lowland 6th: flat 2nd, meadow 3rd, plain 2nd, prairie 4th

loyal 5th: constant 4th, dedicated 6th, devoted 5th, faithful 3rd, honest 3rd, sincere 4th, steady 3rd, true 1st, trusted 2nd

luck 1st: chance 2nd, destiny 5th, fate 3rd, fortune 3rd

lucky K: fortunate 4th, happy K

lug 1st: carry 1st, drag 5th, haul 4th, pack 1st, pull K, transport 5th

luggage 4th: bag 1st, case 2nd, packs 1st, suitcases 1st

lull 5th: break 1st, delay 5th, gap K, idle 4th, pause 3rd, rest 1st, wait 1st

lumber 1st:

A. boards 1st, logs K, wood 1st

B. drag 3rd, persist 5th, plod 5th

lumbering 1st: awkward 6th, clumsy 6th

lumberman 1st: logger 4th, woodsman 3rd

lump 4th:

A. blend 5th, combine 3rd, group 1st, mix 1st, unite 5th

B. ball K, batch 2nd, bulge 4th, mass 3rd, stack 6th, swelling 3rd

lunatic 6th: absurd 6th, crazy 4th, foolish 2nd, insane 6th, mad K

lunch 1st: buffet 6th, fare 3rd, food K, meal 3rd

lunge 6th: dive 1st, drive 1st, leap 3rd, lurch 5th, plunge 4th, poke 1st

lurch 5th: drive 1st, fall K, lunge 6th, reel 5th, stagger 4th, stumble 4th

lure 5th: attract 5th, bait 3rd, charm 3rd, flirt 6th, invite 3rd, tempt 4th, trap 1st

lurk 5th: hide 1st, prowl 2nd, sneak 4th, tiptoe 4th

lush 6th: generous 4th, lavish 6th, rich 1st, sensual 5th

lust 6th:

A. craving 6th, hunger 2nd, longing 1st, need 1st

B. covet 6th, crave 6th, desire 5th, long 1st, need 1st, passion 6th

luster 4th: brilliance 4th, glitter 4th, glory 3rd, glow 1st, polish 4th, shimmer 5th, shine 1st

luxury 4th: comfort 3rd, ease 3rd, elegance 5th, pleasure 2nd, treat 2nd, . wealth 3rd

ma'am 6th: lady 1st, madam 4th, Mrs. K

machine 1st: device 4th, engine 3rd, instrument 3rd, mechanism 6th, motor 4th, tool 1st

machinery 1st: equipment 5th, gear 1st

mad K:
    A. absurd 6th, crazy 4th, foolish 3rd, insane 6th
    B. angry 1st, annoyed 5th, enraged 6th, fierce 4th, stormy 2nd, upset 3rd,
       violent 5th, wild 2nd
madam 4th: lady 1st, ma'am 6th, Mrs. K
magazine 3rd: journal 2nd, publication 4th
magic 1st: spell 1st, witchcraft 3rd
magician 5th: witch K, wizard 6th
magistrate 6th: judge 1st
magnetize 3rd: attract 5th, drag 3rd, lure 5th, pull K
magnificent 4th: awesome 6th, beautiful 1st, brilliant 4th, glorious 3rd,
    grand 2nd, great 1st, splendid 4th, terrific 5th, wonderful 1st
magnify 3rd: enhance 5th, enlarge 5th, expand 5th, increase 3rd, maximize 6th
maid 3rd: girl K, housekeeper 3rd, servant 3rd
maiden 4th:
    A. girl K, maid 3rd
    B. earliest 2nd, first 1st, initial 6th, original 3rd
mail 1st:
    A. letter 1st, package 4th
    B. deliver 5th, post 1st, send 1st, ship 1st
mailman 1st: postal carrier 5th, postman 1st
maim 4th: cripple 5th, disable 3rd, harm 3rd, hurt K, injure 5th
main 3rd: central 3rd, chief 1st, dominant 5th, first 1st, foremost 6th,
    leading 1st, major 3rd, most 1st, primary 5th, prime 5th, principal 3rd,
    supreme 5th, top K
mainland 5th: continent 4th, shore 2nd
maintain 4th: argue 3rd, assert 6th, believe 1st, claim 2nd, contend 5th,
    continue 2nd, encourage 4th, fix 1st, keep K, preserve 4th, provide 3rd,
    repair 4th, save 1st, say K, service 5th, support 4th
maize 2nd: corn 2nd, yellow K
majesty 4th: magnificence 4th, royalty 3rd
major 3rd: big K, critical 5th, dominant 5th, grand 2nd, huge 1st, important 1st,
    key K, large K, leading 1st, main 3rd, primary 5th, principal 3rd, serious 4th,
    sizeable 2nd, vital 5th
majority 3rd: bulk 4th, mass 3rd, most 1st
make K: assemble 4th, build 1st, cause 2nd, compel 3rd, construct 3rd,
    craft 2nd, create 3rd, develop 5th, earn 2nd, erect 4th, force K, form 1st,
    manufacture 3rd, prepare 1st, produce 2nd
maker 1st: builder 1st, creator 4th, manufacturer 3rd, producer 3rd
male 4th: boy K, chap 4th, gentleman 3rd, fellow 1st, guy 1st, lad K, man K
malice 6th: anger 1st, dislike 3rd, grudge 5th, hate 2nd, spite 3rd
malignant 6th: bad K, harmful 3rd, ominous 6th

malinger 6th: delay 5th, idle 4th, lag 1st, linger 4th, loaf 4th, lounge 6th

mall K: business 2nd, market 1st, shop 1st, store K

malt 2nd: dessert 1st, ice cream 1st, milkshake 2nd

mama 1st: mom K, mother K

mammoth 5th: giant 2nd, great K, huge 1st, immense 4th, massive 5th, vast 4th

man K: chap 4th, citizen 3rd, fellow 1st, gentleman 3rd, guy 1st, human 3rd, individual 3rd, male 4th, person 1st

manage 4th: contend 5th, control 2nd, cope 6th, direct 1st, govern 1st, handle 2nd, lead 1st, operate 3rd, oversee 3rd, run K, supervise 6th

mane 1st: fur K, hair K

manifest 5th:
  A. appear 2nd, develop 5th, display 3rd, exhibit 4th, express 5th, happen 1st, occur 3rd, reveal 4th, show 1st
  B. apparent 3rd, clear 2nd, distinct 5th, plain 2nd, obvious 5th, true 1st

mankind 4th: humanity 3rd, people K, world 1st

manly K: bold 2nd, brave 1st, male 4th, mighty 1st, powerful 2nd, strong K, tough 5th

manner 1st: code 3rd, custom 6th, fashion 3rd, habit 3rd, method 2nd, mode 5th, practice 1st, routine 6th, style 3rd, tone 3rd, use K, way K

mansion 5th: castle 3rd, estate 4th, palace 1st

mantel 4th: ledge 5th, shelf 6th

mantle 4th: cape 4th, cloak 4th, coat 1st, jacket 3rd, shawl 6th, wrap 4th

manufacture 3rd: assemble 4th, build 1st, construct 3rd, develop 5th, fabricate 5th, form 1st, make K, produce 2nd

manure 5th: fertilizer 5th

manuscript 6th: book K

many K: enough 1st, host 4th, legion 6th, lots 1st, numerous 4th, plenty 1st

map 1st: chart 1st, design 5th, outline 4th, plan 1st, plot 4th

mar 6th: damage 5th, harm 3rd, hurt 1st, injure 5th, spoil 4th

marble 4th:
  A. agate 4th, alabaster 4th
  B. ball K, orb 4th, sphere 6th

march 1st: advance 2nd, continue 2nd, depart 5th, go K, hike 3rd, leave 1st, parade 2nd, progress 4th, stride 5th, tramp 4th, walk K

mare 4th: horse K, mount 2nd

margin 5th: border 1st, boundary 4th, edge 1st, limit 3rd, rim 1st

marine 5th: sea K, water 1st

mark 1st:
  A. brand 2nd, imprint 4th, note 1st, print 1st, sign 1st, stamp 2nd

B. accent 6th, approval 4th, clue 2nd, dent 1st, emblem 5th, feature 3rd, flag 3rd, grade 2nd, level 3rd, name K, notice 1st, quality 4th, signature 6th, spot 1st

market 1st: bazaar 5th, fair 1st, shop 1st, store K

marrow 5th: center 2nd, core 6th, essence 6th, heart K, spirit 2nd

marry 1st: attach 5th, blend 5th, bond 3rd, combine 3rd, couple 3rd, cross 1st, join 3rd, mate 4th, pair 1st, unite 5th, wed K

marsh 5th: bog 5th, mud 1st, swamp 4th

marshal 5th:
A. officer 1st, police 1st
B. assemble 4th, call 1st, gather 1st, group 1st, order 1st, organize 4th, rally 5th

martyr 6th:
A. sacrifice 4th
B. victim 4th

marvel 4th: miracle 5th, wonder 1st

marvelous 4th: excellent 1st, good K, great 1st, mysterious 3rd, super 1st, unique 6th, wonderful 1st

mash 4th: beat 1st, crush 4th, pound 2nd, squash 2nd, squeeze 5th

mask 2nd:
A. costume 4th, cover 1st, disguise 5th
B. camouflage 6th, conceal 4th, cover 1st, disguise 5th, hide 1st, obscure 6th, pretend 2nd, shield 4th

mason 5th: bricklayer 4th

mass 3rd: abundance 5th, bulk 4th, collection 4th, lot K, lump 4th, majority 3rd, much 1st, plenty 1st, size 1st, stack 3rd, stock 1st, total 2nd, whole 1st

massacre 6th: butcher 4th, destroy 2nd, kill 1st, murder 3rd, slaughter 5th, slay 4th

massive 5th: big K, giant 2nd, huge 1st, immense 4th, large K, mammoth 5th, powerful 2nd

master 1st:
A. conquer 4th, defeat 5th, dominate 5th, learn 1st
B. ace 2nd, artist 1st, champion 4th, expert 5th, guide 1st, leader 2nd, lord 2nd, ruler 2nd, teacher 1st

mat K: carpet 4th, mattress 6th, pad K, rug 1st

match 3rd:
A. compare 3rd, copy 3rd, equal 2nd, meet K, sort 2nd
B. bout 6th, competition 5th, contest 4th, copy 3rd, equal 2nd, for 4th, game 1st, like K, mate 4th, opponent 5th, tie 1st

matching 3rd: alike 1st, comparable 3rd, equal 2nd, same 1st, similar 4th

mate 4th:
A. join 3rd, marry 1st, unite 5th, wed K

B. associate 5th, blend 5th, buddy 4th, equal 2nd, friend 1st, match 3rd, pal 1st

material 5th:
   A. important 1st, physical 5th, real 1st, vital 5th
   B. cloth 1st, fabric 5th, matter 1st, substance 5th

mathematical 5th: exact 2nd, numerical 5th, precise 5th

mathematics 5th: addition 3rd, arithmetic 3rd, math 3rd

matter 1st: affair 2nd, business 2nd, concern 3rd, elements 3rd, issue 4th, material 5th, stuff 1st, substance 5th

mattress 6th: bed K, mat K, pad K

mature 5th:
   A. age 1st, develop 5th, evolve 5th, grow 1st, unfold 2nd
   B. adult 1st, aged 1st, experienced 3rd, grown 1st, mellow 6th, ripe 1st

maturity 6th: adulthood 2nd, age 1st

maxim 6th: moral 3rd, proverb 3rd, rule 2nd, saying 1st, teaching 1st, truth 1st

maximum 6th:
   A. ceiling 4th, extreme 5th, most 1st
   B. best K, biggest 1st, greatest 1st, largest 1st, most 1st, top K

may K: allowed 2nd, can K

maybe 1st: perhaps 1st, possibly 2nd

mayor 1st: leader 2nd, manager 4th

me K: I K, myself 1st, self 3rd

meadow 3rd: field 2nd, grassland 1st, mead 6th

meal 3rd: banquet 4th, breakfast 1st, dinner 2nd, feast 1st, food K, lunch 1st, supper 2nd

mean 1st:
   A. imply 5th, intend 6th, plan 1st
   B. awful 3rd, bad K, base 1st, cheap 3rd, common 2nd, cruel 5th, little K, small 1st, tough 5th, unkind 2nd

mean (average) 5th: average 3rd, halfway 3rd, middle 2nd, standard 3rd

meaning 3rd: content 3rd, explanation 2nd, goal 4th, importance 1st, intent 5th, message 1st, purpose 1st, sense 1st, significance 6th

measure 2nd:
   A. divide 4th
   B. degree 5th, extent 4th, fit K, guide 1st, law 1st, length 2nd, portion 4th, rule 2nd, scope 6th, share 2nd, size 1st, standard 3rd, test 3rd

meat 1st: beef 2nd, food K

mechanic 5th: engineer 4th, operator 5th

mechanical 6th: automatic 6th, robotic 2nd

mechanism 6th: apparatus 6th, engine 3rd, machine 1st, motor 4th

medal 6th: award 5th, honor 1st, prize 3rd, recognition 4th, reward 4th, ribbon 4th, trophy 6th

meddle 6th: fiddle 4th, interfere 4th, intrude 6th, poke 1st, pry 6th

mediate 5th: arrange 3rd, bargain 4th, settle 2nd, umpire 1st

medicine 4th: cure 4th, drug 1st, prescription 6th, remedy 4th, treatment 5th

meditate 6th: consider 2nd, contemplate 6th, ponder 6th, reflect 4th, think 1st

medium 5th:

    A. average 3rd, common 2nd, mean 1st, middle 2nd, ordinary 3rd

    B. agency 5th, agent 5th, channel 4th, instrument 3rd, psychic 6th

meek 2nd: humble 4th, mild 4th, modest 4th, tame 4th

meet K:

    A. adjoin 6th, confer 4th, connect 3rd, date 1st, encounter 4th, fill 1st, fit K, fulfill 4th, greet 3rd, join 3rd, link 5th, match 3rd, satisfy 3rd, see K, unite 5th, visit 1st, welcom 1st

    B. competition 4th, contest 4th, encounter 4th, game 1st

    C. desirable 5th, equal 2nd, just 1st, proper 3rd, right K, useful 2nd

melancholy 6th: depressed 5th, gloomy 3rd, meditative 6th, sad K, sorrow 4th, woeful 4th

mellow 6th:

    A. soften 2nd, tame 4th, temper 4th

    B. aged 1st, gentle 3rd, mature 5th, mild 4th, musical 5th, ripe 1st, soft K, tame 4th

melody 4th: harmony 4th, music K, song K, tune 1st

melon 3rd: fruit 2nd

melt 2nd: defrost 4th, warm 1st

member 1st: associate 5th, individual 3rd, limb 4th, part 1st

memory 3rd: recall 3rd, reminder 3rd

menace 5th:

    A. attack 3rd, frighten 2nd, threaten 5th

    B. danger 1st, hazard 6th, threat 5th

mend 1st: correct 3rd, cure 4th, fix 1st, heal 3rd, patch 4th, remedy 4th, repair 4th

mental 5th: logical 6th, psychological 6th, thinking 2nd

mention 5th: indicate 4th, quote 5th, refer to 5th

menu 6th: fare 3rd, list 2nd

merchandise 6th: goods K, products 4th, stock 1st, wares 5th

merchant 3rd: dealer 2nd, seller 1st, trader 2nd

mercy 4th: care K, charity 4th, forgiveness 3rd, grace 3rd, kindness 2nd, tenderness 3rd

mere 3rd: only K, simply 2nd

merit 4th:

    A. deserve 4th

    B. excellence 2nd, quality 4th, value 2nd, worth 3rd

merry 3rd: bright 1st, cheerful 3rd, festive 5th, gay 1st, happy K, joyful 2nd, sunny 1st

mess 1st: confusion 4th, clutter 4th, difficulty 5th, disorder 2nd, jam K, tangle 3rd

message 1st: intent 5th, letter 1st, meaning 1st, understanding 1st

meter 2nd:
  A. dial 5th
  B. indicate 4th, measure 2nd

method 2nd: action 1st, fashion 3rd, form 1st, mode 5th, order 1st, plan 1st, procedure 4th, process 4th, routine 6th, system 2nd, way K

metropolitan 6th: central 2nd, downtown 1st

microscope 4th: lens 1st, magnifier 4th

middle 2nd:
  A. center 2nd, core 6th, halfway 3rd
  B. central 3rd, halfway 3rd, medium 5th

might 1st: authority 3rd, force 1st, muscle 4th, power 1st, strength 2nd

migrant 4th: drifter 2nd, traveler 2nd, wanderer 4th

mild 4th: gentle 3rd, kind K, mellow 6th, soft K, tender 3rd

milestone 5th: event 3rd, marker 1st, occasion 3rd

military 3rd: army 1st, soldiers 3rd

mill 1st:
  A: crush 4th, grind 4th
  B. factory 1st, plant K

mimic 6th: ape K, copy 3rd, imitate 5th, mime 6th

mince 6th: chop 2nd, slice 5th

mind 1st:
  A. attend 3rd, care 1st, comply 6th, consider 2nd, heed 4th, listen 1st, look K, obey 3rd, object 1st, observe 3rd, watch 1st
  B. attitude 5th, bent K, brain 3rd, brilliance 4th, head 1st, intellect 4th, learning 1st, mood 3rd, self 3rd, sense 1st, slant 6th, spirit 2nd, wit 1st

mingle 4th: blend 5th, combine 3rd, connect 3rd, join 3rd, mix 1st, stir 3rd, unite 5th

miniature 6th: little K, small 1st, tiny 2nd

minimum 6th: base 1st, bottom 1st, least 2nd, lowest 2nd, smallest 2nd

minister 4th: aid 2nd, clergy 6th, cleric 6th, pastor 4th, priest 4th

minnow 4th: fish K

minor 5th:
  A. assistant 4th, child K, teenager 3rd, youth 2nd
  B. casual 5th, lesser 1st, little K, low K, petty 6th, picky 1st, secondary 3rd, slight 4th, small 1st

minstrel 5th: musician 4th, singer 1st

mint 5th:
  A. fortune 3rd
  B. fresh 2nd, new K, perfect 3rd, unused 2nd
minus 1st: deduct 2nd, from K, less 1st, subtract 1st, take 1st
minute 1st: invisible 6th, little K, small 1st, tiny 2nd
miracle 5th: blessing 3rd, marvel 4th, wonder 1st
mirror 4th: glass 1st, lens 1st, reflection 4th
mirth 5th: amusement 4th, cheer 3rd, delight 3rd, glee 5th, happiness 2nd,
  joy 1st, laughter 2nd, merriment 3rd
mischief 4th: adventure 3rd, harm 3rd, joke 1st, prank 5th, trouble 1st
miserable 4th: burden 5th, misfortune 5th, pitiful 3rd, poor K, sad K,
  sadness 1st, shabby 4th, sorrow 4th
misery 4th: agony 5th, distress 5th, pain 2nd, suffering 2nd
misfortune 5th: accident 4th, burden 5th, curse 3rd, disaster 6th, evil 3rd,
  hardship 5th, tragedy 5th, trouble 1st
mislead 5th: cheat 3rd, deceive 5th, misdirect 2nd, trick 1st
miss K:
  A. girl K, lass 1st
  B. long for 1st, regret 5th
  C. disregard 4th, fail K, fall short 1st, overlook 4th
mission 5th: assignment 5th, commission 2nd, concern 3rd, effort 2nd, goal 4th,
  job K, purpose 2nd, task 3rd
mist 1st: cloud 1st, fog 1st, light rain 1st, steam 2nd, vapor 3rd
mistake 1st: error 4th, misunderstanding 2nd, slip 3rd
mistreat 3rd: abuse 6th, hurt K, wrong 1st
mistress 4th: female 4th, lady 1st, lover 1st, woman K
misunderstanding 2nd: disagreement 2nd, dispute 6th, falling out 2nd,
  mistake 1st
misuse 3rd: abuse 6th, mistreat 3rd
mitten 1st: glove 4th
mix 1st:
  A. combination 3rd, compound 4th, mess 1st
  B. blend 5th, combine 3rd, merge 4th, mingle 4th, scramble 4th, stir 3rd,
    unite 5th
mixed 1st: amid 4th, between 1st
mixture 4th: blend 5th, combination 3rd, compound 4th
mix-up 2nd: complicate 6th, confuse 4th, rearrange 3rd, scramble 4th
moan 5th: cry 1st, groan 3rd, sigh 3rd, wail 5th, weep 4th, whine 5th
mob 4th: crowd 2nd, gang 1st, group 1st, herd 2nd, horde 6th, pack 1st
mobile 6th: loose 3rd, moveable 2nd, moving 1st, restless 4th
mobilize 6th: drive 1st, motivate 6th, move K, propel 6th, push 1st, rally 5th,
  start 1st

moccasin 2nd: boot 1st, shoe 1st, slipper 5th

mock 4th:

    A. fake 1st, false 3rd, imitation 5th, pretend 2nd, sham 5th

    B. ape 5th, copy 3rd, imitate 5th, jeer 5th, mimic 6th, sneer 6th, tease 3rd

mode 5th:

    A. fad K, fashion 3rd, style 3rd

    B. agency 5th, channel 4th, condition 3rd, instrument 3rd, manner 2nd, means 1st, mechanism 6th, method 2nd, process 4th, state 1st, tone 3rd, vein 4th, way K

model 3rd:

    A. demonstrate 6th, pose 2nd

    B. classic 5th, hero 1st, ideal 3rd, idol 6th

    C. copy 3rd, example 2nd, image 4th, miniature 6th, mock-up 6th, pattern 3rd, reproduction 5th, sample 5th, symbol 5th, test 3rd, typical 6th

moderate 4th:

    A. cheap 3rd, inexpensive 3rd, reasonable 3rd

    B. chair 1st, lead 1st, preside 6th, regulate 5th

    C. gradual 3rd, mild 4th, reasonable 1st, temperate 4th

    D. ease 3rd, lessen 2nd, lighten 1st, soften 1st

modern 2nd: contemporary 5th, late K, new K, recent 3rd

modest 4th: humble 4th, meek 2nd, moderate 4th, plain 2nd, proper 3rd, pure 3rd, reasonable 1st, shy 1st, simple 2nd, temperate 5th, timid 5th

modify 5th: adapt 4th, adjust 5th, alter 4th, change 2nd, edit 3rd, fix 1st, move K, reform 5th, vary 4th

moist 4th: damp 5th, juicy 1st, misty 1st, watery 1st, wet K

moisture 3rd: dampness 5th, mist 1st, water K, wetness 2nd

mold 5th:

    A. decay 5th, fungus 5th

    B. cast 2nd, fashion 3rd, form 1st, shape 1st

molecule 5th: particle 5th, piece 1st

moment 1st:

    A. importance 1st

    B. instant 3rd, minute 1st, occasion 3rd, second 1st

momentum 6th: energy 4th, impulse 5th, movement 2nd

monarch 5th: king 1st, lord 3rd, queen 1st, ruler 2nd

monastery 5th: abbey 6th, convent 6th

money K: cash 2nd, coins 3rd, currency 3rd, funds 4th

monk 4th: abbot 6th, brother 1st, friar 5th, hermit 5th

monopoly 6th: controlling 2nd, exclusive 6th

monster 1st: beast 3rd, creature 3rd, giant 2nd

monstrous 5th:

    A. giant 2nd, gigantic 5th, huge 1st, immense 4th, massive 5th, vast 4th

B. awful 3rd, offensive 4th, enormous 5th, outrageous 6th, uncivilized 4th, wicked 4th

monument 2nd: legacy 5th, memorial 5th, shrine 5th, statue 4th

mood 3rd: attitude 5th, climate 4th, feeling 1st, humor 4th, outlook 2nd, spirit 2nd, temper 4th

moon 1st: satellite 6th

moor 5th: anchor 4th, secure 3rd

mop 1st: bathe 3rd, clean 1st, launder 6th, scour 6th, scrub 6th, wash 1st, wipe 1st

mope 5th: brood 4th, sulk 5th

moral 3rd:
   A. belief 1st, ethic 5th, truth 1st, virtue 4th
   B. decent 6th, ethical 5th, honest 3rd, honorable 3rd, pure 3rd, responsible 4th, right K, stable 4th, upright 4th, virtuous 4th

more K: above 1st, added 1st, additional 3rd, besides 1st, extra 1st, further 2nd, greater 1st, other 1st, over 1st, superior 4th, surplus 6th

moreover 3rd: additionally 3rd, also K, besides 1st, furthermore 3rd

morning 1st: a.m. 6th, daylight 1st, morn 1st, sunrise 2nd

morsel 5th: bit 1st, bite 1st, dab 1st, dot K, particle 5th, piece 1st, sample 5th, snack 2nd, speck 4th, taste 1st

mortal 4th:
   A. deadly 1st, fatal 4th
   B. alive 3rd, human 3rd, living 1st

mortgage 6th: borrow 2nd, debt 3rd, loan 4th, obligation 6th, payment 1st

mosque 5th: church 1st, house of God 1st, sanctuary 6th, temple 3rd

moss 1st: algae 5th, fungus 5th

most 1st: almost all K, best K, greatest 1st, larger 1st, majority 3rd, prime 5th, superior 4th, usually 3rd

mother K:
   A. care 1st, protect 4th, raise 1st, root 3rd, source 4th, start 1st
   B. mama 1st, mom K, parent 3rd

motion 3rd:
   A. bid 1st, offer 2nd, proposal 4th, request 4th
   B. change 2nd, flow 1st, gesture 4th, move K, movement 2nd, progress 4th, signal 4th

motivate 6th: animate 6th, compel 3rd, drive 1st, encourage 4th, excite 4th, force 1st, inspire 4th, move K, persuade 5th, prompt 4th, propel 6th, provoke 6th, rouse 4th, spark 5th, spur 4th, start 1st, stimulate 6th, urge 4th

motive 5th: aim 3rd, cause 2nd, goal 4th, intention 6th, motivation 6th, principle 4th, reason 2nd

motor 4th: engine 3rd, machine 1st

motto 6th: saying 1st

mound 2nd: heap 3rd, hill 1st, hump 3rd, mount 2nd, pile 1st, stack 6th

mount 2nd:

    A. horse K, steed 4th

    B. ascend 4th, climb 1st, crest 4th, hill 1st, increase 3rd, rise 1st, scale 3rd

mountain 2nd: hill 1st, mount 2nd, peak 4th

mourn 4th: cry 1st, grieve 5th, lament 6th, sorrow 4th, weep 4th

mouth 1st: access 6th, entrance 3rd, inlet 4th, opening 1st

move K:

    A. strategy 6th, tactic 6th

    B. impress 5th, motivate 6th, persuade 5th, sadden 3rd

    C. adjust 5th, advance 2nd, change 2nd, continue 2nd, leave 1st, plan 1st, push 1st, shift 4th

movement 2nd: action 1st, animation 6th, change 2nd, drift 2nd, gesture 4th, motion 3rd, progress 4th, traffic 5th

movie 1st: film 4th, moving picture 1st

moving 1st: active 3rd, animated 6th, mobile 6th

much 1st: full K, lot K, many K, myriad 6th, plenty 1st

mud 1st: dirt 1st

multiply 2nd: breed 4th, double 3rd, enlarge 5th, expand 5th, grow K, increase 3rd

mumble 4th: babble 6th, murmur 4th, mutter 4th, whisper 1st

municipal 6th: city K, civic 3rd, civil 3rd, public 1st

murder 3rd: butcher 4th, execute 5th, finish 1st, kill 1st, shooting 3rd, slaughter 5th, slay 4th, strangle 6th

murmur 4th: babble 6th, gossip 5th, mumble 4th, mutter 4th, rumor 5th, whisper 1st

muscle 4th: energy 4th, force 1st, might 1st, power 1st, strength 2nd

museum 4th: exhibit hall 4th, gallery 5th

music K: harmony 4th, melody 4th, rhythm 6th, song K, tune 1st

musical 5th: harmonious 4th, melodious 4th, tuneful 1st

musician 4th: performer 4th, player 1st, singer 1st

musket 5th: gun K, rifle 4th

muss 1st: crease 5th, disorder 3rd, displace 2nd, disturb 6th, fold 1st, mess 1st, wrinkle 3rd

must 1st: essential 6th, have to K, requirement 3rd

muster 6th: assemble 4th, call 1st, cause 2nd, collect 3rd, crowd 2nd, enlist 6th, gather 1st, generate 4th, group 1st, mass 3rd, rally 5th, recruit 6th

mute 6th: dumb 1st, gag 1st, quiet K, silence 3rd, silent 3rd, speechless 2nd

mutiny 6th: challenge 4th, dare 2nd, defy 6th, revolt 5th, treason 4th

mutt 4th: canine 5th, dog K, hound 2nd

mutter 4th: babble 6th, grumble 5th, mumble 4th, murmur 4th, whisper 1st

mutton 5th: lamb 1st, sheep 1st

mutual 5th: common 2nd, joint 4th, shared 2nd

muzzle 6th:
  A. mouth 1st, nose 1st, snout 5th
  B. gag 1st, restraint 5th, silence 3rd

myriad 6th: bunch 3rd, extensive 4th, legion 6th, many K, numerous 4th, plenty 1st, thousands 1st, tons 1st

myself 1st: me K, I K

mystery 1st:
  A. miracle 5th, secret 1st, wonder 1st
  B. problem 1st, puzzle 4th, question 1st, riddle 1st

mystic 4th: concealed 4th, hidden 1st, mysterious 4th, private 3rd, secret 1st, spiritual 5th

myth 4th: fable 5th, fantasy 5th, fiction 5th, legend 5th, tale 3rd

nab 1st: arrest 3rd, capture 3rd, catch 1st, clutch 4th, get K, grab 4th, seize 3rd, steal 3rd, take 1st

nag 1st: annoy 5th, badger 2nd, bother 2nd, complain 4th, fault 3rd, fuss 1st, gripe 5th, grumble 5th, mutter 4th, object 1st, pester 2nd, scold 5th

nail 2nd:
  A. attach 5th, connect 3rd, fasten 4th, join 3rd, staple 6th, tack 1st
  B. capture 3rd, catch 1st, get K, seize 3rd
  C. grab 4th, hit K, nab 1st, peg 1st, pin K, strike 2nd

naked 4th: bare 3rd, exposed 4th, plain 2nd, stark 1st, stripped 3rd, uncovered 2nd

name K:
  A. alias 6th, reputation 5th, signature 6th, term 3rd, title 3rd
  B. celebrity 5th, star K
  C. appoint 3rd, call 1st, identify 4th, label 3rd, select 4th, specify 5th

nap K: recline 6th, rest 1st, sleep 1st

napkin 5th: cloth 1st, towel 6th

napping 1st: asleep 3rd, resting 1st, sleeping 1st

narrate 6th: explain 2nd, express 5th, inform 5th, read K, recite 5th, relate 4th, report 1st, reveal 4th, review 4th, state 1st, tell K

narrow 2nd:
  A. limit 3rd, reduce 3rd, select 4th, taper 5th
  B. ignorant 4th, limited 3rd, strict 6th
  C. focused 5th, slender 4th, small 1st, thin 2nd, tight 1st

nation 1st: clan 5th, country K, empire 4th, government 1st, land K, race 1st, realm 4th, society 3rd, state 1st, tribe 3rd

native 1st: citizen 3rd, domestic 5th, local 3rd, national 2nd, natural 2nd, original 3rd

natural 2nd:
> A. basic 5th, common 2nd, genuine 5th, honest 3rd, native 1st, normal 5th, plain 2nd, real 1st, simple 2nd, wild 2nd
>
> B. automatic 6th, expected 3rd, instinct 5th, unforced 3rd, usual 3rd

naturalist 6th: nature lover 1st, ranger 1st

nature 1st:
> A. outside 1st, universe 4th, world 1st
>
> B. character 2nd, core 6th, disposition 5th, division 4th, essence 6th, fiber 3rd, heart K, make up K, personality 5th, quality 4th, spirit 2nd, substance 5th, temperament 4th, tendency 5th, tone 3rd, type 1st

naught 5th: defeat 5th, empty 3rd, failure 2nd, none 1st, nothing 1st, ruin 5th, void 6th, zero K

naughty 5th: bad 1st, bratty 3rd, playful 1st, wicked 4th

navigate 5th: command 2nd, direct 1st, guide 1st, journey 3rd, pilot 5th, sail 1st, steer 5th

nay 4th: against 1st, no K

near 1st: about K, approach 3rd, around 1st, beside 1st, close K, nearby 1st

nearing 1st: approaching 3rd, coming K

nearly 1st: almost 1st, barely 3rd, hardly 1st

neat K: clean K, ordered 1st, plain 2nd, straight 3rd, tidy 2nd

necessary 1st: basic 5th, essential 6th, important 1st, must 1st, needed 1st, required 2nd, vital 5th

need 1st:
> A. charge 2nd, duty 1st
>
> B. demand 5th, desire 5th, emergency 5th, lack 1st, miss K, necessity 3rd, poverty 5th, require 1st, want K
>
> C. defect 5th, fault 3rd, flaw 2nd

needle 3rd:
> A. annoy 5th, bug K, pester 2nd, pick on 1st, tease 3rd
>
> B. pin K, point 1st, sew 2nd

negative 6th: against 1st, complaining 4th, critical 5th, denying 5th, harmful 3rd, opposing 3rd, opposite 3rd, unfavorable 3rd

neglect 4th: abandon 4th, absence 5th, carelessness 5th, disregard 4th, exclude 6th, forget 1st, ignore 5th, laziness 4th, miss K, negligence 4th, omission 6th, omit 6th, overlook 4th, pass 2nd, shirk 6th, slight 4th

neighbor 2nd:
> A. acquaintance 4th, person next door 1st
>
> B. border 1st, connect 3rd, meet K, touch 1st

neighborhood 2nd: area 3rd, closeness 1st, district 4th, locale 3rd, nearness 2nd, region 4th, section 4th, suburbs 6th

nervous 1st: afraid 1st, alarmed 3rd, anxious 4th, concerned 3rd, edgy 2nd, excitable 4th, excited 4th, hysterical 6th, restless 4th, scared 1st, tense 5th, timid 5th, troubled 1st, uncertain 3rd, uneasy 3rd, upset 3rd, worried 1st

nest 1st: brood 4th, den 1st, dwelling 4th, home K, refuge 5th, retreat 4th, roost 2nd, shelter 4th

net 3rd:
A. bag 1st, trap 1st
B. attain 6th, earn 2nd, gain 2nd, get K, obtain 5th, profit 4th, return 2nd, take 1st, win 1st, worth 3rd, yield 4th

nettle 4th: anger 3rd, annoy 5th, bother 2nd, disturb 6th, irk 6th, irritate 6th, pester 2nd, pick on 1st, upset 3rd, vex 5th

neutral 6th:
A. pale 3rd, uncolored 3rd
B. detached 5th, fair 1st, free K, impartial 6th, impersonal 3rd, independent 3rd, indifferent 3rd, objective 2nd, peaceful 2nd

never K: at no time 1st, not ever K

nevertheless 4th: anyway 1st, but K, however 3rd, nonetheless 5th, notwithstanding 4th, so K, still 1st

new K: contemporary 5th, first 1st, fresh 2nd, green K, latest 1st, modern 2nd, novel 5th, original 3rd, pioneer 4th, raw 1st, recent 3rd, unique 6th, unknown 3rd, unused 3rd, unusual 3rd, young 1st

newspaper 1st: bulletin 3rd, journal 2nd, publication 4th

next K:
A. following 1st, future 5th, latter 3rd
B. adjoining 6th, beside 1st, closest 1st, later 1st, nearest 2nd

nibble 4th: bite 1st, chew 1st, eat K, gnaw 1st, snack 2nd

nice 1st: agreeable 2nd, charming 3rd, cordial 6th, correct 3rd, good K, likable 1st, pleasant 3rd, polite 4th, refined 6th, sweet K

night 1st: dark 1st, evening 1st, sunset 1st, twilight 1st

nip 1st:
A. cut K, snip 2nd, stop K, stunt 6th, wither 5th
B. piece 1st, pinch 4th, sample 5th
C. bite 1st, consume 4th, drink 1st, gulp 1st, sip 1st, snack 2nd

no K: denial 5th, deny 5th, nay 4th, never K, refusal 2nd, rejection 5th

noble 3rd:
A. aristocrat 6th, gallant 4th, gentleman 3rd, gentlewoman 3rd, grand 2nd, imperial 5th, lady 1st, lofty 5th, lordly 3rd, majestic 4th, regal 6th, royal 3rd
B. ethical 5th, heroic 5th, honest 3rd, honorable 3rd, pure 3rd, true 1st, worthy 3rd

nobody 1st: no one k, not anyone 1st

nod 1st: assent 6th, consent 3rd, cue 2nd, gesture 4th, greet 3rd, motion 3rd, salute 4th, signal 4th

noise 1st: blast 2nd, clamor 6th, commotion 5th, din 6th, racket 2nd, shout 1st, sound 1st, yell K

noisy 5th: babbling 6th, blasting 2nd, harsh 5th, loud 1st, loud-mouthed 1st, riotous 6th, shouting 1st

nominate 5th: appoint 3rd, choose 3rd, designate 5th, elect 3rd, induct 5th, name K, ordain 6th, present K, select 4th, submit 4th

none 1st: no one K, not a one K, nothing 1st, zero K

nonetheless 5th: anyway 1st, but K, however 3rd, notwithstanding 4th, still 1st, yet 1st

nonfiction 5th: actual 3rd, fact 1st, history 2nd

nonsense 5th: absurdity 6th, babble 6th, folly 4th, foolishness 4th, garbage 6th, junk 3rd, ridiculousness 6th, senselessness 3rd, silliness 1st, stupidity 4th

nook 6th: cabinet 4th, cave 1st, chest 2nd, closet 2nd, crack 4th, cubby 4th, gap K, hole 1st

normal 5th: average 3rd, common 2nd, customary 6th, everyday 1st, familiar 3rd, healthy 1st, medium 5th, natural 2nd, ordinary 3rd, regular 3rd, routine 6th, standard 3rd, typical 6th, usual 3rd

nose 1st:
A. beak 4th, muzzle 6th, snout 5th
B. feel K, flair 6th, gift K, insight 2nd, knack 4th, talent 2nd

notable 5th:
A. big shot 1st, celebrity 5th, name K, star K
B. celebrated 4th, famous 2nd, outstanding 2nd, rare 4th, remarkable 4th, significant 6th, special 2nd, strange 1st, unusual 3rd, well-known 1st

notch 5th:
A. degree 5th, grade 2nd
B. carve 4th, chip 5th, cut K, dent 1st, groove 5th, mark 1st, tab K

note 1st:
A. bill 1st, check 1st, currency 3rd, money K
B. card 1st, letter 1st, memo 3rd, reminder 3rd
C. comment 5th, notice 1st, observe 3rd, record 2nd, remark 4th, see K, state 1st, watch 1st
D. honor 1st, recognize 3rd

nothing 1st: empty 3rd, naught 6th, none 1st, void 6th, zero K

notice 1st:
A. announcement 4th, poster 3rd
B. be aware 3rd, concern 3rd, consider 2nd, feel K, mark 1st, observe 3rd, recognize 3rd, regard 4th, remark 4th, see K, sense 1st, watch 1st, witness 3rd

noticeable 3rd: apparent 3rd, clear 2nd, evident 5th, observable 3rd, recognizable 3rd

notify 3rd: alert 5th, caution 5th, let know 1st, remind 3rd, report 1st, tell K, warn 3rd

notion 5th: belief 2nd, clue 2nd, concept 4th, fancy 3rd, idea 1st, guess 1st, guide 1st, hint 1st, idea 1st, impulse 5th, judgment 3rd, mind 1st, opinion 3rd, thought 1st, view 2nd, whim 6th

nourish 6th: feed 1st, help K, maintain 4th, mother K, parent 3rd, promote 5th, protect 4th, support 4th, sustain 5th

novel 5th:
    A. different 4th, fresh 2nd, latest 1st, modern 2nd, new K, original 3rd, strange 1st
    B. book K, history 2nd, fiction 5th, story 1st, tale 3rd

novice 5th: amateur 5th, beginner 2nd, student 3rd

now K: at once 1st, current 3rd, immediately 3rd, instantly 3rd, promptly 4th, quickly 1st, right away K, soon K

nuclear 6th:
    A. atomic 5th
    B. central 3rd, core 6th, focal 5th

nucleus 4th: center 2nd, core 6th, essence 6th, focus 5th, heart K, marrow 2nd, mass 3rd

nuisance 6th: annoyance 5th, bother 2nd, pain 2nd, pest 1st, problem 1st, worry 1st

number K:
    A. itemize 5th, list 2nd
    B. amount 2nd, calculation 5th, count 1st, figure 2nd, numeral 5th, quantity 4th, sum 1st, total 2nd

numeral 5th: figure 2nd, number K

numerous 4th: abundant 5th, assorted 5th, countless 5th, extensive 4th, great K, infinite 5th, many K, numberless 1st, several 1st, various 4th

nun 1st: sister 1st

nurse K:
    A. attendant 4th, governess 2nd
    B. aid 2nd, attend 3rd, care for 1st, feed 1st, help K, nourish 6th, suckle 6th

nut K:
    A. bolt 4th, peg 1st, pin K, stud 6th
    B. acorn 4th, grain 3rd, seed 1st
    C. zealot 6th

nuzzle 1st: caress 1st, cuddle 5th, hold 1st, hug 1st, nestle 2nd, pet 1st, snuggle 5th

nymph 6th: elf 1st, fairy 2nd, mermaid 4th, sea-maiden 4th

oath 5th: declaration 5th, pledge 5th, promise 1st, vow 4th, word K

obey 3rd: comply 6th, conform 6th, execute 5th, follow 1st, mind 1st, observe 3rd, serve 1st

object 1st:

    A. argue 3rd, complain 4th, disagree 3rd, grumble 5th, mind 1st, protest 4th

    B. aim 3rd, goal 4th, intention 5th, target 5th

    C. article 2nd, body 1st, element 3rd, item 5th, piece 1st, thing K

objective 2nd:

    A. fair 1st, impartial 6th

    B. aim 3rd, end K, goal 4th, intent 5th

obligation 6th: burden 5th, commitment 4th, duty 1st, guarantee 6th, pledge 5th, promise 1st, responsibility 4th, tie 1st

oblige 6th: accommodate 6th, aid 2nd, assist 4th, help K, please K

obscure 6th:

    A. clouded 1st, dark 1st, dim 1st, gloomy 3rd

    B. doubtful 5th, mysterious 3rd, mystic 4th, puzzling 4th, unclear 2nd, unknown K, vague 5th, veiled 3rd

    C. concealed 4th, invisible 6th, nameless 3rd, remote 5th, secret 1st

observe 3rd:

    A. eye 1st, examine 5th, inspect 5th, notice 1st, see K, spy 4th, study 2nd, view 2nd, watch 1st

    B. comply 6th, mind 1st, obey 3rd, understand 1st

    C. celebrate 4th, honor 1st, keep K, remember 1st

obstacle 5th: bar 3rd, barrier 6th, challenge 4th, fence 1st, hurdle 5th, interference 4th, plight 6th, problem 1st, restriction 6th

obstinate 5th: determined 5th, firm 2nd, inflexible 6th, persistent 5th, rigid 5th, stubborn 5th, unbending 3rd

obtain 5th: accomplish 2nd, achieve 5th, acquire 4th, attain 6th, buy K, earn 2nd, gain 2nd, get K, procure 5th, secure 3rd, win 1st

obvious 5th: apparent 3rd, clear 2nd, distinct 5th, evident 5th, marked 1st, noticeable 3rd, plain 2nd, prominent 5th, visible 4th

occasion 3rd:

    A. celebration 4th, festivity 5th, holiday K

    B. cause 2nd, chance 2nd, event 3rd, incident 5th, moment 1st, occurrence 4th

occupation 6th: business 2nd, career 4th, employment 5th, job K, profession 5th, task 3rd, trade 2nd, work K

occupy 3rd:

    A. capture 3rd, conquer 4th, seize 3rd

    B. absorb 5th, dwell 4th, fill 1st, live 1st, reside 5th

occur 3rd: appear 2nd, come about 2nd, develop 5th, exist 3rd, happen 1st, pass 2nd

ocean 1st:
    A. immense 4th, infinity 5th, lots K
    B. deep 1st, sea 1st, tide 1st
odd 4th: funny 1st, lone 2nd, one K, only K, peculiar 4th, single 3rd, sole 4th, strange 1st, uncommon 3rd, unique 6th, unusual 3rd, weird 1st
odor 3rd: fragrance 5th, scent 3rd, smell 3rd
off K:
    A. inaccurate 6th, incorrect 4th, wrong 1st
    B. disconnected 4th, not on 1st
    C. odd 4th, strange 1st, unusual 3rd
    D. distant 4th, far 1st, far away 3rd
offend 4th: anger 1st, annoy 5th, insult 5th, irritate 6th, outrage 6th, provoke 6th, shock 1st, sin 1st, slight 4th, upset 3rd
offensive 4th:
    A. aggressive 6th, attacking 4th, hostile 4th
    B. abusive 6th, disagreeable 3rd, disgusting 5th, displeasing 3rd, irritating 6th
offer 2nd:
    A. extend 4th, give 1st, present K, volunteer 5th
    B. attempt 2nd, try K, venture 4th
    C. approach 3rd, bid 1st, proposal 4th, suggest 2nd
office 1st:
    A. department 2nd, division 4th, job K, position 2nd, post 1st
    B. appointment 3rd, branch 2nd, capacity 6th, duty 1st, rank 3rd, task 3rd, unit 5th
officer 1st: director 2nd, executive 5th, official 3rd
official 3rd:
    A. real 1st, standard 3rd
    B. authority 3rd, clerk 2nd
    C. established 3rd
often 1st: common 2nd, frequently 4th, much 1st, regular 3rd, repeated 4th, routine 6th, usual 3rd
oh 1st: goodness 1st, my K
oil K:
    A. canvas 6th, painting 2nd, picture K
    B. annoint 6th
    C. fat 1st, grease 5th
O.K. K or okay 1st: acceptable 4th, accurate 6th, all right K, correct 3rd, good K, satisfactory 4th, well K
old K: aged 1st, ancient 3rd, antique 6th, dead 1st, elderly 5th, former 6th, late 1st, long-lived 1st, ongoing 2nd, past 1st, primitive 5th, stale 2nd, worn 3rd
older 1st: advanced 2nd, elder 5th, first 1st, mature 5th, senior 6th

omen 6th: indication 4th, sage 5th, sign 1st, warning 3rd

ominous 6th: bad K, fearful 2nd, ghostly 1st, malignant 6th, menacing 5th, odd 4th, scary 1st, strange 1st, threatening 5th

omit 6th: bar 3rd, cancel 6th, exclude 6th, forget 1st, leave out 1st, miss K, neglect 4th, remove 2nd, skip 2nd

on K: at K, atop 3rd

once 1st: before 1st, earlier 2nd, former 6th, late 1st, one time 2nd, past 1st

one K:

A. entire 3rd, undivided 4th, united 5th, whole 1st

B. individual 3rd, single 3rd

oneself 3rd: myself 2nd, yourself 2nd

only K: a K, alone 1st, but K, except 2nd, exclusive 6th, however 3rd, individual 3rd, just 1st, lone 2nd, merely 3rd, odd 4th, one K, simply 2nd, single 3rd, sole 4th, unique 6th, yet 1st

onward 3rd: ahead 1st, along 1st, before 1st, beyond 1st, forth 2nd, forward 3rd, in front 1st

open K:

A. earnest 4th, frank 4th, honest 3rd, sincere 4th

B. accessible 6th, bare 3rd, begin 1st, big K, due 2nd, expand 5th, exposed 4th, launch 5th, naked 4th, natural 2nd, owed 3rd, plain 2nd, roomy 2nd, simple 2nd, spacious 3rd, start 1st, unblock 2nd, uncover 2nd, unlock 2nd, vast 4th, visible 4th, wide 1st, widen 1st, windy 1st

opera 4th: music drama 5th

operate 3rd: act K, behave 4th, conduct 3rd, function 4th, manage 4th, work K

operation 3rd: action 1st, battle 2nd, engagement 5th, function 4th, method 2nd, performing 4th, process 4th, use K

operator 5th: conductor 3rd, flier 2nd, manager 4th, mechanic 5th, pilot 5th, user 1st, worker 1st

opinion 3rd: advice 3rd, angle 3rd, belief 1st, bias 6th, conviction 5th, counsel 5th, feeling 1st, judgment 2nd, ruling 2nd, slant 6th, suggestion 2nd, view 2nd, voice 1st

opponent 5th: challenger 4th, competitor 4th, contestant 4th, enemy 2nd, foe 4th, rival 4th

opportunity 3rd: break 1st, chance 2nd, freedom 3rd, means 4th, moment 1st, occasion 3rd, opening 1st, possibility 2nd, room 1st

oppose 3rd: argue 3rd, attack 3rd, challenge 4th, contest 4th, contrast 4th, counter 5th, defy 6th, dispute 6th, resist 4th

opposite 3rd: conflicting 4th, contrary 4th, counter 5th, different 1st, opposed 3rd, reverse 5th, unlike 2nd

oppress 6th: abuse 6th, beat down 1st, burden 5th, crush 4th, exploit 6th, persecute 6th

or K: else 1st, if not 1st, otherwise 3rd,

oracle 6th: authority 3rd, mastermind 2nd, prophecy 4th, prophet 4th, psychic 6th, revelation 4th, seer 1st, vision 4th, visionary 5th, wizard 6th

orbit 4th: circle K, course 3rd, curve 3rd, distance 4th, extent 4th, flight path 2nd, length 2nd, reach 1st, route 4th, scope 6th

ordain 6th: approve 4th, authorize 3rd, establish 3rd, legislate 5th, order 1st, rule K

order 1st:
  A. arrange 3rd, direction 1st, group 1st, method 2nd, organize 4th, pattern 3rd, plan 1st, rank 3rd, series 4th
  B. ask for K, boss K, command 2nd, demand 5th, summon 4th
  C. contract 3rd

ordinary 3rd: average 3rd, common 2nd, familiar 3rd, normal 5th, regular 3rd, standard 3rd, typical 6th, usual 3rd

ore 4th: metal 3rd, rock 1st

organ 4th: journal 2nd, newspaper 1st, publication 4th, voice 1st

organic 6th: live 1st, living 1st, natural 2nd

organism 6th: animal K, being 1st, body 1st, cell 1st, creature 3rd, thing K

organize 4th: arrange 3rd, catalog 5th, classify 5th, group 1st, order 1st, plan 1st, sort 1st, structure 4th

orient 5th: locate 3rd, place 1st

original 3rd:
  A. basic 5th, earliest 2nd, first 1st, fundamental 4th, introductory 5th, primary 5th
  B. clever 3rd, creative 4th, different 1st, new K, novel 5th, unique 6th

ornament 4th: accessory 6th, adorn 6th, decoration 3rd, garnish 6th, trim 4th, trimming 5th

orphan 5th: lone 2nd

other 1st: added 1st, additional 2nd, another 1st, different 1st, distinct 5th, extra 1st, further 2nd, more K, separate 3rd, spare 3rd, surplus 6th

otherwise 3rd: else 1st, if not 1st, or 1st

ought 1st: should 1st

ourselves 3rd: us K, we K

out K: dead 1st, done 1st, expired 6th, free K, not in K, outside 1st, over K, unconscious 6th

outcome 4th: consequence 4th, effect 3rd, end K, payoff 2nd, result 2nd

outcry 4th: demonstration 6th, noise 1st, protest 4th, scream 1st, yell K

outer 5th: exterior 5th, outside 1st, outward 6th

outlandish 6th: excessive 5th, extravagant 6th, extreme 5th, outrageous 6th, peculiar 4th, strange 1st, unbelievable 2nd, weird 1st

outline 4th: chart 1st, essence 6th, form 1st, format 4th, framework 4th, pattern 3rd, plan 1st, profile 5th, shape 1st, skeleton 4th, sketch 5th

outrage 6th: anger 1st, corruption 6th, cruelty 5th, dishonor 3rd, fury 4th, offense 4th, range 4th, scandal 6th, uproar 5th, wrath 4th

outside 1st: beyond 1st, exterior 5th, farther 3rd, front 1st, outdoor 2nd, past 1st, surface 3rd

outstanding 2nd:
A. celebrated 4th, dominant 5th, excellent 1st, famous 2nd, great 1st, important 1st, super 1st, wonderful 1st
B. due 2nd, owed 3rd, unpaid 2nd

outward 6th: evident 5th, exterior 5th, outer 5th, outside 1st, visible 4th

outwit 6th: best K, defeat 5th, fool 2nd, outsmart K, trick 1st, win 1st

over K: above 1st, across 1st, complete 3rd, done 1st, ended 1st, finished 1st, gone 1st, greater 1st, more K, past 1st, through 1st

overflow 5th: excess 5th, flood 2nd, run over 1st, spill 1st, submerge 5th, surplus 6th, swamp 4th

overlook 4th:
A. direct 1st, manage 4th, oversee 1st, supervise 6th
B. forget 1st, ignore 5th, miss K, neglect 4th, omit 6th, pass 2nd, skip 2nd

oversee 1st: direct 1st, manage 4th, overlook 4th, regulate 5th, run K, supervise 6th, watch over 1st

overtake 5th: advance 2nd, approach 3rd, come up 1st, equal 2nd, match 3rd, near 1st, outdo 2nd, pass K, reach 1st

overthrow 2nd: conquer 4th, crush 4th, defeat 5th, destroy 2nd, down K, lick 1st, overcome 3rd, ruin 5th, topple 6th, upset 3rd, vanquish 6th

overwhelm 5th: amaze 5th, awe 6th, conquer 4th, crush 4th, daze 5th, defeat 5th, destroy 2nd, drown 1st, flood 2nd, overpower 2nd, shock 1st, stun 4th, swamp 4th

owe 3rd: payable 2nd

own 1st: admit 4th, allow 2nd, confess 4th, concede 6th, have K, individual 3rd, keep K, personal 3rd, possess 3rd, retain 5th

oxygen 4th: air 1st

ozone 5th: air 1st, atmosphere 4th

pace 3rd:
A. rate 1st, speed 3rd, stride 5th
B. step 1st, walk K

pack 1st:
A. bag 1st, batch 2nd, bundle 5th, gear 1st, kit 1st, pouch 1st, sack 1st, team 1st
B. bag 1st, box K, bunch 3rd, carry 1st, crowd 2nd, fill K, haul 4th, insert 6th, load 2nd, stow 6th, stuff 1st, tote 5th

package 4th:
A. bundle 5th, parcel 4th
B. box K, close K, enclose 4th, pack 1st, seal K, wrap 3rd

pad K:
    A. pack 1st
    B. carpet 4th, mat 5th, pallet 5th, pillow 4th
paddle 1st:
    A. spank 2nd
    B. oar 1st
page 1st:
    A. paper K, sheet 1st
    B. announce 3rd, call 1st, summon 4th
pageant 6th: celebration 4th, ceremony 5th, festival 5th, parade 2nd, show 1st
pagoda 5th: temple 3rd
pail 2nd: bucket 3rd, pan K, pot K, tin 1st, tub 1st
pain 2nd:
    A. annoy 5th, bother 2nd, distress 5th, hurt 1st
    B. ache 5th, agony 5th, anguish 6th, bother 2nd, distress 5th, grief 5th,
        hurt 1st, injury 5th, sorrow 4th, suffering 2nd, trouble 1st, woe 4th
paint 2nd:
    A. color K, cover 1st, dye 2nd
    B. color K, dye 2nd
pair 1st:
    A. couple 3rd, two K
    B. combine 3rd, join 3rd, set K, unite 5th, wed K
pal K: buddy 4th, friend 1st
palace 1st: castle 3rd, estate 4th, mansion 5th
pale 3rd: dim 1st, light K, weak 3rd, white K
pallet 5th: bed K, cot 1st, pad K
palm 4th: hand 1st
pamphlet 6th: booklet 1st, circular 4th, program 4th
pan K: container 5th, pot K
pane 5th: glass 1st, part 1st, sheet 1st, window 1st
panel 6th:
    A. curtain 5th, divider 4th, part 1st
    B. committee 5th, jury 4th
pang 6th: ache 5th, pain 2nd, regret 5th
panic 1st: alarm 3rd, fear 1st, fright 2nd, horror 4th, scare 1st,
    terror 3rd
pantry 5th: closet 2nd, food room 1st
pants 1st: jeans 1st, trousers 5th
papa 1st: dad K, daddy K, father K, pop K
paper K:
    A. page 1st, stationery 5th
    B. composition 4th, essay 5th, papyrus 4th, report 1st, theme 4th

parade 2nd: display 3rd, exhibit 4th, march 1st, procession 4th, show 1st, walk K

paradise 4th: delight 3rd, glory 3rd, heaven 1st, joy 1st

paragraph 6th: part 1st, passage 4th, verse 4th

parallel 5th: associated 5th, equal 2nd, even 1st, like K, related 4th, same K, similar 4th, uniform 1st

paralysis 6th: disability 3rd, immovable 3rd, inaction 2nd, rigid 5th

paralyze 6th: daze 5th, disable 3rd, freeze 4th, shock 1st, stun 4th

paranormal 5th: psychic 6th

parcel 4th:
  A. assign 5th, divide 4th
  B. box K, bunch 3rd, bundle 5th, carton 4, lot K, package 4th, plot 4th, portion 4th

pardon 4th: clear 2nd, excuse 3rd, forgive 2nd, free K, release 5th, relief 4th

parent 3rd:
  A. nourish 6th, raise 1st
  B. creator 3rd, elder 5th, founder 2nd, guardian 2nd, inventor 2nd

parish 6th: district 4th, region 4th, ward 5th

park 1st: field 2nd, forest 1st, garden K, green K, square 2nd, woods 1st

parlor 4th: living room 1st, salon 6th

parrot 1st: copy 3rd, echo 4th, imitate 5th, mimic 6th, repeat 4th

parson 6th: clergy 6th, minister 4th, pastor 4th, priest 4th, reverend 4th

part 1st:
  A. divide 4th, divorce 4th, go K, leave 1st, separate 3rd, share 2nd
  B. break 1st, detail 5th, measure 2nd, percentage 4th, piece 1st, portion 4th, role 6th, section 4th, unit 5th

partial 6th:
  A. biased 6th, favored 2nd, inclined 5th, prejudiced 6th, unfair 3rd
  B. incomplete 3rd, unfinished 3rd

particle 5th: atom 5th, bit 1st, dot K, fragment 6th, grain 2nd, morsel 5th, scrap 3rd, shred 5th, speck 4th, spot 1st

particular 4th: careful 1st, cautious 5th, choosy 3rd, exact 2nd, individual 3rd, part 1st, personal 3rd, select 4th, selective 4th, single 3rd, special 2nd, specific 5th, unique 6th

partition 6th:
  A. assign 5th, divide 4th, separate 3rd
  B. curtain 5th, division 4th, fence 1st, exclude 6th, panel 6th, portion 4th, wall 1st

partner 5th: associate 5th, friend 1st, mate 4th

party K:
  A. bunch 3rd, group 1st, member 1st, partner 5th, team 1st
  B. affair 2nd, ball K, celebration 4th, ceremony 5th, festival 5th

passion 6th: desire 5th, emotion 4th, excitement 4th, intensity 6th, love K, rage 4th, temper 4th

passport 6th: identification 4th, pass 2nd, permit 3rd

past 1st:
    A. beyond 1st, farther 3rd
    B. ancient 3rd, before 1st, behind 1st, earlier 2nd, extinct 5th, former 6th, gone 1st, late 1st, left 1st, old K, once 1st, previous 5th, prior 5th

paste 1st:
    A. adhere 6th, bond 3rd, fasten 4th, join 3rd, seal K, stick K
    B. adhesive 6th, cement 4th, glue 1st

pastel 4th: delicate 5th, pale 3rd, soft K

pastime 6th: amusement 4th, entertainment 4th, game K, hobby 3rd, play K, sport 1st

pastor 4th: clergy 6th, minister 4th, parson 6th, priest 4th, reverend 4th

pasty 5th: doughy 5th, gluey 2nd, sticky K

pat K: dab 1st, tap K, touch 1st

patch 4th:
    A. cover 1st, fix 1st, mend 1st, repair 4th
    B. land K, piece 1st, rag 1st, scrap 3rd

patent 4th:
    A. claim 2nd, grant 2nd, invention 3rd, license 5th, permission 3rd, register 4th, right K
    B. apparent 3rd, evident 5th, obvious 5th, open K, plain 2nd, true 1st

path 1st: direction 1st, journey 3rd, passage 4th, road K, route 4th, street 1st, trail 2nd

pathetic 6th: emotional 4th, moving 1st, sad K, touching 1st

patient 4th: calm 3rd, cooperative 5th, easy 1st, quiet K, sympathetic 4th, tolerant 5th

patriot 4th: loyalist 5th, nationalist 2nd

patrol 1st:
    A. guard 1st, policeman 1st
    B. defend 5th, explore 4th, guard 1st, invade 5th, police 1st, protect 4th, watch 1st

patron 5th: backer 1st, buyer 1st, client 6th, customer 5th

patter 6th: routine 6th, speech 2nd, talk K

pattern 3rd:
    A. copy 3rd, follow 1st, imitate 5th, match 3rd, mimic 6th
    B. copy 3rd, design 5th, example 2nd, form 1st, guide 1st, model 3rd, order 1st, outline 4th, plan 1st, series 4th, standard 3rd, system 2nd, trend 2nd

pause 3rd:
    A. break 1st, delay 5th, rest 1st, stay 1st, stop K, wait 1st

B. break 1st, delay 5th, gap K, halt 4th, lag 1st, period 2nd, rest 1st, stop K, wait 1st

pave 5th: cement 4th, cover 1st

pavilion 5th: canopy 6th, shelter 4th

paw 1st: foot 1st, hit K, strike 2nd

pay K:

    A. spend 2nd, yield 4th

    B. payment 1st, salary 3rd, wage 3rd

pea 1st: dab 1st, dot K, pellet 6th, speck K

peace 1st: calm 3rd, harmony 4th, quiet K, rest 1st

peak 4th: crest 4th, crown 1st, height 4th, hill 1st, summit 5th, top K

peal 6th: chime 6th, clang 4th, ring 1st

pearl 4th: drop K, jewel 5th, seed 1st

peasant 4th: commoner 3rd, farmer K, worker 1st

pebble 4th: gravel 4th, pellet 6th, rock K, stone 2nd

peck 1st: fault 3rd, pick 1st, poke 1st, scold 5th

peculiar 4th: curious 3rd, funny 1st, odd 4th, outstanding 2nd, puzzle 4th, special 2nd, strange 1st, unique 6th, unusual 3rd, weird 1st

peddler 5th: merchant 3rd, salesman 6th, seller 1st

peek 2nd: eye 1st, glance 3rd, look K

peel 2nd:

    A. open K, strip 3rd

    B. bark 3rd, case 2nd, crust 4th, shell 1st, skin 1st

peep 4th: crack 4th, glance 3rd, peek 2nd

peer 1st:

    A. equal 2nd, friend 1st, like K, match 3rd, partner 5th

    B. classmate 4th, examine 5th, explore 4th, gape 5th, gaze 5th, hunt 2nd, inquire 3rd, look K, observe 3rd, stare 3rd

peg 1st:

    A. connect 3rd, join 3rd, nail 2nd, pin K, spike 4th, tack 1st

    B. bolt 4th, nail 2nd, pin K, spike 4th, tack 1st

pellet 6th: bead K, dot K, pea 1st, pebble 4th

pen 1st:

    A. marker 2nd, quill 6th

    B. barn K, cage 1st, jail 4th, stable 4th

    C. author 3rd, compose 4th, write K

penalty 5th: loss K, pain 2nd, punishment 4th

penetrate 5th: enter 2nd, move K, pierce 4th, poke 1st, stab 5th, stir 3rd

peninsula 6th: cape 4th, point 1st

penny 1st: cent 1st

pension 6th: allowance 5th, retirement 4th

perceive 6th: comprehend 5th, detect 4th, feel K, know 1st, notice 1st, observe 3rd, realize 2nd, recognize 3rd, see K, sense 1st, understand 1st, view 2nd

percent 4th: part 1st, portion 4th, section 4th

perch 4th:

A. sit K

B. bar 3rd, seat 1st

perfect 3rd: accurate 6th, best K, complete 3rd, exact 2nd, excellent 1st, faultless 3rd, ideal 3rd, model 3rd, proper 3rd, pure 3rd, whole 1st

perform 4th: accomplish 2nd, achieve 5th, act K, complete 4th, do K, execute 5th, fulfill 2nd, gain 2nd, run K, work K

perfume 3rd: cologne 5th, fragrance 5th, scent 3rd, smell 3rd

perhaps 1st: maybe 1st, possibly 2nd

peril 5th: danger 1st, hazard 6th, menace 5th, risk 4th, threat 5th

period 2nd: age 1st, cycle 6th, era 6th, pause 3rd, term 3rd, time 1st

periodic 4th: alternate 5th, occasional 4th, rare 4th, regular 3rd

perish 4th: cease 3rd, decay 5th, die 2nd, pass 2nd

permanent 5th: constant 4th, continuous 2nd, durable 6th, enduring 4th, eternal 4th, fastened 4th, fixed 1st, lasting 1st, set K, stable 4th

permit 3rd: allow 2nd, let K, license 5th, pass 2nd, support 4th, tolerate 5th

perpetual 6th: constant 4th, continuous 4th, endless 2nd, eternal 4th, permanent 5th, undying 4th

perplex 6th: bewilder 3rd, confuse 4th, puzzle 4th, stump 3rd

persecute 6th: harass 2nd, oppress 6th, pick on 1st, provoke 6th, tease 3rd, torture 5th

persist 5th: assert 6th, continue 2nd, endure 4th, insist 5th, last K, remain 1st, stay 1st, survive 5th

person 1st: human 3rd, individual 3rd

personal 3rd: close K, individual 3rd, intimate 5th, near 1st, own 1st, private 3rd, secret 1st

personality 5th: celebrity 5th, identity 5th, influence 5th, name K, spirit 2nd

perspire 6th: sweat 3rd

persuade 5th: affect 4th, bend K, cause 2nd, convert 4th, convince 4th, influence 5th, inspire 4th, lead 1st, motivate 6th, move 1st

pester 2nd: annoy 5th, badger 2nd, bother 2nd, irk 6th, irritate 6th, nettle 5th, vex 5th

pestilence 6th: curse 3rd, disease 5th, plague 5th

pet 1st:

A. favorite 3rd, special 2nd

B. cuddle 5th, pat K, stroke 1st

petrify 4th: frighten 5th, horrify 1st, scare 1st, shock 1st, surprise 1st, terrify 3rd

petroleum 6th: fuel 4th, gas 1st, oil K

petticoat 6th: slip 3rd, underwear 2nd

petty 6th: light K, little K, meaningless 3rd, minor 5th, poor K, scant 6th, slight 4th, small 1st, sparse 3rd, worthless 3rd

pewter 5th: lead 1st, metal 3rd, tin 1st

phase 6th: aspect 5th, condition 3rd, level 3rd, side K, stage 3rd, state 1st, step 1st

phenomenon 6th: event 3rd, experience 4th, marvel 4th, miracle 5th, wonder 1st

philosophy 5th: belief 1st, knowledge 2nd, logic 6th, principles 4th, thinking 1st

phonograph 5th: record player 2nd

photograph 5th: photo 5th, picture K, slide 2nd, snapshot 2nd

phrase 5th:
A. put into words 1st, say K, speak 1st, state 1st
B. expression 5th, sentence 1st, words K

physical 5th: body 1st, concrete 4th, material 5th, real 1st, substantial 5th

pick 1st:
A. choose 3rd, elect 3rd, remove 2nd, select 4th, separate 3rd, sort 2nd
B. jab 1st, peck 1st
C. best K, decide 1st, favorite 3rd, finest 1st, preference 3rd

picket 3rd:
A. protest 4th, strike 2nd
B. fence 1st, guard 1st

picnic 5th: cookout 2nd, outing 1st

picture K:
A. imagine 2nd, see K, view 2nd
B. art K, drawing 1st, illustration 4th, image 4th, painting 2nd, photograph 5th, print 1st, sketch 5th

piece 1st: bit 1st, bite 1st, fragment 6th, ingredient 4th, measure 2nd, morsel 5th, object 1st, part 1st, patch 4th, portion 4th, rag 1st, scrap 3rd, section 4th, strip 3rd

pier 4th: dock 1st, landing 1st, wharf 5th

pierce 4th: cut K, drill 2nd, penetrate 5th, poke 1st, punch 4th, stab 5th, wound 3rd

pile 1st:
A. collect 3rd, gather 1st, group 1st, heap 4th, stack 6th
B. hill 1st, mound 2nd, reserve 3rd, store K, supply 2nd

pilgrim 5th: pioneer 4th, settler 2nd, traveler 1st

pill 1st: bead K, dot K, pea 1st

pillar 5th: column 4th, pole 1st, post 1st, support 4th

pillow 4th:
    A. soften 2nd, support 5th
    B. pad K
pilot 5th:
    A. flyer 1st, guide 1st
    B. experiment 3rd, test 3rd, untested 3rd
pimple 5th: blemish 5th, boil 3rd, bump 2nd, spot 1st
pin K:
    A. attach 5th, buckle 6th, clasp 4th, clip 2nd, connect 3rd, fasten 4th, join 3rd, staple 6th
    B. bolt 4th, brooch 4th, buckle 6th, fastener 4th, peg 1st, shaft 4th
pinch 4th:
    A. difficulty 5th, hardship 5th, trouble 1st
    B. bit 1st, dab 1st, piece 1st, spot 1st
    C. bind 2nd, catch 1st, pull K, squeeze 5th
pine 1st: crave 6th, desire 5th, long 1st, want K, yearn 6th
pioneer 4th:
    A. create 3rd, invent 2nd, lead 1st, start 1st
    B. first 1st, introductory 5th, original 3rd
    C. guide 1st, scout 1st
pious 6th: devoted 5th, holy 5th, religious 4th, spiritual 5th
pipe 1st: channel 4th, cylinder 6th, hose 6th, tube 3rd
pirate 5th: robber 1st, rogue 5th
pistol 5th: gun 1st, revolver 5th
pit 1st:
    A. compete 4th, match 3rd, oppose 3rd
    B. hole 1st, mine 1st, tomb 5th, trap 1st
pitch 2nd:
    A. fling 6th, send K, throw 1st, toss 2nd
    B. angle 3rd, incline 5th, slant 6th, slope 3rd
    C. frequency 4th, tone 3rd
piteous 6th: emotional 4th, sad K, tender 3rd, to be pitied 3rd, touching 1st
pity 3rd:
    A. dishonor 2nd, regret 5th, shame 3rd
    B. compassion 6th, kindness 3rd, mercy 4th, sympathy 4th, understanding 1st
pivot 5th: turn 1st, turning point 1st, wheel 1st
place 1st:
    A. class 1st, position 2nd, rank 3rd, standing 1st
    B. put K, set K, sit K
    C. identify 4th, recall 3rd, recognize 3rd

D. area 3rd, facility 5th, location 3rd, office 1st, point 1st, scene 1st, site 5th, spot 1st

plague 5th:
    A. annoy 5th, bother 2nd, pester 2nd, tease 3rd, torment 5th
    B. curse 3rd, disease 5th, evil 3rd, trouble 1st

plain 2nd:
    A. bare 3rd, naked 4th, natural 2nd, pure 3rd, simple 2nd
    B. average 3rd, basic 5th, modest 4th, ordinary 3rd, regular 3rd, usual 3rd
    C. candid 4th, frank 4th
    D. ugly 4th, unattractive 5th
    E. clear 2nd, evident 5th

plait 5th: braid 2nd, weave 4th

plan 1st:
    A. design 5th, map 1st, procedure 4th
    B. arrange 3rd, intend 6th, organize 4th, scheme 5th, shape 1st

plane 1st: aircraft 1st, airplane 1st, even 1st, flat 2nd, flat surface 3rd, jet K, level 3rd

planet 4th: satellite 6th, world 1st

plank 5th: beam 3rd, block 1st, board 1st

plant K:
    A. flora 6th, flower K, greenery 3rd, root 3rd, seed 1st
    B. bury 3rd, cultivate 6th, farm K, grow 1st, raise 1st
    C. anchor 4th, moor 5th
    D. establish 3rd, insert 6th, place 1st, promote 5th

plantation 5th: farm K, ranch 5th

plaque 5th: award 5th, badge 5th, sign 1st

plaster 4th: cement 4th, coat 1st, cover 1st

plastic 3rd:
    A. artificial 6th, man-made 1st
    B. adjustable 5th, elastic 6th, flexible 6th, soft K, yielding 4th

plate K:
    A. dish 1st, platter 6th
    B. armor 4th, coat 1st, cover 1st, shell 1st, shield 4th

plateau 6th: level 3rd, mesa 6th, plane 1st

platform 4th: deck 1st, landing 1st, stage 3rd

platter 6th: dish 1st, plate K

play K:
    A. act K, entertainment 4th, show 1st
    B. amusement 4th, pastime 6th, recreation 5th
    C. excess 5th, give 1st, leeway 5th, stretch 4th
    D. amuse oneself 3rd, compete 4th, have fun K

player 1st: athlete 5th, sportsman 1st, sportswoman 1st

playground 1st: park 1st, recreation area 5th

plea 5th:
    A. argument 3rd, defense 5th
    B. excuse 3rd, reason 1st
    C. appeal 3rd, beg 1st, prayer 3rd, request 4th

plead 3rd: appeal 3rd, argue 3rd, ask K, beg 1st, beseech 5th, request 4th

pleasant 3rd: agreeable 2nd, fair 1st, friendly 1st, mild 4th, nice 1st,
    pleasing 2nd

please K: amuse 4th, content 3rd, delight 3rd, entertain 4th, gratify 4th,
    satisfy 3rd, soothe 5th

pleasure 2nd: amusement 4th, contentment 3rd, delight 3rd, enjoy 2nd, joy 1st

pleat 5th: crease 5th, fold 1st

pledge 5th:
    A. declare 5th, guarantee 6th, promise 1st, swear 4th, vow 4th
    B. agreement 3rd, commitment 4th, compact 5th, contract 3rd, oath 5th,
      obligation 6th, promise 1st

plentiful 2nd: more than enough 1st. *See* plenty.

plenty 1st: abundant 5th, ample 5th, armload 2nd, enough 1st, excess 5th
    full K, heaps 4th, loads 2nd, lots K, luxury 4th, many K, much 1st,
    numerous 4th, quantity 4th, resources 5th, wealth 3rd

plight 6th: circumstances 6th, condition 3rd, difficulty 5th, problem 1st,
    situation 4th, state 1st

plod 5th: continue 2nd, grind 4th, lumber 1st, persist 5th, walk K

plop 1st: collapse 5th, drop K, fall 1st

plot 4th:
    A. land K, lot K, parcel 4th, property 3rd
    B. bring about 1st, devise 4th, figure 4th, plan 1st, scheme 5th
    C. chart 1st, design 5th, frame 3rd, plan 1st, scheme 5th, strategy 6th

plow 4th:
    A. plunge 4th, push 1st, shove 5th
    B. cultivate 6th, farm K, prepare 1st, till 1st

pluck 1st:
    A. backbone 4th, nerve 1st, spirit 2nd, vigor 5th
    B. persist 5th, pick 1st, pull K, remove 2nd, tug 1st

plug 5th:
    A. ad 4th, commercial 5th, promotion 5th
    B. block 1st, close K, cork 6th, cover 1st, stop K, stuff 1st
    C. grind 4th, persist 5th, plod 5th, publicize 4th

plume 6th:
    A. boast 4th, brag 3rd, glory 3rd, preen 2nd
    B. feather 2nd, quill 6th

plump 6th: chubby 2nd, fat 1st, heavy 1st, stout 4th

plunder 5th:
  A. fortune 3rd, reward 4th, spoils 4th, take 1st, treasure 4th
  B. devastate 6th, ravage 6th, rob K, seize 3rd
plunge 4th: dip 1st, dive 1st, drive 1st, fall K, hurry 1st, leap 3rd, rush 2nd, sink 3rd, stab 5th, submerge 5th
plural 4th: many K, more than one K
plus 1st: add K, addition 3rd, also K, and K, besides 1st, extra 1st, further 2nd, increase 3rd, too 1st
ply 6th:
  A. handle 2nd, practice 1st, use K
  B. layer 4th, thickness 2nd
  C. furnish 4th, give K, provide 3rd, supply 1st
  D. follow 1st, inclination 5th, prejudice 6th, turn 1st
p.m. 6th: afternoon 1st, evening 1st
poach 6th:
  A. hunt 2nd, raid 6th, steal 3rd
  B. boil 3rd, cook 1st
pocket 1st:
  A. bag 1st, pouch 1st, purse 4th
  B. rob K, steal 3rd, take 1st
poem 3rd: rhyme 6th, sonnet 6th, verse 4th
point 1st:
  A. focus 5th, issue 4th, question 1st
  B. address K, location 3rd, place 1st, position 2nd, spot 1st
  C. dot K, end K, peak 4th, tip 1st
  D. aim 3rd, intent 5th, meaning 3rd, purpose 1st, reason 1st
  E. aim 3rd, direct 1st, show 1st
poise 6th:
  A. attitude 5th, bearing 1st, presence 2nd
  B. balance 3rd, calm 3rd, confidence 6th, coolness 2nd, ease 3rd, self-control 3rd, tact 6th
poison 3rd:
  A. harmful substance 5th, impurity 4th
  B. contaminate 6th, foul 4th, pollute 3rd
poke 1st: force 1st, jog 2nd, push 1st, shove 5th
polar 3rd: conflicting 4th, contrary 4th, different 1st, opposed 3rd, opposite 3rd
pole K: bar 3rd, column 4th, post 1st, rod 1st, shaft 4th
police 1st:
  A. guard 1st, patrol 1st, protect 4th, regulate 5th, watch 1st
  B. authority 3rd, cop K, guard 1st, officer 1st, the law 1st
policeman 1st: authority 3rd, cop K, guard 1st, law enforcer 5th, officer 1st

policy 5th: course 3rd, direction 1st, guarantee 6th, guide 1st, instruction 4th, manner 1st, rule 2nd, strategy 6th, system 2nd, way K

polish 4th:
A. clean K, refine 6th, rub 1st, smooth 2nd, wax K
B. elegance 5th, poise 6th, refinement 6th, style 3rd
C. glaze 6th, gleam 1st, luster 4th, radiance 6th, shine 1st, sparkle 5th

polite 4th: kind K, mannerly 2nd, pleasant 3rd, refined 6th, respectful 2nd

political 4th: civil 3rd, official 3rd, public 1st

poll 5th:
A. ask K, examine 5th, gather 1st, inquire 3rd, question 1st, survey 5th, test 3rd
B. cast a ballot 6th, elect 3rd, vote 2nd

pollute 3rd: contaminate 6th, destroy 2nd, dirty 1st, harm 3rd, poison 3rd, taint 6th

pomp 6th: display 3rd, glory 3rd, parade 2nd, ritual 6th, splendor 4th

pond 1st: basin 4th, lagoon 5th, lake 1st, pool 1st

ponder 6th: consider 2nd, contemplate 6th, examine 5th, meditate 5th, think 1st, weigh 1st

pool 1st:
A. lagoon 5th, lake 1st, pond 1st
B. combine 3rd, gather 3rd, mound 2nd, share 2nd

poor K:
A. ill 1st, lean 3rd, sick 1st
B. bad K, scarce 4th, slight 4th
C. needy 1st, not rich 1st, pitiful 3rd, unfortunate 4th

pop K:
A. dad K, father K
B. break 1st, burst 3rd, explode 3rd

popular 3rd:
A. common 2nd, current 3rd, familiar 3rd, normal 5th, ordinary 3rd, standard 3rd, usual 3rd
B. admired 5th, approved 4th, desired 5th, liked K, wanted 1st

population 3rd: census 6th, inhabitants 6th, natives 1st, people K, residents 5th

porch 3rd: balcony 6th, walk K

pore 6th: consider 2nd, dwell 4th, examine 5th, read K, search 1st

porridge 5th: cereal 1st, gruel 6th, mush 5th

port 3rd: dock 1st, harbor 2nd, landing 1st, pier 4th, shelter 4th, wharf 5th

porter 5th: bearer 1st, carrier 5th, doorman 2nd, loader 2nd, servant 3rd

portion 4th:
A. destiny 5th, fate 3rd, fortune 3rd, future 5th, luck 1st

B. cut K, fraction 4th, parcel 4th, part K, piece 1st, section 4th, serving 1st, share 2nd

portrait 5th: drawing 1st, figure 4th, image 4th, likeness 1st, mask 2nd, model 3rd, painting 2nd, photograph 5th, picture K, profile 5th, sketch 5th

position 2nd:

A. level 3rd, rank 3rd

B. duty 1st, job K, occupation 6th

C. manner 1st, pose 2nd, stance 2nd

D. belief 1st, opinion 3rd, policy 5th, stand 1st

E. angle 3rd, location 3rd, place 1st, post 1st, site 5th, slant 6th, spot 1st

positive 2nd:

A. beneficial 3rd, helpful 2nd, production 4th

B. absolute 3rd, agreement 2nd, certain 1st, conclusion 3rd, confident 6th, decided 1st, for K, good K, sound 1st, sure 1st

possess 3rd: cling 4th, control 2nd, have K, hold 1st, keep K, maintain 4th, occupy 3rd, own 1st, retain 5th

possible 1st: able 3rd, chance 2nd, imaginable 2nd, likely 1st, may K, thinkable 2nd

post 1st:

A. after 1st, later 1st

B. base 1st, camp 1st, headquarters 3rd, position 2nd, station 1st

C. advise 3rd, inform 5th, mail 1st, notify 3rd, send K

D. column 4th, leg 1st, pillar 5th, pole 1st, stake 1st, stud 6th

postcard 1st: note 1st, scene 1st, view 2nd

postpone 6th: delay 5th, put off 1st

pot K: cauldron 6th, container 5th, kettle 4th, pan K, saucepan 5th

pouch 1st: bag 1st, cheek 2nd, pocket 1st, purse 4th, sack 1st

poultry 6th: chickens 1st, fowl 4th, hens 1st

pounce 5th: attack 3rd, dine 1st, fall K, jump K, leap 3rd, spring 1st, surprise 1st

pound 2nd: batter 1st, beat 1st, bruise 5th, buffet 6th, hit K, smash 3rd

pour 3rd:

A. crowd 2nd, stampede 5th, swarm 4th

B. empty 3rd, flow 1st, serve 1st, spill 1st, tip 1st

poverty 5th: distress 5th, need 1st, poor K, scarce 4th, shortage 2nd, want K

powder 3rd:

A. beat 1st, pound 2nd, refine 6th

B. dust 2nd, flour 3rd, grain 3rd, sand 1st

power 1st: ability 3rd, authority 3rd, capacity 6th, command 2nd, control 2nd, energy 4th, force 1st, might 1st, muscle 4th, strength 1st, talent 2nd

powerful 2nd: authoritative 3rd, forceful 2nd, intense 6th, mighty 1st, strong K, supreme 5th

practical 4th: functional 4th, performable 4th, plain 2nd, possible 2nd, realistic 5th, reasonable 2nd, useful 2nd, workable 3rd

practice 1st:

    A. business 2nd, profession 5th, trade 1st

    B. exercise 1st, habit 3rd, method 2nd, perform 4th, polish 4th, repeat 4th, sharpen 1st, study 1st, train K, work K

prairie 4th: flat land 1st, meadow 3rd ·

praise 4th: adore 4th, commend 6th, compliment 5th, flatter 4th, glorify 3rd, honor 1st

prank 5th: caper 4th, joke 1st, mischief 4th, sport 1st, trick 1st

pray 3rd: appeal 3rd, ask K, beg 1st, beseech 5th, plead 3rd, request 4th

prayer 3rd: appeal 3rd, devotion 5th, plea 5th, request 4th, worship 4th

preach 4th: advice 3rd, caution 5th, lecture 5th, moralize 3rd, sermon 5th

precaution 5th: anticipation 6th, care 1st, caution 5th, preparation 2nd, prevention 3rd

precede 6th: anticipate 6th, begin 1st, go before 1st, head 1st, introduce 5th, lead 1st, preface 6th, start 1st, usher 6th

precious 4th: beloved 4th, cherished 5th, costly 1st, dear 1st, expensive 3rd, exquisite 6th, loved 1st, priceless 2nd, rare 4th, sweet 1st, valuable 3rd

precipice 6th: brink 6th, cliff 2nd, drop 1st, edge 1st, ledge 5th, rim 1st

precise 5th: accurate 6th, correct 3rd, exact 2nd, literal 6th, neat K, specific 5th, strict 6th

predict 6th: anticipate 6th, estimate 5th, expect 2nd, figure 2nd, forecast 4th, foresee 6th, foretell 6th, guess 1st, judge 1st, prophesy 4th, see K

preen 2nd: adorn 6th, dress 1st, groom 5th, plume 6th, take pride 3rd

preface 6th: begin 1st, beginning 2nd, foreword 1st, introduce 5th, lead 1st, precede 6th, start 1st

prefer 3rd:

    A. advance 2nd, offer 2nd, promote 5th, raise 1st

    B. choose 3rd, elect 3rd, fancy 3rd, favor 2nd, like K, pick 1st, select 4th

prehistoric 5th: ancestral 5th, ancient 3rd, early 1st, original 3rd, primitive 5th

prejudice 6th: assumption 5th, belief 1st, bias 6th, partial 6th, sexism 3rd, slant 6th, subjective 2nd

preliminary 6th: basic 5th, beginning 1st, elementary 3rd, introductory 5th, opening 1st, presume 6th, prior 6th, surmise 6th, theory 5th

premise 6th: argument 3rd, assumption 5th, basis 5th, given 1st, idea 1st, presume 6th, surmise 6th, theory 5th

preoccupy 5th: absorb 5th, abstract 6th, bother 1st, engage 5th, forget 1st, involved 6th, lost K, occupied 3rd

prepare 1st: arrange 3rd, create 3rd, equip 5th, form 1st, furnish 3rd, make K, provide 3rd, qualify 4th, ready 1st, study 2nd, supply 2nd

prescribe 6th: assign 5th, command 2nd, direct 1st, impose 4th, offer 2nd, order 1st, require 2nd, suggest 2nd

present K:
A. favor 2nd, gift 1st, grant 2nd, offering 2nd
B. award 5th, bestow 5th, confer 4th, contribute 4th, display 3rd, exhibit 4th, give K, offer 2nd, show 1st
C. alive 3rd, attending 3rd, existing 3rd
D. now K, this moment 1st, today K

preserve 4th:
A. can K, jam K, jelly 1st
B. care for 1st, conserve 5th, guard 1st, protect 4th, rescue 4th, save 1st, secure 3rd, shelter 4th, treat 2nd

preside 6th: captain 2nd, chair 1st, control 2nd, direct 1st, head K, judge 1st, lead 1st, manage 4th, organize 4th, run K

president 1st: boss K, chief 1st, head 1st

press 1st:
A. journalist 3rd, reporter 2nd
B. clasp 4th, condense 6th, cram 5th, crowd 2nd, depress 5th, flatten 2nd, grip 4th, iron 2nd, jam K, level 3rd, pack 1st, pat K, poke 1st, push 1st, shove 5th, squeeze 5th

pressure 4th: demand 5th, press 1st, push 1st, strain 4th, stress 6th, tension 5th, weight 1st

presume 6th: assume 5th, conclude 3rd, gather 1st, guess 1st, judge 1st, suppose 2nd, surmise 6th, think 1st

pretend 2nd: act K, deceive 5th, fake 1st, imagine 2nd, imitate 5th, lie 1st, make believe 1st, mask 2nd, play K

pretext 5th: alibi 6th, cover up 1st, deception 5th, defense 5th, device 4th, excuse 3rd, reason 1st, trick 1st

pretty 1st:
A. fairly 1st, reasonably 2nd, somewhat 1st
B. attractive 5th, beautiful 1st, delicate 5th, fair 1st, good-looking 1st, handsome 3rd

prevail 5th: affect 4th, conquer 4th, dominate 5th, endure 4th, get K, induce 5th, overcome 2nd, reign 4th, succeed 2nd, win 1st

prevent 3rd: avoid 3rd, bar 3rd, block 1st, dam K, forbid 4th, hinder 6th, prohibit 6th, stop K

previous 5th: earlier 1st, first 1st, former 6th, preceding 6th

prey 4th: catch 1st, chase 1st, game K, kill 1st, stalk 4th, target 5th, use K, victim 4th

price K: amount 2nd, charge 2nd, cost 1st, expense 3rd, fee 4th, payment 1st, penalty 5th, tab K, toll 6th, value 2nd, wages 3rd, worth 3rd

prick 5th: bore 2nd, compel 3rd, cut K, drill 2nd, excite 4th, move K, pierce 4th, provoke 6th, punch 4th, slit 5th, stab 5th, stick K, stimulate 6th

pride 2nd: arrogance 6th, conceit 5th, self-importance 3rd, vanity 5th

priest 4th: clergy 6th, cleric 6th, father K, minister 4th, pastor 4th, rabbi 4th

prim 5th: clean 1st, formal 4th, grim 4th, modest 4th, neat K, proper 3rd, pure 3rd, rigid 5th, sour 2nd, straight 3rd

primary 5th: base 1st, beginning 1st, earliest 1st, first 1st, fundamental 4th, head K, initial 6th, key K, leading 1st, oldest 1st, original 3rd, primitive 5th, start 1st

prime 5th: basic 5th, beginning 1st, best K, bloom 4th, excellent 1st, first 1st, good K, health K, primary 5th, principal 3rd, splendid 4th, superb 6th, superior 4th, top K, youth 2nd

primitive 5th: basic 5th, early 1st, original 3rd, plain 2nd, primary 5th, savage 5th, simple 2nd, uncivilized 4th

prince 1st: monarch 5th, nobleman 3rd, royalty 3rd

princess 1st: monarch 5th, noblewoman 3rd, royalty 3rd

principal 3rd: capital 2nd, central 3rd, director 1st, ethic 5th, head 1st, idea 1st, main 3rd, major 3rd, master 1st, money K, most important 1st, prime 5th, star K, superior 4th

principle 4th: basis 5th, ethics 5th, fundamentals 4th, guide 1st, law 1st, regulation 5th, rule K, source 4th, standard 3rd, truth 1st

print 1st: impress 5th, imprint 4th, mark 1st, stamp 2nd, type 1st

prior 5th: before 1st, earlier 2nd, former 6th, preceding 6th, previous 5th

prison 3rd: cage 4th, cell 1st, dungeon 5th, jail 4th, vault 5th

private 3rd:
  A. exclusive 6th, individual 3rd, nonpublic 2nd, restricted 6th
  B. alone 1st, confidential 6th, quiet K, remote 5th, secret 1st, solitary 5th, withdrawn 2nd
  C. confidential 6th, hidden 1st, intimate 5th, personal 3rd, secret 1st

privateer 6th: pirate 5th

privilege 5th: advantage 3rd, allowance 5th, authority 3rd, benefit 3rd, due 2nd, entitle 5th, entitlement 5th, freedom 3rd, liberty 3rd, license 5th, permission 3rd, power 1st, right K

prize 3rd:
  A. appreciate 5th, cherish 5th, desire 5th, hope K, treasure 4th, value 2nd
  B. aim 3rd, award 5th, gift 1st, honor 1st, payment 1st, present K, recognition 3rd, reward 4th, trophy 6th, winnings 1st

probably 4th: chance 2nd, expectation 2nd, likely 1st, possible 1st, risky 4th, surely 1st

problem 1st: challenge 4th, complexity 6th, mystery 1st, puzzle 4th, question 1st, riddle 1st, unknown 1st

proceed 4th: advance 2nd, continue 2nd, extend 4th, go K, move along 1st, pass 2nd, progress 4th, pursue 5th

process 4th:
   A. develop 5th, grow K, handle 2nd, make K, prepare 1st, refine 6th
   B. action 1st, development 5th, formula 6th, growth 1st, mechanism 6th, method 2nd, movement 2nd, procedure 4th, routine 6th, style 3rd, system 2nd, way 1st

procession 4th: line K, march 1st, parade 2nd, stream 1st, train 1st

proclaim 4th: advertise 4th, announce 3rd, broadcast 5th, declare 5th, inform 5th, report 1st, state 1st

procure 5th: acquire 4th, attain 6th, buy K, earn 2nd, gain 2nd, gather 1st, get K, obtain 5th, pick up 1st, receive 1st, secure 3rd

prod 6th: bug 1st, drive 1st, poke 1st, prick 5th, prompt 4th, push 1st, remind 3rd, stick K, stimulate 6th

produce 2nd:
   A. construct 3rd, create 3rd, generate 4th, make K, manufacture 3rd, turn out 1st,
   B. crops 2nd, food K, product 4th, yield 4th

product 4th: crop 2nd, goods K, item 5th, result 2nd

production 4th: creation 3rd, formation 4th, goods K, making 1st

profess 5th: allege 6th, assert 6th, claim 2nd, declare 5th, state 1st

profession 5th: business 2nd, career 4th, employment 5th, job K, occupation 6th, pursuit 5th, specialty 3rd, work K

professor 4th: doctor 1st, educator 3rd, instructor 4th, teacher 1st

profile 5th: portrait 5th, shape 1st, side view 1st

profit 4th: benefit 3rd, gain 2nd, income 4th, yield 4th

profound 6th: deep 1st, important 1st, intense 6th, moving 1st, thoughtful 2nd, wise 1st

program 4th:
   A. aim 3rd, approach 3rd, design 5th, intent 5th, plan 1st
   B. calendar 1st, entertainment 4th, event 3rd, presentation 4th, schedule 6th

progress 4th:
   A. breakthrough 2nd, growth 1st, movement 2nd
   B. advance 2nd, change 2nd, develop 5th, go on K, grow 1st, improve 3rd, proceed 4th

prohibit 6th: ban K, bar 3rd, block 1st, deny 5th, forbid 4th, prevent 3rd, stop K

project 4th:
   A. aim 3rd, intend 6th
   B. cast 2nd, shoot 3rd, stick out 1st, throw 1st
   C. design 5th, program 4th, scheme 5th, undertaking 1st, work K

prolong 5th: carry on 1st, continue 2nd, draw out 1st, lengthen 2nd, pull K, stretch 4th

promenade 5th:
    A. path 1st, sidewalk 1, walkway 2nd
    B. march 1st, parade 2nd, saunter 6th, stroll 5th, walk K

prominent 5th:
    A. projecting 4th, raised 1st
    B. famous 2nd, important 1st, outstanding 2nd, well-known K

promise 1st:
    A. assurance 3rd, commitment 4th, contract 3rd, guarantee 6th, oath 5th, pledge 5th, vow 4th, word K
    B. assure 3rd, commit 4th, profess 5th, swear 4th, vow 4th

promote 5th:
    A. advance 2nd, further 2nd, graduate 4th
    B. advertise 4th, encourage 4th, support 4th, uphold 6th

promotion 5th:
    A. advance 2nd, move up K, raise 1st
    B. help K, encourgement 4th, support 4th
    C. ad 4th, advertisement 4th

prompt 4th:
    A. animate 6th, force 1st, push 1st, stimulate 6th, urge 4th
    B. alert 5th, fast 1st, instant 3rd, on time 1st, rapid 4th, ready 1st, timely 1st

pronounce 4th: announce 3rd, declare 5th, proclaim 4th, report 1st, say K, speak 1st, talk K, voice 1st

proof 4th: demonstration 6th, evidence 5th, show 1st, support 4th

prop 5th:
    A. lean against 3rd, rest 1st
    B. assurance 3rd, hold up 1st, support 4th, sustain 5th, uphold 6th

propel 6th: compel 3rd, move K, prod 6th, project 4th, push 1st, send K, start 1st

proper 3rd: correct 3rd, fitting 2nd, formal 4th, mannerly 2nd, right K, strict 6th, suitable 2nd

property 3rd:
    A. character 2nd, feature 3rd, mark 1st, quality 4th, trait 6th
    B. belongings 2nd, capital 2nd, holdings 1st, land K

prophet 4th: forecaster 2nd, preacher 4th, predictor 6th, seer 1st

proportion 4th: balance 3rd, part 1st, percent 4th, portion 4th, ratio 6th, relationship 4th, share 2nd, uniform 1st

propose 4th: advance 2nd, aim 3rd, ask K, design 5th, intend 5th, plan 1st, present K, submit 4th, suggest 2nd

proprietor 6th: manager 4th, owner 2nd, possessor 3rd

prospect 4th: chance 2nd, expectation 3rd, forecast 4th, intention 5th, outlook 2nd, possibility 2nd, probability 4th, view 2nd

prosper 5th: benefit 3rd, bloom 4th, do well 1st, flourish 4th, gain 2nd, money K, profit 4th, succeed 2nd, thrive 6th

protect 4th: conserve 5th, defend 5th, guard 1st, keep K, preserve 4th, save 1st, secure 3rd, shelter 4th, shield 4th

protection 4th: armor 4th, defense 5th, guard 1st, security 3rd

protest 4th:
A. demonstration 6th, strike 2nd, walk out 1st
B. complain 4th, demonstrate 6th, gripe 5th, object 1st, oppose 3rd

proud 2nd: arrogant 6th, lofty 5th, satisfied 3rd, see K, vain 4th

prove 1st: demonstrate 6th, show 1st

provide 3rd: distribute 6th, furnish 3rd, give 1st, maintain 4th, stock 1st, supply 2nd, yield 4th

province 6th: area 3rd, domain 5th, orbit 4th, realm 4th, region 4th, sphere 6th, territory 3rd

provision 4th: equipment 5th, means 1st, stock 1st, supplies 1st

provoke 6th: anger 1st, disturb 6th, move K, press 1st, prompt 4th, push 1st, start 1st, torment 5th

prow 5th: bow 1st, front 1st, nose 1st

prowess 6th: bravery 1st, courage 4th, force 1st, power 1st, strength 1st, talent 2nd

prowl 2nd: roam 4th, rove 6th, search 1st, sneak 6th, stroll 5th, wander 3rd

prudent 6th: careful 1st, cautious 5th, economical 4th, moderate 4th, modest 4th, polite 4th, proper 3rd, reasonable 1st, sensible 6th

prune 3rd: cut K, shape 1st, shorten 1st, thin 2nd, trim 4th

pry 6th:
A. examine 5th, impose 4th, inquire 3rd, investigate 5th, question 1st, spy 4th
B. force 1st, lift 1st, open K, tear 4th

psalm 6th: chant 5th, hymn 5th, poem 3rd, song K, verse 4th

psychic 6th: mental 5th, spiritual 5th, supernatural 3rd

pub 1st: bar 3rd, inn 4th, tavern 5th

public 1st: common 2nd, general 2nd, national 2nd, not secret 1st, open K, outside 1st, society 3rd, universal 4th

publication 4th: ad 4th, announcement 3rd, issue 4th, printed material 5th

publicity 4th: ad 4th, advertisement 4th, notice 1st, promotion 5th

publicize 4th: advertise 4th, announce 3rd, broadcast 5th, publish 4th

publish 4th: advertise 4th, air 1st, broadcast 5th, declare 5th, issue 4th, make public 1st, print 1st, produce 2nd, report 1st reveal 4th

puff 2nd:
A. boast 4th, magnify 3rd, praise 4th, publicize 4th, show off 1st
B. air 1st, blow up 1st, breath 1st, gasp 4th

pull K: draw K, haul 4th, lower 2nd, lug 1st, tow 1st, transport 5th

pulp 6th: batter 1st, flesh 3rd, fruit 2nd, jam K, mash 4th, paste 1st, squash 2nd, wood 1st

pulse 5th: beat 1st, heart rate 1st, pace 3rd, throb 5th

pump 4th:
    A. cross-examine 5th, question 1st
    B. blow up 1st, enlarge 5th, expand 5th, swell 3rd

punch 4th: beat 1st, box K, cuff 1st, drill 2nd, hit K, pound 2nd, smash 3rd, strike 2nd

punish 4th: correct 3rd, discipline 6th, fine 1st, imprison 6th, penalize 5th

pup K: dog K, puppy K

pupil 4th: beginner 2nd, devotee 5th, follower 1st, scholar 5th, student 3rd, trainee 2nd

purchase 3rd:
    A. grasp 4th, hold 1st, perch 4th, stand 1st
    B. acquire 4th, attain 6th, buy K, gain 2nd, invest 5th, trade 2nd

pure 3rd:
    A. innocent 5th, moral 3rd, proper 3rd, sincere 4th, virtuous 4th
    B. clean 1st, clear 2nd, complete 3rd, genuine 5th, perfect 3rd, spotless 2nd

Puritan 1st: moralist 3rd, prim 5th, proper 3rd, prude 6th, strict 6th

purpose 1st: aim 3rd, design 5th, goal 4th, idea 1st, intent 6th, meaning 1st, mission 5th, object 1st, objective 2nd, plan 1st, reason 2nd, resolve 5th, target 5th, will K

purse 4th:
    A. award 5th, gift K, means 5th, prize 3rd
    B. bag 1st, pouch 1st, wallet 6th

pursuit 5th: chase 1st, hunt 2nd, quest 3rd, run K

push 1st: get going 1st, move K, press 1st, propel 6th, shove 5th

pushy 1st: aggressive 6th, bossy 1st, forceful 2nd

put K: drop K, lay 1st, locate 3rd, place 1st, position 2nd, set K, stand K

puzzle 4th:
    A. game 1st, mystery 1st, riddle 1st
    B. bewilder 3rd, challenge 4th, confuse 4th, consider 2nd, ponder 6th, question 1st, study 1st, think 1st

pyramid 5th:
    A. cone 1st, triangle 1st
    B. build 1st, compound 4th, increase 3rd, rise 1st, soar 6th

quack K:
    A. cheat 3rd, hoaxer 5th, pretender 2nd
    B. affected 4th, fake 1st, false 3rd, put-on K
    C. gobble 4th, honk 1st

quaint 5th:
  A. charming 3rd, homey 1st, picturesque 2nd, small-town K
  B. curious 3rd, odd 4th, peculiar 4th, queer 4th, ridiculous 6th, strange 1st, unusual 3rd, weird 1st

quake 4th:
  A. shock 1st, tremor 6th
  B. jar K, jostle 6th, reel 5th, rock K, shake 1st, shudder 4th, stir 3rd, tremble 3rd, wobble 4th

Quaker 1st: puritan

qualify 4th:
  A. adapt 4th, coach 4th, enable 4th, instruct 4th, prepare 1st, ready 1st, supply 1st, teach 1st, test 3rd, train K
  B. distinguish 6th, name K, regard 4th
  C. able 3rd, capable 4th, pass 2nd

quality 4th:
  A. excellence 2nd, greatness 1st, superior 4th
  B. characteristic 6th, class 1st, condition 3rd, grade 2nd, feature 3rd, property 3rd, rank 3rd, tone 3rd, worth 3rd

quantity 4th:
  A. amount 2nd, capacity 6th, content 3rd, extent 4th, large amount 2nd, mass 4th, measure 2nd, number K, sum 1st, volume 3rd, weight 1st
  B. allowance 5th, dose 1st, handful 1st, portion 4th

quarrel 4th:
  A. argue 3rd, blow up 1st, contest 4th, disagree 3rd, dispute 6th, have words K
  B. broil 4th, conflict 4th, difference of opinion 4th, feud 6th, variance 4th

quarry 6th:
  A. dig 1st, mine 1st, pit 1st, seek 1st
  B. game K, hunted animal 2nd, prey 4th, victim 4th

quarter 1st:
  A. area 3rd, neighborhood 2nd, part 1st, region 4th, territory 3rd
  B. fourth 1st, one-fourth 1st, twenty-five percent 4th
  C. ease 3rd, help K, locate 3rd, mercy 4th, pity 3rd

quay 5th: dock 1st, landing 1st, pier 4th, wharf 5th

queen K:
  A. empress 4th, majesty 4th, noble 3rd, princess 1st, ruler 2nd
  B. ideal 3rd, perfection 3rd, pink 1st, star K

queer 4th: abnormal 5th, astonishing 4th, comical 5th, curious 3rd, faint 3rd, gamble 5th, insane 6th, odd 4th, original 3rd, peculiar 4th, quaint 5th, ruin 5th, spoil 4th, strange 1st, suspicious 4th, uncommon 2nd, unusual 3rd

quench 6th: choke 1st, crush 4th, defeat 5th, drown 1st, ease 3rd, extinguish 5th, fill 1st, flood 2nd, hit the spot 1st, nip 1st, put out K, quiet K, satisfy 3rd, smother 6th, subdue 6th, topple 6th

query 6th:
  A. ask K, challenge 4th, examine 5th, inquire 3rd, investigate 5th, raise 1st, suspect 5th
  B. confusion 4th, doubt 1st, question 1st, reservation 3rd, survey 5th

quest 3rd:
  A. aim 3rd, campaign 3rd, goal 4th, hunt 2nd, journey 3rd, objective 2nd, point 1st, pursuit 5th
  B. chase 1st, hunt 2nd, pursue 5th, search 1st, seek 1st

question 1st:
  A. ask K, challenge 4th, doubt 1st, examine 5th, inquire 3rd, raise 1st, suspect 5th
  B. issue 4th, mystery 1st, problem 1st, puzzle 4th, query 6th, uncertainty 2nd

quick 1st:
  A. active 3rd, alert 5th, alive 3rd, energetic 4th, keen 4th, lively 1st, skillful 2nd, spirited 2nd, vigorous 5th
  B. apt 5th, brief 3rd, fast 1st, immediate 3rd, prompt 4th, rapid 4th, speedy 3rd, sudden 1st

quiet K:
  A. calm 3rd, grave 3rd, hushed 3rd, immobile 6th, inactive 3rd, meek 2nd, modest 4th, motionless 3rd, mute 3rd, noiseless 2nd, peaceful 2nd, reserved 3rd, secretive 2nd, silent 3rd, simple 2nd, sleeping K, sleepy 1st, slumbering 4th, soundless 2nd, still 1st, unexcited 4th
  B. break 1st, delay 5th, interval 6th, pause 3rd, rest 1st, silence 3rd
  C. choke 1st, prevent 3rd, quench 6th, smother 6th

quill 6th: feather 2nd, needle 3rd, nib 4th, pen 1st, plume 6th, point 1st, spine 4th

quilt 6th:
  A. piece 1st, sew 2nd
  B. bedspread 2nd, blanket 3rd, comforter 3rd, cover 1st

quit 1st: abandon 4th, cease 3rd, depart 5th, discard 6th, discontinue 4th, down K, emigrate 6th, end K, flee 5th, give up 1st, leave 1st, lessen 2nd, move K, pause 3rd, quiet down K, reject 5th, resign 5th, stop K, surrender 5th, vacate 2nd, yield 4th

quite 1st: actually 3rd, certainly 1st, completely 3rd, considerably 2nd, excessively 5th, highly 1st, in fact K, indeed 1st, really 1st, totally 2nd, truly 1st, very K

quiver 4th:
  A. container 5th, holder 1st

B. beating 1st, flapping 4th, jump K, move K, pounding 2nd, shake 1st, shiver 1st, start 1st, tremble 3rd, tremor 6th, vibrate 5th, waving 1st

quoit 6th: crop 2nd, stick K, whip 4th

quote 5th:

A. chorus 5th, passage 4th, selection 4th, words K

B. charge 2nd, evaluate 2nd, price K, value 2nd

C. call to mind 1st, cite 6th, copy 3rd, mimic 6th, note 1st, parrot 1st, proclaim 4th, recite 5th, refer to 5th, remember 1st, repeat 4th, reproduce 5th, retell 3rd, state 1st

race 1st:

A. competition 3rd, contest 4th

B. clan 5th, family K, nation 1st, people K, stock 1st, tribe 3rd

C. bolt 4th, dart 1st, hurry 1st, run K, speed 3rd

rack 1st:

A. agonize 5th, extend 4th, hang 2nd, hurt K, pain 2nd, torment 5th, torture 5th, wound 3rd

B. display 3rd, form 1st, frame 3rd, holder 1st, stand K, structure 4th

radiant 6th: bright 1st, brilliant 4th, dazzling 5th, gleaming 1st, glowing 1st, lighted 1st, magnificent 4th, shining 3rd, sparkling 5th, splendid 4th, sunny 1st

radiate 6th:

A. beam 3rd, glitter 4th, glow 1st, sparkle 5th

B. circulate 4th, scatter 3rd, send out 1st, spread 2nd

radical 6th: complete 3rd, extreme 5th, far 1st, severe 4th, total 2nd

radio 1st: beam 3rd, broadcast 5th, transmit 6th

radius 6th: arc 4th, arch 4th, circle K, section 4th

rafter 6th: beam 3rd, support 4th

rag 1st: fragment 6th, part 1st, patch 4th, piece 1st, scrap 3rd, shred 5th, towel 6th

rage 4th:

A. rave 5th, roar 1st, storm 2nd, yell K

B. anger 1st, craze 4th, fad 4th, fit K, fury 4th, madness 3rd, passion 6th, violence 5th, wrath 4th

ragged 5th: jagged 5th, ripped 1st, shabby 4th, torn 2nd, worn 3rd

raid 6th:

A. attack 3rd, invade 5th, storm 2nd

B. assault 4th, invasion 5th, seizure 3rd

rail 2nd: fence 1st, picket 3rd, post 1st, track 1st

railroad 2nd: rails 2nd, tracks 1st, train K

rain 1st: flood 2nd, mist 1st, pour 3rd, raindrops 2nd, rainfall 2nd, shower 4th, sprinkle 3rd, storm 2nd

raise 1st:
> A. cultivate 6th, develop 5th, farm K, grow K, hoe 2nd, nurse K, plant K, rear 3rd, spade 6th
>
> B. build 1st, construct 3rd, erect 4th, fabricate 5th
>
> C. elevate 2nd, heave 5th, hoist up 6th, lift 1st

rake 1st: comb 2nd, dig 1st

rally 5th:
> A. collect 3rd, gather 1st, muster 6, unite 5th
>
> B. assembly 4th, conference 4th, convention 6th, group 1st, meeting 1st

ram K: beat 1st, cram 5th, crowd 2nd, drive K, force 1st, hammer 2nd, hit K, pack 1st, pound 2nd, push 1st, strike 2nd

ramble 6th: babble 6th, chatter 1st, rave 5th, rove 6th, stroll 5th, talk K, walk K, wander 3rd

ramp 6th: access 6th, elevate 2nd, grade 2nd, hill K, incline 5th, slant 6th, slope 3rd

rampart 6th: barrier 6th, block 1st, wall 1st

ranch 5th: farm K

random 6th: accidental 4th, aimless 3rd, careless 5th, casual 5th, chance 2nd, stray 3rd

range 3rd:
> A. grass K, meadow 3rd
>
> B. roam 4th, rove 6th, sweep 4th, wander 3rd
>
> C. arrange 3rd, classify 2nd, file 1st, grade 2nd, group 1st, order 1st, rank 3rd, rate 1st
>
> D. circuit 4th, distance 4th, extent 4th, reach 1st

ranger 1st: forester 2nd

rank 3rd: class 1st, grade 2nd, level 3rd, place 1st, position 2nd, range 3rd, station 1st

ransom 6th:
> A. bribe 5th, cost K, penalty 5th, price K, purchase 3rd
>
> B. buy back 1st, free K, pay off 1st, redeem 6th
>
> C. freedom 3rd, redemption 6th, release 5th, rescue 4th

rap 1st: belt 2nd, crack 4th, hit K, knock 3rd, pat K, slap 2nd, strike 2nd, tap K

rapid 4th: brisk 6th, fast 1st, hasty 2nd, prompt 4th, quick 1st, speedy 3rd, swift 4th, urgent 6th

rapture 6th: happiness 2nd, joy 1st, paradise 4th, pleasure 2nd, thrill 4th

rare 4th:
> A. bloody 1st, uncooked 2nd, underdone 2nd
>
> B. excellent 1st, exceptional 2nd, extraordinary 5th, few 1st, fine 1st, infrequent 4th, marvelous 4th, remarkable 4th, scarce 4th, uncommon 2nd, unique 6th, unusual 3rd

rascal 5th: bad boy 1st, brat 3rd, creep 1st, imp 5th, rat K, rogue 5th, scamp 4th, villain 5th

rash 6th:
A. break out 2nd, hives 2nd, irritation 6th
B. bold 2nd, careless 5th, hasty 2nd, thoughtless 2nd

rate 1st:
A. grade 2nd, judge 1st, place 1st, rank 3rd, sort 1st
B. pace 3rd
C. charge 2nd, cost K, estimate 5th, fare 3rd, price K, toll 6th, value 2nd

rather 1st:
A. better 1st, preferably 3rd, sooner 1st
B. quite 1st, somewhat 1st, very K

ratify 6th: approve 4th, certify 6th, support 4th

ratio 6th: fraction 4th, part 1st, percentage 4th, proportion 4th, quota 5th, share 2nd

rattle 2nd: bewilder 3rd, clatter 5th, confuse 4th, disturb 6th, racket 2nd, upset 3rd

ravage 6th: damage 5th, desolate 6th, destroy 2nd, devastate 6th, lay waste 2nd, ruin 5th, wreck 4th

rave 5th: go mad K, howl 4th, rage 4th, roar 1st, storm 2nd, wander 3rd, yell K

ravenous 6th: devouring 5th, fierce 4th, greedy 5th, hungry 2nd, piggish 1st, starving 5th

ravine 5th: gorge 5th, gulf 4th, valley 2nd

ravish 6th:
A. charm 3rd, delight 3rd, enchant 6th
B. abduct 6th, abuse 6th, assault 4th, attack 3rd, kidnap 2nd, seize 3rd, steal 3rd

raw 1st:
A. bloody 1st, fresh 2nd, rare 4th, uncooked 2nd
B. green K, not ripe 1st
C. exposed 4th, natural 2nd, rough 4th, untrained 2nd

ray 1st: beam 3rd, flame 3rd, gleam 1st, radiation 6th, stream 3rd

razor 6th: blade 2nd, edge 1st, knife 1st, shaver 1st

reach 1st:
A. distance 4th, expanse 5th, extension 4th, space 1st, stretch 4th, sweep 4th
B. approach 3rd, extend 4th, gain 2nd, get K, grasp 4th, seize 3rd, span 6th, stretch out 4th, touch 1st

react 5th: answer K, reply 1st, respond 5th, return 1st

read K: go over 1st, review 4th, skim 6th, study 2nd

ready 1st:
A. equipped 5th, fit K, prepared 1st, willing 1st
B. arrange 3rd, done 1st, order 1st, prepare 1st, provide 3rd

real 1st:
    A. concrete 4th, material 5th, natural 2nd, physical 5th
    B. actual 3rd, genuine 5th, just 1st, pure 3rd, simple 1st, sincere 4th, true K

reality 5th: actual 3rd, concrete 4th, fact 1st, life 1st, realness 2nd, truth 1st

realize 2nd: comprehend 5th, discover 1st, figure out 2nd, know 1st,
    perceive 6th, recognize 3rd, take in 1st

realm 4th: area 3rd, empire 4th, kingdom 3rd, orbit 4th, place 1st, province 6th,
    region 4th, section 4th, territory 3rd, zone 4th

reap 4th: crop 2nd, cut K, gather 1st, harvest 4th, prune 3rd, trim 4th

rear 3rd:
    A. back 1st, behind 1st, heel 3rd, tail 1st
    B. bring up 1st, erect 4th, raise 1st

reason 1st:
    A. alibi 6th, basis 5th, cause 2nd, excuse 3rd
    B. deduce 6th, explain 2nd, figure 4th, review 4th, think 1st, understand 1st
    C. intelligence 4th, sanity 6th, sense 1st

reassure 6th: assure 3rd, back up 1st, encourage 4th, hearten 1st, inspire 4th,
    support 4th, uplift 2nd

rebuke 4th:
    A. refutation 5th, reproach 6th, scolding 5th
    B. lecture 5th, refute 3rd, reproach 6th, scold 5th

recall 3rd: recognize 3rd, recollect 6th, remember 1st, review 4th

receipt 5th: bill 1st, ticket 1st

receive 1st: accept 3rd, acquire 4th, catch 1st, gain 2nd, get K, inherit 5th,
    obtain 5th, take in 1st

recent 3rd: current 3rd, fresh 2nd, late K, latest 1st, modern 2nd, new K

reception 5th:
    A. greeting 3rd, welcome 1st
    B. acceptance 3rd, admission 4th, gathering 1st, party K

recess 2nd: break 1st, holiday K, interval 6th, lull 5th, pause 3rd, rest 1st,
    vacation 2nd

recipe 4th: directions 1st, formula 6th, plan 1st, process 4th, system 2nd

recite 5th:
    A. narrate 6th, recount 6th, relate 4th, speak 1st, state 1st
    B. chant 5th, mimic 6th, perform 4th, quote 5th, rehearse 6th, repeat 4th,
    say by heart 1st

reckless 5th: careless 5th, dangerous 6th, daring 2nd, foolish 2nd,
    impulsive 5th, rash 6th, thoughtless 2nd, wild 2nd

reckon 5th:
    A. add K, calculate 5th, compute 1st, count 1st, figure 4th, number K
    B. conclude 3rd, consider 2nd, judge 1st, rate 1st, think 1st, value 2nd

reclaim 6th: clean 1st, recover 4th, reform 5th, rescue 4th, restore 5th, save 1st

recline 6th: lay 1st, lie 1st, lounge 6th, repose 6th

recognize 3rd: comprehend 5th, identify 4th, know 1st, perceive 6th, realize 2nd, recall 3rd, remember 1st, see K, understand 1st

recollect 6th: recall 3rd, recognize 3rd, remember 1st, review 4th

recommend 5th: advise 3rd, approve 4th, back 1st, favor 1st, offer 2nd, promote 5th, propose 4th, suggest 2nd, support 4th

recompense 6th:
  A. compensation 6th, fee 4th, payment 1st, reward 4th, salary 3rd, satisfaction 3rd, wages 3rd
  B. compensate 6th, pay K, recover 4th, repay 3rd, reward 4th

reconcile 6th:
  A. harmonize 4th, heal 3rd, make up 1st, mend 1st, reunite 5th
  B. accept 3rd, adjust 5th, resign 5th, resolve 5th, settle 2nd, submit 4th

record 2nd:
  A. chornicle 6th, log K, note 1st, register 4th, report 1st, set down K, write K
  B. account 3rd, achievement 5th, chronicle 6th, diary 3rd, history 2nd, journal 2nd, register 4th, report 1st

recount 6th: narrate 6th, recite 5th, relate 4th, report 1st, review 4th, tell K

recourse 6th:
  A. backup 1st, retreat 4th
  B. action 1st, course 3rd, plan 1st, resource 5th, way K

recover 4th:
  A. find K, get back 1st, regain 6th, rescue 4th, restore 5th, retrieve 6th, save 1st
  B. get better 1st, get well 1st, heal 3rd, mend 1st, revive 6th

recreation 5th: entertainment 4th, exercise 1st, fun K, game K, hobby 3rd, pastime 2nd, play K, relaxation 4th, rest 1st

recruit 6th: call 1st, enlist 6th, gather 1st, impress 5th, summon 4th

recur 6th: continue 2nd, persist 5th, reappear 2nd, repeat 4th, return 2nd

redeem 6th: exchange 4th, free K, offset 2nd, pay off 1st, purchase 3rd, ransom 6th, recover 4th, regain 6th, restore 5th, retrieve 6th, save 1st

redouble 6th: concentrate 5th, heighten 4th, intensify 6th, try harder 1st

reduce 3rd:
  A. abbreviate 6th, cut K, diminish 6th, lessen 3rd, limit 3rd, shorten 1st, trim 4th
  B. ease 3rd, relax 4th, restrain 5th

reef 5th: bank 1st, bar 3rd, flat 2nd, ledge 5th, ridge 5th

reel 5th:
  A. bobbin 4th, spool 2nd, wheel 1st

B. lurch 5th, pitch 2nd, rock K, roll 1st, rotate 6th, spin 1st, sway 3rd, waver 5th, whirl 4th

refer 5th: ask K, call on 1st, direct 1st, indicate 4th, mean 1st, mention 5th, quote 5th, signify 6th, site 5th, specify 5th

refine 6th: civilize 4th, clean 1st, clear 2nd, cultivate 6th, elevate 2nd, finish 1st, improve 3rd, polish 4th, purify 3rd, sensitize 5th, sharpen 1st

reflect 4th: contemplate 6th, copy 3rd, deliberate 6th, display 3rd, exhibit 4th, illustrate 4th, intimate 5th, mirror 4th, remember 1st, reproduce 5th, reverse 5th, show 1st, think 1st, turn 1st

reflex 6th: habit 3rd, reaction 5th, response 6th

reform 5th: better 1st, change 2nd, correct 3rd, improve 3rd, make over 1st, redo 1st, repair 4th, reshape 3rd, restore 5th, revolutionize 5th

refrain 6th:
    A. avoid 3rd, cease 3rd, discontinue 4th, halt 4th, hold 1st, quit 1st, renounce 6th, resist 4th, restrain 5th, stop K
    B. chorus 5th, repetition 4th

refresh 6th: awaken 3rd, energize 4th, motivate 6th, pick up 1st, prompt 4th, renew 2nd, rest 1st, restore 5th, revive 6th

refrigerator 2nd: cooler 1st, freezer 4th, icebox 1st

refuge 5th: hiding 1st, protection 4th, retreat 4th, sanctuary 6th, security 3rd, shelter 4th

refuse 2nd: decline 6th, forbid 4th, reject 5th

refute 5th: deny 5th, expose 4th

regain 6th: get back 1st, recover 4th, repossess 3rd, retrieve 6th

regal 6th: imperial 5th, majestic 4th, noble 3rd, royal 3rd, stately 2nd

regard 4th:
    A. behold 3rd, detect 4th, look K, notice 1st, perceive 6th, see K, view 1st, witness 3rd
    B. contemplate 6th, think 1st
    C. admire 5th, cherish 5th, esteem 5th, honor 1st, praise 4th, respect 2nd, treasure 4th, value 2nd, worship 4th

regiment 5th: company 2nd

region 4th: area 3rd, arena 5th, district 4th, location 3rd, place 1st, quarter 1st, realm 4th, section 4th, site 5th, sphere 6th, territory 3rd, zone 4th

register 4th:
    A. catalog 5th, enlist 6th, enter 2nd, list 2nd, record 2nd, sign 1st
    B. journal 2nd, record 2nd, roll 1st

registration 5th: certificate 6th, list 2nd, permit 3rd, record 2nd, ticket 1st

regret 5th:
    A. apologies 6th, grief 5th, remorse 6th, shame 3rd, sorrow 4th, woe 4th, worry 1st
    B. grieve 5th, lament 6th, miss K, mourn 4th, repent 6th

regular 3rd: common 2nd, customary 6th, even 1st, habitual 3rd, normal 5th, orderly 2nd, ordinary 3rd, routine 6th, typical 6th, uniform 1st, usual 3rd

regulate 5th: accustom 4th, adapt 4th, adjust 5th, alter 4th, control 2nd, correct 3rd, direct 1st, govern 1st, manage 4th, modify 5th, operate 3rd, rule K, run K

rehearse 6th: drill 2nd, practice 1st, prepare 1st, recite 5th, repeat 4th, review 4th, train 6th

reheat 6th: cook 1st, warm 1st

reign 4th:
  A. administer 6th, control 2nd, dominate 5th, govern 1st, lead 1st, prevail 5th, rule 2nd
  B. era 6th, period 2nd

reins 1st: bridle 4th, control 2nd, hold 1st, restrain 5th

reject 5th:
  A. decline 6th, forbid 4th, refuse 2nd, say no to K, turn down 1st
  B. discard 6th, eliminate 5th, rid 1st, toss 2nd

rejoice 4th: celebrate 4th, delight 3rd, glory 3rd, party K, triumph 5th

relate 4th:
  A. communicate 5th, narrate 6th, recite 5th, repeat 4th, say K, tell K
  B. associate 5th, connect 3rd, link 5th

relation 4th:
  A. association 5th, connection 3rd, similarity 4th, tie-in 1st
  B. family K, relative K

relative 4th:
  A. fitting 2nd, regarding 4th, related 4th, relating to 4th
  B. blood 1st, family K, kin 1st, relation 4th

relax 4th: bend K, ease 3rd, free K, lessen 2nd, loosen 5th, release 5th, soften 1st, weaken 3rd, yield 4th

relay 6th:
  A. communicate 5th, report 1st, say K, tell K
  B. give 1st, hand off 1st

release 5th:
  A. announcement 3rd
  B. freedom 3rd, loosening 5th
  C. excuse 3rd, free K, let out K, liberate 3rd, lose K, unfasten 4th, untie 3rd

relic 5th: antique 6th, fossil 4th, heirloom 5th, remains 1st, trace 3rd

relief 4th:
  A. break 1st, recess 2nd, rest 1st
  B. aid 2nd, assistance 4th, comfort 3rd, help K, rescue 4, support 4th

relieve 4th: aid 2nd, assist 4th, calm 3rd, ease 3rd, help K, lessen 2nd, lose K, relax 4th, rest 1st, soothe 5th

religion 4th: belief 1st, church 1st, creed 6th, cult 5th, faith 3rd, sect 5th

relish 6th:

    A. appetite 4th, delight 3rd, enjoyment 2nd, liking 1st, pleasure 2nd, taste 1st, zest 6th

    B. approve 4th, delight in 3rd, enjoy 2nd

    C. appetizer 4th, pickle 1st

reluctant 6th: afraid 1st, cautious 5th, hesitant 4th, resistant 4th, shy 1st, unwilling 3rd

rely 5th: believe in 1st, count on 1st, depend 3rd, lean on 3rd, trust 1st

remain 1st: abide 5th, continue 2nd, dwell 4th, endure 4th, exist 3rd, inhabit 6th, last K, linger 4th, reside 5th, rest 1st, stay 1st, survive 5th, tarry 5th, wait 1st

remark 4th:

    A. comment 5th, declare 5th, mention 5th, note 1st, notice 1st, observe 3rd, perceive 6th, say K, speak 1st, state 1st, voice 1st

    B. comment 5th, saying 1st, statement 2nd

remedy 4th:

    A. correct 3rd, cure 4th, heal 3rd

    B. cure 4th, medicine 4th, tonic 2nd, treatment 5th

remember 1st: recall 3rd, recognize 3rd, recollect 6th, recover 4th, reflect 4th, retrieve 6th

remind 3rd: cue 2nd, hint 1st, prompt 4th, review 4th, suggest 2nd

remnant 6th: carry-over 1st, piece 1st, remains 2nd, rest 1st, scrap 3rd, trace 3rd, waste 1st

remonstrate 6th:

    A. scold 5th

    B. argue 3rd, challenge 4th, complain 4th, oppose 3rd, protest 4th

remorse 6th: grief 5th, guilt 4th, regret 5th, repentance 6th, sadness 1st, shame 1st, sorrow 4th, woe 4th, worry 1st

remote 5th:

    A. obscure 6th, pointless 2nd, strange 1st, vague 5th

    B. distant 4th, far 1st, foreign 5th, removed 2nd

    C. slight 4th, slim 5th, small K, tiny 2nd

remove 2nd:

    A. dethrone 6th, kill 1st, cut K, subtract 1st, take away 1st

    B. bare 3rd, clean 1st

renaissance 5th: awakening 3rd, rebirth 3rd, renewal 4th, revival 6th

rend 4th: divide 4th, rip K, shred 5th, slice 5th, split 4th, tear 2nd

renew 4th:

    A. begin again 1st, repeat 4th, resume 5th

    B. make anew 3rd, modernize 3rd, refresh 6th, repair 4th

renounce 6th: abandon 4th, avoid 3rd, deny 5th, disown 3rd, forego 5th, forsake 6th, give up 1st, shun 6th, stop K

renown 5th: eminence 6th, fame 3rd, importance 1st, noted 2nd, popularity 3rd, respect 2nd

rent K:
  A. hire 3rd, lease 6th, let K
  B. fee 4th, payment 1st
  C. crack 4th, damage 5th, hole K, rip 1st, tear 2nd

repair 4th:
  A. correction 3rd, improvement 3rd, renewal 4th, restoration 5th
  B. correct 3rd, cure 4th, fix 1st, mend 1st, renew 4th, restore 5th, right K

repeat 4th:
  A. duplicate 6th, playback 1st
  B. copy 3rd, duplicate 6th, echo 4th, recur 6th, redo 1st, reproduce 5th

repel 6th:
  A. disgust 5th, revolt 5th, sicken 2nd
  B. oppose 3rd, push 1st, put off 1st, reject 5th, repulse 6th, resist 4th

repent 6th:
  A. make amends 4th, make up for 1st
  B. grieve 5th, lament 6th, mourn 4th, regret 5th

replace 5th:
  A. follow 1st, substitute 5th, succeed 2nd
  B. displace 3rd, replenish 6th, restore 5th

replenish 6th: provide 3rd, refill 1st, reload 2nd, renew 1st, replace 5th, supply 1st

reply 1st:
  A. acknowledgment 5th, answer 1st, comment 5th, reaction 5th, response 5th
  B. answer 1st, comment 5th, respond 5th

report 1st:
  A. announce 3rd, communicate 5th, relay 6th, repeat 4th, tell K
  B. account 3rd, article 2nd, log K, news 1st, paper K, relation 4th, review 4th, rumor 5th, telling 1st

repose 6th:
  A. lounge 6th, relax 4th
  B. ease 3rd, nap K, peace 1st, recess 2nd, rest 1st, sleep K, vacation 2nd

represent 4th: illustrate 4th, image 4th, picture K, portray 5th, present K, symbolize 5th, typify 6th

reproach 6th:
  A. blame 2nd, disapproval 4th, scolding 5th
  B. blame 2nd, criticize 5th, disapprove 4th, scold 5th, shame 3rd

reproduce 5th: breed 4th, copy 3rd, duplicate 6th, match 3rd, multiply 2nd, redo 1st, renew 4th, repeat 4th, restore 5th

reptile 4th: lizard 1st, serpent 5th, snake 5th

repulse 6th:
   A. deny 5th, put off 1st
   B. denial 5th, rejection 5th, repelling 6th
   C. defeat 5th, drive away 1st, repel 6th

reputation 5th: fame 3rd, honor 1st, name K, rank 3rd, repute 5th, standing 1st

request 4th:
   A. appeal 3rd, ask K, beg 1st, demand 5th, plead 5th
   B. appeal 3rd, demand 5th, plea 5th

require 1st: demand 5th, force 1st, lack 1st, need 1st, order 1st, want K

requisition 6th:
   A. call K, command 2nd, demand 5th, order 1st, request 4th
   B. ask K, order 1st, request 4th, seize 3rd, take over 1st

rescue 4th:
   A. delivery 5th, freedom 3rd, liberty 3rd, salvation 6th
   B. deliver 5th, free K, liberate 3rd, release 5th, save 1st

research 5th:
   A. exploration 4th, investigation 5th, search 1st, study 1st
   B. explore 4th, inquire 3rd, investigate 5th

resemble 4th: be like 1st, be similar to 4th, favor 2nd, look like 1st, match 3rd, mimic 6th, seem like 1st

resent 5th: be irritated 6th, dislike 3rd, envy 4th

reserve 3rd:
   A. conserve 5th, put aside 3rd, retain 5th, save 1st, withhold 2nd
   B. backup 2nd, extra 1st, spare 3rd
   C. composure 4th, formality 4th
   D. stock 1st, store K, supply 2nd

reside 5th: dwell 4th, inhabit 6th, live 1st, occupy 3rd

residence 5th: address K, domicile 5th, dwelling 4th, habitation 6th, home K, house K, location 3rd, lodging 4th

resident 5th:
   A. dwelling 4th, inhabiting 6th, living 1st
   B. dweller 4th, inhabitant 6th, lodger 5th, occupant 3rd, tenant 5th

resign 5th:
   A. depart 5th, leave 1st, quit 1st, retire 4th
   B. accept 3rd, give up 1st, submit 4th, surrender 5th, yield 4th

resin 5th: amber 5th, copal 5th, gum 1st, pitch 2nd, tar 1st

resist 4th: defy 6th, fight K, interfere 4th, oppose 3rd, repel 6th, stop K, withstand 2nd

resolution 5th:
   A. bill 1st, declaration 5th, outcome 4th, proposal 2nd, ruling 1st, verdict 6th
   B. desire 5th, determination 5th, proposal 2nd, purpose 2nd, resolve 5th, will K

resolve 5th:
A. decide 1st, determine 5th, propose 4th, solve 4th, will K
B. break up 1st, separate 3rd
C. determination 5th, effort 2nd, purpose 2nd, resolution 5th, stubbornness 5th

resort 5th:
A. aid 2nd, choice 3rd, recourse 6th
B. hotel 3rd, refuge 5th, retreat 4th
C. come to 1st, lower 1st, try K, use K

resource 5th: aid 2nd, backup 2nd, help K, reserve 3rd, support 4th

resourceful 5th: clever 3rd, creative 3rd, enterprising 5th, inventive 2nd, original 3rd

respect 2nd:
A. admiration 5th, consideration 2nd, courtesy 4th, politeness 4th, reverence 4th
B. compliment 5th, esteem 5th, honor 1st, regard 4th, venerate 6th

respecting 4th:
A. concerning 3rd, considering 2nd
B. admiring 5th, honoring 2nd, venerating 6th

respiration 6th: breath 1st, breathing 1st, gasping 4th, wheezing 5th

respite 6th:
A. internal 6th, pause 3rd, rest 1st
B. ease 3rd, relax 4th, relieve 4th

respond 5th: acknowledge 5th, answer 1st, react 5th, reply 2nd, retort 5th

responsible 4th: accountable 3rd, answerable 2nd, dependable 3rd, liable 6th, reasonable 2nd, reliable 5th, sensible 6th, stable 4th

rest 1st:
A. ease 3rd, pause 3rd, peace 1st, quiet K, sleep K
B. place 1st, put K, relax 4th, remain 2nd, settle 2nd

restaurant 5th: cafe 4th, cafeteria 5th, coffeehouse 2nd, delicatessen 5th

restless 4th:
A. sleepless 1st
B. agitable 5th, excitable 4th, nervous 1st, restive 5th, uneasy 3rd
C. changing 2nd, moving 1st, wandering 3rd

restore 5th: cure 4th, fix 1st, mend 1st, patch 4th, re-establish 3rd, remodel 3rd, renew 3rd, repair 4th, replace 5th

restrain 5th: contain 5th, control 2nd, delay 5th, deter 5th, hinder 6th, holdback 1st, prevent 3rd, stop K

restrict 6th: bound 2nd, cage 1st, limit 3rd, localize 3rd

result 2nd:
A. conclude 3rd, finish 1st
B. arise 4th, emerge 5th, follow 1st

C. answer K, conclusion 3rd, consequence 4th, effect 3rd, end K, outcome 4th, product 4th

resume 5th: advance 2nd, continue 2nd, proceed 4th, restart 1st, return 2nd

retain 5th:
  A. employ 5th, hire 3rd
  B. memorize 3rd, remember 1st
  C. hold 1st, keep K, reserve 3rd, save 1st

retire 4th:
  A. go to bed K, rest 1st
  B. give up work 1st, resign 5th
  C. depart 5th, leave 1st, retreat 4th, withdraw 2nd

retort 5th:
  A. answer K, reply 2nd, response 5th
  B. answer K, reply 2nd, respond 5th

retreat 4th:
  A. flee 5th, leave 1st, retire 4th, withdraw 2nd
  B. departure 5th, escape 1st, privacy 3rd, protection 4th, rest 1st, sanctuary 6th, shelter 4th

retrieve 6th: acquire 4th, recover 4th, redeem 6th, remedy 4th, rescue 4th, restore 5th

return 1st:
  A. give back 1st, replace 5th, restore 5th
  B. gain 2nd, profits 4th, yield 4th
  C. reverse 5th
  D. reappear 2nd, reoccur 3rd
  E. duplication 6th, recurrence 6th
  F. answer K, response 5th
  G. reply 2nd, respond 5th

reveal 4th:
  A. acknowledge 5th, tell K
  B. bare 3rd, exhibit 4th, expose 4th, show 1st

revenge 5th: bitterness 3rd, get back at 1st, get even with 1st, repayment 1st, satisfaction 3rd, spite 3rd

revenue 6th: cash 2nd, earnings 2nd, gain 2nd, income 4th, payment 1st, profits 4th, wealth 3rd

reverence 4th: awe 6th, honor 1st, regard 4th, respect 2nd, worship 4th

reverend 4th:
  A. holy 5th, honorable 3rd, worthy 3rd
  B. clergy 6th, minister 4th, pastor 4th, priest 4th

reverse 5th:
  A. backward 4th, contrasting 4th, opposite 3rd
  B. contrary 4th, opposite 3rd

C. cancel 6th, change 2nd, conflict 4th, counter 5th, turn 1st

review 4th:
- A. examine 5th, reconsider 2nd, skim 6th
- B. study 1st, survey 5th

revive 6th:
- A. recall 3rd
- B. freshen 2nd, heal 3rd, mend 1st, rally 5th, rebuild 3rd, recover 4th, remodel 3rd, renew 4th, restore 5th, start 1st

revolt 5th:
- A. go against 1st, oppose 3rd
- B. disgust 5th, dislike 1st, sicken 2nd
- C. mutiny 6th, riot 6th, uprising 5th

revolution 5th:
- A. mutiny 6th, revolt 5th, riot 6th, uprising 5th
- B. circulation 4th, curl 2nd, loop 5th, rotation 6th, turn 1st

revolve 5th:
- A. recur 6th, return 1st
- B. circle 1st, circulate 4th, rotate 6th, spin 1st, turn 1st

revolver 5th: gun K, pistol 5th

reward 4th:
- A. compensate 6th, pay K, tip 1st
- B. award 5th, bonus 6th, gain 2nd, gift 1st, outcome 4th, payment 1st, present 2nd, result 2nd

rhyme 6th: lyric 6th, poem 3rd, song K, verse 4th

rhythm 5th:
- A. flow 1st, harmony 4th
- B. beat 1st, pulse 5th, rate 1st, time 1st, throb 5th

rib 1st: joke 1st, needle 3rd, tease 3rd

ribbon 4th: band 1st, headband 2nd, sash 6th, strip 3rd

rich K:
- A. bright 1st, vivid 6th,
- B. wealthy 3rd
- C. fattening 2nd, heavy 1st, sweet 1st
- D. elegant 5th, extravagant 6th, lavish 6th, ornate 4th, precious 4th, valuable 4th

rid 1st: eliminate 5th, free K, relieve 4th, remove 2nd

riddle 1st: mystery 1st, problem 1st, puzzle 4th, question 1st, secret 1st

ride K:
- A. drive K, journey 3rd, spin 1st, trip 1st
- B. mount 2nd, sit on K
- C. annoy 5th, bother 2nd, tease 3rd
- D. drive K, journey 3rd, tour 3rd, travel 3rd

ridge 5th: crest 4th, hill 1st, ledge 5th, mound 5th

ridicule 6th:

    A. contempt 5th, mockery 4th, teasing 3rd

    B. mock 4th, scorn 4th, tease 3rd

ridiculous 6th: absurd 6th, comical 5th, foolish 2nd, impossible 3rd, senseless 2nd, stupid 4th, unreasonable 2nd, untrue 1st

rifle 4th: look K, sort 2nd

rig 1st:

    A. clothe 1st, dress K, equip 5th, furnish 4th, supply 2nd

    B. equipment 5th, outfit 2nd

    C. carriage 5th, vehicle 6th

    D. adapt 4th, convert 4th, fit K, modify 5th, tailor 4th

right K:

    A. accurate 6th, correct 3rd, exact 2nd, precise 5th, true 1st

    B. ethical 5th, good K, honest 3rd, moral 3rd, polite 4th, proper 3rd

    C. license 5th, permission 3rd, privilege 5th, title 3rd

    D. adjust 5th, fix 1st, mend 1st, remedy 4th

rigid 5th:

    A. harsh 5th, severe 4th, stern 4th, strict 6th, stubborn 5th, unbending 2nd

    B. controlled 2nd, exact 2nd, firm 2nd, hard 1st, set K, solid 3rd, stiff 3rd, tight 1st

rim 1st: border 1st, boundary 4th, brink 6th, curb 3rd, edge 1st, limit 3rd, lip 1st

ring 1st:

    A. gang 1st, group 1st

    B. band 1st, circle K, loop 5th

    C. clang 4th, chime 6th, toll 6th

    D. revolve 5th, spin 1st

    E. sound 1st, tone 3rd

rinse 3rd:

    A. bath 1st, cleaning K, shower 4th, wash 1st

    B. clean K, launder 6th, wash 1st, wet K, wipe 1st

riot 6th:

    A. celebration 4th, merrymaking 3rd, party K

    B. fight K, revolt 5th

    C. crazy 4th, disorder 3rd, fun 3rd, panic 1st, wild 2nd

rip K:

    A. crack 4th, cut K, slit 5th, tear 2nd

    B. cut K, rend 4th, shred 5th, slash 6th, tear 2nd

ripe 1st: aged 1st, mature 5th, mellow 6th, ready 1st

ripen 1st: age 1st, develop 5th, mature 5th, mellow 6th, season 2nd

ripple 4th:

    A. ruffle 6th, wrinkle 3rd

B. splash 1st, swell 3rd, wave K

rise 1st:

    A. arise 4th, ascend 4th, climb 1st, stand 1st

    B. happen 1st, occur 3rd, pass 2nd

    C. hill 1st, incline 5th, lift 1st, mound 2nd, slope 3rd

    D. appearance 2nd, coming K

    E. awaken 3rd

    F. expansion 5th, gain 2nd

    G. come up 1st, develop 5th, expand 5th, grow K, increase 3rd, raise 1st, swell 3rd

risk 4th:

    A. endanger 6th, threaten 5th

    B. adventure 3rd, chance 2nd, danger 1st, gamble 5th, hazard 6th, menace 5th, peril 5th

    C. attempt 2nd, bet 1st, dare 2nd, gamble 5th, try K, wager 3rd

rite 6th:

    A. command 2nd, law 1st, order 1st, rule 2nd

    B. celebration 4th, ceremony 5th, custom 6th, ritual 6th, tradition 5th

ritual 6th: ceremony 5th, custom 6th, rite 6th, service 5th, tradition 5th

rival 4th:

    A. competing 5th, competitive 5th, opposing 5th

    B. equal 2nd, match 3rd

    C. challenger 4th, enemy 2nd, opponent 5th

    D. challenge 4th, contend 5th, fight K

river K: branch 2nd, creek 4th, waterway 2nd, stream 1st

road K:

    A. freeway 2nd, highway 4th, lane 4th, street 1st

    B. means 1st, method 2nd, path 1st, route 4th, way K

roadbed 1st:

    A. path 1st, route 4th

    B. base 1st, foundation 5th

roam 4th: drift 2nd, ramble 6th, rove 6th, stroll 5th, travel 1st, walk K, wander 3rd

roar 1st:

    A. boom 1st, crash 2nd, rumble 3rd, thunder 3rd

    B. bellow 4th, cry K, growl 4th, howl 4th, laugh loudly 1st, scream 1st, shriek 4th, wail 5th, yell K

roast 4th:

    A. joke 1st, mock 4th, tease 3rd

    B. bake 1st, broil 4th, cook 1st, heat 1st

rob K: cheat 3rd, plunder 5th, steal 3rd, take 1st, thieve 3rd

robe 4th:
   A. adorn 6th, attire 6th, clothe 1st, drape 5th, garb 5th
   B. cape 4th, cloak 4th, coat 1st, dress K, frock 4th, gown 4th, tunic 6th
robust 5th: athletic 5th, dynamic 5th, energetic 4th, hardy 5th, healthy 1st, hearty 5th, powerful 2nd, sound 1st, stout 4th, sturdy 2nd, well 1st
rock K:
   A. disturb 6th, stun 4th, upset 3rd
   B. roll 1st, shake 1st, sway 3rd, swing 1st, wobble 4th
   C. boulder 5th, pebble 4th, stone 2nd
rocket K:
   A. fire K, launch 5th, shoot 3rd
   B. spacecraft 2nd
   C. hurry 1st, rush 2nd, speed 3rd
rod 1st:
   A. gun K, pistol 5th, revolver 5th
   B. bar 3rd, cane 3rd, pole 1st, staff 4th, stick K, wand 3rd, whip 4th
rogue 5th: knave 5th, rascal 5th, troublemaker 2nd, villain 5th, wretch 6th
role 6th: character 2nd, part 1st, position 2nd, use K
roll 1st:
   A. coil 5th, scroll 5th
   B. ripple 4th, rock K, rotate 6th, spill 1st, spin 1st, toss 2nd, turn 1st, upset 3rd, wave K
   C. list 2nd
   D. roar 1st, rumble 3rd, thunder 3rd, thundering 3rd
   E. reel 5th, spool 2nd
   F. biscuit 6th, bun 2nd
   G. circle K, loop 5th, revolve 5th
romance 5th:
   A. affair 2nd, wooing 6th
   B. fiction 5th, novel 5th, story K, tale 3rd
   C. court 3rd, flirt 6th, love K
roof 1st:
   A. dwelling 4th, home K, house K
   B. canopy 6th, ceiling 4th, cover 1st, shade 2nd, top K
room K:
   A. capacity 6th
   B. expanse 5th, freedom 3rd, space 1st
   C. dwell 4th, live 1st, lodge 4th, rent K, reside 5th
   D. apartment 1st, chamber 5th, compartment 6th
roost 2nd:
   A. perch 4th, sit on 1st
   B. home 1st, perch 4th, rest 1st, seat 1st

root 3rd:

    A. fasten 4th, plant K, set K, settle 2nd

    B. dig K, pry 6th, search 1st

    C. cheer 3rd, support 4th

    D. beginning 2nd, fundamental 4th, heart K, origin 3rd, principle 3rd, source 4th

    E. anchor 4th, base 1st, footing 1st, foundation 5th, ground 1st

rope 1st:

    A. bind 2nd, catch 1st, fasten 4th, join 3rd, lash 4th, tie 1st

    B. cable 1st, cord 4th, line K

rot 1st:

    A. decay 5th, spoil 4th

    B. corrupt 6th, poison 3rd, ruin 5th

    C. nonsense 5th

    D. contamination 6th, infection 6th, pollution 3rd

rotate 6th:

    A. change 2nd, shift 4th, switch 4th

    B. circle K, cycle 6th, revolve 5th, spin 1st, turn 1st

rote 2nd: groove 5th, habit 3rd, ritual 6th, routine 6th

rough 4th:

    A. basic 5th, brief 3rd, plain 1st, simple 2nd, sketchy 5th, unfinished 3rd

    B. difficult 5th, tough 5th

    C. bumpy 2nd, coarse 4th, harsh 5th, irregular 6th, rugged 5th, uneven 3rd

    D. primitive 5th

    E. impolite 4th, rude 2nd, unmannered 2nd

round K:

    A. circuit 4th, revolution 5th, turn 1st

    B. arch 4th, bend K, curve 3rd

    C. circular 4th, oval 1st

    D. complete 3rd, entire 3rd

    E. circle K, disk 2nd, sphere 6th

rouse 4th: call K, challenge 4th, excite 4th, inspire 4th, provoke 6th, rally 5th, stimulate 6th, stir 3rd, thrill 4th, wake up 1st

roust 5th: awaken rudely 3rd, prod 6th

route 4th:

    A. direct 1st, guide 1st, send 1st, steer 5th

    B. course 3rd, highway 4th, passage 4th, path 1st, road K, trail 2nd, way K

routine 6th:

    A. habit 3rd, method 2nd, procedure 4th, process 4th, practice 1st, rote 2nd, system 2nd

    B. accustomed 4th, automatic 6th, average 3rd, common 2nd, established 3rd, familiar 3rd, normal 5th, regular 3rd, typical 6th, usual 3rd

rove 6th: ramble 6th, roam 4th, stroll 5th, travel 1st, walk K, wander 3rd

row K:

    A. chain 3rd, column 4th, layer 4th, line K, order 1st, rank 3rd, series 4th

    B. oar 1st, paddle 1st

    C. argue 3rd, fight K, quarrel 4th

    D. argument 3rd, battle 2nd, dispute 6th, fight 1st

royal 3rd: imperial 5th, majestic 4th, noble 3rd, regal 6th

rub 1st: brush 2nd, clean 1st, knead 4th, pet 1st, polish 4th, scour 6th, scrub 6th, stroke 1st, wipe 1st

rubbish 5th:

    A. debris 5th, garbage 5th, junk 3rd, litter 2nd, remains 2nd, rot 1st, trash 2nd, waste 1st

    B. foolishness 2nd, garbage 5th, nonsense 5th, trash 2nd

rude 2nd: abrupt 5th, fresh 2nd, impolite 4th, rough 4th, thoughtless 2nd, uncivil 3rd, unmannerly 2nd

ruffle 6th:

    A. disorder 3rd

    B. agitate 5th, bewilder 3rd, confuse 4th, disturb 6th, upset 3rd

    C. crease 5th, ripple 4th

    D. edging 1st, trim 4th

rug 1st: carpet 4th, mat K, pad K

rugged 5th:

    A. durable 6th, powerful 2nd, strong K, sturdy 3rd, tough 5th

    B. rocky 1st, rough 4th, uneven 2nd

    C. demanding 5th, difficult 5th, forceful 3rd, harsh 5th

ruin 5th:

    A. destruction 6th, downfall 3rd, failure 3rd, fall K, finish 1st

    B. collapse 5th, corrupt 6th, decay 5th, destroy 2nd, spoil 4th, upset 3rd

rule K:

    A. code 3rd, guide 1st, rite 6th, saying 1st, standard 3rd, truth 1st

    B. law 1st, policy 5th, principle 4th

    C. administer 6th, command 2nd, control 2nd, decide 1st, dominate 5th, find K, govern 1st, judge 1st, manage 4th

rumble 3rd:

    A. boom 1st, crash 2nd, thunder 3rd

    B. growl 4th, roar 1st

rumor 5th:

    A. gossip 5th, tell K

    B. gossip 5th, news 1st, report 1st, tale 3rd, talk K

run K:

    A. escape 2nd, flee 5th

    B. course 3rd, trip 1st, way K

C. chain 3rd, pattern 3rd, series 4th

D. competition 4th, event 3rd, game 1st, meet K

E. conduct 3rd, direct 1st, manage 4th, operate 3rd

F. flow 1st, leak 6th, melt 2nd

G. gallop 4th, jog 2nd, race 1st, rush 2nd, speed 3rd, sprint 5th

rural 5th: country 1st, farm K, outback 1st, outland 2nd, rustic 3rd

rush 2nd:

A. flow 1st, motion 3rd, surge 5th

B. assault 4th, attack 3rd

C. fast 1st, hasty 2nd, quick 1st

D. hurry 1st, race 1st, run K, scramble 4th, speed 3rd

rust 2nd:

A. age 1st, decay 5th, wear 1st

B. stain 4th

rustle 3rd: disturb 6th, move K, ripple 4th, whisper 1st

rut 1st:

A. habit 3rd, routine 6th, system 2nd

B. crack 4th, groove 5th, path 1st

saber 5th: blade 2nd, knife 1st, sword 4th

sable 5th: black K, dark K, jet K

sack 1st:

A. bag 1st, case 2nd, pack 1st, pouch 1st

B. discharge 3rd, fire K, terminate 6th

C. abuse 6th, attack 3rd, plunder 5th, ravage 6th, rob K

sacred 4th: blessed 3rd, godly 1st, holy 5th, pure 3rd, religious 4th, spiritual 5th

sacrifice 4th:

A. forfeit 6th, give up 1st, offer 2nd, reject 5th, surrender 5th, yield 4th

B. gift K, loss K, offering 2nd

sad K: depressed 5th, down K, grim 4th, pitiful 3rd, serious 4th, unhappy 1st, woeful 4th

saddle 4th:

A. perch 4th, seat 1st

B. burden 5th, impose 4th, load 2nd, strain 4th

sadness 1st: depression 6th, gloom 3rd, grief 5th, sorrow 4th

safe K:

A. guarded 1st, protected 4th, secure 3rd, sound 1st, unharmed 3rd, unhurt 2nd

B. cautious 5th, harmless 3rd, wary 5th

C. strong box 2nd, vault 5th

D. accurate 6th, believable 3rd, certain 1st, dependable 3rd, reliable 5th, true 1st

sag 1st: dip 1st, drip 2nd, droop 5th, fall K, lower 1st, sink 3rd, slide 2nd, slip 3rd, slump 5th, wilt 4th

saga 6th: adventure 3rd, fantasy 6th, legend 5th, story K, tale 3rd

sage 4th: clever 3rd, enlightened 4th, just 1st, knowing 1st, prudent 6th, wise 1st

sail 1st:
    A. outing 1st, trip 1st, voyage 4th
    B. coast 2nd, drift 2nd, float 1st

sailor 3rd: mariner 5th, seaman 2nd

saint 3rd: angel 4th, holy person 5th, model 3rd

sake 3rd: account 3rd, behalf 6th, benefit 3rd, cause 2nd, gain 2nd, goal 4th, good K, interest 1st, motive 5th, objective 2nd, purpose 2nd, reason 2nd, welfare 5th

salary 3rd: commission 2nd, earnings 1st, income 4th, pay K, wage 3rd

sale 1st:
    A. bargain 4th, discount 3rd, special 2nd
    B. deal 2nd, exchange 4th, trade 2nd

salesperson 6th: clerk 2nd, representative 4th, seller 1st

sally 5th:
    A. depart 5th, go K, leave 1st, set out 1st
    B. expedition 4th, journey 3rd, trip 1st, venture 4th

saloon 6th: bar 3rd, lounge 6th, pub 1st, tavern 5th

salt 1st: flavor 4th, season 2nd

salute 4th: address K, bow 1st, cheer 3rd, greet 3rd, hail 4th, honor 1st, nod 1st, recognize 3rd, welcome 1st

salvation 6th: deliverance 5th, freedom 3rd, liberation 3rd, release 5th, rescue 4th

same K: alike 1st, constant 4th, duplicate 6th, equal 2nd, equivalent 6th, even 1st, identical 6th, like K, matching 3rd

sample 5th:
    A. taste 1st, test 3rd, try K
    B. case 2nd, example 2nd, illustration 4th, member 2nd, model 3rd, part 1st, piece 1st, portion 4th, section 4th

sanction 6th: approve 4th, authorize 3rd, back 1st, conform 6th, consent 3rd, license 5th, permit 3rd, support 4th, warrant 5th

sand 1st:
    A. gravel 4th
    B. finish 1st, grate 4th, grind 4th, polish 4th

sane 6th: logical 6th, normal 5th, reasonable 2nd, sensible 6th, sound 1st, stable 4th

sap 1st: drain 5th, exhaust 4th, wear 1st

sapling 5th: bush 2nd, tree K, young tree 1st

sash 6th: band 1st, belt 2nd, ribbon 4th

satellite 6th: moon 1st

satisfy 3rd:
    A. baby K, comfort 3rd, content 3rd, delight 3rd, please K, spoil 4th
    B. achieve 5th, answer 1st, complete 3rd, do K, fill 1st, finish 1st, fulfill 2nd, meet K, pay K, settle 2nd

sauce 5th: flavoring 4th, relish 6th, seasoning 2nd, topping 1st

saunter 6th: ramble 6th, roam 4th, rove 6th, stroll 5th, walk K, wander 3rd

sausage 4th: breakfast meat 1st, frank 4th, meat 1st

saute 4th: cook 1st, fry 1st

savage 5th: angry 1st, fierce 4th, primitive 5th, uncivilized 4th, untame 4th, violent 5th, wild 2nd

save 1st:
    A. rescue 4th, salvage 6th
    B. economize 4th, maintain 4th, preserve 4th
    C. but K, except 2nd
    D. accumulate 6th, collect 3rd, protect 4th, store K

savior 6th: deliverer 5th, liberator 3rd, rescuer 4th

savor 6th:
    A. flavor 4th, salt 1st, season 2nd
    B. enjoy 2nd, sample 5th, taste 1st

savory 6th: flavorful 4th, juicy 1st, moist 4th, tasty 1st, tender 3rd

saw K: cut K, divide 4th, split 4th

say K:
    A. choice 3rd, opinion 3rd, turn 1st
    B. announce 3rd, assert 6th, claim 2nd, express 5th, speak 1st, state 1st, swear 4th, talk K

scale 3rd:
    A. coat 1st, cover 1st, peel 2nd, skin 1st
    B. climb 1st

scamper 4th: dart 1st, move quickly 2nd, run K, rush 2nd, sprint 5th

scandal 6th: crime 2nd, dishonor 2nd, disturbance 6th, misconduct 3rd, outrage 6th, shame 3rd

scant 6th: bare 3rd, few 1st, inferior 5th, lacking 1st, limited 3rd, scarce 1st, short 1st

scar 5th: fault 3rd, flaw 2nd

scarce 4th: barely 3rd, few 1st, hardly 1st, rare 4th, scant 6th, seldom 4th, uncommon 3rd, unusual 3rd, wanting 1st

scare 1st: alarm 3rd, fright 2nd, frighten 5th, horrify 4th, shock 1st, startle 4th, terrify 3rd

scared 1st: frightened 5th, nervous 1st, on edge 1st

scarf 6th: sash 6th, shawl 6th, tie 1st

scatter 3rd: drop 1st, litter 2nd, spread 2nd

scene 1st:

    A. area 3rd, arena 5th, locale 4th, place 1st, setting 1st, site 5th, theater 3rd

    B. event 3rd, incident 5th, occurrence 3rd, spectacle 5th

scent 3rd: bouquet 6th, fragrance 5th, odor 3rd, perfume 3rd, smell 3rd

schedule 6th:

    A. arrange 3rd, organize 4th, plan 1st

    B. book K, calendar 1st, dates 1st, list 2nd, listing 2nd, program 4th

scheme 5th:

    A. organize 4th, plan 1st, prepare 1st, think out 1st

    B. design 5th, intent 5th, plan 1st, project 4th, purpose 1st, strategy 6th

scholar 5th: intellectual 4th, learner 1st, pupil 4th, student 3rd

school K:

    A. educate 3rd, teach 1st, train K, tutor 6th

    B. group 1st, institute 5th

schoolwork 1st: homework 1st

science 3rd: information 5th, knowledge 2nd, methods 2nd, principles 4th

scoff 6th: jeer 5th, laugh at 1st, ridicule 6th, sneer 6th

scold 5th: accuse 4th, blame 2nd, charge 2nd, complain 4th, criticize 5th, fault 3rd

scoop 4th:

    A. facts 1st, information 5th, report 2nd

    B. ladle 4th, spoon 1st

    C. bucket 3rd, dig 1st, shovel 1st

scope 6th:

    A. glass 1st, lens 1st, microscope 4th, telescope 4th

    B. amount 2nd, degree 5th, extent 4th, measure 2nd, range 3rd, size 1st, span 6th

scorch 6th: bake 1st, burn 3rd, roast 4th, toast 5th

score 1st: amount 2nd, count 1st, grade 2nd, mark 1st, rate 1st, record 2nd, sum 1st, total 2nd

scorn 4th: attack 3rd, contempt 5th, insult 5th, mock 4th, reject 5th, slight 4th, tease 3rd

scour 6th:

    A. look K, search 1st, separate 3rd, sift 4th, sort 1st

    B. clean 1st, scrape 4th, scrub 6th, wash 1st

scourge 6th: bad luck 1st, curse 3rd, evil 3rd, misfortune 3rd, plague 5th

scout 1st:

    A. escort 5th, guide 1st, leader 1st

    B. examine 5th, explore 4th, investigate 5th, observe 3rd, spy 4th, survey 5th

scramble 4th:

    A. hurry 1st, race 1st, rush 2nd

B. clash 5th, fight K, struggle 1st

C. blend 5th, confuse 4th, disorder 3rd, mix 1st

scrap 3rd:

    A. abandon 4th, discard 6th, junk 3rd

    B. argument 3rd, battle 2nd, disagreement 3rd, quarrel 4th

    C. fragment 6th, part 1st, patch 4th, piece 1st, rag 1st, remainder 2nd, shred 5th

scrapbook 3rd: album 1st, chronicle 6th, record 2nd

scrape 4th:

    A. bind 2nd, difficulty 5th, fix 1st, trouble 1st

    B. brush 2nd, clean 1st, cut K, graze 5th, hurt 1st, irritate 6th, rub 1st, scour 6th, scratch 4th, scrub 6th, shave 1st

scratch 4th:

    A. cut K, scrape 4th, shave 1st

    B. cut K, scar 5th, wound 3rd

scream 1st: cry 1st, roar 1st, screech 5th, shout 1st, yell K

screech 1st: *See* scream.

screen 5th:

    A. barrier 6th, blind 3rd, cover 1st, shade 2nd

    B. guard 1st, hide 1st, protect 4th, shield 4th

    C. filter 5th, sieve 5th

screw 3rd:

    A. fasten 4th, turn 1st, twist 1st

    B. bolt 4th, clamp 5th, fastener 4th

scroll 5th:

    A. list 2nd, manuscript 6th, paper K

    B. move K, unroll 1st

scrub 6th: brush 2nd, clean 1st, rub 1st, scour 6th, scrape 4th, wash 1st, wipe 1st

scuff 5th: brush 2nd, rub 1st, scrape 4th

sculptor 4th: artist 2nd, carver 4th

sculpture 4th: figure 2nd, statue 4th

scuttle 4th: damage 5th, destroy 2nd, ruin 5th, wreck 4th

sea K: abundance 5th, a lot K, host 4th, ocean 1st

seal K:

    A. brand 2nd, label 3rd, mark 1st, stamp 2nd

    B. cement 4th, close K, glue 1st, secure 3rd, shut 1st, stick K, tape 1st

seam 5th: connection 3rd, joint 4th

search 1st:

    A. quest 3rd, scouting 1st

    B. examine 5th, explore 4th, hunt 2nd, inspect 5th, investigate 5th

season 2nd:

    A. flavor 4th, salt 1st, spice 3rd

    B. age 1st, cycle 5th, period 2nd, span 6th, term 3rd, time 1st

    C. accustom 4th, harden 2nd, ripen 2nd, toughen 5th

seat 1st:

    A. lead 1st, place 1st, put K

    B. assign 5th, elect 3rd

    C. bench 4th, chair 1st, couch 4th

second 1st:

    A. instant 3rd, moment 1st

    B. following 1st, next K, other 1st, runner-up 2nd

secret 1st:

    A. code 3rd, mystery 1st, puzzle 4th

    B. concealed 4th, covered 1st, hidden 1st, private 3rd, unknown 2nd

secretary 4th: assistant 4th, clerk 2nd, helper 1st

section 4th: area 3rd, division 4th, part 1st, piece 1st, portion 4th

secure 3rd:

    A. acquire 4th, get K

    B. attach 5th, close K, fix 1st, lock 1st, tape 1st

    C. defend 5th, guard 1st, protect 4th

    D. comfortable 3rd, guarded 1st, protected 4th, safe 1st

see K: look K, notice 1st, observe 3rd, view 2nd, watch 1st

seed 1st:

    A. child K, heir 4th, offspring 2nd

    B. beginning 1st, start 1st

    C. center 2nd, core 6th, pit 1st

seek 1st: explore 4th, hunt 2nd, investigate 5th, look K, pursue 5th, search 1st

seem 1st: appear 2nd, look like K

seep 4th: drain 5th, drip 2nd, leak 6th, soak 5th

seesaw 1st: bounce 6th, change 2nd, shift 4th, rotate 6th, up and down K

seize 3rd: catch 1st, clasp 4th, get K, grab 4th, grasp 4th, handle 2nd, hold 1st, pull K, steal 3rd, take 1st

seldom 4th: few 1st, not often 1st, not usual 3rd, occasional 3rd, rarely 4th, scarce 4th, uncommon 3rd, unusual 3rd

select 4th: choose 3rd, pick 1st, put aside 3rd

self 3rd: being 1st, I K, individual 3rd, me K, person 1st

selfish 5th: childish 4th, grabby 4th, greedy 5th, mean 1st, miserly 5th, taking 1st, unsharing 3rd

sell K: bargain 4th, market 1st, merchandise 6th, offer 2nd, trade 2nd

senate 1st: legislature 5th, ruling body 2nd

send K: convey 4th, deliver 5th, direct 1st, mail 1st, ship 1st, transmit 6th

senior 6th: aged 1st, chief 1st, elder 5th, first 1st, higher 1st, older 1st, over K, superior 4th

sensation 5th:
A. marvel 4th, spectacle 5th, wonder 1st
B. awareness 3rd, emotion 4th, feeling 1st, impression 5th, passion 6th, sense 1st

sense 1st:
A. feeling 1st, instinct 5th, judgement 3rd, opinion 3rd
B. intent 5th, meaning 1st, message 1st
C. intelligence 4th, mind 1st, understanding 1st

sensible 6th: intelligent 4th, objective 2nd, practical 4th, realistic 5th, reasonable 3rd, sane 6th, thoughtful 2nd, wise 1st

sensitive 5th:
A. irritated 6th, painful 3rd, sore 4th, touchy 1st
B. clever 3rd, delicate 5th, emotional 4th, feeling 1st, knowing 1st, psychic 6th, secret 1st

sensitivity 5th:
A. allergy 5th, reaction 5th
B. compassion 6th, concern 3rd, emotion 4th, sympathy 4th, understanding 1st

sentence 1st:
A. condemn 4th, fine 1st, judge 1st
B. finding 1st, judgment 3rd, ruling 2nd, tax K, verdict 6th

sentiment 5th:
A. attitude 5th, belief 1st, feeling 1st, opinion 3rd
B. affection 4th, caring 1st, emotion 4th, passion 6th, warmth 1st

sentinel 5th: guard 1st, lookout 2nd, patrol 1st, sentry 5th, watch 1st

sentry 5th: guard 1st, lookout 2nd, watch 1st

separate 3rd:
A. divide 4th, part 1st, pull apart 3rd, sort 1st
B. different 1st, distinct 5th, exclusive 6th, free K, independent 3rd, individual 3rd, lone 2nd, sole 4th

serene 6th: calm 3rd, composed 4th, even 1st, gentle 3rd, peaceful 2nd, quiet K, still 1st, tranquil 6th, unchanging 3rd

serf 6th: peasant 4th, servant 3rd, slave 3rd, worker 1st

series 4th: chain 3rd, line K, order 1st, pattern 3rd, routine 6th, row K, run K, trend 2nd

serious 4th:
A. earnest 4th, grim 4th, sad K, sober 4th, solemn 5th, stern 4th, thoughtful 2nd
B. acute 6th, alarming 3rd, critical 5th, dangerous 6th, scary 1st
C. important 1st, significant 6th

sermon 5th: instruction 4th, lecture 5th, lesson 3rd, preaching 4th, talk K

serpent 5th: snake 5th

servant 3rd: aide 5th, assistant 4th, attendant 3rd, employee 5th, helper K

serve 1st: assist 4th, attend 3rd, help K, lend a hand 1st, obey 3rd, provide 3rd, supply 1st, wait on 1st

service 1st:
 A. install 6th, maintain 4th, repair 4th, upkeep 2nd
 B. ceremony 5th, observance 3rd, rite 6th, ritual 6th
 C. assistance 4th, attention 2nd, courtesy 4th, favor 2nd, kindness 2nd

session 6th: assembly 4th, conference 4th, meeting 1st, period 2nd

set K:
 A. agreed 2nd, established 3rd, regular 3rd, routine 6th, usual 3rd
 B. group 1st, series 4th
 C. prepared 1st, primed 5th, ready 1st

settle 2nd:
 A. decide 1st, determine 5th, find K, judge 1st
 B. drop 1st, lower 1st, sink 3rd
 C. arrange 3rd, calm 3rd, establish 3rd, order 1st, quiet K, set K, straighten 3rd

several 1st: few 1st, numerous 4th, some K, three K, various 4th

severe 4th:
 A. plain 2nd, prim 5th, prudish 6th, unadorned 6th
 B. hard K, harsh 5th, rigid 5th, stern 4th, strict 6th
 C. dangerous 6th, extreme 5th, violent 5th
 D. demanding 5th, difficult 5th, hard K, intense 6th

sew 2nd: fix 1st, mend 1st, stitch 6th

shabby 4th: dirty 1st, faded 1st, inferior 5th, poor K, run down 1st, worn 3rd

shade 2nd:
 A. blend 5th, color K, hue 6th, tone 3rd
 B. blind 3rd, protect 4th, screen 1st, shield 4th
 C. degree 5th, slight 4th, touch 1st
 D. blot out 4th, cloud 1st, obscure 6th, shadow 3rd

shadow 3rd:
 A. chase 1st, follow 1st, tail 1st, trace 3rd, track 1st, trail 2nd
 B. dim 1st, shade 2nd
 C. cloud 1st, confuse 4th, obscure 6th
 D. darkness 1st, gloom 3rd, sadness 1st

shaft 4th:
 A. beam 3rd, glimmer 6th, ray 1st
 B. passage 4th, path 1st, tunnel 2nd
 C. pole 1st, rod 1st, tube 3rd
 D. cheat 3rd, deceive 5th, offend 4th

shaggy 5th: hairy 1st, raggedy 5th

shake 1st: agitate 5th, jar K, jog 2nd, loosen 5th, move K, quake 4th, rattle 2nd, rock K, stir 3rd, upset 3rd, vibrate 5th

shall 1st: should 1st, will K, would 1st

shallow 4th:
  A. not deep 1st
  B. meaningless 3rd, silly 1st, surface 3rd, vain 4th

shaman 5th: healer 3rd, magician 5th, witch 1st, wizard 6th

shame 3rd:
  A. burden 5th, guilt 4th, remorse 6th, sorrow 4th
  B. blame 2nd, disgrace 4th, dishonor 3rd, fault 3rd, humiliate 4th

shape 1st:
  A. figure 4th, form 1st, outline 4th
  B. carve 1st, conceive 4th, craft 2nd, design 5th, devise 4th, fashion 3rd, make K, mold 5th, sculpt 5th
  C. condition 3rd, fitness 3rd, state 1st

share 2nd:
  A. due 2nd, portion 4th
  B. cooperate 5th, lend K, use K

sharp 1st:
  A. alert 5th, bright 1st, clever 3rd, crafty 2nd, keen 4th, knowing 1st, quick 1st, sly 4th, smart 1st
  B. acid 4th, sour 2nd, tart 5th
  C. accurate 6th, acute 6th, clear 2nd, exact 2nd, precise 5th
  D. high K, piercing 4th, pointed 1st
  E. cutting 1st, harsh 5th, hurtful 1st

shatter 5th: break 1st, burst 3rd, destroy 2nd, fracture 4th, fragment 6th, smash 3rd

shave 1st:
  A. brush 2nd, graze 5th, scrape 4th, skim 6th, touch 1st
  B. crop 2nd, cut K, reduce 3rd, trim 4th

shawl 6th: cape 4th, cloak 4th, scarf 6th, wrap 3rd

she K: female 4th, girl K, her K

sheaf 6th: batch 2nd, bundle 5th, pile 1st

shear 5th: clip 2nd, crop 2nd, cut K, lop 1st, shave 1st, trim 4th

sheer 5th:
  A. absolute 3rd, full K, perfect 3rd, pure 3rd, total 2nd, very K
  B. sharp 1st, steep 2nd, vertical 6th
  C. delicate 5th, filmy 4th, transparent 5th

sheet 1st:
  A. coating 1st, cover 1st, film 4th, layer 4th, top K
  B. page 1st, paper K, tissue 5th

shelf 6th: ledge 5th, reef 5th, sill 1st

shell 1st:

    A. bullet 4th, shot 1st

    B. armor 4th, covering 1st, plate K, protection 4th, shield 4th

    C. bark 3rd, body 1st, case 2nd, coat 1st, frame 3rd, skin 1st

shelter 4th:

    A. conceal 4th, cover 1st, harbor 2nd, hide 1st, protect 4th, shield 4th

    B. enclosure 4th, housing 1st, lodging 4th, port 3rd, refuge 5th, retreat 4th, room K

shepherd 4th: conduct 3rd, direct 1st, guide 1st, lead 1st, pilot 5th, steer 4th

shield 4th:

    A. armor 4th, barrier 6th, defense 5th, protection 4th, shell 1st

    B. mask 2nd, plate K

    C. conceal 4th, cover 1st, defend 5th, disguise 5th, protect 4th, screen 1st, shelter 4th

shift 4th: adjust 5th, alter 4th, change 2nd, move K, rearrange 3rd, reverse 5th, transfer 5th, turn 1st, vary 4th

shimmer 5th: gleam 1st, glitter 4th, luster 4th, radiance 6th, reflect 4th, shine 1st, sparkle 5th

shine 1st: glaze 6th, gleam 1st, glitter 4th, polish 4th, reflect 4th, shimmer 5th, sparkle 5th

ship 1st:

    A. export 5th, mail 1st, move K, send 1st, shift 4th, transfer 5th

    B. ark 2nd, boat 1st, craft 2nd, freighter 4th, liner K, vessel 4th

shipment 5th: cargo 5th, freight 4th, load 2nd, package 4th

shirk 6th: avoid 3rd, duck K, put off 1st

shirt 1st: blouse 1st, tee 1st, top K

shiver 1st: quake 4th, shake 1st, shudder 4th, tremble 3rd, vibrate 5th

shock 1st:

    A. horror 4th, surprise 1st, thrill 4th

    B. amaze 5th, astonish 4th, jar K, offend 4th, scare 1st, startle 4th, stun 4th

shoe K: boot 1st, footwear 1st, slipper 5th

shoot 3rd:

    A. branch 2nd, growth 2nd, spurt 5th

    B. fling 6th, launch 5th, throw 2nd, toss 2nd

    C. fire K, hit K, kill 1st, wound 3rd

shop 1st:

    A. buy K, purchase 3rd, seek 1st

    B. booth 5th, business 2nd, market 1st, store K

shoplift 3rd: pocket 1st, rob K, steal 3rd, take 1st

shore 1st:

    A. beach 1st, coast 2nd

B. base 1st, brace 5th, foundation 5th, prop 5th, strengthen 2nd, support 4th

short 1st:

    A. brief 3rd, low K, small K

    B. incomplete 3rd, lacking 1st

    C. abrupt 5th, rude 2nd, sharp 1st, tactless 6th

    D. fast 1st, hasty 2nd, sudden 1st

shortly 1st: directly 1st, immediately 3rd, presently 2nd, promptly 4th, quickly 1st, soon K

shot 1st:

    A. attempt 2nd, chance 2nd, effort 2nd, opportunity 3rd, try 1st

    B. tired 5th, useless 2nd

    C. bullet 4th, lead 1st, round 1st, shell 1st

shoulder 1st: bear K, burden 5th, carry 1st, lift 1st, push 1st, shove 5th, transport 5th

shout 1st:

    A. cheer 3rd, cry K, howl 4th, yelp 6th

    B. bellow 4th, call 1st, hail 4th, scream 1st, yell K

shove 5th:

    A. push 1st, thrust 4th

    B. drive 1st, force 1st, move K, press 1st, push 1st

shovel 1st:

    A. dig 1st, groove 5th, mine 1st, trench 5th

    B. backhoe 2nd, bulldozer 1st, plow 4th, scoop 4th, spade 6th

show 1st:

    A. act K, drama 5th, performance 4th, theater 3rd

    B. demonstration 6th, display 3rd, exhibition 4th, pretense 2nd

    C. demonstrate 6th, display 3rd, exhibit 4th, present K, prove 1st, reveal 4th

showroom 4th: display room 3rd, merchandise display 6th, sales floor 1st

shred 5th:

    A. rip 1st, slice 5th, splinter 6th, tear 2nd

    B. bit 1st, dab 1st, end K, fragment 6th, particle 5th, piece 1st, rag 1st, scrap 3rd

shrewd 6th: careful 1st, clever 1st, crafty 2nd, intelligent 4th, prudent 6th, sharp 1st, sly 4th, smart 1st, wary 5th

shriek 4th: cry 1st, scream 1st, shout 1st, yell K

shrill 5th: acute 6th, high K, piercing 4th, sharp 1st

shrine 5th: memorial 4th, monument 2nd, statue 4th, temple 3rd, tomb 5th

shrink 5th:

    A. hesitate 4th, recoil 5th, retire 4th, retreat 4th

    B. collapse 5th, compress 6th, contract 3rd, dry 1st, reduce 3rd, waste 1st, wilt 4th, wither 5th

shroud 6th:
> A. camouflage 6th, cloak 4th, conceal 4th, cover 1st, darken 2nd, disguise 5th, envelope 5th, hide 1st
>
> B. mask 2nd, pretense 2nd, sheet 1st, shield 4th, veil 3rd, wrap 3rd

shrub 4th: bush 2nd, hedge 4th, thicket 4th

shrug 4th: show indifference 5th, toss one's head 3rd, turn aside 3rd

shudder 4th:
> A. pulse 5th, shake 1st, shiver 1st, vibrate 5th
>
> B. quake 4th, quiver 4th, tremble 3rd

shun 6th: avoid 3rd, disregard 4th, exclude 6th, ignore 5th, neglect 4th, omit 6th, pass 2nd, skip 2nd

shut 1st:
> A. block 1st, stop K
>
> B. closed 1st, fastened 4th, latched 6th
>
> C. close 1st, lock 1st, secure 3rd, slam 5th

shutter 4th: blind 3rd, shade 2nd, window cover 2nd

shuttle 5th: carry 1st, haul 4th, transport 5th

shy K:
> A. avoid 3rd, retreat 3rd, shrink 5th
>
> B. insufficient 3rd, scant 6th, scarce 4th, short 1st
>
> C. afraid 1st, bashful 4th, doubtful 5th, hesitant 4th, modest 4th, reluctant 6th, timid 5th, uncertain 2nd, unsure 2nd

sick K:
> A. offended 4th, revolted 5th, shocked 1st, upset 3rd
>
> B. hurt K, ill 1st, injured 5th, not healthy 1st, unwell 2nd

sickle 6th: blade 2nd, knife 1st, reaper blade 4th

side K:
> A. angle 3rd, aspect 5th, view 2nd
>
> B. squad 6th, support 4th, team 1st
>
> C. back 1st, border 1st, curb 3rd, edge 1st, face 1st, margin 5th, surface 3rd, wall K

sidekick 1st: companion 3rd, friend 1st, pal K, partner 5th

sidewalk 1st: path 1st, pavement 5th, walk K

siege 5th:
> A. contain 5th, surround 3rd
>
> B. attack 3rd, campaign 3rd, encirclement 5th

sieve 5th: filter 5th, screen 1st, sifter 4th, strainer 4th

sift 4th: comb 2nd, filter 5th, pick 1st, screen 1st, select 4th, separate 3rd, search 1st, sieve 5th, sort 2nd

sigh 3rd:
> A. deep breath 1st, sob 1st, wail 5th
>
> B. groan 3rd, moan 5th, sob 1st

sight 1st:
  A. perception 6th, picture K, scene 1st, spot 1st, view 2nd, vision 4th
  B. rarity 4th, spectacle 5th, wonder 1st
  C. focus 5th, look K, notice 1st, see K

sign 1st:
  A. clue 2nd, hint 1st, indicator 4th, key K, lead 1st, mark 1st, pointer 1st, signal 4th, symbol 5th, tip 1st, token 5th, trace 3rd
  B. autograph 6th, character 2nd
  C. flag 3rd, indicate 4th, show 1st, signal 4th
  D. announcement 4th, banner 3rd

signal 4th:
  A. alarm 3rd, bell K, clue 2nd, cue 2nd, hint 1st, pointer 1st, sign 1st, symptom 6th
  B. indicate 4th, warn 3rd
  C. caution 5th, directional 1st, guiding 1st, warning 3rd

signature 6th:
  A. acceptance 3rd, approval 4th
  B. autograph 6th, label 3rd, logo 4th, mark 1st, name K, symbol 5th

significant 6th: essential 6th, formidable 6th, huge 1st, important 1st, impressive 5th, meaningful 3rd, momentous 6th, substantial 5th, vital 5th

signify 6th: identify 4th, indicate 4th, mean 1st, represent 4th, show 1st, signal 4th, symbolize 5th

silent 3rd:
  A. dumb 1st, mute 6th, speechless 2nd
  B. calm 3rd, peaceful 1st, quiet K, still 1st

silk 3rd: fiber 3rd, soft fabric 5th

silly 1st: absurd 6th, comic 5th, crazy 4th, foolish 3rd, funny 1st, humorous 4th, mindless 2nd

similar 4th: alike 1st, comparable 3rd, equal 2nd, like K, matching 3rd, parallel 5th, related 4th, same 1st, uniform 1st

simmer 4th: boil 3rd, bubble 2nd, cook 1st, stew 2nd

simple 1st:
  A. natural 2nd, primitive 5th, undeveloped 5th
  B. foolish 2nd, innocent 5th, modest 4th, slow 1st, stupid 4th
  C. basic 6th, childish 3rd, clear 2nd, direct 1st, easy 1st, elementary 3rd, frank 4th, logical 6th, plain 2nd, understandable 3rd

simulate 6th: affect 4th, copy 3rd, imitate 5th, pretend 2nd

sin 1st:
  A. err 6th, misbehave 4th, offend 4th, wrong 1st
  B. crime 2nd, dishonor 3rd, evil 3rd, fault 3rd, offense 4th, vice 4th

since 1st:
  A. because K, due to 2nd

B. after 1st, subsequent 6th

sincere 4th: direct 1st, earnest 4th, frank 4th, genuine 5th, honest 3rd, open K, real 1st, true 1st, truthful 2nd

sinew 6th: muscle 4th, power 1st, strength 1st

sing 1st:
    A. glorify 3rd, honor 1st, praise 4th
    B. carol 3rd, chant 5th, chirp 2nd, harmony 4th

single 3rd:
    A. divorced 4th, unmarried 2nd, widowed 4th
    B. alone 1st, distinct 5th, exclusive 6th, lone 2nd, odd 4th, one K, only K, separate 3rd, sole 4th, solitary 5th, solo 5th, unique 6th

sink 3rd:
    A. collapse 5th, drop K, fall K, settle 2nd, tilt 5th
    B. basin 4th, tub 1st, washbowl 2nd

sip 1st:
    A. drink 1st, lick 1st, nip 1st, sample 5th
    B. drink 1st, sample 5th, suck 1st, taste 1st

sir 1st: knight 2nd, man K

sire 4th:
    A. father K, mate 4th, parent 3rd
    B. breed 4th, create 3rd, originate 3rd

sister 1st: female 4th, girl K

sit K: model 3rd, perch 4th, pose 2nd, relax 4th, rest 1st, roost 2nd

site 5th: area 3rd, arena 5th, location 3rd, place 1st, scene 1st, spot 1st

sitting 1st:
    A. period 2nd, session 6th
    B. lounging 6th, relaxing 4th, resting 1st

situation 4th:
    A. environment 6th, place 1st, setting 1st
    B. circumstance 6th, condition 3rd, difficulty 5th, position 2nd, problem 1st, rank 3rd, state 1st

size 1st: amount 2nd, extent 4th, magnitude 4th, measure 2nd, quantity 4th, scope 6th

skate 1st: coast 2nd, glide 4th, skim 6th, slide 2nd

skeleton 4th: bones 1st, frame 3rd, outline 4th, shape 1st, structure 4th

sketch 5th:
    A. draw K, outline 4th
    B. drawing 1st, illustration 4th, study 1st
    C. performance 4th, scene 1st, story K

skill 2nd: ability 3rd, aptitude 5th, art K, craft 2nd, education 3rd, grace 5th, knowledge 2nd, mastery 2nd, practice 1st, talent 2nd

skim 6th:
  A. brush 2nd, scrape 4th, touch 1st
  B. cream 1st, remove 2nd, take 1st
  C. coast 2nd, fly 1st, glide 4th, skate 1st, slide 2nd
  D. glance at 3rd, scan 6th

skin 1st:
  A. cut K, hurt K, scrape 4th
  B. peel 2nd, shave 1st, strip 3rd
  C. bark 3rd, case 2nd, coating 1st, covering 1st, fur K, hide 1st, outside 1st, peel 2nd, shell 1st, surface 3rd, wrapper 3rd

skinny 1st: bony 1st, gaunt 6th, lean 3rd, narrow 2nd, slender 4th, slim 5th, thin 2nd

skip 2nd:
  A. disregard 4th, exclusion 6th, oversight 2nd
  B. bounce 6th, caper 1st, jump K, hop K, leap 3rd, spring 1st
  C. exclude 6th, ignore 5th, miss K, omit 6th, pass 2nd

skirt 3rd:
  A. avoid 3rd, hedge 4th
  B. clothing 1st, garment 4th
  C. approach 3rd, border 1st, edge 1st

skull 5th: face 1st, head 1st, skeleton 4th

skunk K:
  A. beat 1st, best K, outdo K, win 1st
  B. cheat 3rd, fool 2nd, trick 1st

sky K: atmosphere 4th, heavens 1st, space 1st

skyline 5th: horizon 4th, outline of buildings 4th

skyrocket 3rd: bomb 5th, explosive 3rd, fireworks 1st, rocket K

slab 5th: block 1st, board 1st, piece 1st, plank 5th, slice 5th

slam 5th:
  A. close K, fling 6th, shut 1st
  B. hit K, knock 3rd
  C. bang 3rd, crash 2nd
  D. smash 3rd, strike 2nd

slant 6th:
  A. incline 5th, misrepresent 4th, pitch 2nd, slope 3rd, tilt 5th
  B. angle 3rd, attitude 5th, belief 1st, bias 6th, hill 1st, leaning 3rd, opinion 3rd, ramp 6th, view 2nd

slap 2nd:
  A. box K, cuff 1st, strike 2nd
  B. clap 2nd, hit K, knock 3rd, rap 1st, smack 6th, spank 2nd
  C. insult 5th, jeer 5th

slash 6th:
   A. break 1st, crack 4th, wound 3rd
   B. condense 6th, edit 3rd, reduce 3rd, shorten 1st
   C. beat 1st, lash 4th, whip 4th
   D. drop K, reduction 3rd
   E. line K, streak 5th, stroke 1st
   F. cut K, pierce 4th, punch 4th, rip 1st, slice 5th, slit 5th, tear 2nd

slate 1st:
   A. book K, plan 1st, program 4th, schedule 6th
   B. arrange 3rd, list 2nd, organize 4th, register 4th
   C. blackboard 2nd, chalkboard 5th

slaughter 5th:
   A. butchering 4th, killing 1st, massacre 6th, murder 3rd
   B. butcher 4th, execute 5th, kill 1st, slay 4th

slave 3rd:
   A. labor 2nd, toil 4th, work K
   B. bondsman 3rd, serf 6th, servant 3rd

slay 4th: execute 5th, kill 1st, murder 3rd, slaughter 5th

sled 5th:
   A. glide 4th, ride K, slide 2nd
   B. sledge 6th

sledge 6th: hammer 2nd, sled 5th

sleek 3rd:
   A. polish 4th, shine 1st
   B. elegant 5th, neat K, oily 1st, polished 4th, shiny 1st, smooth 2nd

sleep K:
   A. nap K, repose 6th, rest 1st, slumber 4th
   B. nap K, nod 1st, retire 4th, snooze 4th

sleeve 5th: envelope 5th, file 1st, folder 1st

slender 4th: bony 1st, gaunt 6th, lank 5th, light K, narrow 2nd, skinny 1st, slight 4th, slim 5th, small 1st, thin 2nd

slice 5th:
   A. bit 1st, lot K, part 1st, piece 1st, portion 4th, section 4th, share 2nd
   B. carve 4th, cut K, measure 2nd, rip 1st, shred 5th, slash 6th, tear 2nd

slide 2nd:
   A. chute 5th, shaft 4th, trough 6th, tube 3rd
   B. picture K, transparency 5th
   C. coast 2nd, descend 6th, dip 1st, dive 1st, drop 1st, fall K, float 1st, glide 4th, plunge 4th, skim 6th, slip 3rd, sneak 4th, tumble 4th

slight 4th:
   A. attack 3rd, insult 5th, offend 4th
   B. casual 5th, minor 5th, petty 6th, unimportant 2nd

C. ignore 5th, omit 6th

D. delicate 5th, faint 3rd, feeble 4th, frail 6th, light K, little K, narrow 2nd, slender 4th, slim 5th, thin 2nd, weak 3rd

slim 5th:

A. diet 4th, reduce 3rd

B. casual 5th, marginal 5th, petty 6th

C. lank 5th, narrow 2nd, skinny 1st, slender 4th, slight 4th, thin 2nd

slip 3rd:

A. accident 4th, error 4th, mistake 1st

B. stumble 4th, trip 1st, tumble 4th

C. drift 2nd, glide 4th, skim 6th, slide 2nd

D. drop 1st, fall K, settle 2nd

E. fall K, spill 1st

F. err 6th, fumble 5th

G. decline 6th, dip 1st

H. card 1st, note 1st, paper K

I. petticoat 6th, underdress 2nd, underwear 1st

J. lapse 6th, miss K, pass K

slipper 5th: house shoe 1st, moccasin 2nd, shoe 4th

slit 5th:

A. crack 4th, opening 1st, tear 2nd, trench 5th

B. cut K, rip 1st, slash 6th, slice 5th

slither 4th: crawl 1st, creep 1st, glide 4th, skim 6th, slide 2nd, snake 5th, sneak 4th

slob 5th: messy person 1st, tramp 4th

slope 3rd:

A. bluff 6th, hill 1st, ramp 6th, rise 1st, slant 6th, tilt 5th

B. angle 3rd, bank 1st, grade 2nd, incline 5th, pitch 2nd

slouch 6th:

A. lazybones 4th, loafer 4th, lounger 6th

B. bend K, droop 5th, hunch over 6th, slump 5th, stoop 5th

slow 1st:

A. backward 4th, dull 1st, stupid 4th

B. inactive 3rd, unhurried 2nd

C. endless 2nd, long 1st

D. crawling 1st, gradual 3rd, hesitant 4th, methodical 4th, unhasty 3rd

slugger 5th: batter 1st, fighter 1st, hitter 1st

slumber 4th:

A. repose 6th, snooze 4th

B. nap K, nod 1st, rest 1st, sleep K

slump 5th:

A. decline 6th, fall K, plunge 4th

B. bend K, bow 1st, collapse 5th, dip 1st, drop 1st, lower 1st, sag 1st, slide 2nd, slip 3rd

sly 4th:
    A. secret 1st, sneaky 4th, subtle 6th, tricky 1st
    B. artful 3rd, clever 3rd, crafty 2nd, foxy 1st, sharp 1st, shifty 4th, shrewd 6th

smack 6th:
    A. accurate 6th, exact 2nd, right K
    B. blow 1st, hit K, punch 4th, slap 2nd
    C. bang 3rd, box K, clap 2nd, knock 3rd, jar K, rap 1st, spank 2nd, strike 2nd

small K:
    A. minor 5th, unimportant 2nd
    B. brief 3rd, compact 5th, limited 3rd, nominal 5th, token 5th
    C. grudging 5th, mean 1st, petty 6th
    D. little K, mini 6th, miniature 6th, narrow 2nd, slight 4th, thin 1st, tiny 2nd

smart 1st:
    A. hurt K, pinch 4th, sting 4th
    B. painful 2nd, sore 4th
    C. fashionable 3rd, stylish 3rd, trendy 2nd
    D. alert 5th, brilliant 4th, clever 3rd, intelligent 4th, knowing 1st, quick 1st, sharp 1st, sly 4th, wise 1st, witty 2nd

smash 3rd:
    A. accident 4th, blow 1st, crash 2nd, hit K, impact 6th, wreck 4th
    B. defeat 5th, overthrow 2nd
    C. break 1st, destroy 2nd, destruct 6th, knock 3rd, shatter 5th, slam 5th, splinter 6th, strike 2nd

smear 3rd:
    A. blacken 1st, defame 4th, libel 6th
    B. defamation 4th, false accusation 4th
    C. blot 4th, soil 2nd, spot 1st
    D. blur 4th, dirty 1st, spread 2nd, stain 4th

smell 3rd:
    A. scent 3rd, sniff 4th
    B. detect 4th, perceive 6th, sense 1st
    C. fragrance 5th, odor 3rd, savor 6th

smile 1st:
    A. beam 3rd, grin 1st, laugh 1st
    B. grin 1st, laugh 1st

smite 5th: attack 3rd, beat 1st, hit K, strike 2nd
smog 5th: fog 1st, fumes 3rd, gases 1st, pollution 3rd
smoke 1st:
    A. breath in 1st, puff 2nd
    B. burn 3rd, rage 4th, steam 2nd

C. cloud 1st, exhaust 4th, fog 1st, smog 5th

smooth 2nd:
  A. polished 4th, silky 3rd, shiny 1st, sleek 3rd, soft K
  B. mellow 6th, mild 4th, poised 6th
  C. even 1st, flat 2nd, level 3rd
  D. flatten 4th, plane 1st
  E. easy K, simple 1st
  F. improve 3rd, polish 4th, soften 1st
  G. calm 3rd, hush 3rd, soothe 5th
  H. charming 3rd, cultured 6th, elegant 5th, flowing 1st, refined 6th

smother 6th:
  A. dampen 5th, put out 1st
  B. cover 1st, wrap 3rd
  C. conceal 4th, mask 2nd, suppress 5th
  D. dull 1st, mute 6th, soften K
  E. choke 1st, gag 1st, strangle 6th, suffocate 6th

smuggle 6th: sneak in 4th, transport illegally 5th

snack 2nd:
  A. nip 1st, taste 1st
  B. bite 1st, food K, meal 3rd

snail 1st: crawl 1st, creep 1st, inch 1st

snap 2nd:
  A. catch 1st, clip 2nd, fastener 4th, pin K
  B. clasp 4th, hook 4th, link 5th
  C. crack 4th, pop K
  D. break 1st, click 2nd

snare 6th:
  A. bag 1st, hook 4th, pit 1st, trap 1st
  B. attract 5th, bait 3rd, capture 3rd, catch 1st, entrap 3rd, lure 5th, tangle 3rd, tempt 4th

snarl 5th:
  A. confusion 4th, disarray 5th, disorder 3rd, mess 1st, tangle 3rd
  B. bark 3rd
  C. menace 5th, snap at 2nd, threaten 5th
  D. complicate 6th, entangle 4th, knot 4th, twist 1st

snatch 4th: catch 1st, grab 4th, nab 1st, seize 3rd, steal 3rd, take 1st

sneak 4th:
  A. prowler 2nd, snake 5th
  B. creep 1st, glide 4th, hide 1st, shrink 5th, slip 3rd, slither 4th, steal 3rd

sneer 6th:
  A. insult 5th, jeer 5th, put-down 1st
  B. mock 4th, taunt 5th, torment 5th

sniff 4th: perceive 6th, scent 3rd, smell 3rd, track 1st, whiff 5th

snooze 4th:
  A. sleep K, slumber 4th
  B. nap K, rest 1st

snore 6th: breathe loudly 1st, saw logs 1st

snorkel 5th:
  A. dive 1st, swim K
  B. breathing tube 3rd, swimmer's air supplier 1st

snort 5th:
  A. grunt 3rd, honk 1st
  B. grunt 3rd, honk 1st, sniff 4th

snout 5th: beak 4th, bill 1st, muzzle 6th, nose 1st

snow K:
  A. blizzard 4th, white ice K
  B. coax 6th, deceive 5th, trick 1st

snowball K:
  A. enlarge 5th, grow 1st, increase 3rd
  B. pressed snow 1st, rolled snow 1st

snowstorm 3rd: blizzard 4th, heavy downpour 3rd

snuff 6th:
  A. scent 3rd, smell 3rd, sniff 4th
  B. dampen 5th, put out 1st

snug 6th: comfortable 3rd, content 3rd, secure 3rd, soft K

snuggle 5th: cradle 4th, cuddle 5th, hold 1st, hug 1st, love K, nuzzle 1st

so K:
  A. extremely 5th, very K
  B. positive 2nd, real 1st, true K
  C. also K, consequently 4th, hence 3rd, therefore 2nd, thus 1st, too 1st

soak 5th: spray 2nd, water down 1st, wet K

soap 4th:
  A. cleaner 1st, scrub 6th
  B. clean K, wash 1st

soar 6th: arise 4th, ascend 4th, fly K, lift 1st, rise 1st

sob 1st: cry 1st, moan 5th, wail 5th, weep 4th

sober 4th:
  A. calm 3rd, quiet K, subdue 6th
  B. earnest 4th, grave 3rd, logical 6th, moderate 4th, reasonable 3rd, sensible 6th, serious 4th, solemn 5th

soccer 1st: ball game 1st, field game 2nd, football 1st

social 1st: collective 4th, friendly 1st, neighborly 2nd, public 1st

society 3rd: association 5th, club 1st, colony 3rd, community 2nd, company 2nd, institution 5th, organization 4th, people K, public 1st, tribe 3rd, union 3rd, culture 6th

sock 1st:
  A. foot covering 1st, slipper 5th
  B. hit K, punch 4th, strike 2nd

socket 6th: holder 1st, hollow 3rd, opening 1st

sod 6th: grass 1st, land K, mud 1st, turf 5th

sodden 6th:
  A. dull 1st, lifeless 2nd, sober 4th, solemn 5th
  B. dripping 1st, soaked 5th, spongy 3rd, wet K

soft K: calm 3rd, comfortable 3rd, cottony 2nd, flexible 6th, gentle 3rd, luxurious 4th, mild 4th, movable 2nd, mushy 5th, silky 3rd, smooth 2nd, tender 3rd, velvety 4th

soil 2nd:
  A. blot 4th, darken 2nd, dirty 1st, smear 3rd, stain 4th, taint 6th
  B. dirst 1st, earth 1st, ground 1st, land K, mud 1st

soldier 3rd: brave 1st, fighter K, hero 1st, knight 2nd, trooper 3rd, warrior 4th

sole 4th: exclusive 6th, individual 3rd, lone 2nd, odd 4th, one K, particular 4th, separate 3rd, single 3rd, solitary 5th, unique 6th

solemn 5th: dire 6th, earnest 4th, grave 3rd, important 1st, profound 6th, serious 4th, sober 4th

solid 3rd: close K, compact 5th, firm 2nd, hard 1st, reliable 5th, rigid 5th, secure 3rd, set K, sound 1st, strong K, thick 2nd, tight 1st, trusted 1st

solitary 5th: abandoned 4th, alone 1st, deserted 1st, desolate 6th, exclusive 6th, forsaken 6th, individual 3rd, lone 2nd, one K, only K, single 3rd, sole 4th, unique 6th, unusual 3rd

solution 5th:
  A. fluid 6th, liquid 3rd, mixture 4th
  B. answer 1st, conclusion 3rd, cure 4th, explanation 4th, key K, relief 4th, remedy 4th, resolution 5th, result 2nd

solve 4th: determine 5th, examine 5th, explain 2nd, penetrate 5th, resolve 5th

some K: a few 1st, any 1st, several 1st, various 4th

somebody 1st: being 1st, human 3rd, individual 3rd, person 1st, someone 1st

someday 1st: at last 1st, eventually 5th, finally 3rd, ultimately 6th

someone 1st: being 1st, human 3rd, individual 3rd, person 1st, somebody 1st

something 1st: article 2nd, element 3rd, item 5th, object 1st, part 1st, thing K

sometimes 1st: now and then 1st, occasionally 6th, once in a while 1st

somewhere 1st: place 1st, unspecified location 5th

son K: boy K, junior 4th, heir 4th, lad K

song K: air 1st, melody 4th, poem 3rd, rhyme 6th, tune 1st, verse 4th

sonic 2nd: audible 6th, noisy 1st, of the speed of sound 3rd

sonnet 6th: poem 3rd, rhyme 6th, verse 4th

soon K: directly 1st, presently 2nd, promptly 4th, quickly 1st, rapidly 4th, shortly 1st, swiftly 4th

soothe 5th: calm 3rd, comfort 3rd, compose 4th, lull 1st, quiet K, relieve 4th, soften 1st

sore 4th:
    A. annoyed 5th, irritated 6th, mad K
    B. aching 5th, painful 2nd, sensitive 5th, tender 3rd

sorrow 4th: ache 5th, agony 5th, care 1st, distress 5th, grief 5th, heartache 6th, pain 2nd, regret 5th, remorse 6th, sadness 2nd, suffering 2nd, torment 5th, trouble 1st, woe 4th, worry 1st

sorry 2nd:
    A. hopeless 2nd, inferior 5th, poor K, shabby 4th
    B. contrite 5th, depressed 5th, gloomy 3rd, remorseful 6th, repentant 6th, sad K

sort 1st:
    A. group 1st, organize 4th, systemize 2nd
    B. class 1st, division 4th, kind K, order 1st, section 4th, type 1st

soul 3rd: center 2nd, heart K, individual 3rd, mind 1st, personality 5th, self 3rd, spirit 2nd

sound 1st:
    A. express 5th, pronounce 4th, say K
    B. chime 6th, ring 1st, toll 6th
    C. chord 5th, music K, noise 1st, note 1st, tone 3rd
    D. complete 3rd, correct 3rd, logical 6th, reasonable 3rd, whole 1st, wise 1st
    E. firm 2nd, fit K, healthy 1st, intact 6th, safe 1st, secure 3rd, solid 3rd, strong K, well 1st

soup 1st: broth 4th, chowder 5th

sour 2nd:
    A. disenchant 6th, disillusion 6th
    B. acidify 4th, spoil 4th
    C. acid 4th, sharp 1st, spoiled 4th, tart 5th
    D. gloomy 3rd, glum 4th, sulky 5th, unhappy 2nd

source 4th: author 3rd, authority 3rd, basis 5th, beginning 2nd, cause 2nd, creation 3rd, foundation 5th, fund 4th, maker 1st, origin 3rd, parent 3rd, reason 2nd, reference 5th, root 3rd, seed 1st, start 1st, store K, supply 2nd

sovereign 4th:
    A. emperor 4th, king 1st, master 1st, ruler 2nd
    B. dominant 5th, free K, independent 3rd, lone 2nd, separate 3rd

space 1st:
    A. break 1st, crack 4th, gap K, opening 1st, split 4th
    B. arrange 3rd, rank 3rd

C. area 3rd, atmosphere 4th, capacity 6th, region 4th, room 1st

spade 6th:
  A. dig 1st, trench 5th
  B. scoop 4th, shovel 1st

span 6th:
  A. continuation 2nd, depth 5th, distance 4th, interval 6th, length 2nd
  B. cross 1st, range 3rd, reach 1st, stretch 4th
  C. age 1st, cycle 5th, era 6th, life 1st, period 2nd, season 2nd, stage 3rd, survival 5th, term 3rd

spank 2nd: hit K, paddle 1st, slap 2nd, smack 6th

spar 5th:
  A. battle 2nd, fight K, quarrel 4th
  B. beam 3rd, plank 5th
  C. argue 3rd, box K, combat 5th, struggle 1st

spare 3rd:
  A. free K, rescue 4th, save 1st
  B. extra 1st, more K, other 1st, surplus 6th
  C. conserve 5th, hold onto 1st
  D. bare 3rd, few 1st, poor K, scant 6th
  E. lank 5th, skinny 1st, thin 2nd

spark 3rd:
  A. life 1st, spirit 2nd
  B. beam 3rd, flicker 5th, glimmer 6th, hint 1st, light K, trace 3rd
  C. activate 3rd, awaken 3rd, cause 2nd, excite 4th, generate 4th, ignite 6th, motivate 6th, prompt 4th, stimulate 6th

sparkle 5th:
  A. flash 2nd, gleam 1st, glimmer 6th
  B. glisten 6th, glitter 4th, shimmer 5th, shine 1st, twinkle 4th
  C. animation 6th, energy 4th, spirit 2nd, vigor 5th

spasm 6th: attack 3rd, contraction 3rd, cramp 6th, fit K, seizure 3rd

speak 1st: address K, chat 1st, express 5th, lecture 5th, preach 4th, say K, talk K

spear 4th:
  A. pierce 4th, stab 5th
  B. lance 4th, sword 4th

spearhead 5th:
  A. lead 1st, pioneer 4th
  B. forefront 4th, front 1st, head 1st

special 2nd:
  A. bargain 4th, deal 2nd, sale 1st
  B. different 1st, favorite 3rd, individual 3rd, odd 4th, personal 3rd, pet 1st, remarkable 4th, select 4th, specific 5th, unique 6th, unusual 3rd

species 5th: class 1st, division 4th, family K, group 1st, kind K, order 1st, set K, type 1st, variety 4th

specific 5th: certain 1st, clear 2nd, detailed 5th, distinct 5th, exact 2nd, individual 3rd, particular 4th, precise 5th, special 2nd

specimen 5th: case 2nd, example 2nd, illustration 4th, representative 4th, sample 5th

speck 4th: bit 1st, dab 1st, dot K, drop 1st, fragment 6th, particle 5th, pinch 4th, scrap 3rd, tad 1st

spectacle 5th: demonstration 6th, event 3rd, marvel 4th, scene 1st, sensation 5th, vision 4th, wonder 1st

spectator 5th: attender 3rd, onlooker 2nd, patron 5th, tourist 5th, viewer 2nd, watcher 1st

spectrum 6th: assortment 5th, extent 4th, range 3rd, reach 1st, scope 6th, variety 4th

speculate 6th: assume 5th, bet 1st, chance 2nd, consider 2nd, contemplate 6th, gamble 5th, imagine 2nd, ponder 6th, presume 6th, propose 4th, suggest 2nd, suppose 2nd, surmise 6th, theorize 5th, think 1st, wager 3rd

speech 2nd: address K, conversation 5th, language 2nd, lecture 5th, speaking 1st, statement 3rd, talk K

speed 3rd:
A. haste 3rd, hurry 1st, rate 1st, swiftness 4th
B. race 1st, run K, rush 2nd, sprint 5th, zoom 4th

spell 1st:
A. mean 1st, signify 6th, write out 1st
B. cycle 5th, period 2nd, span 6th, term 3rd
C. charm 3rd, enchantment 6th, magic 1st
D. relieve 4th, replace 5th, substitute 5th

spend 2nd: consume 4th, dispose of 5th, employ 5th, exhaust 4th, expend 3rd, finish 1st, use K, waste 1st

sphere 6th:
A. ball K, globe 4th, orb 4th
B. area 3rd, domain 5th, kingdom 3rd, realm 4th, territory 3rd

spice 3rd:
A. flavor 4th, improve 3rd, season 2nd
B. herb 5th, incense 5th, perfume 3rd, scent 3rd

spike 4th:
A. pierce 4th, prick 5th, stick K
B. bolt 4th, nail 2nd, peg 1st, pin K, stud 6th

spill 1st:
A. fall K, tumble 4th
B. confess 4th, exclaim 3rd, report 1st
C. flood 2nd, overflow 5th, pour 3rd, surge 5th

spin 1st:
  A. circle K, curl 2nd, loop 5th, revolve 5th, rotate 6th, turn 1st, twirl 3rd
  B. drive 1st, ride K
spine 4th:
  A. backbone 4th, ridge 5th
  B. courage 4th, determination 5th, resolution 5th
spire 6th: crown 1st, peak 4th, point 1st, summit 5th, tip 1st
spirit 2nd:
  A. bravery 2nd, courage 4th, daring 2nd, initiative 6th, strength 1st
  B. heart K, mind 1st, nature 1st, soul 3rd, wit 1st
  C. atmosphere 4th, attitude 5th, character 2nd, mood 3rd
spirits 2nd: alcohol 5th, liquor 5th
spiritual 5th: goodly 1st, heavenly 1st, pure 3rd, sacred 4th, unearthly 3rd
spit 3rd:
  A. sprinkle 3rd, sputter 3rd
  B. point 1st, spear 4th
  C. hiss 3rd, jeer 5th, sneer 6th
  D. pierce 4th, spear 4th
spite 3rd:
  A. grudge 5th, hate 2nd, hostility 4th, malice 6th, resentment 5th
  B. annoy 5th, hurt K, injure 5th, needle 3rd, pester 2nd, plague 5th, tease 3rd
splash 1st:
  A. shower 4th, squirt 4th, stain 4th
  B. smear 3rd, spot 1st, spray 2nd, sprinkle 3rd
splendid 4th: beautiful 1st, brilliant 4th, elegant 5th, glorious 3rd, great 1st,
  magnificent 4th, outstanding 2nd, superb 6th, terrific 5th, wonderful 1st
splendor 4th: brilliance 4th, distinction 5th, glory 3rd, luster 4th
splinter 6th:
  A. bit 1st, fragment 6th, piece 1st, shred 5th
  B. break 1st, shatter 5th, smash 3rd
split 4th:
  A. apart 3rd, parted 1st
  B. break 1st, crack 4th, gap K, space 1st
  C. chop 2nd, cut K, divide 4th, divorce 4th, escape 2nd, flee 5th, leave 1st,
  open K, run K, separate 3rd, slice 5th
splotch 5th:
  A. smear 3rd, soil 2nd, splash 1st
  B. blot 4th, patch 4th, spot 1st, stain 4th
spoil 4th:
  A. baby K, humor 4th, indulge 5th
  B. corrupt 6th, decay 5th, destroy 2nd, devastate 6th, disintegrate 5th,
  harm 3rd, ravage 6th, rot 1st, ruin 5th

spoke 1st:
    A. addressed 1st, chatted 1st, conversed 5th, said K, talked 1st
    B. handle 2nd, ladder bar 3rd, rod 1st
spool 2nd: cylinder 6th, wheel 1st
spoon 1st: dipper 1st, ladle 4th, scoop 4th
sport 1st:
    A. frolic 6th, play K
    B. cheer 3rd, contest 4th, exercise 1st, fun K, game 1st
sportsman 1st: athlete 5th, fair player 1st, fisherman 1st, good loser 1st, graceful winner 3rd, hunter 2nd
sportswoman 1st: athlete 5th, fair player 1st, good loser 1st, graceful winner 3rd
spot 1st:
    A. area 3rd, location 3rd, place 1st, point 1st, position 2nd, scene 1st, site 5th
    B. blemish 5th, blot 4th, dab 1st, mess 1st
    C. detect 4th, glimpse 4th, locate 3rd, see K, sight 1st
    D. mark 1st, smear 3rd, stain 4th
    E. ad 4th, commercial 5th, promotion 5th
spout 5th:
    A. chute 5th, drain 5th, lip 1st, nose 1st, tube 3rd
    B. erupt 4th, explode 3rd, jet K, shoot 3rd, spurt 5th, squirt 4th, tap K
sprawl 6th: expand 5th, extend 4th, fan out K, flare 6th, spread 2nd, stretch 4th, unfold 2nd
spray 2nd:
    A. explode 3rd, hose 6th, spout 5th, sprinkle 3rd, spurt 5th, squirt 4th
    B. jet K, mist 1st, shower 4th, splash 1st
spread 2nd:
    A. apply 2nd, rub 1st
    B. depth 5th, distance 1st, expansion 5th, range 3rd, sprawl 6th
    C. array 5th, organize 4th, set K
    D. farm K, ranch 5th
    E. blanket 3rd, cover 1st
    F. arrangement 3rd, layout 2nd
    G. broaden 3rd, enlarge 5th, expand 5th, extend 4th, fan K, flare 6th, open K, scatter 3rd, stretch 4th
spring K:
    A. coil 5th, flexibility 6th, hop 4th, skip 2nd, stretchiness 4th
    B. appear 2nd, jump K, leap 3rd, pop up 1st
sprinkle 3rd:
    A. misting 1st, scattering 3rd, spitting 3rd
    B. dust 2nd, powder 3rd, rain 1st, shower 4th, spray 2nd, spread 2nd

sprint 5th:
  A. race 1st, run K
  B. hurry 1st, speed 3rd
spruce 3rd:
  A. evergreen tree 4th, pine 1st
  B. neat K, sleek 3rd, trim 3rd
spur 4th:
  A. arouse 4th, dig 1st, encourage 4th, prod 6th, prompt 4th, urge 4th
  B. claw 1st, hook 4th, spike 4th, stimulus 6th
spurt 5th:
  A. flow 1st, jet K, squirt 4th
  B. ejaculate 6th, shoot 3rd, spout 5th, surge 5th
sputter 3rd: bubble 2nd, foam 4th, shower 4th, spit 3rd, spray 2nd
spy 4th:
  A. agent 5th, detective 4th, informer 5th
  B. bug 1st, examine 5th, investigate 5th, observe 3rd, scout 1st
squadron 6th: division 4th, fleet 6th, formation 4th, troop 3rd
square 2nd:
  A. block 1st, cube 4th
  B. fair 1st, honest 3rd, just 1st
  C. park 1st, place 1st
  D. accurate 6th, equal 2nd, even 1st, exact 2nd, right K
  E. agree 2nd, conform 6th, corresond 5th, fit K, harmonize 4th
squash 2nd: bruise 5th, compact 5th, compress 6th, crush 4th, jam K, mash 4th, pack 1st, press 1st, push 1st, squeeze 5th, stomp 4th, trample 5th
squat 5th:
  A. fat 1st, short 1st, stout 4th
  B. bend K, crouch 5th, hunch 6th, shrink 5th, sit K
squawk 2nd: complain 4th, cry 1st, howl 4th, scream 1st, shriek 4th, wail 5th, whine 5th, yell K
squeak 2nd:
  A. creak 4th, peep 4th
  B. cry K, whimper 5th, yelp 6th
squeeze 5th:
  A. clasp 4th, compression 6th, crowding 2nd, hug 1st
  B. compact 5th, compress 6th, crush 4th, drain 5th, embrace 4th, hold 1st, mash 4th, milk 1st, press 1st, squash 2nd, wring 5th
squire 4th:
  A. gentleman 3rd, landlord 4th, owner 2nd
  B. attendant 3rd, escort 5th, partner 5th, servant 3rd
  C. boss K, conduct 3rd, usher 6th
squirm 2nd: move K, slither 4th, snake 5th, writhe 6th

squirrel 1st: accumulate 6th, collect 3rd, gather 1st, save 1st

squirt 4th:

    A. flow 1st, fountain 3rd, spray 2nd

    B. jet K, shoot 3rd, splash 1st, spout 5th, spurt 5th, surge 5th, wet K

stab 5th:

    A. cut K, lunge 6th, pain 2nd, punch 4th, slash 6th spasm 6th, throb 5th

    B. hurt K, lance 4th, penetrate 5th, pierce 4th, spear 4th, thrust 4th, wound 3rd

    C. attempt 2nd, chance 2nd, guess 1st, try 1st

stable 4th:

    A. barn K, stall 5th

    B. consistent 3rd, constant 4th, durable 6th, enduring 4th, even 1st, firm 4th, lasting 1st, permanent 5th, reliable 5th, resolute 5th, sane 6th, secure 3rd, solid 3rd, sound 1st, steady 3rd

stack 6th:

    A. pile 1st, rank 3rd, rate 1st, sort 2nd

    B. bank 1st, cluster 4th, group 1st, heap 4th, mass 3rd, mound 2nd

staff 4th:

    A. equip 5th, furnish 4th, supply 1st

    B. crew 2nd, employees 5th, faculty 6th

    C. baton 5th, cane 3rd, pole 1st, rod 1st, stick K, wand 3rd

stage 3rd:

    A. level 3rd, place 1st, platform 4th, site 5th

    B. perform 4th, present K, produce 2nd

    C. condition 3rd, cycle 5th, period 2nd, phase 6th, span 6th, step 1st, time 1st

stagger 4th:

    A. falter 1st, halt 4th, hesitate 4th, lurch 5th, reel 5th, stumble 4th, sway 3rd, totter 6th, waver 5th

    B. amaze 5th, astonish 4th, awe 6th, confound 6th

stain 4th:

    A. dirty 1st, spot 1st, taint 6th, tint 5th

    B. blemish 5th, blot 4th, color K, dye 2nd, paint 2nd, smear 3rd, soil 2nd

stair 2nd: steps 1st, riser 2nd

stake 1st:

    A. bet 1st, claim 2nd, finance 4th, risk 4th

    B. cane 3rd, pole 1st, post 1st, rod 1st, stick K

    C. bankroll 2nd, fortune 3rd, fund 4th, interest 3rd, money K, prize 3rd, reward 4th, share 2nd

stalagmite 5th: calcium deposit 6th, cave floor formation 4th

stale 2nd: foul 4th, musty 2nd, old K, rusty 2nd, spoiled 4th, sour 2nd, tired 2nd

stalk 4th:

    A. bunch 3rd, stem 2nd, trunk 4th

B. chase 1st, follow 1st, hunt 2nd, pursue 5th, seek 1st, shadow 3rd, track 1st, trail 2nd

stall 5th:

A. barn K, bed K, crib 2nd, pen 1st

B. delay 5th, pause 3rd

C. cage 1st, park 1st, room K

D. arrest 3rd, block 1st, falter 1st, halt 4th, hesitate 4th, put off 1st, stop K, waver 5th

stalwart 6th:

A. hero 1st, loyalist 5th, soldier 3rd

B. bold 2nd, brave 1st, courageous 4th, daring 2nd, fearless 3rd, firm 2nd, forceful 3rd, gallant 4th, hearty 5th, heroic 5th, mighty 1st, powerful 2nd, robust 5th, rugged 5th, stout 4th, strong K, sturdy 3rd, tough 5th, valiant 6th

stammer 6th: echo 4th, hesitate 4th, pause 3rd, repeat 4th

stamp 2nd:

A. pound 2nd, strike 2nd

B. imprint 4th, mint 5th, press 1st, print 1st

C. brand 2nd, impression 5th, mark 1st, seal 5th

stampede 5th:

A. flee 5th, run K, scatter 3rd

B. race 1st, riot 6th, rush 2nd

stand K:

A. abide 5th, accept 3rd, allow 3rd, endure 4th, permit 3rd, remain 1st, tolerate 5th

B. belief 1st, policy 5th, post 1st, station 1st

C. position 2nd, put K, rise 1st, set K

standard 3rd:

A. flag 3rd

B. example 2nd, guideline 3rd, ideal 3rd, mean 1st, model 3rd, normal 5th, pattern 3rd, plan 1st, principle 4th, rule K

C. accepted 3rd, average 3rd, basic 5th, common 2nd, conventional 6th, established 3rd, official 3rd, regular 3rd, traditional 5th, uniform 1st

stanza 5th: chapter 3rd, paragraph 6th, passage 4th, verse 4th

staple 6th:

A. essence 6th, product 4th, resource 5th

B. peg 1st, pin K, spike 4th, tack 1st

C. attach 5th, bolt 4th, clip 2nd, fasten 4th, nail 2nd

D. basic 5th, core 6th, essential 6th

star K:

A. heavenly body 2nd, planet 4th

B. celebrity 5th, lead 1st, principal 3rd

C. feature 3rd, present K, promote 5th

D. chief 1st, famed 3rd, superior 4th

starch 6th:

    A. make rigid 5th, stiffen 3rd

    B. formailty 4th, manners 1st, precision 5th, stiffness 3rd

stare 3rd:

    A. blank look 4th, gaze 5th

    B. eye 1st, gape 5th, observe 3rd, peer 1st, study 1st

start 1st:

    A. scare 1st, shock 1st, surprise 1st

    B. activate 4th, begin 1st, bolt 4th, create 3rd, ignite 6th, invent 2nd, jump K, launch 5th, originate 3rd

    C. introduction 5th, outset 1st

startle 4th: alarm 3rd, bolt 4th, bump 2nd, jar K, jump K, panic 1st, scare 1st, shock 1st, surprise 1st

starve 5th: die 2nd, fast 1st, hunger 2nd, perish 4th

state 1st:

    A. allege 6th, argue 3rd, assert 6th, claim 2nd, comment 5th, declare 5th, explain 2nd, express 5th, narrate 6th, remark 4th, tell K

    B. condition 3rd, disposition 5th, feeling K, level 3rd, mode 5th, phase 6th, plight 6th, quality 4th, situation 4th, standing 1st, temper 4th

    C. federal 4th, formal 4th, national 1st, solemn 5th

    D. country 1st, land K, nation 2nd, province 6th

station 1st:

    A. establish 3rd, install 6th

    B. location 3rd, office 1st, position 2nd, rank 3rd, standing 1st, stop K

statue 4th: bust 6th, figure 4th, image 4th, monument 2nd

stature 6th: fame 3rd, height 4th, merit 4th, rank 3rd, reputation 5th, size 1st, standing 1st

stay 1st:

    A. delay 5th, interval 6th, lull 5th, standstill 1st

    B. suspension 5th

    C. brace 5th, column 4th, support 4th

    D. halt 4th, pause 3rd, postpone 6th, stop K, wait 1st

    E. dwell 4th, live 1st, persist 5th, remain 2nd, reside 5th, visit 1st

steady 3rd:

    A. fix 1st, settle 2nd, stabilize 4th

    B. balanced 3rd, calm 3rd, composed 4th, consistent 3rd, constant 4th, cool 1st, dependable 3rd, endless 2nd, even 1st, faithful 4th, loyal 5th, orderly 1st, ready 1st, regular 3rd, reliable 5th, routine 6th, stable 4th, trusty 1st, uniform 1st

steak 2nd: beef 2nd, fish K, meat 1st, slice 5th

steal 3rd:
> A. bargain 4th, sale 1st
> B. creep 1st, defraud 6th, grab 4th, plunder 5th, rob K, seize 3rd, sneak 4th, take 1st, thieve 3rd

steam 2nd:
> A. boil 3rd, drive 1st
> B. energy 4th, might 1st, power 1st
> C. fog 1st, fume 3rd, mist 1st, vapor 3rd

steed 4th: horse K, mount 2nd, stallion 5th

steel 2nd:
> A. brace 5th, toughen 5th
> B. blade 2nd, knife 1st, sword 4th

steep 2nd:
> A. brew 6th, soak 5th, wet K
> B. cliff 2nd, height 4th, hill K
> C. sheer 5th, sudden 1st
> D. costly 1st, expensive 3rd

stem 2nd:
> A. base 1st, origin 3rd, source 4th, stalk 4th
> B. check 1st, oppose 3rd, resist 4th, stop K

step 1st:
> A. go K, move K, stride 5th, walk K
> B. action 1st, degree 5th, grade 2nd, interval 6th, level 3rd, phase 6th, rank 3rd, stage 3rd
> C. riser 2nd, stair 2nd

stereoscope 5th: depth simulator 6th, eye test instrument 3rd

stern 4th: brutal 6th, fierce 4th, firm 2nd, grim 4th, hard 1st, harsh 5th, resolute 5th, rigid 5th, serious 4th, severe 4th, steadfast 4th, stiff 3rd, strict 6th, tough 5th

stew 2nd:
> A. chowder 5th, soup 1st
> B. boil 3rd, brood 4th, fret 5th, fuss 1st, simmer 4th, worry 1st

stick K:
> A. bar 3rd, bat K, cane 3rd, pole 1st, rod 1st, staff 4th, stake 1st
> B. adhere 6th, bond 3rd, cement 4th, fasten 4th, glue 1st, join 3rd, paste 1st, seal 5th
> C. pierce 4th, stab 5th

sticker K: adhesive paper 6th, label 3rd

sticky K:
> A. awkward 6th, delicate 5th, tricky 1st
> B. adhesive 6th, gummy 1st, tacky 1st

stiff 3rd:
    A. body 1st, dead person 1st
    B. awkward 6th, firm 2nd, formal 4th, hard 1st, obstinate 5th, rigid 5th,
        solid 3rd, stern 4th, tense 5th, tight 1st, tough 5th
still 1st:
    A. subsequently 6th, until now 1st
    B. gag 1st, hush 3rd, quiet K, silence 3rd, suppress 5th
    C. calm 3rd, dead 1st, fixed 1st, idle 4th, inactive 3rd, silent 3rd,
        stationary 3rd, steady 3rd
    D. but K, however 3rd, though 1st, yet 1st
stimulate 6th: amuse 4th, arouse 4th, cue 2nd, entertain 4th, excite 4th,
    inspire 4th, interest 3rd, prompt 4th, provoke 6th, rouse 4th, spark 3rd,
    start K, stir 3rd, thrill 4th
sting 4th:
    A. cheat 3rd, scheme 5th
    B. bite 1st, injury 5th
    C. hurt 1st, pain 2nd
stir 3rd:
    A. agitate 5th, animate 6th, arouse 4th, awaken 3rd, bother 2nd, convince 4th,
        cue 2nd, excite 4th, prompt 4th, remind 3rd, suggest 2nd, upset 3rd
    B. beat 1st, blend 5th, mix 1st, shake 1st
    C. action 1st, activity 3rd, bustle 6th, commotion 5th, excitement 4th,
        fuss 1st, interest 3rd, movement 2nd, turmoil 5th
stitch 6th:
    A. pain 2nd, pang 6th
    B. embroider 5th, fix 1st, repair 4th, sew 2nd
stock 1st:
    A. ancestry 5th, breed 4th, ownership 3rd, relation 4th
    B. basic 5th, essential 6th, staple 6th
    C. animals K, cattle 3rd
    D. goods 1st, store K, supply 1st, wares 5th
    E. fill 1st, furnish 3rd, pile 1st, replace 5th
stockade 6th:
    A. block 1st, surround 3rd
    B. brig 6th, defense 5th, enclosure 4th, fort 5th, jail 4th, pen 1st, prison 3rd
stocking 4th: footwear 2nd, hose 6th, sock 1st
stomach 2nd:
    A. accept 3rd, allow 2nd, bear K, endure 4th, permit 3rd, tolerate 5th
    B. appetite 4th, desire 5th, liking 1st
    C. abdomen 6th, belly 5th
stomp 4th: crush 4th, stamp 2nd, trample 5th
stone 2nd: boulder 5th, jewel 5th, pebble 4th, rock K

stool 2nd: bench 4th, chair 1st, seat 1st, toilet 2nd

stoop 5th:

    A. bow 1st, droop 5th, humility 4th, slouch 6th, yielding 4th

    B. deck 1st, porch 3rd

    C. bend K, descend 6th, duck 1st, hunch 6th, lower 1st, patronize 5th,
       sink 3rd, submit 4th

stop K:

    A. stay 1st, visit 1st

    B. location 3rd, station 1st

    C. block 1st, cancel 6th, conclude 3rd, finish 1st, quit 1st, suspend 5th,
       terminate 6th

    D. end K, halt 4th, pause 3rd, rest 1st

stoplight 1st: brake light 1st, traffic signal 5th

store K:

    A. business 2nd, market 1st, shop 1st

    B. put away 1st, reserve 3rd, save 1st

    C. bank 1st, deposit 5th, fund 4th, goods 1st, source 4th, stock 1st, supply 1st

storm 2nd:

    A. anger 1st, charge 2nd, rage 4th

    B. attack 3rd, commotion 5th, disorder 3rd

    C. rain 1st, thundershower 3rd, torrent 5th

story K:

    A. deck 1st, floor 2nd, level 3rd

    B. adventure 3rd, fable 5th, fantasy 6th, fib 1st, gossip 5th, legend 5th, lie 2nd,
       narration 6th, novel 5th, saga 6th, tale 3rd, yarn 2nd

stout 4th:

    A. ale 2nd, beer 5th

    B. athletic 5th, chubby 2nd, fat 1st, firm 2nd, heavy 1st, large K,
       muscular 4th, powerful 2nd, strong K, sturdy 3rd

stove 1st: burner 3rd, furnace 4th, oven 1st, range 3rd

stovepipe 4th: chimney 2nd, smoke chute 5th

stow 6th:

    A. carry K, contain 5th, hold 1st

    B. box K, crate 5th, pack 1st, store K

straight 3rd:

    A. fair 1st, honest 3rd, just 1st, proper 3rd, traditional 5th

    B. frankly 4th, honestly 3rd

    C. direct 1st, even 1st, neat K, ordered 1st, plain 2nd, pure 3rd

strain 4th:

    A. injure 5th, labor 2nd, pull K, stretch 4th, struggle 1st, tense 5th,
       tighten 1st, try K, work K

    B. melody 4th, subject 1st, theme 4th

C. burden 5th, effort 2nd, pressure 4th, stress 6th, tension 5th

D. family K, stock 1st, tribe 3rd

strait 5th:

A. difficult 5th, tight 1st

B. difficulty 5th, problem 1st

C. arm K, bay K, channel 4th, inlet 4th, narrows 2nd, road K, street 1st

strand 5th:

A. abandon 4th, desert 1st

B. braid 2nd, twine 3rd, weave 4th

C. beach 1st, coast 2nd

D. cable 1st, cord 4th, fiber 3rd, line K, rope 1st, string 1st

strange 1st: foreign 5th, not known 1st, novel 5th, odd 4th, peculiar 4th, queer 4th, unusual 3rd, weird 1st

stranger 1st: foreigner 5th, outsider 1st

strangle 6th: choke 1st, smother 6th, suffocate 6th

strap 5th:

A. beat 1st, whip 4th

B. band 1st, belt 2nd, tie 1st

C. bind 2nd, fasten 4th, lash 4th

strategy 6th: course 3rd, design 5th, direction 1st, logic 6th, plan 1st, plot 4th, proposal 4th, scheme 5th, tactics 6th

straw 2nd: hay K, reed 4th, stalk 4th, stem 2nd

stray 3rd:

A. deserter 1st, homeless 2nd, orphan 5th

B. lost K, roaming 4th

C. drift 2nd, roam 4th, wander 3rd

streak 5th:

A. layer 4th, line K, mark 1st, strip 3rd

B. hurry 1st, run K

C. bleach 4th, stain 4th

stream 1st:

A. flow 1st, glide 4th, march 1st, pour 3rd

B. brook 2nd, creek 4th, current 3rd, movement 2nd

street 1st: access 6th, avenue 3rd, lane 4th, path 1st, road K, route 4th

strength 1st:

A. ability 3rd, gift 1st, skill 2nd, talent 2nd

B. concentration 5th, endurance 4th, force 1st, magnitude 4th, might 1st, muscle 4th, power 1st, spirit 2nd

strenuous 6th: demanding 5th, difficult 5th, hard 1st, heavy 1st, labored 2nd, rough 4th, severe 4th, tough 5th, trying 1st

stress 6th:

A. annoy 5th, bother 2nd

B. anxiety 4th, burden 5th, distress 5th, pressure 4th, strain 4th, weight 1st, worry 1st

C. accent 6th, emphasis 5th, importance 1st

D. feature 3rd, highlight 2nd

stretch 4th:

A. period 2nd, term 3rd

B. enlarge 5th, expand 5th, extend 4th, flex 6th, prolong 5th, span 6th, tense 5th, tighten 2nd

C. excess 5th, give 1st, reach 1st

stricken 6th: hit K, overwhelmed 5th, tortured 5th, wounded 3rd

strict 6th: careful 1st, exact 2nd, firm 2nd, harsh 5th, narrow 2nd, precise 5th, prim 5th, rigid 5th, severe 4th, stern 4th, tough 5th, zealous 6th

stride 5th:

A. gait 6th, step 1st

B. march 1st, pace 3rd, walk K

strife 5th: battle 2nd, clash 5th, conflict 4th, dispute 6th, fight 1st

strike 2nd:

A. assault 4th, attack 3rd, club 1st, dispute 6th, hammer 2nd, invade 5th, raid 6th, storm 2nd, surprise 1st

B. coin 3rd, imprint 4th, mint 5th, print 1st, stamp 2nd

C. blow 1st, hit K, knock 3rd, slap 2nd

D. boycott 6th, picket 3rd, walkout K

E. ignite 6th, light K, spark 3rd

string 1st:

A. row K, run K, series 4th, train K

B. arrange 3rd, order 1st, rank 3rd

C. cable 1st, chain 3rd, cord 4th, line K, rope 1st, row K, run K, series 4th, thread 2nd

D. bind 2nd, fasten 4th, tie 1st

strip 3rd:

A. band 1st, bar 3rd, ribbon 4th, tape 1st

B. bare 3rd, expose 4th, peel 2nd, remove 2nd, reveal 4th, skin 1st, uncover 2nd, undress 2nd

stripe 1st:

A. blaze 1st, line K, streak 5th

B. band 1st, layer 4th, ribbon 4th, stream 1st

strive 5th: advance 2nd, aim 3rd, argue 3rd, attempt 2nd, compete 4th, contend 5th, contest 4th, dispute 6th, fight K, labor 2nd, oppose 3rd, progress 4th, resist 4th, struggle 1st, toil 4th, try K, work K

stroke 1st:

A. attack 3rd, seizure 3rd, spasm 6th

B. blow 1st, hit K, kick 1st

C. feel K, pet 1st, rub 1st

D. cheer 3rd, commend 6th, flatter 4th, preen 2nd, recognize 3rd

stroll 5th:

A. hike 3rd, saunter 6th, walk K

B. ramble 6th, roam 4th, wander 3rd

strong K: athletic 5th, durable 6th, effective 4th, forceful 3rd, heavy 1st, intense 6th, massive 5th, mighty 1st, muscular 4th, powerful 2nd, severe 4th, sturdy 3rd, vital 5th

structure 4th:

A. arrange 3rd, build 1st, form 1st, organize 4th

B. building 1st, frame 3rd, pattern 3rd, shape 1st

struggle 1st:

A. battle 2nd, clash 5th, combat 5th, effort 2nd, fight K, quarrel 4th, trial 4th

B. compete 4th, conflict 4th, contest 4th, dispute 6th, oppose 3rd, scramble 4th, spar 5th, strive 5th, toil 4th, try K, war 1st, work K, wrestle 6th

strut 5th: boast 4th, brag 3rd, crow 2nd, march 1st, parade 2nd, step 1st, stride 5th, swagger 5th, walk K

stubble 6th: beard 4th, grass K, growth 1st

stubborn 5th: arrogant 6th, defiant 6th, determined 5th, firm 2nd, hard 1st, obstinate 5th, persistent 5th, pushy 1st, resolute 5th, rigid 5th, tough 5th, unbending 3rd

stud 6th:

A. buck 1st, horse K

B. bolt 4th, button 1st, cleat 5th, peg 1st, pin K, spike 4th

student 3rd: beginner 2nd, learner 1st, pupil 4th, scholar 5th

studio 5th: broadcast station 5th, school K, work space 1st

study 1st:

A. consider 2nd, explore 4th, inquire 3rd, investigate 5th, search 1st

B. class 1st, course 3rd, research 5th, subject 3rd

C. den 1st, sanctuary 6th, school K

stuff 1st:

A. cram 5th, fill 1st, jam K, load 2nd, pack 1st

B. content 3rd, matter 1st, property 3rd, substance 5th, things K

stumble 4th: bewilder 3rd, err 6th, fall K, hesitate 4th, stagger 4th, stump 3rd, trip 1st, tumble 4th

stump 3rd:

A. clip 2nd, shorten 1st, trim 4th

B. amaze 5th, bewilder 3rd, puzzle 4th

C. base 1st, behind 1st, bottom 1st, end K, stem 2nd, trunk 4th

stun 4th: amaze 5th, astonish 4th, awe 6th, confound 6th, dazzle 5th, disable 3rd, freeze 4th, horrify 4th, outrage 6th, shock 1st, stagger 4th, stop K, surprise 1st

stunt 6th:
    A. check 1st, shorten 1st
    B. act K, deed 1st, event 3rd, exploit 6th, feat 1st, trick 1st
stupid 4th: dull 1st, dumb 1st, foolish 3rd, pointless 2nd, silly 1st, simple 2nd, slow 1st
sturdy 3rd: durable 6th, fit K, forceful 3rd, hardy 5th, healthy 1st, powerful 2nd, robust 5th, sound 1st, stout 4th, strong K, tough 5th, well 1st
style 3rd:
    A. design 5th, make K, plan 1st
    B. elegance 5th, fad K, flair 6th, polish 4th
    C. approach 3rd, class 1st, fashion 3rd, manner 2nd, tone 3rd, type 1st
subdue 6th: calm 3rd, conquer 4th, crush 4th, defeat 5th, dominate 5th, exploit 6th, hush 3rd, quiet K, reduce 3rd, silence 3rd, suppress 5th, soften 1st, vanquish 6th
subject 1st:
    A. course 3rd, issue 4th, object 1st, study 2nd, target 5th, text 6th, theme 4th, topic 5th
    B. citizen 3rd, dependent 3rd, national 2nd
    C. expose 4th, humble 4th, treat 2nd
sublime 6th:
    A. ideal 3rd, model 3rd, perfection 3rd
    B. elevated 2nd, great 1st, heavenly 1st, lofty 5th, magnificent 4th, superb 6th
submarine 5th: ship 1st, underwater vessel 4th
submerge 5th: cover 1st, drown 1st, lower 1st, sink 3rd, subside 6th
submit 4th:
    A. present K, propose 4th, refer 5th
    B. comply 6th, conform 6th, fall K, follow 1st, obey 3rd, surrender 5th, yield 4th
subsequent 6th: after 1st, behind 1st, beyond 1st, following 1st, future 5th
subside 6th: cease 3rd, decline 6th, ease 3rd, fall K, reduce 3rd, relax 4th, settle 2nd, shrink 5th, sink 3rd, slide 2nd, submerge 5th
substance 5th: basis 2nd, content 3rd, depth 5th, elements 3rd, essence 6th, fiber 3rd, heart K, ingredients 4th, intent 5th, mass 3rd, material 5th, matter 1st, nature 1st, significance 6th, weight 1st
substantial 5th: ample 5th, generous 4th, important 1st, impressive 5th, objective 3rd, real 1st
substitute 5th:
    A. agent 5th, alternate 5th, equivalent 6th, fake 1st, false 3rd, mock 4th, recourse 6th, stand-in 1st
    B. exchange 4th, replace 5th, switch 4th

subtle 6th: careful 1st, crafty 2nd, delicate 5th, gentle 3rd, logical 6th, mysterious 2nd, refined 6th, sensitive 5th, skillful 3rd, slight 4th, sly 4th, tactful 6th, vague 5th

subtract 1st: minus 1st, reduce 3rd, take away 1st

suburb 6th: border 1st, edge 1st, fringe 5th

success 2nd: achievement 5th, fame 3rd, triumph 5th, victory 4th, win 1st

succession 6th:
A. descent 6th, family K
B. chain 3rd, following 1st, line K, order 1st, pattern 3rd, procession 4th, row K, run K, series 4th, string 1st

such 1st: akin 1st, alike 1st, comparable 3rd, equivalent 6th, like K, related 4th, same 1st, similar 4th

suck 1st: drain 5th, draw K, drink 1st, pull K, sip 1st

suckling 6th: baby K, newborn 2nd

sudden 1st: abrupt 5th, fast 1st, impulsive 5th, immediate 3rd, instant 3rd, quick 1st, rapid 4th, startling 4th, surprising 1st, swift 4th, unexpected 3rd

suffer 2nd: accept 3rd, allow 2nd, bear K, concede 6th, endure 4th, experience 4th, grieve 5th, hurt 1st, let K, permit 3rd, tolerate 5th, undergo 2nd

suffering 2nd: agony 5th, distress 5th, endurance 4th, misery 4th, pain 2nd, patience 4th, trial 4th, grief 5th

suffice 6th: answer 1st, do K, meet K, qualify 4th, satisfy 3rd

sufficient 3rd: ample 5th, competent 6th, effective 4th, enough 1st, plenty 1st

suffocate 6th: choke 1st, smother 6th, strangle 6th, suppress 5th

sugar 1st: flavor 4th, sweeten K

suggest 2nd: convey 4th, hint 1st, imply 5th, indicate 4th, mention 5th, offer 2nd, resemble 4th

suggestion 2nd:
A. advice 3rd, idea 1st, opinion 3rd, thought 1st
B. hint 1st, sprinkling 3rd, tinge 5th, trace 3rd

suit 1st:
A. adapt 4th, adjust 5th, content 3rd, fit K, modify 5th, please K, satisfy 3rd
B. clothes 1st, costume 4th, fashion 3rd, outfit 2nd
C. case 2nd, legal action 5th, trial 4th
D. attire 6th, dress K, equip 5th

suitcase 1st: bag 1st, baggage 3rd, case 2nd, grip 4th, luggage 4th

suitor 5th: admirer 5th, boyfriend 1st, lover 1st

sulky 5th: angry 1st, brooding 4th, cross 1st, gloomy 3rd, glum 4th, moody 3rd, sour 2nd, sullen 5th, surly 6th

sullen 5th: angry 1st, brooding 4th, crabby 2nd, cross 1st, glum 4th, moody 3rd, sulky 5th, surly 6th, touchy 1st

sulphur 4th: element 3rd, yellow crystals 3rd

sultan 5th: king K, sovereign 4th

sum 1st:

A. add K, count 1st

B. addition 3rd, all K, amount 2nd, balance 3rd, result 2nd, total 2nd, whole 1st

summit 5th: crest 4th, crown 1st, height 4th, hill 1st, peak 4th, top K

summon 4th:

A. recall 3rd, remember 1st, revive 6th

B. announce 3rd, assemble 4th, call 1st, cluster 4th, collect 3rd, gather 1st, greet 3rd, group 1st, marshal 5th, mass 3rd, muster 6th, order 1st, page 1st, rally 5th

sun K: daylight 1st, fireball 2nd, light K, star K

sundown 2nd: dusk 5th, nightfall 2nd, sunset 1st

sundry 6th: assorted 5th, many K, various 4th

sunlit 2nd: bright 1st, clear 2nd, fair 1st, glowing 1st, light K

sunny 1st:

A. bright 1st, glowing 1st, radiant 6th, shining 1st

B. cheerful 3rd, cheery 3rd, fair 1st, favorable 3rd, merry 3rd, promising 1st, warm 1st

sunset 1st: dusk 5th, nightfall 2nd, sundown 2nd

suntan 2nd: browning 1st, tan K

super 1st: excellent 1st, exceptional 3rd, fantastic 6th, great 1st, marvelous 4th, remarkable 4th, stunning 4th, terrific 5th, tremendous 4th, wonderful 1st

superb 6th: excellent 1st, fine 1st, outstanding 2nd, superior 4th

superintendent 5th: boss K, chief 1st, director 1st, foreman 6th, manager 4th

superior 4th:

A. boss K, chief 1st, foreman 6th, senior 6th, supervisor 6th

B. champion 4th, standout 2nd

C. above 1st, best K, better 1st, excellent 1st, finest 1st, greater 1st, leading 1st, outstanding 2nd, over 1st, prime 5th, principal 3rd, select 4th, superb 6th, top K

supernatural 5th: ghostly 1st, magical 1st, marvelous 4th, mystical 4th

superstition 5th: belief 1st, fable 5th, illusion 6th, myth 4th, tradition 5th, witchcraft 2nd

supervise 6th: administer 6th, boss K, direct 1st, govern 1st, guide 1st, lead 1st, manage 4th, oversee 2nd, regulate 5th

supper 2nd: dinner 2nd, meal 3rd

supple 6th: agile 6th, elastic 6th, flexible 6th, movable 3rd, plastic 3rd, pliable 6th, soft K

supply 1st:

A. arm K, deliver 5th, equip 5th, fill 1st, furnish 3rd, give 1st, nourish 6th, outfit 2nd, provide 3rd

B. fund 4th, reserve 3rd, stock 1st, store K, source 4th

support 4th:

    A. approval 4th, base 1st, beam 3rd, comfort 3rd, foundation 5th, helper 1st

    B. aid 2nd, assist 4th, back 1st, brace 5th, keep K, lift 1st, maintain 4th, nourish 6th, persuade 5th, promote 5th, sustain 5th

suppose 2nd: assume 5th, believe 1st, dream 1st, guess 1st, imagine 2nd, infer 5th, presume 6th, suggest 2nd, suspect 5th, think 1st, trust 1st

suppress 5th: ban K, bar 3rd, choke 1st, crush 4th, dominate 5th, forbid 4th, outlaw 2nd, prevent 3rd, prohibit 6th, put down K, smother 6th, stop K, subdue 6th

supreme 5th: best K, chief 1st, dominant 5th, first 1st, foremost 4th, greatest 1st, head 1st, highest 2nd, primary 5th, principal 3rd, top K

sure K: accurate 6th, certain 1st, confident 6th, convinced 4th, dependable 3rd, effective 3rd, positive 2nd, reliable 5th, secure 3rd, stable 4th

surf 4th: current 3rd, surge 5th, tide 1st, waves 2nd

surface 3rd: appearance 2nd, cover 1st, face 1st, front 1st, outside 1st, rise 1st, side K, skin 1st, tip K

surge 5th:

    A. flow 1st, rise 1st, stream 1st, swell 3rd

    B. crest 4th, flood 2nd, pulse 5th, rush 2nd, wave 1st

surgeon 5th: doctor 1st, operator 5th

surly 6th: angry 1st, brooding 4th, gloomy 3rd, impolite 4th, mean 1st, rude 2nd, sullen 5th

surmise 6th:

    A. guess 1st, opinion 3rd, view 2nd

    B. assume 5th, believe 1st, conclude 3rd, consider 2nd, gather 1st, imagine 2nd, judge 1st, presume 6th, suggest 2nd, suppose 2nd, think 1st

surmount 6th: ascend 4th, clear 2nd, climb 1st, conquer 4th, defeat 5th, leap 3rd, mount 2nd, overcome 2nd, scale 3rd, vault 5th

surpass 6th: beat 1st, better 1st, eclipse 4th, exceed 4th, excel 6th, pass 2nd, top K

surplus 6th:

    A. excess 5th, extra 1st, unused 1st

    B. overflow 5th, spare 3rd

surprise 1st:

    A. blow 1st, marvel 4th, sensation 5th, wonder 1st

    B. alarm 3rd, amaze 5th, ambush 6th, astonish 4th, shock 1st, stagger 4th, stun 4th

surrender 5th:

    A. compliance 6th, concession 6th, fall K, submission 4th

    B. bow 1st, comply 6th, concede 6th, forfeit 6th, give up 1st, resign 5th, submit 4th, yield 4th

surround 3rd: circle K, compass 4th, enclose 4th, frame 3rd

surrounding 3rd:

    A. around 1st, circling 1st, near 1st

    B. belt 2nd, border 1st, enclosure 4th

survey 5th:

    A. report 1st, research 5th

    B. examine 5th, explore 4th, inquire 3rd, inspect 5th, investigate 5th, question 1st, review 4th, study 1st

survive 5th: continue 2nd, endure 4th, last K, live 1st, outlast 2nd, outlive 2nd, persist 5th, stay 1st

suspect 5th:

    A. distrust 3rd, fear 1st, mistrust 3rd, question 1st, suspect 5th

    B. doubtful 5th, uncertain 1st

    C. guess 1st, imagine 2nd, suppose 2nd, think 1st

    D. accused 4th, prisoner 3rd

suspend 5th:

    A. dangle 5th, hang 2nd

    B. bar 3rd, delay 5th, halt 4th, interrupt 3rd, postpone 6th, stop K

suspicion 4th: clue 2nd, concern 3rd, distrust 3rd, doubt 5th, fear 1st, feeling 1st, guess 1st, hint 1st, hunch 6th, instinct 5th, mistrust 3rd, sense 1st

sustain 5th: defend 5th, feed 1st, maintain 4th, nourish 6th, provide 3rd, support 4th, uphold 6th

swagger 5th: boast 4th, brag 3rd, march 1st, parade 2nd, strut 5th

swallow 1st:

    A. consume 4th, drink 1st, eat K

    B. bite 1st, consumption 4th, drinking 1st, eating 1st

    C. accept 3rd, allow 2nd, believe 1st, endure 4th, permit 3rd, tolerate 5th

swamp 4th:

    A. drown 1st, flood 2nd, overflow 5th

    B. bog 5th, marsh 5th

swarm 4th:

    A. crowd 2nd, overrun 2nd, throng 5th

    B. cluster 4th, horde 6th, host 4th, many K, mass 3rd, mob 4th, numerous 4th

swarthy 6th: black K, brown K, chocolate 4th, dark 1st

sway 3rd:

    A. authority 3rd, bend K, influence 5th, tilt 5th, vibration 5th

    B. affect 4th, charm 3rd, convert 4th, convince 4th, persuade 5th, pitch 2nd, reel 5th, rock K, roll 1st, swing 1st, toss 2nd, wave 1st, wheel 1st, win 1st

swear 4th:

    A. condemn 4th, curse 3rd

B. guarantee 6th, pledge 5th, promise 1st, vow 4th

sweat 3rd:

    A. fret 5th, slavery 3rd, toil 4th, work K

    B. labor 2nd, perspire 6th, strain 4th, strive 5th, worry 1st

sweater 3rd: jacket 3rd, pullover 1st

sweep 4th:

    A. drive K, movement 2nd, stroke 1st

    B. blow 1st, carry K, force 1st, move K

    C. brush 2nd, clean K, mop 1st, wipe 1st

    D. range 3rd, reach 1st, realm 4th, scope 6th, width 4th

sweet K: appealing 3rd, dear 1st, fresh 2nd, honey 1st, pleasant 3rd,
    precious 4th, pure 3rd, sugary 1st

sweetmeat 5th: candy K, cream 1st, kiss K, pie K, sweet K

sweetness 2nd: gentleness 3rd, perfume 3rd, sugariness 2nd, tastiness 2nd

sweets 1st: candy K, treats 2nd

swell 3rd:

    A. elegant 5th, fine 1st, stylish 3rd, superior 4th

    B. hill K, increase 3rd, lump 4th, spread 2nd

    C. enlarge 5th, expand 5th, fatten 2nd, grow 1st, peak 4th, rise 1st, roll 1st,
    surge 5th

swift 4th:

    A. alert 5th, bright 1st, intelligent 4th, smart 1st

    B. brief 3rd, fast 1st, hasty 2nd, immediate 3rd, instant 3rd, quick 1st,
    rapid 4th, speedy 3rd, sudden 1st

swim K: crawl 1st, float 1st, glide 4th, skim 6th

swine 5th: animal K, boar 5th, hog K, monster 1st, pig K, slob 5th

swing 1st:

    A. jab 1st, punch 4th

    B. lurch 5th, reel 5th, wave K

    C. direct 1st, guide 1st, manage 4th

    D. range 3rd, scope 6th, sweep 4th

    E. beat 1st, pulse 5th, rhythm 5th

    F. dangle 5th, hang 2nd, move K, pitch 2nd, rock K, suspend 5th, sway 3rd,
    turn 1st

swish 2nd:

    A. swing 1st, wave K, whip 4th, whisk 4th

    B. hiss 3rd, hum 1st, murmur 4th, rustle 3rd, sigh 3rd, whir 6th, whisper 1st,
    whistle 4th

switch 4th:

    A. exchange 4th, replace 5th, turn 1st

    B. rod 1st, stick K, whip 4th

    C. hit K, strike 2nd

D. change 2nd, substitute 5th, trade 2nd

swoop 4th:

    A. descent 6th, dive 1st, plunge 4th

    B. clutch 4th, grab 4th, lift 1st, seize 3rd

    C. descend 6th, dip 1st, pounce 5th

sword 4th: blade 2nd, cutlass 6th, knife 1st, saber 5th

syllable 6th: letters 1st, word part 1st

symbol 5th: character 2nd, emblem 5th, image 4th, model 3rd, sign 1st, signal 4th, token 5th

sympathy 4th: accord 4th, approval 4th, compassion 6th, harmony 4th, kindness 2nd, mercy 4th, pity 3rd, sensitivity 5th, understanding 1st, unity 5th

symphony 6th: music K, orchestra 6th, performance 6th, piece 1st, recital 5th

symptom 6th: evidence 5th, feature 3rd, sign 1st, signal 4th, symbol 5th, trait 6th

syrup 4th:

    A. sap 1st, sugary water 1st

    B. sentimentality 5th, sweetness 2nd

system 2nd: arrangement 3rd, method 2nd, order 1st, pattern 3rd, plan 1st, procedure 4th, routine 6th, scheme 5th

tab K:

    A. account 3rd, bill 1st, credit 5th, statement 3rd

    B. flap 4th, label 3rd, loop 5th, mark 1st, notch 5th

table K:

    A. chart 1st, column 4th, list 2nd

    B. board 1st, desk 2nd, shelf 6th, stand K

tablecloth 4th: covering 1st, linen 4th, spread 2nd

tablespoon 4th: ladle 4th, measurer 2nd, scoop 4th, server 1st

tack 1st:

    A. bolt 4th, nail 2nd, pin K, staple 6th

    B. angle 3rd, course 3rd, direction 1st, path 1st

    C. shift 4th, turn 1st

    D. attach 5th, connect 3rd, fasten 4th

tackle 4th:

    A. equipment 5th, gear 1st, outfit 2nd

    B. attack 3rd, attempt 2nd, seize 3rd, take on 1st, try 1st

tact 6th: diplomacy 5th, grace 3rd, poise 6th, polish 4th, regard 4th, skill 2nd, subtlety 6th

tactics 6th: execution 5th, handling 2nd, plans 1st, strategies 6th

tag K:

    A. follow 1st, pursue 5th, trail 2nd

    B. flap 4th, name K, sticker K, tab K, term 3rd

C. call 1st, label 3rd, ticket 1st, title 3rd, touch 1st

tail 1st:

A. back 1st, end K, last 1

B. chase 1st, follow 1st, hunt 2nd, pursue 5th, near 3rd, shadow 3rd, track 1st, trail 2nd

tailor 4th:

A. costumer 4th, dressmaker 2nd, seamstress 5th

B. adapt 4th, create 3rd, conform 6th, fashion 3rd, fit K, modify 5th, sew 2nd, shape 1st

taint 6th:

A. flaw 2nd, infection 6th, pollution 3rd, stain 4th, trace 3rd

B. contaminate 6th, corrupt 6th, defile 6th, dirty 1st, discolor 3rd, poison 3rd, ruin 5th, soil 4th, spoil 4th

take K:

A. bear K, bring 1st, carry 1st

B. endure 4th, put up with K, stand K, tolerate 5th

C. earnings 2nd, obtainment 2nd, profits 4th, seizure 3rd

D. consume 4th, eat K

E. accept 3rd, acquire 4th, collect 3rd, rob K, seize 3rd, steal 3rd

tale 3rd: fable 5th, fantasy 6th, fib 1st, fiction 5th, invention 2nd, legend 5th, lie 2nd, myth 4th, story K

talent 2nd: ability 3rd, aptitude 5th, art K, craft 2nd, flair 6th, genius 4th, gift 1st, skill 2nd

talk K:

A. chat 1st, conference 4th, lecture 5th, presentation 4th, speech 2nd

B. address K, discuss 5th, gossip 5th, rumor 5th, speak 1st

tall K: big K, elevated 2nd, giant 2nd, high K, long 1st, soaring 6th

tame 4th:

A. meek 2nd, mild 4th, yielding 4th

B. govern 1st, restrict 6th, temper 4th, train K

tan K:

A. darken 1st, sun K, toast 5th

B. beige 3rd, bronze 4th, brown K, copper 4th

tangle 3rd:

A. involve 6th, snare 6th, twist 1st

B. confusion 4th, disorder 3rd, mess 1st, snarl 5th

tank 5th:

A. armored car 4th, combat vehicle 6th

B. bowl 1st, container 5th, holder 1st, jug 1st, pool 1st, vessel 4th

tankard 6th: cup 1st, glass 1st, mug 1st, vessel 1st

tap K:

A. drain 5th, explore 4th, open K

B. plug 5th, valve 6th

C. bump 2nd, knock 3rd, rap 1st

D. hit K, pat K, strike 2nd

tape 1st:

A. photograph 5th, record 2nd

B. adhesive 6th, band 1st, roll 1st, seal K, strip 3rd

C. adhere 6th, bind 2nd, close K, wrap 3rd

taper 5th:

A. compress 6th, ease 3rd, narrow 2nd, slow down 1st, thin 1st

B. candle 2nd, light K, wick 1st

tapestry 6th: curtain 5th, hanging 2nd, weaving 4th

tar 1st: asphalt 5th, gum K, resin 5th

target 5th: aim 3rd, center 2nd, goal 4th, focus 5th, mission 5th, prey 4th, quarry 6th, subject 1st, task 3rd, victim 4th

tariff 5th: fee 4th, tax K, toll 6th

tarpaulin 6th: canvas 6th, covering 1st

tarry 5th: await 5th, delay 5th, linger 4th, remain 2nd, stay 1st, wait 1st

tart 5th:

A. pie K, puff 2nd

B. acid 4th, biting 1st, sharp 1st, sour 2nd

task 3rd: assignment 5th, goal 4th, job K, labor 1st, mission 5th, objective 2nd, work K

taste 1st:

A. appetite 4th, flavor 4th, fondness 4th, liking 1st

B. fashion 3rd, style 3rd

C. experience 4th, sample 5th, savor 6th, sip 1st

taught 2nd: coached 4th, explained 2nd, instructed 4th, trained 1st, tutored 6th

taunt 5th:

A. insult 5th, jeer 5th, scorn 4th, sneer 6th

B. annoy 5th, badger 2nd, bother 2nd, mock 4th, needle 3rd, tease 3rd, torment 5th

tavern 5th: bar 3rd, pub 1st, saloon 6th

tawny 6th: dark 1st, golden 1st, light brown 1st, tan K

tax K:

A. burden 5th, charge 2nd, duty 1st, fee 4th, tariff 5th

B. demand 5th, load 2nd, strain 4th, toll 6th

taxi 1st:

A. glide 4th, ride K

B. cab K, fare 3rd

teach 1st: acquaint 4th, coach 4th, educate 3rd, explain 2nd, inform 5th, instruct 4th, school K, train K, tutor 6th

teacher 1st: educator 3rd, example 2nd, guide 1st, instructor 4th, model 3rd, professor 4th, tutor 6th

team 1st: band 1st, crew 2nd, group 1st, pack 1st, unit 5th

tear 2nd:

A. break 1st, cut K

B. cry K, weep 4th

C. bead K, drop K

D. divide 4th, pull K, remove 2nd, rip 1st, shred 5th, split 4th, tug 1st

tease 3rd: annoy 5th, badger 2nd, bait 3rd, bother 2nd, jeer 5th, kid 1st, mock 4th, needle 3rd, pester 2nd, taunt 5th

teaspoon 2nd: ladle 4th, measurer 2nd, scoop 4th, stirrer 3rd

tedious 6th: boring 2nd, dull 1st, long 1st, slow 1st, tiresome 3rd

tee 1st:

A. begin 1st, set up K, start 1st

B. holder 1st, mound 2nd, peg 1st, support 4th

teen 2nd: adolescent 5th, juvenile 5th, minor 5th, teenager 3rd, youth 2nd

teenager 3rd: adolescent 5th, juvenile 5th, minor 5th, teen 2nd, youth 2nd

teeth 1st: fangs 5th, points 1st, spikes 4th, tips 1st, tusks 5th

telegram 4th: bulletin 3rd, cable 1st, message 1st, wire 3rd

telephone 2nd:

A. line K, phone 2nd

B. call 1st, dial 5th, ring 1st

telescope 4th:

A. condense 6th, cut K, reduce 3rd, shorten 1st

B. binoculars 6th, glass 1st, lens 1st, scope 6th

television 5th:

A. broadcast 5th, transmission 6th

B. cabinet 4th, set K, TV K

tell K: announce 3rd, brief 3rd, confide 6th, expose 4th, express 5th, gossip 5th, inform 5th, mention 5th, recount 6th, reveal 4th, share 2nd, state 1st

telling 1st: convincing 4th, forceful 3rd, influential 5th, persuasive 5th, revealing 4th

temper 4th:

A. mellow 6th, moderate 4th, regulate 5th, restrain 5th, soften 2nd, tame 4th

B. anger 1st, emotions 4th, feeling 1st, mood 3rd, passion 6th, rage 4th

temperature 5th: climate 4th, condition 3rd, heat 1st, warmth 3rd

temple 3rd: chapel 4th, church 1st, sanctuary 6th, shrine 5th

temporary 5th: brief 3rd, fleeting 6th, passing 2nd, reserve 3rd, short 1st

tempt 4th: appeal 3rd, attract 5th, charm 3rd, coax 6th, court 3rd, draw K, encourage 4th, excite 4th, influence 5th, invite 3rd, lure 5th, magnetize 3rd, prompt 4th, summon 4th, tease 3rd, woo 6th

temptation 5th: attraction 5th, bait 3rd, coaxing 6th, dare 2nd, fascination 5th, invitation 3rd, lure 5th, magnet 3rd, persuasion 5th, trap 1st

tenant 5th:
  A. lease 6th, pay K, rent 1st
  B. guest 3rd, holder 2nd, inhabitant 6th, lodger 4th, occupant 6th, occupier 6th, owner 2nd, renter 1st, resident 5th

tend K:
  A. incline 5th, influence 5th, look to K, point to 1st
  B. care for 1st, comfort 3rd, guard 1st, help K, nurse K, protect 4th, relieve 4th, serve 1st

tendency 5th: appetite 4th, attraction 5th, bearing K, bent K, course 3rd, direction 1st, drift 2nd, impression 5th, leaning 3rd, likeliness 2nd, path 1st, pattern 3rd, tone 3rd, trend 2nd

tender 3rd:
  A. affectionate 4th, agreeable 2nd, caring 1st, gentle 3rd, kind K, loving 1st, mild 4th, romantic 5th, soft K
  B. caretaker 4th, observer 3rd, sitter 2nd
  C. delicate 5th, painful 3rd, sensitive 5th, shaky 2nd, sore 4th, touchy 1st
  D. extend 4th, offer 2nd, present K, yield 4th

tenement 6th: apartment 1st, dwelling 4th, house K, lodge 4th, residence 5th, room 1st

tense 5th:
  A. frightened 5th, nervous 1st, restless 4th, shy K, timid 5th, trembling 3rd, uneasy 2nd, worried 1st
  B. draw K, firm 2nd, flex 6th, pull K, rigid 5th, stiff 3rd, stretch 4th, tight 1st, unyielding 4th

tent 1st: booth 5th, canopy 6th, canvas 6th

term 3rd:
  A. call 1st, expression 5th, label 3rd, name K, phrase 5th, word K
  B. administration 6th, cycle 5th, interval 6th, length 2nd, period 2nd, rule K, season 2nd, span 6th, stage 2nd, time 1st

terminate 6th: close K, complete 3rd, conclude 3rd, end K, finish 1st, fire K, halt 4th, kill 1st, lapse 6th, limit 3rd, stop K

terrace 5th: plain 2nd, platform 4th, porch 3rd

terrible 1st: awful 3rd, dreadful 6th, fearful 2nd, foul 4th, frightful 3rd, grim 4th, gross 3rd, hateful 3rd, horrible 4th, offensive 4th, shocking 1st, violent 5th, ugly 4th

terrific 5th: delightful 3rd, excellent 1st, fantastic 6th, glorious 4th, great 1st, magnificent 4th, marvelous 4th, outstanding 2nd, splendid 4th, super 1st, superb 6th, superior 4th, wonderful 1st

terrified 3rd: frightened 4th, horrified 4th, scared 1st, stunned 4th

terrify 3rd: alarm 3rd, frighten 2nd, horrify 4th, panic 1st, scare 1st, shock 1st, stun 4th

territory 3rd: area 4th, neighborhood 2nd, quarter 1st, region 4th, zone 4th

terror 3rd:
A. beast 3rd, monster 1st
B. alarm 3rd, fear 1st, fright 2nd, horror 4th, panic 1st, shock 1st

test 3rd:
A. criteria 5th, examination 5th, guideline 2nd
B. attempt 2nd, examine 5th, experiment 3rd, explore 4th, judge 1st, measure 2nd, question 1st, search 1st, trial 4th, try K

tether 6th:
A. cable 1st, chain 3rd, connection 3rd, rope 1st, tie 1st
B. attach 5th, bind 2nd, bridle 6th, check 1st, fasten 4th, line K, restrain 5th, secure 3rd

text 6th: book K, contents 3rd, grammar 6th, idea 1st, matter 1st, subject 1st, words K, writing 1st

texture 6th: build 1st, composition 4th, feel K, formation 4th, frame 3rd, grain 3rd, make K, net 3rd, pile 1st, touch 1st, weave 4th

thank 1st: acknowledge 5th, appreciate 5th, credit 5th, recognize 3rd, reward 4th, tip 1st

that K: it K, thing K

that's 1st: that is 1st, that was 1st

thatch 4th: cover 1st, plants 1st, roof 1st, shelter 4th

the K: a K, it K, one K

theater 3rd:
A. company 2nd, drama 5th
B. arena 5th, hall 1st, movie palace 1st

thee 2nd: you K

theme 4th:
A. issue 4th, main idea 1st, opinion 3rd, point 1st, strain 4th, subject 1st, substance 5th, thread 2nd, topic 5th
B. composition 4th, essay 5th, paper K, report 1st, story K

then K: after 1st, behind 1st, beyond 1st, following 1st, later 1st

thence 4th: from here K, since 1st, therefore 1st

theory 5th: assumption 5th, belief 1st, code 3rd, idea 1st, opinion 3rd, philosophy 5th, principle 4th, school K, science 3rd

therefore 1st: so K, thence 4th, thus 1st

thermometer 6th: instrument 3rd, temperature 5th

they K: the boys K, the girls K, the group 1st, the individuals 3rd, them 1st

thick 2nd:
A. abundant 5th, crowded 2nd, full K, plentiful 2nd
B. slow 1st, stupid 4th

C. broad 3rd, compact 5th, jelled 5th, solid 3rd, tight 1st, wide 1st

D. chummy 6th, intimate 5th

E. deep 1st, extreme 5th, mysterious 2nd

thicket 4th: bush 2nd, jungle 4th, shrubbery 4th, woods 1st

thief 3rd: bandit 3rd, burglar 1st, pirate 5th, robber 1st, smuggler 6th, sneak 4th, trickster 5th

thin 1st:

A. light K, watery 2nd

B. delicate 5th, sheer 5th, transparent 5th

C. gentle 3rd, little K, quiet K, scarce 4th, weak 3rd

D. bony 1st, fragile 6th, lean 3rd, narrow 2nd, skinny 1st, slender 4th, slim 5th, withered 5th

thing K: action 1st, anything 1st, article 2nd, calling 1st, design 5th, element 3rd, fashion 3rd, goal 4th, ingredient 4th, item 5th, object 1st, situation 4th, task 3rd, trend 2nd

things K: doings 1st, equipment 5th, goods K, matters 1st, possessions 3rd, stuff 1st, tools 1st, utensils 6th, works K

think 1st: acknowledge 5th, assert 6th, assume 5th, believe 1st, conceive 4th, consider 2nd, contend 5th, feel K, imagine 2nd, intend 6th, maintain 4th, ponder 6th, propose 4th, reason 2nd, speculate 6th, suppose 2nd, view 1st

thirsty 2nd: arid 6th, craving 6th, dry 1st, eager 5th, longing 2nd, needing moisture 3rd, yearning 6th

this K: it K, that K

thorough 4th: careful 1st, complete 3rd, deliberate 6th, entire 3rd, exact 2nd, fine 1st, global 4th, nice 1st, patient 4th, perfect 3rd, total 2nd

those 1st: them 1st

though 1st: although 2nd, but K, however 3rd

thought 1st: concept 4th, guess 1st, hope K, idea 1st, imagination 3rd, judgment 2nd, memory 3rd, mind 1st, notion 5th, purpose 1st, suspicion 4th

thoughtful 2nd:

A. deep 1st, focusing 5th, pondering 6th, serious 4th, substantial 5th, thinking 1st

B. careful 1st, considerate 3rd, generous 4th, kind K, sympathetic 4th, tender 3rd

thrash 4th: batter 1st, beat 1st, blow 1st, crush 4th, defeat 5th, overwhelm 5th, spank 2nd, trample 5th, whip 4th

thread 2nd:

A. braid 2nd, fuse 4th

B. plot 4th, subject 1st, theme 4th, thought 1st

C. cord 4th, fiber 3rd, line K, strain 4th, strand 1st, string 1st, twine 3rd, yarn 2nd

threat 5th: alarm 3rd, danger 1st, hazard 6th, menace 5th, notice 1st, peril 5th, quicksand 1st, risk 4th, warning 3rd

thresh 6th:

    A. clean 1st, seed 1st, separate 3rd

    B. beat 1st, paddle 1st, spanking 2nd, thrash 4th, whipping 4th

threshold 5th:

    A. approach 3rd, door 1st, entrance 3rd, frontier 5th, opening 1st

    B. beginning 1st, edge 1st, start 1st, verge 6th

thrift 6th: cheapness 3rd, conservative 5th, economy 4th, moderation 4th, tightness 2nd

thrill 4th: arouse 4th, charm 3rd, delight 3rd, excitement 4th, impress 5th, inspire 4th, move K, please K, stimulate 6th, stir 3rd, throb 5th, tickle pink 2nd, tingle 4th, touch 1st

thrive 6th: develop 5th, flourish 4th, flower K, grow K, progress 4th, prosper 5th, ripen 2nd, succeed 2nd

throat 1st: neck 1st

throb 5th: beat 1st, pound 2nd, pulse 5th, surge 5th, tremble 3rd

throne 4th: emperor 4th, king K, queen K, royal seat 3rd, ruler 1st

throng 5th: crowd 2nd, flock 2nd, gang 1st, group 1st, herd 2nd, jam K, mass 3rd, mob 4th, pack 1st, press 1st, shove 5th, swarm 4th

through 1st:

    A. complete 3rd, conclude 3rd, done 1st, ended K, finished 1st, over 1st

    B. direct 1st, straight 3rd

    C. among 1st, between 1st, beyond 1st, inside K, under K

throw 1st:

    A. blanket 3rd, comforter 3rd, cover 1st, quilt 6th

    B. bounce 6th, bump 2nd, cast 2nd, deliver 5th, fling 6th, hurl 5th, launch 5th, pitch 2nd, rid 1st, toss 2nd, unseat 3rd

thrust 4th:

    A. assault 4th, attack 3rd, offensive 4th

    B. ambition 4th, drive K, force 1st, jab 1st, plunge 4th, propel 6th, punch 4th, push 1st, ram K, shove 5th, stab 5th

thunder 3rd: bellow 4th, boom 1st, clap 2nd, crash 2nd, roar 1st, rumble 3rd, shout 1st, yell K

thus 1st: for example 2nd, so K, thence 4th, therefore 2nd, wherefore 4th, whereupon 4th

thy 3rd: your 1st

thyself 5th: yourself 2nd

tick 1st: beat 1st, check 1st, click 2nd, go K, snap 2nd, sound 1st, strike 2nd, stroke 1st, succeed 2nd, tap K, throb 5th, work K

ticket 1st: admission 4th, ballot 6th, citation 6th, fare 3rd, label 3rd, notice 1st, tag K, token 5th

tickets 1st: attaches 5th, designates 5th, labels 3rd

tide 1st: breakers 4th, current 3rd, direction 1st, drift 2nd, flow 1st, stream 1st, swell 3rd, tendency 5th

tie 1st:

A. association 5th, bond 3rd, connection 3rd, membership 5th, obligation 6th

B. draw K, equal 2nd, even 1st

C. attach 5th, band 1st, bind 2nd, chain 3rd, fasten 4th, join 3rd, lash 4th, link 5th, marry 1st, restrain 5th, restrict 6th, secure 3rd, wrap 3rd

D. cord 4th, deadlock 3rd, strap 5th

tight 1st:

A. cheap 3rd

B. close K, confining 6th, fixed 1st, limited 3rd, restricted 6th, sealed 1st, secure 3rd

C. compact 5th, crowded 2nd, difficult 5th, fast 1st, firm 2nd, hard 1st, mean 1st, rigid 5th, solid 3rd, stiff 3rd, tense 5th, thick 2nd

tile 1st:

A. clay 1st, stone 2nd

B. cover 1st

till 1st:

A. box K, drawer 2nd, safe K

B. before K, until 1st

C. cultivate 6th, dig up 1st, farm K, plant K, plow 4th, weed 1st

tilt 5th:

A. bank 1st, grade 2nd, hill K, incline 5th, slope 3rd

B. angle 3rd, bend K, flex 6th, lean 3rd, list 2nd, rise 1st, roll 1st, slant 6th, tip 1st, twist 1st

timber 5th:

A. duck 2nd, look out K

B. beam 3rd, board 1st, log 1st, lumber 1st, plank 5th, pole K, rafter 6th, wood 1st

time 1st:

A. count K, measure 2nd, set K

B. beat 1st, pulse 5th, rhythm 5th

C. age 1st, break 1st, era 6th, instant 3rd, interval 6th, leisure 5th, length 2nd, moment 1st, occasion 3rd, opportunity 3rd, pause 3rd, period 2nd, point 1st, season 2nd, span 6th, stage 3rd, term 3rd

timid 5th:

A. afraid 1st, cowardly 4th, fearful 1st, frightened 5th, scared 1st

B. bashful 4th, demure 5th, hesitant 4th, quiet K, reluctant 6th, sheepish 1st, shy 1st

tin 1st: can K

tinge 5th:

    A. glimmer 6th, little bit 1st, nip 1st, pinch 4th, touch 1st, trace 3rd

    B. flavor 4th, season 2nd, smell 3rd, spice 3rd, sprinkle 3rd, suggest 2nd, whisper 1st

    C. color K, dye 2nd, hint 1st, shade 2nd, stain 4th

tingle 4th:

    A. crawl 1st, quake 4th, quiver 4th, shake 1st, tickle 2nd

    B. excitement 4th, thrill 4th, tremor 6th

tinker 5th:

    A. mend 2nd, patch 4th, repair 4th

    B. dabble 2nd, fiddle 4th, toy 1st, trifle 5th

    C. fixer 2nd, mender 2nd

    D. bungle 6th, damage 5th

tinkle 5th: chime 6th, jingle 2nd, murmur 4th, ring 1st, sound 1st, whisper 1st

tint 5th: bleach 4th, cast 2nd, color K, darken 1st, dye 2nd, hue 6th, paint 2nd, pastel 3rd, shade 2nd, stain 4th, tinge 5th, tone 3rd

tiny 2nd: delicate 5th, dwarf 4th, little K, miniature 6th, minor 5th, minute 1st, petty 6th, slight 4th, small 1st

tip 1st:

    A. clue 2nd, cue 2nd, guide 1st, hint 1st, key K, lead 1st, warn 3rd

    B. bend K, tilt 5th, turn 1st

    C. bonus 6th, commission 2nd, reward 4th

    D. crest 4th, edge 1st, end K, peak 4th, point 1st, summit 5th, top K

tiptoe 4th: creep 1st, sneak 4th

tire 2nd: annoy 5th, bore 2nd, bother 2nd, disable 3rd, drain 5th, exhaust 4th, fatigue 5th, irritate 6th, weary 4th

tissue 5th: cloth 1st, coat 1st, cover 1st, fabric 5th, film 4th, lace 1st, layer 4th, net 3rd, sheet 1st

title 3rd:

    A. claim 2nd, deed 1st, right K, share 2nd

    B. call 1st, label 3rd, name K, term 3rd

    C. banner 3rd, heading 1st

to K: into 1st, opposite 3rd

toast 5th:

    A. celebrate 4th, drink 1st, honor 1st, pledge 5th, praise 4th, roast 4th, salute 4th

    B. bake 1st, bread 2nd, brown K, warm 1st

tobacco 4th: cigar 4th, cigarette 4th, smoke 1st

today K: current 3rd, now 1st, present 2nd

together 1st: as one K, collective 4th, jointly 4th, mutual 5th, side by side 1st, successive 2nd, united 5th

toil 4th:
  A. net 3rd, snare 6th, trap 1st
  B. effort 2nd, exertion 6th, grind 4th, labor 2nd, persist 5th, strain 4th, struggle 1st, work K
toilet 2nd: bathroom 1st, outhouse K, potty 1st, throne 4th
token 5th:
  A. indifferent 5th, little K, slight 4th, small 1st, unenthusiastic 4th
  B. badge 5th, emblem 5th, example 2nd, gift 1st, guarantee 6th, keepsake 3rd, mark 1st, omen 6th, pledge 5th, relic 5th, reminder 3rd, sign 1st, symbol 5th
told K: informed 5th, remarked 4th, reported 2nd, said K
tolerate 5th: accept 3rd, admit 4th, allow 2nd, endure 4th, favor 1st, ignore 5th, let K, permit 3rd, stand K, suffer 2nd
toll 6th:
  A. chime 6th, peal 6th, ring 1st, sound 1st, strike 2nd
  B. cost 1st, duty 1st, expense 3rd, fee 4th, pay 1st, penalty 5th, tax K
tomb 5th: grave 3rd, memorial 3rd, resting place 1st, shrine 5th
tomfoolery 5th: folly 4th, joking 2nd, mischief 4th, monkey business 2nd, nonsense 5th, oddity 4th, rot 1st, silliness 3rd, strangeness 2nd
tomorrow 1st: future 5th, the next day K
ton 1st: abundance 5th, huge 1st, mass 3rd, weighty 2nd
tone 3rd:
  A. attitude 5th, feeling 1st, humor 4th, impression 5th, manner 2nd, mood 3rd, quality 4th, spirit 2nd, temper 4th
  B. cast 2nd, chime 6th, color K, flavor 4th, hue 6th, peal 6th, shade 2nd, tinge 5th, tint 5th
  C. jingle 2nd, noise 1st, note 1st, pitch 2nd, ring 1st, sound 1st, swing 1st
tongue 3rd: accent 6th, dialect 5th, language 2nd, lick 1st, speech 2nd, taste 1st, vocabulary 6th, voice 1st
tonic 2nd: healthful 1st, medicine 4th, refresher 6th, stimulating 6th, strengthening 2nd
tonight 1st: now K, this evening 1st, today K
too 1st: also K, and K, as well 1st, besides 1st, furthermore 3rd, likewise 2nd, moreover 2nd, plus 1st, with K
took 1st: achieved 5th, captured 3rd, gained 2nd, swallowed 1st, used 1st
tool 1st: agent 5th, alter 4th, device 4th, drill 2nd, fit K, implement 6th, instrument 3rd, machine 1st, medium 5th, utensil 6th, vehicle 6th
toolbox 5th: compartment 6th, holder 1st, storage box 2nd
toot 1st: blow 1st, honk 1st, sound 1st
tooth 1st: dent 1st, fang 5th, point 1st, spine 4th, tusk 5th
toothpaste 2nd: brush 2nd, cleaner 1st, soap 4th

top K:
  A. cover 1st, lid 1st
  B. ace 2nd, best K, better 1st, champion 4th, chief 1st, dominant 5th, finest 1st, first 1st, greatest 2nd, key K, leading 1st, main 3rd, major 3rd, maximum 6th, primary 5th, principal 3rd, supreme 5th
  C. beat 1st, pass 2nd, surpass 6th
  D. cap K, crest 4th, crown 1st, head 1st, peak 4th, point 1st, summit 5th, tip 1st

topic 5th: argument 3rd, idea 1st, issue 4th, question 1st, statement 2nd, subject 1st, theme 4th, theory 5th

topple 6th: collapse 5th, cut K, defeat 5th, fall K, knock down 3rd, spill 1st, tip 1st, tumble 4th, upset 3rd

torch 5th: burn 3rd, flame 3rd, flashlight 3rd

torment 5th:
  A. agony 5th, anguish 6th, distress 5th, misery 4th, pain 2nd, sorrow 4th, suffering 2nd, torture 5th, woe 4th
  B. annoy 5th, badger 2nd, bend K, corrupt 6th, persecute 6th, punish 4th, twist 1st

tornado 6th: funnel cloud 3rd, gale 2nd, storm 2nd, twister 1st, winds 1st

torrent 5th: abundance 5th, flood 2nd, flow 1st, rush 2nd, stream 1st

torture 5th:
  A. abuse 6th, agony 5th, misery 4th, suffering 2nd, torment 5th
  B. hurt 1st, injure 5th, persecute 6th, punish 4th

toss 2nd:
  A. fling 6th, pitch 2nd, throw 1st
  B. cast 2nd, lurch 5th, mingle 4th, mix 1st, rock K, roll 1st, stir 3rd, sway 3rd

total 2nd:
  A. complete 3rd, entire 3rd, whole 1st
  B. addition 3rd, all K, amount 2nd, balance 3rd, mass 3rd, quantity 4th, result 2nd, score 1st
  C. add K, count 1st, number K, plus 1st, sum 1st

tote 5th:
  A. bag 1st, load 2nd, suitcase 1st
  B. bear K, carry 1st, haul 4th, transport 5th

totter 6th: limp 5th, lurch 5th, pitch 2nd, reel 5th, rock K, stagger 4th, sway 3rd, toss 2nd

touch 1st:
  A. hint 1st, shade 2nd, sprinkle 3rd, suggestion 2nd, tinge 5th, trace 3rd, whisper 1st
  B. brush 2nd, dab 1st, explore 4th, feel K, handle 2nd
  C. contact 4th, pat K, sensation 5th, stroke 1st

touching 1st:
    A. against 1st, meeting 1st
    B. affecting 4th, exciting 4th, thrilling 4th
tough 5th: bad K, cruel 5th, demanding 5th, difficult 5th, durable 6th, firm 2nd, hard 1st, harsh 5th, mean 1st, rigid 5th, rough 4th, rugged 5th, severe 4th, stern 4th, stiff 3rd, strict 6th, strong K, taxing 1st, trying 1st
tour 3rd:
    A. explore 4th, survey 5th, travel 1st, visit 1st
    B. circuit 4th, journey 3rd, trip 1st
tourist 5th: foreigner 5th, traveler 1st, visitor 2nd
tournament 5th: competition 4th, contest 4th, game 1st, match 3rd, meet K, race 1st
tow 1st: drag 5th, draw K, haul 4th, pull K, tug 1st
toward 1st:
    A. almost K, near 1st
    B. onward 3rd, to K
towel 6th:
    A. dry 1st, rub 1st
    B. cloth 1st, linen 4th, paper K
tower 3rd:
    A. ascend 4th, soar 6th, uprise 2nd
    B. castle 3rd, column 4th, pillar 5th, pyramid 5th
towhead 4th: blond 5th, flaxen-haired 6th
town K: city K, downtown 1st, metropolis 6th, village 2nd
toxic 2nd: dangerous 6th, deadly 1st, harmful 3rd, poisonous 3rd
toy K:
    A. game 1st, plaything 1st
    B. imaginary 2nd, miniature 6th
    C. fiddle 4th, flirt 6th, fool 2nd, jest 4th, kid 1st, play K, sport 1st, tease 3rd, tinker 5th
trace 3rd:
    A. copy 3rd, draw K
    B. chase 1st, hunt 2nd, pursue 5th, seek 1st, tail 1st, track 1st, trail 2nd
    C. image 4th, sketch 5th
    D. breath 1st, clue 2nd, glimmer 6th, hint 1st, lead 1st, mark 1st, relic 5th, remnant 6th, shade 2nd, shadow 3rd, sign 1st, spark 3rd, sprinkle 3rd, suggestion 2nd, touch 1st, whisper 1st
track 1st:
    A. line K, path 1st, railway 2nd, road K, route 4th
    B. chase 1st, follow 1st, hunt 2nd, pursue 5th, seek 1st, shadow 3rd, trace 3rd, trail 2nd

trade 1st:
  A. deal 2nd, exchange 4th, sell K, switch 4th, transfer 5th
  B. business 2nd, commerce 6th, enterprise 5th, industry 5th, job K,
     profession 5th, work K

tradition 5th: belief 1st, custom 6th, habit 3rd, practice 1st, rite 6th, ritual 6th,
  routine 6th, superstition 5th, way K

traffic 5th:
  A. conveyance 4th, movement 2nd, transport 5th
  B. bargain 4th, deal 2nd, trade 2nd
  C. business 2nd, commerce 6th

tragedy 5th: calamity 6th, disaster 6th, drama 5th, misfortune 5th

trail 2nd:
  A. path 1st, road K, route 4th, track 1st
  B. chase 1st, drag 5th, follow 1st, hunt 2nd, pursue 5th, seek 1st, shadow 3rd,
     tail 1st, trace 3rd

train K:
  A. locomotive 5th, rail 2nd
  B. chain 3rd, line K, order 1st, row K, run K, series 4th, string 1st
  C. aim 3rd, condition 3rd, drill 2nd, educate 3rd, focus 5th, instruct 4th,
     point 1st, teach 1st

trait 6th: characteristic 6th, feature 3rd, manner 2nd, mark 1st, quality 4th,
  sign 1st, symptom 6th

traitor 4th: betrayer 5th, informer 5th

tramp 4th:
  A. beggar 2nd, derelict 6th, drifter 2nd
  B. firm walk 2nd, plodding 5th, stroll 5th
  C. hike 3rd, march 1st, stomp 4th, tread 4th, walk K

trample 5th: crush 4th, defy 6th, squash 2nd, stomp 4th, tramp 4th

tranquil 6th: calm 3rd, collected 3rd, cool 1st, peaceful 2nd, quiet K,
  relaxed 4th, serene 6th, still 1st

transfer 5th:
  A. relocation 3rd, removal 2nd, sale 1st
  B. deed 1st, lease 6th
  C. assign 5th, convey 4th, exchange 4th, move K, sell K, shift 4th, ship 1st,
     trade 2nd

transform 5th: alter 4th, change 2nd, evolve 6th, modify 5th

transit 6th: change 2nd, going 1st, journey 3rd, movement 2nd, shift 4th,
  transport 5th

translate 5th: explain 2nd, interpret 5th, render 4th

transmit 6th: air 1st, beam 3rd, broadcast 5th, carry 1st, conduct 3rd,
  convey 4th, forward 3rd, funnel 3rd, pass 2nd, radiate 6th, relay 6th, send 1st,
  ship 1st, spread 2nd

transom 6th: crosspiece 2nd, window 1st

transparent 5th:
    A. direct 1st, honest 3rd, obvious 5th, plain 2nd
    B. clear 2nd, crystal 3rd, filmy 4th, sheer 5th

transport 5th:
    A. charm 3rd, delight 3rd, fascinate 5th
    B. ecstacy 6th, thrill 4th
    C. bus K, ship 1st, transit 6th, truck 1st
    D. carry 1st, convey 4th, haul 4th, move K, send 1st

trap 1st:
    A. lure 5th, snare 6th, trick 1st
    B. bag 1st, cage 1st, capture 3rd, catch 1st, imprison 5th, tempt 4th

trash 2nd:
    A. destroy 2nd, wreck 4th
    B. garbage 5th, junk 3rd, litter 2nd, refuse 2nd, rubbish 5th, waste 1st

travel 1st:
    A. movement 2nd, transit 6th
    B. go K, journey 3rd, move K, roam 4th, tour 3rd, venture 4th, wander 3rd

traverse 5th: cross 1st, pass 2nd, roam 4th, rove 6th, stray 3rd, tour 3rd, travel 1st, wander 3rd, voyage 4th

tray 1st: base 1st, dish 1st, plate K, platter 6th, server 1st

treacherous 6th: dangerous 6th, dishonest 3rd, evil 3rd, false 3rd, hostile 4th, shaky 1st, sneaky 4th, traitorous 4th

tread 4th:
    A. step 1st, stomp 4th, walk K
    B. march 1st, oppress 6th, pace 3rd, plod 5th, trample 5th

treason 4th: betrayal 5th, mutiny 6th, revolt 5th, riot 6th

treasure 4th:
    A. bank 1st, collect 3rd, save 1st
    B. fortune 3rd, prize 3rd, riches 1st, wealth 3rd
    C. adore 4th, cherish 5th, honor 1st, idolize 6th, love K, value 2nd

treat 2nd:
    A. cure 4th, heal 3rd
    B. cope 6th, handle 2nd, manage 4th, use K
    C. prepare 1st, process 4th, ready 1st
    D. extra 1st, gift 1st
    E. amuse 4th, cheer 3rd, entertain 4th
    F. candy K, morsel 5th, snack 2nd
    G. buy K, finance 1st, fund 4th

treatment 5th:
    A. behavior 4th, handling 2nd, use K
    B. cure 4th, remedy 4th

C. preparation 2nd, processing 4th

treaty 4th: agreement 3rd, bargain 4th, compact 5th, contract 4th, deal 2nd, pledge 5th, promise 1st, understanding 1st

treble 6th: high K, shrill 5th

tree K:
A. evergreen 4th, sapling 5th, shrub 4th
B. corner 2nd, trap 1st

tremble 3rd: pulse 5th, quake 4th, quiver 4th, shake 1st, vibrato 5th

tremendous 4th:
A. excellent 1st, extraordinary 5th, fantastic 6th, great 1st, marvelous 4th, super 1st, superb 6th, terrific 5th, wonderful 1st
B. big K, enormous 4th, giant 2nd, huge 1st, immense 4th, massive 5th, vast 4th

tremor 6th: quake 4th, quiver 4th, shake 1st, shudder 4th, tremble 3, vibrate 5th

trench 5th:
A. gorge 5th, groove 5th, furrow 5th
B. canal 4th, channel 4th, cut K, furrow 6th, rut 1st, slit 5th

trend 2nd:
A. drift 2nd, incline 5th, lean 3rd, tend K
B. course 3rd, direction 1st, drift 2nd, fad K, fashion 3rd, mood 3rd, pattern 3rd, run K, tendency 5th

trespass 6th:
A. intrude 6th, invade 5th, sin 1st
B. crime 2nd, intrusion 6th, invasion 5th, offense 4th, wrong 1st

trial 4th:
A. developmental 6th, experimental 4th
B. examination 5th, inquiry 3rd, study 1st
C. attempt 2nd, care 1st, struggle 1st, test 3rd, try K, worry 1st

tribe 3rd: clan 5th, class 1st, company 2nd, family K, group 1st, race 1st, species 5th, stock 1st

tribunal 6th: court 3rd, panel 6th, session 6th, trial 4th

tribute 5th: award 5th, compliment 5th, credit 5th, honor 1st, medal 6th, praise 4th, recognition 3rd, reward 4th

trick 1st:
A. cheat 3rd, confuse 4th, fool 2nd, trap 1st
B. act K, deception 5th, feat 1st, hoax 5th, joke 1st, lie 2nd, plot 4th, prank 5th

trickery 5th: betrayal 5th, deceit 5th, fraud 6th, shrewdness 6th

tried K: dependable 3rd, proved 1st, reliable 5th, sure 1st, tested 3rd

trifle 5th:
A. fragment 6th, hint 1st, suggestion 2nd, tease 3rd, tinge 5th, trace 3rd

B. chatter 1st, talk K

C. junk 3rd, plaything 1st, toy K

D. flirt 6th, play K, tinker 5th

trigger 6th:

A. starter 1st, stimulus 6th

B. activate 4th, generate 4th, prompt 4th, provoke 6th, spark 3rd, start 1st

trim 4th:

A. adorn 6th, decorate 3rd, garnish 6th

B. border 1st, edge 1st, fringe 5th, lace 4th, ornament 4th, ribbon 4th, ruffle 6th

C. clip 2nd, crop 2nd, cut K, fit K, shave 1st

D. neatness 1st, organization 4th

E. clip 2nd, scrap 3rd

F. conditioned 3rd, neat K, orderly 1st, sleek 3rd

trinket 6th: amusement 4th, decoration 3rd, ornament 4th, plaything 1st, toy K

trip 1st:

A. drop K, error 4th, fall K, mistake 1st, slip 3rd, stumble 4th

B. adventure 3rd, expedition 4th, journey 3rd, tour 3rd, voyage 4th

C. err 6th, lurch 5th, spill 1st, tumble 4th

triumph 5th:

A. master 1st, prevail 5th, rejoice 4th, win 1st

B. achievement 5th, celebration 4th, conquest 4th, defeat 5th, success 2nd, victory 4th

troll 1st: beast 3rd, creature 3rd, dwarf 4th, fairy 4th, monster 1st

troop 3rd:

A. assemble 4th, gather 1st, swarm 4th, unite 5th

B. band 1st, company 2nd, crowd 2nd, group 1st, herd 2nd, mass 3rd, mob 4th

trophy 6th: award 5th, keepsake 4th, prize 3rd, relic 5th, token 5th

tropical 5th: boiling 3rd, burning 3rd, hot 1st, oppressive 6th, warm 1st

trot 5th:

A. gallop 4th, jog 2nd, pace 3rd

B. hurry 1st, ride K, run K, step 1st

troth 6th: engagement 5th, fidelity 6th, pledge 5th, promise 1st

trouble 1st:

A. annoy 5th, bother 2nd, concern 3rd, distress 5th, worry 1st

B. bind 2nd, care 1st, conflict 4th, difficulty 5th, dispute 6th, effort 2nd, misfortune 5th, pain 2nd, problem 1st, sorrow 4th, struggle 1st, trial 4th, upset 3rd, vex 5th

troublemaker 1st: agitator 5th, gossip 5th, meddler 6th, provoker 6th, rioter 6th

trough 6th:
   A. canal 4th, channel 4th, cut K, furrow 6th, gorge 5th, groove 5th, gully 6th, ravine 5th, trench 5th
   B. feedbox 2nd, manger 4th
trousers 5th: breeches 5th, jeans 1st, pants 1st
truant 6th:
   A. avoider 3rd, deserter 1st, neglecter 4th
   B. absent 5th, gone 1st, missing 1st
truce 6th: agreement 2nd, peace 1st, rest 1st, treaty 4th
truck 1st:
   A. van K, vehicle 6th
   B. carry 1st, cart 1st, convey 4th, freight 4th, haul 4th, move K, ship 1st, transport 5th
trudge 5th:
   A. march 1st, tramp 4th, walk K
   B. creep 1st, lag 1st, plod 5th, walk K
true K:
   A. accurate 6th, actual 3rd, constant 4th, devoted 5th, direct 1st, exact 2nd, factual 2nd, faithful 3rd, genuine 5th, honest 3rd, legitimate 6th, loyal 5th, precise 5th, real 1st, right K, rightful 2nd
   B. honestly 3rd, sincerely 4th
trunk 4th:
   A. box K, chest 2nd, luggage 4th, suitcase 1st
   B. nose 1st, snout 5th
   C. body 1st, framework 4th, stalk 4th, stem 2nd
trust 1st:
   A. belief 1st, confidence 6th, faith 3rd
   B. expect 3rd, rely 5th, understand 1st
truth 1st: actuality 4th, fact 1st, honesty 3rd, reality 5th
try K:
   A. annoy 5th, bother 2nd, distress 5th, disturb 6th, irritate 6th, strain 4th, worry 1st
   B. attempt 2nd, judge 1st, tackle 4th, test 3rd
   C. chance 2nd, effort 2nd, struggle 1st
tryout 2nd: attempt 2nd, demonstration 6th, performance 4th, test 3rd
tub 1st: barrel 4th, basin 4th, bath 1st, bowl 1st, bucket 3rd, pail 2nd, vessel 4th
tube 3rd: channel 4th, cylinder 6th, pipe 1st, shaft 4th, straw 4th, tunnel 2nd
tuck 1st:
   A. crease 5th, dart 1st, fold 1st, pleat 5th
   B. cover 1st, hide 1st, insert 6th, pin K, stuff 1st
tuft 3rd: bunch 3rd, bush 2nd, cluster 4th, puff 2nd, stand K

tug 1st:
    A. effort 2nd, labor 1st, pull K
    B. drag 5th, draw K, haul 4th, tow 1st
tumble 4th:
    A. collapse 5th, slip 3rd, stumble 4th, trip 1st
    B. dive 1st, drop 1st, fall K, flow 1st, plunge 4th, topple 6th, upset 3rd
tummy K: abdomen 6th, belly 5th, stomach 2nd
tumor 6th: cancer 6th, growth 1st, swelling 3rd
tumult 6th: agitation 5th, commotion 5th, confusion 4th, disorder 3rd, excitement 4th, fury 4th, fuss 1st, noise 1st, passion 6th, turmoil 5th, uproar 5th, violence 5th
tune 1st: harmony 4th, melody 4th, song K, strain 4th
tunic 6th: garment 4th, jacket 3rd, robe 4th
tunnel 2nd:
    A. build 1st, make K, mine 1st
    B. burrow 5th, chute 5th, tube 3rd
turban 5th: headdress 2nd, scarf 6th
turbulent 5th: agitated 5th, excited 4th, fierce 4th, frantic 5th, furious 4th, stormy 2nd, violent 5th, wild 2nd
turf 5th: area 3rd, grass 1st, land K, region 4th, sod 6th, space 1st, territory 3rd, zone 4th
turmoil 5th: bother 2nd, confusion 4th, disorder 3rd, excitement 4th, fight K, noise 1st, stir 3rd, tangle 3rd, whirl 4th
turn 1st:
    A. revolve 5th, rotate 6th, spin 1st, swing 1st, twirl 3rd, twist 1st, veer 6th
    B. attempt 2nd, chance 2nd, opportunity 3rd, try K
    C. circle K, movement 2nd
    D. difference 1st, shift 4th
    E. alter 4th, change 2nd, deviate 4th, reverse 5th
turret 5th: spire 6th, tower 3rd
tusk 5th: fang 5th, tooth 1st
tussle 6th:
    A. combat 5th, conflict 4th, contest 4th
    B. fight K, struggle 1st, wrestle 6th
tutor 6th:
    A. coach 4th, drill 2nd, guide 1st, prepare 1st, school K
    B. educator 3rd, instructor 4th, leader 1st, teacher 1st, trainer K
TV K: screen 1st, television 5th
twain 6th: couple 3rd, pair 1st, two K
twang 6th:
    A. ringing 1st, shrillness 5th
    B. chime 6th, pang 6th, pluck 1st, ring 1st

C. suggestion 2nd, trace 3rd

twice 3rd: double 3rd, two times 1st

twig 4th: branch 2nd, limb 4th, sprout 5th, stem 2nd, stick 4th

twine 3rd:
A. braid 2nd, knit 4th, weave 4th
B. cord 4th, line K, rope 1st, string 1st

twinkle 4th:
A. flash 2nd, flicker 5th, glimmer 6th, sparkle 5th, wink 2nd
B. blink 6th, gleam 1st, glisten 6th, glitter 4th, pulse 5th, shimmer 5th, shine 1st

twirl 3rd:
A. coil 5th, spin 1st, turn 1st, whirl 4th
B. curl 2nd, loop 5th, reel 5th, revolve 5th, ring 1st, rotate 6th

twist 1st:
A. bend K, cord 4th, twine 3rd
B. coil 5th, connect 3rd, curl 2nd, join 3rd, loop 5th, revolve 5th, rotate 6th, snarl 5th, spin 1st, tangle 3rd, tighten 2nd, turn 1st, twirl 3rd, wind 1st

type 1st:
A. class 1st, copy 3rd, grade 2nd, order 1st, sort 1st
B. breed 4th, division 4th, family K, flavor 4th, group 1st, kind K, set K, species 5th, style 3rd, variety 4th

typewriter 1st: keyboard 1st, writing machine 1st

typical 6th: average 3rd, characteristic 6th, common 2nd, general 2nd, model 3rd, normal 5th, ordinary 3rd, regular 3rd, routine 6th, usual 3rd

tyranny 6th: cruelty 5th, domination 5th, harshness 5th, oppression 6th, sovereignty 4th

tyrant 5th: emperor 4th, king K, master 1st, monarch 5th, sovereign 4th

ugly 4th: awful 3rd, bad K, evil 3rd, frightening 3rd, grim 4th, hideous 6th, horrible 1st, plain 2nd, repulsive 6th, revolting 5th, shocking 1st, terrible 1st, unattractive 6th, vile 6th

ultimate 6th:
A. best K
B. crest 4th, height 4th, summit 5th, terminal 6th
C. extreme 5th, farthest 3rd, final 3rd, furthest 3rd, last K, peak 4th, remotest 5th, top K

umpire 1st:
A. judge 1st, mediator 5th, moderator 4th
B. decide 1st, judge 1st, mediate 5th, settle 2nd

unanimous 6th: agreed 2nd, complete 3rd, solid 3rd, uniform 1st, united 5th

unbidden 6th:
A. free K, voluntary 5th, willing 5th
B. unasked 2nd, uninvited 3rd, unwelcome 2nd

uncanny 6th:

    A. amazing 5th, astonishing 4th, extraordinary 5th, fantastic 6th, incredible 6th, marvelous 4th, remarkable 4th, unbelievable 2nd, wonderful 1st

    B. odd 4th, ominous 6th, peculiar 4th, queer 4th, strange 1st, unreal 2nd, unusual 3rd, weird 1st

unceremonious 4th:

    A. casual 5th, easy K, familiar 3rd, free K, informal 5th, natural 2nd, relaxed 4th

    B. abrupt 5th, brief 3rd, careless 5th, hasty 2nd, inconsiderate 3rd, quick 1st, rude 2nd, sharp 1st, short 1st, tactless 6th, unrefined 6th

uncertain 1st: anxious 4th, conditional 3rd, conflicting 4th, dependent 3rd, doubtful 5th, nervous 1st, shy 1st, suspect 5th, suspicious 4th, unstable 4th, unsure 1st, variable 4th, wary 5th

under K: below 1st, beneath 1st, lower 1st, sunken 3rd

underground 4th:

    A. buried 3rd, sunken 3rd

    B. concealed 4th, hidden 1st, secret 1st, undercover 1st

understand 1st: believe 1st, comprehend 5th, conceive 4th, conclude 3rd, decode 5th, determine 5th, estimate 5th, fathom 6th, figure 2nd, grasp 4th, interpret 5th, know 1st, learn 1st, master 1st, perceive 6th, presume 6th, realize 3rd, think 1st

undertaking 1st: adventure 3rd, enterprise 5th, feat 1st, job K, project 4th, task 3rd, venture 4th

undoubtedly 5th: absolutely 3rd, certainly 1st, positively 2nd, really 1st, surely 1st, truly 1st

unfit 1st: forlorn 6th, ill 1st, improper 3rd, melancholy 6th, out of shape 2nd, sickly 1st, unable 3rd, unsuitable 3rd, weak 3rd

unhappy 1st: blue K, cursed 3rd, dejected 5th, depressed 5th, difficult 5th, down K, foolish 2nd, gloomy 3rd, mournful 4th, ominous 6th, sad K, threatening 5th, unfortunate 4th, unlucky 1st, unpleasant 3rd

unidentified 5th:

    A. mysterious 2nd, strange 1st, supernatural 5th, unexplained 3rd, unfamiliar 3rd

    B. disguised 5th, hidden 1st, masked 2nd, nameless 2nd, secret 1st, unknown 2nd, veiled 3rd

uniform 1st:

    A. suit 1st, costume 4th, habit 3rd

    B. alike 1st, certain 1st, consistent 3rd, constant 4th, equivalent 6th, even 1st, identical 6th, like K, matching 3rd, regular 3rd, same 1st, similar 4th, stable 4th, standard 3rd, steady 3rd

union 3rd:
> A. marriage 1st, wedding 3rd
> B. association 5th, blend 5th, bond 3rd, connection 3rd, league 3rd, society 3rd

unique 6th: alone 1st, different 1st, distinctive 5th, exceptional 2nd, extraordinary 5th, individual 3rd, lone 2nd, matchless 3rd, odd 4th, only K, particular 4th, peculiar 4th, rare 4th, select 4th, singular 4th, solitary 5th, special 2nd, strange 1st, uncommon 3rd, unusual 3rd

unison 6th: accord 4th, agreement 3rd, harmony 4th, union 3rd, unity 5th

unit 5th: item 5th, measure 2nd, member 1st, one K, part 1st, piece 1st, portion 4th, quantity 4th

unite 5th: adhere 6th, attach 3rd, band 1st, blend 5th, bond 3rd, cement 4th, clump 3rd, combine 3rd, connect 3rd, couple 3rd, fasten 4th, fuse 4th, join 3rd, knot 4th, link 5th, lock 1st, marry 1st, mate 4th, mix 1st, pool 1st, tie 1st, wed K

unity 5th: accord 4th, agreement 2nd, cooperation 5th, entirety 3rd, harmony 4th, individuality 4th, oneness 2nd, teamwork 2nd, union 3rd, unison 6th, wholeness 2nd

universal 4th: common 2nd, entire 3rd, general 2nd, total 2nd, unlimited 3rd, worldwide 2nd

universe 4th: creation 3rd, heavens 1st, infinity 5th, nature 1st, vast 4th

university 4th: college 4th, institute 5th, school K

unless 2nd: aside 3rd, bar 3rd, but K, except 2nd, excluding 6th, leaving out 2nd, save 1st, without 1st

unlimited 3rd: boundless 3rd, countless 1st, endless 1st, eternal 4th, infinite 5th

unpaid 2nd: amateur 5th, free K

unreal 1st: artificial 6th, false 3rd, imaginary 3rd, imitation 5th, pretend 2nd

unruly 6th: aggressive 6th, disorderly 2nd, lawless 2nd, restless 4th, stubborn 5th, uncontrollable 3rd, wild 2nd

unusual 3rd: abnormal 5th, alien 5th, curious 3rd, distinct 5th, extraordinary 5th, irregular 3rd, lone 2nd, new K, novel 5th, occasional 3rd, odd 4th, quaint 5th, queer 4th, rare 4th, scarce 1st, singular 4th, special 2nd, strange 1st, uncommon 2nd, unique 6th, weird 1st

unzip 1st: air 1st, expose 4th, loosen 5th, open K, peel 2nd, reveal 4th, speak 1st, unbind 2nd, undo 2nd, unfasten 4th

up K: alert 5th, aware 3rd, excited 4th, familiar 3rd, high K, increase 3rd, informed 5th, intensify 6th, lift 1st, prepared 2nd, raise 1st, ready 1st

uphill 1st: angled 3rd, banked 1st, difficult 5th, hard 1st, inclined 5th, pitched 2nd, slanted 6th, sloped 3rd, steep 2nd, strenuous 6th, tilted 5th, trying 1st

uphold 6th: aid 2nd, back 1st, bolster 4th, brace 5th, carry 1st, champion 4th, defend 5th, maintain 4th, promote 5th, prop 5th, side K, support 4th, sustain 5th

upholster 6th: cover 1st, pad K

upholstery 6th: covering 1st, fabric 5th, padding 1st

upon 1st: at K, atop 3rd, on K, when K

upper 3rd: above 1st, excitement 4th, greatest 1st, higher 1st, leading 2nd, principal 3rd, supreme 5th

upright 4th:
  A. erect 4th, stand up 1st, straight 3rd, upstanding 2nd, vertical 6th
  B. ethical 5th, fair 1st, honest 3rd, just 1st, moral 3rd, noble 3rd, proper 3rd, true K

uproar 5th: agitation 5th, clamor 6th, commotion 5th, conflict 4th, confusion 4th, craze 4th, din 6th, disturbance 6th, excitement 4th, fury 4th, fuss 1st, noise 1st, riot 6th, tumult 6th

upset 3rd: agitate 5th, alarm 3rd, angry 1st, annoyed 5th, anxious 4th, blow 1st, bother 2nd, collapse 5th, confuse 4th, cross 1st, defeat 5th, disorder 2nd, distressed 5th, disturb 6th, excited 4th, failure 3rd, fall K, fluster 6th, fuming 3rd, mad K, overthrow 6th, shake 1st, shock 1st, startle 4th, tip 1st, topple 6th, troubled 1st, turnover 1st

upward 4th: alone K, high K, overhead 1st, rising 1st, striving 5th

urchin 3rd: brat 3rd, child K, kid K, stray 3rd

urge 4th:
  A. desire 5th, hunger 2nd, impulse 5th, longing 1st, yearning 6th
  B. agitate 5th, arouse 4th, assert 6th, coax 6th, demand 5th, drive K, encourage 4th, excite 4th, force 1st, insist 5th, itch 5th, motivate 6th, move K, persuade 5th, prod 6th, prompt 4th, provoke 6th, push 1st, recommend 5th, spur 4th, stimulate 6th, urgency 6th

urgent 6th: acute 6th, burning 3rd, critical 5th, demanding 5th, desperate 5th, dire 6th, grave 3rd, immediate 3rd, important 1st, pressing 1st, serious 4th, severe 4th, vital 5th

use K: apply 2nd, assistance 4th, benefit 3rd, control 2nd, custom 6th, employ 5th, exercise 1st, exploit 6th, function 4th, handle 2nd, help K, manage 4th, operate 3rd, profit 4th, purpose 2nd, routine 6th, service 6th, tradition 5th, utility 6th, utilize 6th

used K: hand-me-down 2nd, old K, ragged 2nd, second hand 1st, worn 3rd, worn out 3rd

useful 2nd: beneficial 3rd, convenient 4th, effective 4th, fitting 1st, good K, handy 1st, helpful 1st, practical 4th, productive 4th, suitable 2nd, usable 1st, valuable 4th, working 1st, worthwhile 3rd

useless 2nd: fruitless 3rd, hopeless 1st, impractical 4th, ineffective 4th, unhelpful 2nd, vain 4th, worthless 3rd

usher 6th:
>A. accompany 3rd, attend 3rd, conduct 3rd, direct 1st, escort 5th, guide 1st, lead 1st, pilot 5th
>B. escort 5th, guide 2nd

usual 3rd: accepted 3rd, average 3rd, casual 5th, common 2nd, established 3rd, everyday 1st, expected 2nd, familiar 3rd, frequent 4th, general 2nd, habitual 4th, normal 5th, ordinary 3rd, predictable 6th, regular 3rd, routine 6th, traditional 5th, typical 6th

utensil 6th: appliance 2nd, container 5th, device 4th, fork 1st, holder 2nd, instrument 3rd, knife 1st, spoon 1st, tool 1st

utilize 6th: adopt 3rd, apply 2nd, control 2nd, employ 5th, exercise 1st, exploit 6th, handle 2nd, manage 4th, occupy 3rd, operate 3rd, service 1st, use K

utter 4th:
>A. air K, express 5th, pronounce 4th, say K, tell K, vent 4th, voice 1st
>B. absolute 3rd, complete 3rd, downright 1st, pure 3rd, total 2nd

vacant 6th: bare 3rd, barren 3rd, blank 4th, clear 2nd, deserted 1st, empty 3rd, free K, hollow 3rd, idle 4th, uninhabited 6th, unused 2nd, void 6th

vacation 2nd:
>A. break 1st, holiday K, jaunt 6th, recess 2nd, repose 6th, rest 1st, trip 1st
>B. explore 4th, travel 1st

vacuum 5th:
>A. clean 1st, suck 1st, sweep 4th
>B. emptiness 3rd, void 6th

vague 5th: blurry 4th, clouded 1st, doubtful 5th, dubious 6th, faint 3rd, foggy 1st, lost K, mysterious 2nd, obscure 6th, pale 3rd, puzzling 4th, questionable 2nd, remote 5th, suspect 5th, uncertain 1st, unclear 2nd, weak 3rd

vain 4th:
>A. arrogant 6th, conceited 5th, haughty 6th, proud 2nd
>B. empty 3rd, foolish 2nd, hollow 3rd, idle 4th, meaningless 3rd, pointless 3rd, shallow 4th, unsuccessful 3rd, useless 3rd, valueless 2nd, worthless 3rd

vale 4th: glen 6th, valley 2nd

valiant 6th: bold 2nd, brave 1st, courageous 4th, daring 2nd, fearless 3rd, gallant 4th, heroic 5th, resolute 5th, spirited 2nd, stalwart 6th, sturdy 3rd

valley 2nd: basin 4th, hollow 3rd, ravine 5th, vale 4th

valuable 4th: costly 1st, dear 1st, expensive 3rd, important 1st, lavish 6th, precious 4th, priceless 2nd, prized 3rd, rare 4th, rich K, treasured 4th, useful 2nd, valued 2nd, worthwhile 3rd

value 2nd:
>A. admire 5th, cherish 5th, esteem 5th, honor 1st, prize 3rd, regard 4th, respect 2nd, treasure 4th, worship 4th
>B. estimate 5th, price K

C. meaning 3rd, purpose 1st, significance 6th

D. cost 1st, gain 2nd, importance 2nd, merit 4th, price K, profit 4th, use K, worth 3rd

vamoose 6th: bolt 4th, depart 5th, exit 3rd, flee 5th, go K, leave 1st

van K: bus K, car K, truck 1st, vehicle 6th, wagon 2nd

vanish 3rd: die out 2nd, disappear 2nd, dissolve 4th, expire 6th, fade 1st, perish 4th, retire 4th

vanity 5th:

A. arrogance 6th, conceit 5th, haughtiness 6th, pride 2nd

B. emptiness 3rd, hollowness 3rd, worthlessness 3rd

vanquish 6th: beat 1st, conquer 4th, crush 4th, defeat 5th, destroy 2nd, dominate 5th, eliminate 5th, enslave 3rd, master 1st, overpower 2nd, overthrow 2nd, ruin 5th, subdue 6th, surpass 6th

vapor 3rd: breath 1st, cloud 1st, fog 1st, fume 3rd, gas 1st, mist 1st, smoke 1st, steam 2nd

various 4th:

A. abundant 5th, many K, multiple 2nd, numerous 4th, several 1st, some K

B. alternate 5th, assorted 5th, different 1st

vary 4th: adjust 5th, alter 4th, assort 5th, change 2nd, contrast 4th, depart 5th, disagree 3rd, dispute 6th, evolve 6th, mix 1st, modify 5th, transform 5th, tune 1st

vase 5th: jar K, pitcher 2nd, pot K

vast 4th: big K, endless 2nd, enormous 4th, extensive 4th, giant 2nd, gigantic 5th, grand 2nd, great 1st, huge 1st, immense 4th, infinite 5th, large K, mammoth 5th, massive 5th, monstrous 2nd, monumental 2nd, roomy 1st, tremendous 4th, wide 1st

vault 5th:

A. bound 2nd, hop K, jump K, leap 3rd

B. arch 4th, bend K, curve 3rd

C. basement 3rd, cellar 1st, chest 2nd, safe 1st, strongbox 2nd, tomb 5th, treasury 4th

veer 6th: bend K, curve 3rd, shift 4th, swing 1st, turn 1st, twist 1st, wheel 1st

vegetable 2nd: green K, plant K, produce 2nd

vehicle 6th:

A. automobile 3rd, car K, carriage 5th, cart 1st

B. agency 5th, agent 5th, channel 1st, instrument 3rd, mechanism 6th, medium 5th, method 2nd, way K

veil 3rd:

A. camouflage 6th, cloak 4th, curtain 5th, mantle 4th, mask 2nd, scarf 6th, shield 4th, shroud 6th

B. camouflage 6th, cloud 1st, conceal 4th, cover 1st, cover up 1st, curtain 5th, envelope 5th, hide 1st, mask 2nd, obscure 6th, shade 2nd, shroud 6th

vein 4th:

    A. blood vessel 4th

    B. bed K, mine 1st, seam 5th

    C. channel 4th, vessel 4th

    D. attitude 5th, fashion 3rd, feeling 1st, flavor 4th, manner 2nd, mind 1st, mode 5th, mood 3rd, spirit 2nd, style 3rd, temper 4th, tone 3rd

vengeance 6th: punishment 4th, revenge 5th

vent 4th:

    A. express 5th, proclaim 4th, reveal 4th, tell K, utter 4th, voice 1st

    B. air 1st

venture 4th:

    A. attempt 2nd, bet 1st, chance 2nd, dare 2nd, endanger 6th, endeavor 4th, gamble 5th, hazard 6th, imperil 5th, risk 4th, speculate 6th, try K, wager 3rd

    B. advance 2nd, presume 6th

    C. adventure 3rd, chance 2nd, enterprise 3rd, experiment 5th, exploration 4th, journey 3rd, project 4th, quest 3rd, stake 1st, trial 4th, undertaking 2nd

verdict 6th: conclusion 3rd, decision 1st, finding 1st, judgment 3rd, opinion 3rd, ruling 2nd, sentence 1st

verge 6th: approach 3rd, border 1st, boundary 4th, brim 5th, brink 6th, edge 1st, end K, fringe 5th, hem 1st, limit 3rd, margin 5th, outline 4th, rim 1st, side K, skirt 3rd, thicket 4th, threshold 5th

verse 4th: line K, poem 3rd, rhyme 6th, song K, stanza 5th

version 6th: account 3rd, edition 3rd, interpretation 5th, rendition 4th, story K, variation 4th

vertical 6th: erect 4th, high K, sheer 5th, steep 2nd, straight 3rd, upright 4th

very K: actually 3rd, exactly 2nd, extremely 5th, genuinely 5th, greatly 1st, highly 1st, quite 1st, rather 2nd, really 1st, sincerely 4th, terribly 1st, thoroughly 1st, truly 1st, unusually 3rd, well 1st

vessel 4th: boat 1st, container 5th, cup 1st, drum 5th, keg 1st, pan K, pot K, ship 1st, tub 1st, vase 5th, vein 4th

vest 3rd: waistcoat 4th

veteran 6th: chief 1st, experienced 4th, expert 5th, master 1st, practiced 1st, professional 5th, ranking 3rd, seasoned 2nd, senior 6th, soldier 3rd, superior 4th

vex 5th: anger 1st, annoy 5th, bother 2nd, bug K, condemn 4th, curse 3rd, enrage 6th, irk 6th, irritate 6th, pester 2nd, provoke 6th, upset 3rd, worry 1st

vexation 5th: anger 1st, annoyance 5th, bother 2nd, care 1st, concern 3rd, discontent 3rd, displeasure 2nd, dissatisfaction 3rd, irritation 6th, nuisance 6th, pest 1st, problem 1st, regret 5th, worry 1st

vibrant 5th: active 3rd, alive 3rd, bright 1st, dynamic 5th, energetic 4th, lively 2nd, spirited 2nd, strong K, vigorous 5th, vital 5th

vibrate 5th: beat 1st, echo 4th, jar K, pulsate 5th, quake 4th, quiver 4th, shake 1st, shiver 1st, shudder 4th, surge 5th, sway 3rd, throb 5th, tremble 3rd, wave K, waver 5th, wobble 4th

vice 4th: corruption 6th, crime 2nd, dishonor 3rd, evil 3rd, fault 3rd, immorality 4th, impurity 4th, offense 4th, sin 1st, weakness 3rd, wickedness 4th, wrong 1st

vicinity 6th: area 3rd, closeness 2nd, district 4th, field 2nd, locality 3rd, nearness 2nd, neighborhood 2nd, range 3rd, reach 1st, section 4th, sphere 6th, surroundings 3rd, zone 4th

vicious 6th: angry 1st, bad K, brutal 6th, cruel 5th, deadly 1st, evil 3rd, fierce 4th, foul 4th, hateful 3rd, horrible 4th, hostile 4th, intense 6th, mean 1st, savage 5th, violent 5th, wicked 4th, wild 2nd

victim 4th: casualty 5th, injured 5th, prey 4th, sufferer 2nd, target 5th

victory 4th: success 2nd, triumph 5th, win 1st

view 1st:

    A. look K, notice 1st, observe 3rd, see K, watch 1st, witness 3rd

    B. picture K, prospect 4th, scene 2nd

    C. comprehend 5th, sight 1st, understand 1st, vision 4th

    D. attitude 5th, belief 1st, bias 6th, opinion 3rd, perception 6th

    E. angle 3rd, aspect 5th, observance 3rd, side 1st

viewpoint 5th: angle 3rd, apsect 5th

vigor 5th: animation 6th, drive 1st, energy 4th, enthusiasm 4th, flair 6th, force 1st, health K, intensity 6th, might 1st, power 1st, punch 4th, spark 3rd, spirit 2nd, strength 1st, tolerance 5th, vitality 5th

vile 6th: awful 3rd, bad K, base 1st, corrupt 6th, dreadful 6th, evil 3rd, hateful 3rd, horrible 1st, immoral 4th, low K, sinful 2nd, terrible 1st, wicked 4th, wretched 6th

village 2nd: community 2nd, settlement 2nd, town 1st

villain 5th: brute 6th, creep 1st, rat K, rogue 5th, snake 1st

violent 5th: brutal 6th, cruel 5th, destructive 5th, fierce 4th, frantic 5th, furious 4th, intense 6th, out of control 2nd, powerful 2nd, savage 5th, severe 4th, stormy 2nd, strong K, terrible 1st, turbulent 5th, wild 2nd

virgin 6th: clean 1st, first 1st, inexperienced 4th, new K, original 3rd, pure 3rd

virtually 6th: almost K, essentially 6th, nearly 1st, practically 4th, substantially 5th

virtue 4th: character 2nd, charity 4th, goodness 1st, honor 1st, innocence 5th, morality 3rd, purity 3rd

visible 4th: apparent 3rd, evident 5th, exposed 4th, noticeable 3rd, observable 3rd, obvious 5th, open K, public 1st, uncovered 2nd, visual 4th

vision 4th:
  A. daydream 2nd, dream 1st, fantasy 6th, illusion 6th
  B. eyesight 1st, sight 1st
  C. ghost 1st, soul 3rd, spirit 2nd
  D. image 4th, perception 6th, prophecy 4th, revelation 4th, visualization 4th
visit 1st:
  A. chat 1st, stop K, talk K
  B. call K, stay 1st, tour 3rd
  C. appear 2nd, attend 3rd, chat 1st, meet K, talk K
vital 5th:
  A. active 3rd, alive 3rd, dynamic 5th, intense 6th, lively 2nd, living 1st,
    powerful 2nd, spirited 2nd, strong K, vibrant 5th, vigorous 5th
  B. central 3rd, critical 5th, essential 6th, important 1st, key K, necessary 1st,
    needed 1st, required 2nd, significant 6th, urgent 6th
vivid 6th:
  A. bright 1st, brilliant 4th, colorful 1st, expressive 5th, radiant 6th,
    splendid 4th, vibrant 5th
  B. detailed 5th, dramatic 5th, impressive 5th, intense 6th, powerful 2nd,
    striking 2nd, strong 1st
vocabulary 6th: dialect 5th, language 2nd, terms 3rd
voice 1st:
  A. call K, language 2nd, sound 1st
  B. air K, announce 3rd, express 5th, mouth 1st, proclaim 4th, pronounce 4th,
    reveal 4th, say K, speak 1st, state 1st, utter 4th, vent 4th
  C. expression 5th, utterance 4th
void 6th:
  A. nothing 1st, opening 1st, space 1st, vacancy 6th, vacuum 5th, zero K
  B. useless 2nd, vain 4th
  C. bare 3rd, blank 4th, empty 3rd, hollow 3rd, vacant 6th
volume 3rd:
  A. amount 2nd, bulk 4th, capacity 6th, content 3rd, mass 3rd, quantity 4th,
    scope 6th, size 1st
  B. amount 2nd, number K, sum 1st, total 2nd
  C. book K, edition 3rd, publication 4th, text 6th
  D. loudness 2nd, sound 1st
volunteer 5th:
  A. bestow 5th, give 1st, grant 2nd, offer 2nd, present K, propose 4th
  B. communicate 5th, tell K
vote 2nd:
  A. appoint 3rd, choose 3rd, elect 3rd, pick 1st, select 4th
  B. ballot 6th, count K, election 3rd, poll 5th

vow 4th:
>   **A.** assure 3rd, commit 4th, guarantee 6th, pledge 5th, promise 1st, swear 4th
>   **B.** guarantee 6th, oath 5th, pledge 5th, promise 1st

voyage 4th:
>   **A.** adventure 3rd, journey 3rd, passage 4th, sail 1st, trip 1st, travel 3rd
>   **B.** adventure 3rd, journey 3rd, roam 4th, tour 3rd, travel 3rd

waddle 5th: rock K, roll 1st, stagger 4th, step 1st, sway 3rd, swing 1st, walk K

waft 5th: blow 1st, breath 1st, carry K, convey 4th, current 3rd, float 1st, fly K, glide 4th, sail 1st

wag 1st: shake 1st, sway 3rd, swing 1st, wave K

wage 3rd: compensation 6th, conduct 3rd, earnings 2nd, fee 4th, hire 3rd, income 4th, pay K, salary 3rd

wagon 2nd: buggy 6th, carriage 5th, cart 1st, coach 4th, stagecoach 4th, van K

wail 5th: bawl 5th, cry 1st, grieve 5th, howl 4th, lament 6th, moan 5th, mourn 4th, scream 1st, shriek 4th, sob 1st, sorrow 4th, weep 4th, whine 5th

wait K: abide 5th, anticipate 6th, attend 3rd, await 5th, delay 5th, expect 2nd, help K, linger 4th, look for 1st, lull 5th, pause 3rd, postpone 6th, remain 2nd, rest 1st, serve 1st, stay 1st, suspend 5th, table 1st

wake 1st:
>   **A.** funeral 4th, session 6th
>   **B.** arouse 4th, awaken 3rd, excite 4th, kindle 5th, rise 1st, rouse 4th, stir 3rd

walk K:
>   **A.** lane 4th, pathway 2nd, sidewalk 1st, trail 2nd
>   **B.** hike 3rd, march 1st, pace 3rd, step 1st, stride 5th, stroll 5th, strut 5th

wall K: barrier 6th, curtain 5th, divider 4th, face 1st, fence 1st, panel 6th, partition 6th, railing 2nd, screen 1st, side K, surface 3rd

wallet 6th: case 2nd, purse 4th

wallow 6th:
>   **A.** delight 3rd, enjoy 2nd, indulge 5th, relish 6th
>   **B.** flop 6th, pitch 2nd, roll 1st, toss 2nd, tumble 4th

waltz 6th: dance 2nd, glide 4th

wan 6th: ashen 3rd, colorless 1st, dim 1st, faint 3rd, gentle 3rd, ghostly 1st, pale 3rd, peaked 5th, thin 1st, weak 3rd

wand 3rd: baton 5th, rod 1st, staff 4th, stick K

wander 3rd: drift 2nd, ramble 6th, range 3rd, roam 4th, rove 6th, shift 4th, stray 3rd, stroll 5th, travel 3rd, veer 6th

want K: absence 5th, crave 6th, demand 5th, desire 5th, fancy 3rd, fault 3rd, flaw 2nd, hunger 2nd, lack 1st, longing 2nd, miss K, need 1st, passion 6th, poverty 5th, require 2nd, shortage 2nd, thirst 2nd, wish 1st, yearn 6th

wanted 1st: desired 5th, marketable 4th, needed 1st, salable 4th

war 1st: arms 2nd, battle 2nd, clash 5th, combat 5th, contest 4th, conflict 4th, fight 1st

warble 6th: chirp 2nd, sing 1st

ward 5th: area 3rd, chamber 5th, district 4th, dormitory 5th,
  guard 1st, hall 1st, region 4th, room K, section 4th, sentinel 5th, watch 1st,
  zone 4th

wardrobe 6th:
  A. attire 6th, clothes 1st, costume 4th, dress K, outfit 1st
  B. bureau 4th, cabinet 4th, chest 2nd, closet 2nd, dresser 2nd

ware 5th: goods 1st, line K, merchandise 6th, products 4th, stock 2nd

warehouse 5th: stock 1st, stockroom 2nd, store K, vault 5th

warm 1st:
  A. heat 1st, hot K, stuffy 2nd
  B. eager 5th, emotional 4th, enthusiastic 4th, lively 1st, violent 5th
  C. affectionate 4th, comfortable 3rd, friendly 1st, kind K, loving 1st

warn 3rd: advise 3rd, alarm 3rd, alert 5th, caution 5th, flag 3rd, inform 5th,
  notify 3rd, recommend 5th, signal 4th, threaten 5th, tip 1st, urge 4th

warning 3rd: advice 3rd, caution 5th, notification 3rd, sign 1st, signal 4th,
  threat 5th

warp 4th: bend K, bias 6th, corrupt 6th, infect 6th, misrepresent 4th,
  prejudice 6th, poison 3rd, slant 6th, twist 1st

warrant 5th: assure 3rd, authorize 3rd, believe 1st, certificate 6th,
  establish 3rd, guarantee 6th, license 5th, permit 3rd, right K, support 4th

warrior 4th: brave 1st, fighter 1st, soldier 3rd, veteran 6th

wary 5th: alert 5th, artful 1st, awake 3rd, careful 1st, cautious 5th, clever 3rd,
  guarded 1st, prudent 6th, suspect 5th, watchful 2nd, wise 1st

wash 1st: bathe 1st, clean 1st, drift 2nd, float 1st, launder 6th, rinse 3rd,
  scour 6th, scrub 6th, shower 4th, wet K

waste 1st: debris 5th, garbage 5th, junk 3rd, litter 2nd, misuse 3rd, rubbish 5th,
  scraps 3rd, throw away 2nd, trash 2nd, wasteland 6th, wilderness 4th, wilt 4th

wasteland 6th: barren 4th, desert 1st, waste 1st, wild 2nd, wilderness 4th

watch 1st:
  A. clock 1st
  B. anticipate 6th, beware 6th, examine 5th, eye K, guard 1st, inspect 5th,
    lookout 2nd, mind 1st, observe 3rd, patrol 1st, police 1st, protect 4th,
    regard 4th, see K, study 2nd, view 1st, witness 3rd

watchful 2nd: alert 5th, attentive 2nd, cautious 5th, on guard 1st

wave K: alert 5th, breaker 4th, curl 2nd, curve 3rd, flag 3rd, flap 4th,
  indicate 4th, motion 3rd, move K, rise 1st, rush 2nd, shake 1st, signal 4th,
  surge 5th, sway 3rd, swell 3rd, swing 1st, tide 1st, twist 1st, wag 1st,
  warn 3rd

waver 5th: delay 5th, falter 1st, hesitate 4th, pause 3rd, shift 4th, stagger 4th,
  stall 5th, stumble 4th, sway 3rd, waffle 4th, weave 4th

wax K: build 1st, develop 5th, enlarge 5th, expand 5th, glaze 6th, grow 1st, increase 3rd, polish 4th, shine 1st, spread 2nd, stretch 4th, swell 3rd

way K:

A. approach 3rd, custom 6th, fashion 3rd, manner 2nd, method 2nd, practice 1st, process 4th, style 3rd, tradition 5th

B. access 6th, avenue 3rd, code 3rd, course 3rd, direction 1st, distance 4th, lane 4th, length 2nd, path 1st, road K, route 4th, street 1st, system 2nd, trail 2nd, use K

weak 3rd: defenseless 5th, delicate 5th, dependent 3rd, exposed 4th, feeble 4th, fragile 6th, frail 6th, helpless 2nd, hesitant 4th, ineffective 4th, lacking 2nd, powerless 2nd, reduced 3rd, slight 4th, spineless 4th

wealth 3rd: abundance 5th, capital 2nd, fortune 3rd, money K, plenty 1st, prosperity 5th, resources 5th, riches 1st, treasure 4th

weapon 4th: ammunition 6th, arm K, defense 5th, shot 1st

wear 1st:

A. decay 5th, destruction 5th, wear-and-tear 3rd

B. attire 6th, clothes 1st, display 3rd, dress K, exhibit 4th, have on 1st, outfit 1st, show 1st, use K, weary 4th

weary 4th: beat 1st, bored 2nd, drain 5th, exhausted 4th, fatigued 5th, impatient 5th, sick K, spent 2nd, tired 2nd, wear 1st, worn 1st

weather 1st:

A. climate 4th, temperature 5th

B. bear K, overcome 1st, resist 4th, stand K, suffer 2nd, survive 5th

weave 4th: build 1st, compose 4th, create 3rd, design 5th, invent 2nd, knot 4th, lace 4th, loom 5th, loop 5th, make up 2nd, produce 2nd, thread 2nd, twist 1st

wed K: associate 5th, attach 5th, blend 5th, bond 3rd, combine 3rd, connect 3rd, couple 3rd, fasten 4th, fuse 4th, join 3rd, link 5th, marry 1st, mate 4th, pair 1st, tie 1st, unite 5th

wedding 1st: ceremony 5th, marriage 2nd, vows 4th

wedge 4th:

A. crowd 2nd, force 1st, jam K, lodge 4th, press 1st, squeeze 5th, stuff 1st

B. access 6th, cut K, crack 4th, device 4th, gap K, groove 5th, notch 5th, opening 1st, opportunity 3rd, prop 5th, slot 5th, split 4th, step 1st, void 6th

weed 1st: clear 2nd, dig 1st, hoe 2nd, pick 1st, pluck 1st, pull K

weep 4th: bawl 5th, cry 1st, grieve 5th, lament 6th, mourn 4th, sob 1st, wail 5th, whimper 5th, whine 5th

weigh 1st:

A. consider 2nd, contemplate 6th, ponder 6th, reason 2nd, reflect 4th, study 2nd, think 1st

B. balance 3rd, measure 2nd

C. mark 1st, note 1st, observe 3rd

weight 1st:
   A. gravity 5th, mass 3rd, pounds 2nd, volume 3rd
   B. concern 3rd, emphasis 5th, importance 2nd, significance 6th, value 2nd
   C. burden 5th, load 2nd, responsibility 4th, stress 6th
   D. anchor 4th
weird 1st: crazy 4th, creepy 2nd, curious 3rd, fantastic 6th, ghostly 1st, odd 4th, peculiar 4th, queer 4th, strange 1st, unaccountable 3rd, unusual 3rd, wild 2nd
welcome 1st:
   A. agreeable 2nd, comfortable 3rd, pleasing 1st
   B. address K, embrace 4th, greet 3rd, hail 4th, hello K, meet K, receive 1st, toast 5th
weld 6th: attach 5th, bolt 4th, bond 3rd, connect 3rd, fasten 4th, link 5th, pin K
welfare 5th:
   A. financial aid 2nd, public assistance 4th
   B. advantage 3rd, benefit 3rd, good K, interest 3rd, sake 3rd
   C. fortune 3rd, happiness 1st, health K, prosperity 5th, success 2nd
well K:
   A. acceptable 3rd, favorable 3rd, satisfactory 3rd, suitable 3rd
   B. fit K, hardy 5th, healthy 1st, sound 1st, sturdy 3rd
   C. fortunate 4th, good K, happy K, nice 1st, very K
   D. flow 1st, run K, spring K
well built 2nd: durable 6th, solid 3rd, strong K, sturdy 3rd
wet K:
   A. damp 5th, dripping 2nd, fluid 6th, liquid 3rd, misty 2nd, moist 4th, rainy 1st, soaked 5th, watery 1st
   B. flood 2nd, rain 1st, shower 4th, vapor 3rd
wharf 5th: breakwater 4th, dock 1st, landing 1st, pier 4th
wheel 1st:
   A. drive 1st, move K, push 1st, reel 5th, roll 1st, spin 1st, stagger 4th, sway 3rd, turn 1st, veer 6th, whirl 4th
   B. band 1st, circle K, disk 2nd, round K
wheeze 5th: cough 5th, gasp 4th, sneeze 5th
when K: at the time 1st, then 1st
whence 4th: from K, where 1st
whenever 3rd: anytime 1st, every time 1st
where 1st: direction 1st, position 2nd, what place 1st
whereas 4th: although 2nd, because K, since 1st, while 1st
wherefore 4th: therefore 1st
whereupon 4th: in consequence of 4th, on which 1st
whether 1st: or 1st
which 1st: that K

whiff 5th:
  A. clue 2nd, hint 1st, suspicion 4th, trace 3rd
  B. blow 1st, breath 1st, breeze 4th, puff 2nd, smell 3rd, sniff 4th
while 1st:
  A. period 2nd, spell 1st, time 1st
  B. although 2nd, as K, at the same time 1st, during 4th, whereas 2nd
whim 6th: craze 4th, dream K, fancy 3rd, impulse 5th, notion 5th
whimper 5th: cry 1st, groan 3rd, moan 5th, sigh 3rd, sob 1st, wail 5th,
  weep 4th, whine 5th
whine 5th:
  A. beg 1st, bemoan 5th, cry 1st, groan 3rd, lament 6th, moan 5th, plead 3rd,
    wail 5th, whimper 5th
  B. complain 4th, gripe 5th, grumble 5th, nag 1st
whip 4th:
  A. batter 1st, beat 1st, blend 5th, mix 1st, stir 3rd
  B. conquer 4th, defeat 5th, lash 4th, pound 2nd, thrash 4th
  C. route 4th, swing 1st, turn 1st, veer 6th
whir 6th:
  A. buzz 5th
  B. fly K, revolve 5th
whirl 4th: circle K, fling 6th, rotate 6th, round K, spin 1st, turn 1st
whisk 4th:
  A. hurry 1st, quickly 1st, rush 2nd, speed 3rd
  B. brush 2nd, clean 1st, dust 2nd, sweep 4th
  C. beat 1st, mix 1st
whiskey 6th: alcohol 5th, liquor 5th, sauce 5th
whisper 1st:
  A. breathe 1st, hum 1st, mumble 4th, murmur 4th, mutter 4th, sigh 3rd,
    tell K
  B. shade 2nd, sprinkle 3rd, tinge 5th, touch 1st
  C. clue 2nd, hint 1st, suggestion 2nd, suspicion 4th
whistle 4th: chirp 2nd, hum 1st, sound 1st
whoever 1st: anybody 1st, anyone 1st, everybody 3rd, everyone 1st
whole 1st:
  A. all K, complete 3rd, entire 3rd, full K, sum 1st, total 2nd, undivided 4th
  B. hearty 5th, perfect 3rd, solid 3rd, strong K
wholesome 5th: clean 1st, fit K, hardy 5th, healthy 1st, helpful 1st, pure 3rd,
  robust 5th, sound 1st, spotless 2nd, sturdy 3rd, well 1st
wholly 5th: completely 3rd, entirely 3rd, fully 1st, thoroughly 1st, totally 2nd
whom 2nd: who K
whoop 6th: call 1st, cheer 3rd, cry 1st, roar 1st, scream 1st, shout 1st, yell K
why K: because K, cause 2nd, reason 2nd

wick 1st: cord 4th, fibers 3rd, fuse 4th

wicked 4th:

    A. awful 3rd, bad K, corrupt 6th, criminal 4th, dishonest 3rd, evil 3rd, immoral 3rd, monstrous 5th, sinful 2nd, unethical 5th, vile 6th, villainous 5th, wrong 1st

    B. dangerous 6th, harsh 5th, severe 4th

wide 1st: ample 5th, broad 3rd, catholic 4th, full K, large 4th, thick 2nd, vast 4th

widespread 5th: broad 3rd, common 2nd, current 3rd, general 2nd, global 4th, fashionable 4th, popular 3rd, rampant 6th, universal 4th

width 4th: capacity 6th, degree 5th, extent 4th, measure 2nd, range 3rd, reach 1st, scope 6th, size 1st, space 1st, span 6th

wield 6th: control 2nd, exercise 1st, handle 2nd, ply 6th, raise 1st, shake 1st, swing 1st, use K

wife 1st: bride 4th, lady 1st, mate 4th

wig 1st: carpet 4th, fall K, hairpiece 2nd, rug 1st

wigwam 5th: home K, house K, hut 4th

wild 2nd:

    A. barren 4th, desert 1st, waste 1st, wasteland 4th, wilderness 4th

    B. agitated 5th, confused 4th, disorderly 3rd, excited 4th, extravagant 6th, fantastic 6th, fierce 4th, frantic 5th, free K, mad K, rambling 6th, reckless 5th, savage 5th, stubborn 5th, uncivilized 4th

wilderness 4th: barren 4th, desert 1st, wasteland 4th

wile 6th: attraction 5th, charm 3rd, design 5th, device 4th, lure 5th, snare 6th, temptation 5th, trap 1st

will K:

    A. ambition 4th, choice 3rd, discipline 6th, goal 4th, persistence 5th, purpose 1st

    B. command 2nd, decide 1st, desire 5th, determine 5th, effect 3rd, order 1st, wish K

    C. free K, impart 6th, leave 1st, resolve 5th

willing 5th: agreeable 2nd, compliant 6th, content 3rd, cooperative 5th, eager 5th, glad 1st, happy K, inclined 5th, obedient 4th, pleased K, unforced 3rd, voluntary 5th

wilt 4th: decay 5th, die 2nd, droop 5th, dry 1st, fade 1st, faint 3rd, sag 1st, shrink 5th, waste 1st, wither 5th

win K:

    A. success 2nd, triumph 5th, victory 4th

    B. ace 2nd, acquaint 4th, best K, capture 3rd, conquer 4th, conquest 4th, defeat 5th, earn 2nd, gain 2nd, get K, master 1st, score 1st, secure 3rd

wince 5th: quiver 4th, shudder 4th, shy K, start 1st, startle 4th, tremble K

wind 1st:

    A. blow 1st, breeze 4th, current 3rd, gale 2nd, gust 5th, puff 2nd, storm 2nd

B. circle K, coil 5th, curl 2nd, curve 3rd, screw 3rd, turn 1st, twist 1st

window 1st: bull's-eye 1st, opening 1st, port 3rd

wine 1st: alcohol 5th, liquor 5th, spirits 2nd

wing 1st:

A. branch 2nd, division 4th, extension 4th, section 4th

B. fly 1st, glide 4th, soar 6th

C. harm 3rd, hit K, hurt K, injure 5th

wink 2nd:

A. instant 3rd, moment 1st

B. hint 1st, sign 1st, signal 4th

C. blink 6th, flash 2nd, flicker 5th, shine 1st, sparkle 5th, twinkle 4th

wipe 1st: brush 2nd, clean 1st, dry 1st, polish 4th, rub 1st, scour 6th, stroke 1st

wire 3rd: cable 1st, rigging 1st, telegraph 4th

wise 1st:

A. competent 6th, educated 3rd, intelligent 4th, just 1st, knowledgeable 3rd, politic 4th, prudent 6th, reasonable 3rd, sage 5th, sensible 6th

B. fashion 3rd, manner 1st, method 2nd, way K

wish K: aim 3rd, desire 5th, fancy 3rd, goal 4th, hope 1st, hunger 2nd, longing 1st, request 4th, want K, whim 6th, will K, yearn 6th

wit 1st:

A. comedy 5th, humor 4th, jest 4th, joke 1st

B. awareness 3rd, intelligence 4th, keenness 4th, perception 6th, reason 2nd, sense 1st

witch K: enchantress 6th, medium 5th, nag 1st, old bat 1st

with K: along 1st, also K, amid 4th, among 1st, and K, besides 1st, furthermore 3rd, inside 1st, moreover 2nd, plus 1st, too 1st, within 3rd

withal 6th: also K, besides 2nd, everything 1st, nevertheless 4th, too 1st

withdraw 2nd: depart 5th, exit 3rd, go K, leave 1st, pull out K, recall 3rd, remove 2nd, resign 5th, retreat 4th, subtract K, surrender 5th, yield 4th

wither 5th: decay 5th, decline 6th, droop 5th, dry 1st, fade 1st, sag 1st, shrink 5th, starve 5th, weaken 3rd, wilt 4th

within 1st: inside 1st, into 1st, inwardly 6th

without 1st: lacking 1st, not K

witness 3rd:

A. behold 3rd, note 1st, observe 3rd, see K, sight 1st, view 1st, watch 1st

B. approve 4th, certify 6th, proof 4th, speak 1st, swear 4th, warrant 5th

wizard 6th: authority 3rd, expert 5th, genius 4th, magician 5th, master 5th, witch K

wobble 4th: flex 6th, lean 3rd, quiver 4th, shake 1st, stagger 4th, tilt 5th, tip 1st, twist 1st

woe 4th:
A. agony 5th, anguish 6th, care 1st, depression 6th, distress 5th, grief 5th, misery 4th, pain 2nd, regret 5th, remorse 6th, sadness 1st, sorrow 4th, suffering 2nd, torment 5th
B. burden 5th, disaster 6th, trial 4th, trouble 1st

woman K: bride 4th, female 4th, individual 3rd, lady 1st, mistress 4th, person 1st, wife 1st

wonder 1st:
A. marvel 4th, miracle 5th, novelty 5th, phenomenon 6th, sight 1st, spectacle 5th
B. awe 6th, curiosity 3rd, doubt 5th, question 1st, suspicion 4th
C. amazement 5th, astonishment 4th, sensation 5th, stare 3rd

wonderful 1st: delightful 3rd, excellent 1st, fantastic 6th, good K, glorious 3rd, great 1st, magnificent 4th, marvelous 4th, outstanding 2nd, phenomenal 6th, splendid 4th, superb 6th, super 1st, terrific 5th, tremendous 4th

wont 5th: custom 6th, fashion 3rd, habit 3rd, manner 2nd, observance 3rd, practice 1st, routine 6th, tradition 5th, use K

woo 6th: attract 5th, beg 1st, court 3rd, encourage 4th, flirt 6th, lure 5th, pursue 5th, romance 5th, tempt 4th, urge 4th

wood 1st: forest 2nd, lumber 1st, trees K, timber 5th, wilderness 4th

word K:
A. oath 5th, pledge 5th, promise 1st, vow 4th
B. account 3rd, expression 5th, gossip 5th, name K, report 1st, story K, talk K, term 3rd
C. demand 5th, law 1st, order 1st, rule K

work K:
A. business 2nd, employment 5th, job K, occupation 6th, profession 5th, role 6th, task 3rd, trade 2nd
B. act 1st, answer 1st, do K, effort 2nd, grind 4th, labor 2nd, operation 3rd, perform 4th, qualify 4th, run K, satisfy 3rd, toil 4th
C. action 1st, book K, composition 4th, essay 5th, manuscript 6th, text 6th

worker 1st: employee 5th, laborer 2nd, master 1st, operator 5th

workman 1st: employee 5th, laborer 2nd, operator 5th

world 1st: globe 4th, nations 1st, sphere 6th

worn 3rd: aged 1st, exhausted 4th, faded 1st, old K, shabby 4th, spent 2nd, tired 2nd, used 1st, weary 4th

worrisome 5th: annoying 5th, provoking 6th, tormenting 5th, troublesome 2nd

worry 1st:
A. alarm 3rd, bother 2nd, concern 3rd, confuse 4th, distress 5th, fret 5th, fuss 1st, sweat 3rd, torment 5th, unease 3rd, woe 4th
B. anxiety 4th, care 1st, doubt 5th, fear 1st, pain 2nd, stress 6th, trial 4th, trouble 1st

worse 1st: inferior 5th, meaner 1st, poorer 1st, weaker 3rd

worship 4th:
  A. church K, temple 3rd
  B. adore 4th, beseech 5th, cherish 5th, devotion 5th, glory 3rd, hail 4th, honor 1st, love K, praise 4th, pray 3rd, respect 2nd, reverence 4th

worst 3rd:
  A. last K, least 2nd, lowest K, poorest 1st
  B. beat 1st, best K, break 1st, defeat 5th, quench 6th

worth 3rd:
  A. cost 1st, merit 4th, price K, rate 1st, significance 6th, value 2nd
  B. character 2nd, excellence 1st, honor 1st, quality 4th, stature 6th

worthless 3rd: fruitless 3rd, immaterial 5th, ineffective 3rd, insignificant 6th, unimportant 2nd, useless 2nd, vain 4th

wound 3rd:
  A. cut K, damage 5th, hurt 1st, injure 5th, pierce 4th, shoot 3rd
  B. ache 5th, blow 1st, bump 2nd, injury 5th, pain 2nd

wow K: amaze 5th, astonish 4th, awe 6th, delight 3rd, floor 2nd, impress 5th

wrap 3rd:
  A. cape 4th, cloak 4th, coat 1st, shawl 6th
  B. close 1st, cover 1st, enclose 4th, envelop 5th, package 4th, tape 1st

wrath 4th: anger 1st, fury 4th, indignation 5th, madness 3rd, outrage 6th, rage 4th, revenge 5th

wreath 4th: circle K, crown 1st, garland 6th, ring 1st

wreck 4th:
  A. crash 2nd, crush 4th, destroy 2nd, devastate 6th, ruin 5th, shatter 5th, sink 3rd, smash 3rd, trash 2nd
  B. accident 4th, collision 6th
  C. remains 2nd, ruins 5th, shell 1st

wrench 6th:
  A. pull K, tear 2nd, tug 1st, turn 1st, twist 1st, yank 2nd
  B. hurt K, pain 2nd, sadness 1st, trouble 1st, worry 1st

wrest 6th: abduct 6th, clutch 4th, grab 4th, grapple 6th, grasp 4th, grip 4th, hold 1st, nab 1st, seize 3rd, snatch 4th, steal 3rd, take 1st, wrench 6th

wrestle 6th: battle 2nd, contend 5th, fight K, grab 4th, grapple 6th, squeeze 5th, struggle 1st, tackle 4th

wretched 6th: broken 1st, crushed 4th, depressed 5th, difficult 5th, fatal 4th, poor K, rotten 1st, sorry 2nd, tragic 5th

wriggle 5th: crawl 1st, slither 4th, snake 5th, squirm 2nd, turn 1st, twist 1st, writhe 6th

wring 5th: exact 2nd, pierce 4th, pull K, rend 4th, squeeze 5th, tug 1st, twist 1st, wound 3rd, wrench 6th, wrest 6th, yank 2nd

wrinkle 3rd: crease 5th, fold 1st, gather 1st, knit 4th, muss 1st, pleat 5th, ridge 5th

writ 6th: citation 6th, summons 4th, ticket 1st

write K: author 3rd, communicate 5th, compose 4th, inscribe 5th, note 1st, rhyme 6th, scratch 4th

writer 1st: author 3rd, composer 4th, correspondent 5th

writhe 6th: bend K, crawl 1st, glide 4th, misshape 1st, slither 4th, snake 5th, squirm 2nd, twist 1st, wriggle 5th

wrong 1st:

    A. corrupt 6th, crime 2nd, error 4th, evil 3rd, fraud 6th, illegal 1st, immoral 3rd, improper 3rd, injustice 3rd, mistake 1st, offense 4th, sin 1st, unethical 2nd, unfair 2nd, unjust 2nd

    B. abuse 6th, exploit 6th, fault 3rd, harm 3rd, injure 5th, persecute 6th, victimize 4th

    C. amiss 3rd, bad K, false 3rd, incorrect 3rd, untrue 2nd, wicked 4th

wrought 5th:

    A. excited 4th

    B. fashioned 3rd, formed 1st, hammered 2nd, manufactured 3rd, turned 1st

yank 2nd: drag 5th, draw K, pull K, tug 1st, wrench 6th

yard K: garden K, grounds 1st, park 1st, pen 1st, plot 4th

yarn 2nd:

    A. cord 4th, fiber 3rd, strand 5th, thread 2nd

    B. fable 5th, fantasy 6th, fiction 5th, myth 4th, story K, tale 3rd

yawn 5th: gape 5th, open wide 1st, stretch 4th, tired 2nd

ye 4th: you K

yea K: yes K

yeah 1st: yes K

year 1st: period 2nd, session 6th, span 6th, term 3rd, time 1st, twelve months 1st

yearn 6th: ache 5th, covet 6th, crave 6th, desire 5th, hunger 2nd, long 1st, need 1st, thrust 4th, want K, wish for K

yeast 2nd:

    A. bubble 2nd, foam K, rise 1st

    B. agitation 5th, confusion 4th, fuss 1st

yell K: alarm 3rd, bellow 4th, call 1st, cry 1st, exclaim 3rd, howl 4th, roar 1st, scream 1st, shout 1st, shriek 4th, signal 4th, wail 5th

yelp 6th: bark 3rd, bay K, cry 1st, howl 4th, shout 1st. *See* yell.

yes K: yea K, yeah 1st

yesterday 3rd: day before K, last night 1st

yet 1st: but K, except 2nd, further 2nd, however 3rd, just 1st, merely 3rd, only K, simply 2nd, still 1st, through 5th

yield 4th:

    A. earnings 2nd, gain 2nd, pay K, profit 4th, result 2nd, return 2nd

    B. crop 2nd, harvest 4th, produce 2nd, product 4th

    C. abandon 4th, bend K, buckle 6th, cave 1st, comply 6th, concede 6th, generate 4th, give 1st, resign 5th, submit 4th, surrender 5th

yip 1st: bark 3rd, cry 1st, yelp 6th

yoke 6th:

    A. band 1st, collar 4th, frame 3rd

    B. chain 3rd, connect 3rd, group 1st, join 3rd, link 5th, team 1st, tie 1st

yon 4th: that K, there 1st, yonder 4th

yonder 4th: beyond 1st, distant 4th, far 1st, far away 3rd, further 2nd, overseas 4th, over there 1st, past 1st, yon 4th

yore 6th: ancient 3rd, earlier 2nd, forgotten 2nd, former 6th, gone 1st, late 1st, long ago 1st, lost 1st, old K, once 1st, past 1st, preceding 6th, prior 5th, time past 1st, vague 5th

you K: thee 2nd, ye 4th

young 1st:

    A. active 3rd, cheerful 3rd, confident 6th, keen 4th, laughing 1st

    B. early 1st, fresh 2nd, green K, immature 5th, innocent 5th, new K, youthful 2nd

yourself 2nd: oneself 3rd, you K

youth 2nd:

    A. child K, juvenile 5th, kid 1st, lad K, minor 5th, teen 2nd

    B. freshness 2nd, vigor 5th

    C. early life 1st

yule 2nd: Christmas K, New Year 1st

zeal 6th: delight 3rd, devotion 5th, ecstasy 6th, enjoyment 3rd, enthusiasm 4th, excitement 4th, fire K, glow 1st, passion 6th, relish 6th, spirited 2nd, warmth 1st, zest 6th

zealous 6th: ambitious 4th, ardent 6th, devoted 5th, eager 5th, emotional 4th, energetic 4th, extreme 5th, fervent 6th, fiery 5th, intense 6th, loyal 5th, passionate 6th, radical 6th, revolutionary 5th

zero K: bottom 1st, none 1st, nothing 1st

zest 6th:

    A. bite 1st, edge 1st, flavor 4th, seasoning 2nd, spice 3rd

    B. delight 3rd, enjoyment 3rd, fervor 6th, fire K, passion 6th, relish 6th, thrill 4th, zeal 6th, zip K

zigazg 3rd: abrupt 5th, angled 3rd, cross 1st, curve 3rd, forked 2nd

zip K:

    A. close 1st

    B. barrel 4th, drive 1st, hurry 1st, rush 2nd, speed 3rd, streak 5th

    C. easy 1st, energy 4th, spirit 2nd, vigor 5th, vitality 5th, zest 6th

zipper K: close K, fastener 4th, seal 2nd, slide 2nd

zone 4th: area 3rd, arena 5th, belt 2nd, district 4th, field 2nd, part 1st, quarter 1st, range 3rd, realm 4th, region 4th, section 4th, space 1st, sphere 6th, territory 3rd, ward 5th

zoo K:

A. confusion 4th, disorder 1st

B. garden K, park 1st

Some Things You'll Need to Know

MORE ON WORDS

Unusual Words. To introduce words not in the child's standard vocabulary — foreign words for example — give the definition first, then the word. Or, you could underline the word the first time it is used. Children (adults too) tend to skip over unfamiliar words without trying to read them, getting the meaning from the context of the sentence. Giving the definition first makes it much easier to actually learn the new word.

Names. Nicknames for your characters can be highly desirable. They can help describe someone's personality or their appearance with little or no exposition: "Hey, Red, come here!" "Go get Pokey so we can get started." They can also set the mood as hostile or friendly or describe the cultural set of an era or a nation. They are also excellent "tags" that help your reader remember or identify a character.

Unless it is important to the story, avoid connecting words like *tiny, little, bitty* and *small* to the names of your protagonists. The *tiny* of Tiny Tim is central to the character and his problem. Believe me, Little Leroy or Bitsy Betty have problems, too, whether you intended them or not. The diminutive name takes away personal power and emasculates.

Nonsexist/Nonracist Terminology. It is good to use generic terminology instead of words that express gender bias. Use *mail carrier* instead of *mailman;* carry that principle to all occupations or positions that end with *man.* Other things to look out for are usage of the pronoun *he,* try to vary it, and stereotypical roles, such as male doctors and female nurses.

Race is another area where you should be sensitive to word usage. Use *African American* instead of *black* and *Native American* instead of *Indian. Asian American* is often preferred to *Oriental.* In all instances, be sensitive to offensive terminology and seek out an authority when in doubt. Children enjoy reading about people like themselves, so it's good to have characters with diverse backgrounds. With the trend toward globalization, this is becoming a more important practice.

Tags. An editor may suggest you use a "tag" to help identify a character. Tags are generally actions or gestures a character typically uses that easily identify the person to the reader. A boy may toss his head when he gossips, a young girl may push up her glasses just before she throws a fast pitch. The tag may be used to build a character, be part of the problem or identify a "mystery" person. For example, a boy may try to hide in the bushes or shadow a suspect while humming the song he always hums or sniffing a chronically runny nose. Nicknames are another good tag you can use to help describe the character.

Word Count. One of the most common reasons magazines reject good manuscripts is the failure to include a word count at the top of the first page. No editor is going to sit and count the number of words in your work to see if it will fit into their format.

THEME AND CONTENT

Character's Ages. The protagonist(s) of your story should be the same age as or a little older than the reader. Establish the age of the protagonist as soon as possible and make sure your characters act appropriately for their ages.

Taboos. While the market is much more flexible than in the past, stay away from any positive portrayal of drugs, tobacco, alcohol, explicit sex, war, crime and violence. Drunkenness particularly should never be portrayed in a humorous light.

You will find certain themes, while not actually taboo, difficult to sell. Animals that talk to people are almost impossible to sell—even as fantasy. 'Lil Toot and The Little Engine That Could aside, anthropomorphizing inanimate objects also makes for a difficult sale. Stories that turn out to be only a dream are not often welcome, especially if waking up is used to solve a plot problem. Things that are too cute, too old-fashioned or too common usually get the cold shoulder, too.

Women and men should be treated the same in all types of stories, as should boys and girls. Again, stay away from stereotyping.

Fantasy. Fantasy is a healthy field for juvenile publishing. However, retelling such classics as Thumbelina or The Goose Girl in modern dress is sure to garner rejection slips instead of praise.

Mystery. There is a great difference between adult and children's mysteries. Violence is generally out for any age group. For preteen readers, murder is out, and so are most dead bodies. The only corpses are generally ancient mummies or legends that lend creeps to a story. Missing treasure, old legends and secrets, theft and even kidnapping have formed the core of wonderful mysteries. Many are even elaborate puzzles the reader is meant to solve.

Science Fiction. Science fiction becomes popular around fourth or fifth grade when it is a venue for fast-paced adventure. By the sixth grade, character development becomes important. It is often a pleasant and charming way of explaining science or giving facts—but make sure its primary goal is to entertain.

Romance. Romance stories are popular with sixth graders on up. Contemporary stories include urban themes such as gangs, alcohol and sex. Today's teens are dealing with some serious situations, and books and stories that accurately reflect their world are popular.

Nonfiction. Nonfiction is popular with readers in the elementary level. Stories about scientific phenomena, the environment, history and technology interest this group. Current events and how-to books are welcome at the elementary and high school level.

AGE GROUPS/READING LEVELS

This section covers the age groupings and categories of books that publishers recognize. First, the age groups:

The Primary Age Group. Includes children from six- to eight-years-old, or first through third grades. This group reads the picture book, picture story and easy to read book. There are more magazines aimed at this age group than at younger children. The *Easy Reader* is meant for the child to read alone and the target sentence length is five to six words, ten words maximum. All the words given in the kindergarten through third-grade word lists are appropriate to use when writing for this group.

The Elementary Level. Includes eight- to twelve-year-olds, or the fourth through sixth graders. The target sentence length is ten words. The longest length acceptable to conservative institutions is about twenty words. Sentence length is more flexible in books than in magazines. Fiction should have a lot of action, and both fiction and nonfiction should deal with the special interests and problems relevant to this age group.

Most books written at the elementary level range between 20,000 and 40,000 words. Most magazines use stories ranging from 700 to 2,000 words and often have a page or two of short-shorts under 100 words.

The High School Level. Includes 13- to 17-year-olds, or seventh- through twelfth-grade readers. However, many readers are somewhat younger and sixth graders often constitute a major portion of the readership. This group uses an adult vocabulary and structure. Most books range from 25,000 to 55,000 words. Longer lengths are permissible. Popular fiction subjects include romance, mystery, suspense (mild horror), the supernatural and humor. More magazines are aimed at this age group than any other. Magazine stories range from 1,000 to 3,500 words. Eighty percent of this market is nonfiction and include age-related problems, interviews and special interests.

Following are the terms commonly used by publishers for the different types of children's books:

Picture Books. There are basically three types of picture books. The first are for babies to three-year-olds, have little text and are often prepared by publishers in-house.

The next type is for toddlers to five-year-olds. These must be kept short enough to be read aloud at one sitting. They should have a happy ending. These picture books must use language that can be read aloud comfortably. Sentence length should also be determined by reading ease. If the book is meant to be an early self-reader, the target sentence length should be five to six words. Try to use mainly kindergarten and first-grade vocabulary. These books should take no more than twenty minutes to read.

The oldest group of picture book readers is the five- to eight-year-olds. These books must have a story to tell. They should have a beginning, a middle and an end. There should be a plot, but it should be simple. Children in this age group still like to be read to, and rhythm keeps them attentive.

Picture books may run from as few as 50 words to 1,500. Most picture books average 500 to 1,000 words. Books for the youngest listeners (through five-years-old) should take no more than twenty minutes to read; about ten to fifteen minutes is preferred. Keep in mind the short attention span of the listener.

Picture Story. Picture stories are the picture books in which text carries the story. These are for the five-to eight-year-old. Picture stories tell a real story and have lots of action. If it is written for an adult to read to a child, sentence length is only restricted to that which is comfortable to read aloud, and the vocabulary should be such that the child can understand it, rather than read it.

The picture story is still heavily illustrated but has a more complicated plot than a picture book.

Easy to Read Books (Also Known as Young Readers). These books are intended for ages six to nine (grades one to three). Manuscripts are 500 to 2,000 words, with 1,000 to 1,500 words preferred. These books are generally about forty-eight pages in length, composed of some blank pages and about thirty-eight pages of text. Sentences should be five to six words in length, with a few up to eight words. When putting your story together, try not to break up phrases between lines. To make sure you haven't done this and that your story is easy to read, read it out loud a few times. These books are for the child to read alone; if your book is meant to be read by an adult to a child, notify the publisher when you submit it.

Hi-Lo Books. The term "Hi-Lo" means *high interest, low reading level.* These books are purchased mainly by schools and are written for people learning to read or slow learners. They use a controlled vocabulary and a sentence length appropriate to the vocabulary level. They use a lot of action and dialogue. Romance, mystery, ethnic and stories dealing with urban problems are often welcome. Most of these books run from 400 to 1,200 words. The sentence structure and length should be the same as that used for the grade level intended. For example, you can write a hi-lo book on the second-grade level, but the story must be mature in theme.

Many publishers want graded hi-lo books but do not supply the word lists. It is here that the graded word lists in this book become invaluable. Sentence length is about ten to twelve words. Stories should be fast paced and have a tightly knit plot.

Young Adult Novels. These books are written for readers aged twelve to eighteen. They are similar to mainstream novels except the protagonist is a teen or young adult and the story is relevant to that age group.

OTHER TYPES OF WRITING

So far I've talked a lot about books and a little about magazines. Here, I'll discuss magazines a bit more and then other types of writing for children.

Features. Feature stories really come into their own at the elementary level. Fourth-, fifth- and sixth-grade magazines often use the feature story style to lend life to science, mathematics and news stories. A feature story is one that allows emotional involvement or entertains as well as informs. Such stories almost always make your audience feel something or want to do something.

Fillers. A filler is a short article or story—usually under 500 words and often under 100. Fillers, such as games, riddles and items of special scientific or human interest, are especially welcome in young children's periodicals. In broadcasting, fillers are short, nonessential stories kept on hand in case a program runs short. If you are helping to produce a children's television or radio news program, keep a number of these on hand and at the bottom of the reader's pile. Trivia about such things as the world's largest pizza or the biggest pair of shoes is interesting and can be carried week after week until needed.

Writing for Television. The existence of public-access cable television channels and the availability of reasonably priced video-taping equipment have created a variety of exciting opportunities for people throughout the country. Even the smallest schools often videotape students presenting a weekly news report or original drama to be shown on these regular television channels or for use in the classroom.

Television news and other productions that narrate silent videos the viewers are watching generally use a forty- to forty-five-space line for the script, typed in a double- or triple-spaced column down the right-hand side of the paper. Common margin settings are thirty for the left margin and seventy for the right margin. The placement allows the left side of the paper to be used to note what video accompanies the text. Each forty-space line takes about two seconds of on-air time to read. Triple spacing makes it easier for the reader to keep their place and the writer to edit the work.

Writing for Radio. Many schools now have their own FM radio broadcasting facilities or access to local college or commercial stations. It's easy to produce material for this medium according to professional industry standards and, like so many other things, its just as easy for the children to learn the correct format as any other. Standard radio broadcast format uses a sixty-five-space line for typing. This line length makes timing your stories easy. Each group of sixteen lines takes about one minute to read aloud (3.75 seconds per line).

Writing in Verse. Verse seems to be everywhere in children's publishing, yet it is sometimes very hard to sell. One of the problems is that verse must sound good when read out loud, and it needs to be easy to read for an extended period of time. Read your work into a tape recorder, have a friend read it to you or take it to a writer's workshop. If you stumble or have trouble reading it smoothly and easily, go back to work. It is a lot easier to sell verse to a magazine because it is generally interspersed with other types of material. A good track record publishing verse in magazines will also make it easier to sell a book written the same way.

Writing Plays. Children's plays can be written one of three ways: 1) with children as actors, 2) with adults as actors but children as the audience and 3) acted by adults or teens for young adults and teens. For younger children, action is important, just as it is in other forms of children's writing. As always, themes and protagonists must correlate with the intended audience.

Bibliographies. Occasionally children's periodicals ask writers to submit lists of reference material to support their facts. Do keep track of your source material—do not submit it with your story until asked for it; unless you know the periodical requires it. Books are another matter, reference material should be cited with any work of nonfiction or fiction that should have accurate factual content.

Bibliography

RECOMMENDED READING

Balkin, Richard. *How to Understand & Negotiate a Book Contract or Magazine Agreement*. Writer's Digest Books.

Carpenter, Lisa, ed. *Children's Writer's & Illustrator's Market*. Writer's Digest Books, 1992.

Wyndham, Lee. *Writing for Children & Teenagers*. Writer's Digest Books.

SOURCES USED FOR WORD LISTS

Ainsworth, Norma Ruedi. *The Ghost at Peaceful End*. Scholastic, 1977.

Batchelor de Garcia, Karen and Randi Slaughter. *An Integrated Skills Approach in Plain English*. Addison-Wesley, 1986.

Beech, Linda Ward and Tara McCarthy. *Communication for Today*. Steck-Vaughn, 1987.

Bolognese, Don. *Squeak Parker*. Scholastic, 1977.

Borisoff, Norman. *Dangerous Fortune*. Scholastic, 1976.

Bunting, Eve. *Going Against Cool Calvin*. Scholastic, 1978.

Granbeck, Marilyn. *Summer at Ravenswood*. Scholastic, 1977.

Henney, R. Lee. *Basic Education: Reading* Book 1. Cambridge, 1977.

Katz, Bobbi. *Action on Ice*. Scholastic, 1976.

Kimberly, Gail. *Star Jewel*. Scholastic, 1979.

Martel, Cruz. *Pirate Kite*. Scholastic, 1978.

Purification, Les. *Karate Ace*. Scholastic, 1976.

Reading for Today, a Sequential Program for Adults. Steck-Vaughn, 1987.

Reading 720 (a sequential reading program for children: levels 5-12). Ginn and Company (Xerox Corp.), 1976.

Roth, Arthur. *Black and White Jones*. Scholastic, 1978.

Stamper, Judith Bauer. *Ghost Town*. Scholastic, 1979.

Stevens, Claire. *Mr. Marvel*. Scholastic, 1978.

Stine, H. William and Megan. *Frozen Danger*. Scholastic, 1981.

Stine, Megan and H. William. *The Mad Doctor*. Scholastic, 1978.

Sunshine, Madeline. *Adventure at the Wax Museum*. Scholastic, 1980.

Sunshine, Madeline. *Midnight Lantern*. Scholastic, 1979.

Thorndike, Edward L., Irving Lorge. *The Teacher's Word Book of 30,000 Words*. Columbia University, 1944.

Tivenan, Bonnie. *Contemporary's New Beginnings in Reading*. Contemporary Books, 1985.

Word List B. Minneapolis Public Schools, 1962.

Other Books of Interest

General Writing Books
Beginnings, Middles and Ends, by Nancy Kress $13.95
Dare to Be a Great Writer, by Leonard Bishop (paper) $14.95
Discovering the Writer Within, by Bruce Ballenger & Barry Lane $18.95
Freeing Your Creativity, by Marshall Cook $17.95
Getting the Words Right: How to Rewrite, Edit and Revise, by Theodore A. Rees Cheney (paper) $12.95
How to Write a Book Proposal, by Michael Larsen (paper) $11.95
How to Write Fast While Writing Well, by David Fryxell $17.95
How to Write with the Skill of a Master and the Genius of a Child, by Marshall J. Cook $18.95
Just Open a Vein, edited by William Brohaugh $6.99
Knowing Where to Look: The Ultimate Guide to Research, by Lois Horowitz (paper) $19.95
Make Your Words Work, by Gary Provost $8.99
On Being a Writer, edited by Bill Strickland (paper) $16.95
Pinckert's Practical Grammar, by Robert C. Pinckert (paper) $3.99
Research & Writing: A Complete Guide and Handbook, by Shah Malmoud (paper) $18.95
Shift Your Writing Career into High Gear, by Gene Perret $16.95
The 30-Minute Writer: How to Write and Sell Short Pieces, by Connie Emerson $17.95
30 Steps to Becoming a Writer, by Scott Edelstein $16.95
The 28 Biggest Writing Blunders, by William Noble $12.95
The 29 Most Common Writing Mistakes & How to Avoid Them, by Judy Delton (paper) $9.95
The Wordwatcher's Guide to Good Writing & Grammar, by Morton S. Freeman (paper) $15.95
The Writer's Book of Checklists, by Scott Edelstein $16.95
The Writer's Digest Guide to Manuscript Formats, by Buchman & Groves $18.95
The Writer's Essential Desk Reference, edited by Glenda Neff $19.95
Write Tight: How to Keep Your Prose Sharp, Focused and Concise, by William Brohaugh $16.95
Writing as a Road to Self-Discovery, by Barry Lane $16.95

Nonfiction Writing
The Complete Guide to Writing Biographies, by Ted Schwarz $6.99
How to Do Leaflets, Newsletters, & Newspapers, by Nancy Brigham (paper) $14.95
How to Write Irresistible Query Letters, by Lisa Collier Cool (paper) $10.95
The Complete Guide to Magazine Article Writing, by John M. Wilson $17.95
The Writer's Complete Guide to Conducting Interviews, by Michael Schumacher $14.95
The Writer's Digest Handbook of Magazine Article Writing, edited by Jean M. Fredette (paper) $11.95
Writing Articles From the Heart: How to Write & Sell Your Life Experiences, by Marjorie Holmes $16.95

Fiction Writing
The Art & Craft of Novel Writing, by Oakley Hall $17.95
Best Stories from New Writers, edited by Linda Sanders $5.99
Characters & Viewpoint, by Orson Scott Card $13.95
The Complete Guide to Writing Fiction, by Barnaby Conrad $18.95
Creating Characters: How to Build Story People, by Dwight V. Swain $16.95

Creating Short Fiction, by Damon Knight (paper) $11.95
Dialogue, by Lewis Turco $13.95
The Fiction Writer's Silent Partner, by Martin Roth $19.95
Get That Novel Started! (And Keep Going 'Til You Finish), by Donna Levin $17.95
Handbook of Short Story Writing: Vol. I, by Dickson and Smythe (paper) $12.95
Handbook of Short Story Writing: Vol. II, edited by Jean Fredette (paper) $12.95
How to Write & Sell Your First Novel, by Collier & Leighton (paper) $13.95
Manuscript Submission, by Scott Edelstein $13.95
Mastering Fiction Writing, by Kit Reed $6.99
Plot, by Ansen Dibell $13.95
Practical Tips for Writing Popular Fiction, by Robyn Carr $17.95
Scene and Structure by Jack Bickham $14.95
Theme & Strategy, by Ronald B. Tobias $13.95
The 38 Most Common Fiction Writing Mistakes, by Jack M. Bickham $12.95
20 Master Plots (And How to Build Them), by Ronald B. Tobias $16.95
Writer's Digest Handbook of Novel Writing, $18.95
Writing the Novel: From Plot to Print, by Lawrence Block (paper) $11.95

Special Interest Writing Books

Armed & Dangerous: A Writer's Guide to Weapons, by Michael Newton (paper) $14.95
Cause of Death: A Writer's Guide to Death, Murder & Forensic Medicine, by Keith D. Wilson, M.D. $15.95
Children's Writer's Word Book, by Alijandra Mogliner $19.95
Comedy Writing Secrets, by Mel Helitzer (paper) $15.95
The Complete Book of Feature Writing, by Leonard Witt $18.95
Creating Poetry, by John Drury $18.95
Deadly Doses: A Writer's Guide to Poisons, by Serita Deborah Stevens with Anne Klarner (paper) $16.95
Editing Your Newsletter, by Mark Beach (paper) $18.95
Families Writing, by Peter Stillman (paper) $12.95
A Guide to Travel Writing & Photography, by Ann & Carl Purcell (paper) $22.95
How to Pitch & Sell Your TV Script, by David Silver $6.99
How to Write & Sell Greeting Cards, Bumper Stickers, T-Shirts and Other Fun Stuff, by Molly Wigand (paper) 15.95
How to Write & Sell True Crime, by Gary Provost $5.99
How to Write Horror Fiction, by William F. Nolan $15.95
How to Write Mysteries, by Shannon OCork $13.95
How to Write Romances, by Phyllis Taylor Pianka $15.95
How to Write Science Fiction & Fantasy, by Orson Scott Card $13.95
How to Write Tales of Horror, Fantasy & Science Fiction, edited by J.N. Williamson (paper) $12.95
How to Write the Story of Your Life, by Frank P. Thomas (paper) $12.95
How to Write Western Novels, by Matt Braun $1.00
The Poet's Handbook, by Judson Jerome (paper) $12.95
Police Procedural: A Writer's Guide to the Police and How They Work, by Russell Bintliff (paper) $16.95
Powerful Business Writing, by Tom McKeown $12.95
Private Eyes: A Writer's Guide to Private Investigators, by H. Blythe, C. Sweet, & J. Landreth (paper) $15.95
Scene of the Crime: A Writer's Guide to Crime-Scene Investigation, by Anne Wingate, Ph.D. $15.95
Successful Scriptwriting, by Jurgen Wolff & Kerry Cox (paper) $14.95
The Writer's Complete Crime Reference, by Martin Roth $19.95
The Writer's Guide to Conquering the Magazine Market, by Connie Emerson $17.95
The Writer's Guide to Creating a Science Fiction Universe, by George Ochoa & Jeff Osier $18.95
The Writer's Guide to Everyday Life in the 1800s, by Marc McCutcheon $18.95
Writing for Children & Teenagers, 3rd Edition, by L. Wyndham & Arnold Madison (paper) $12.95
Writing Mysteries: A Handbook by the Mystery Writers of America, Edited by Sue Grafton, $18.95
Writing the Modern Mystery, by Barbara Norville (paper) $12.95

The Writing Business

Business & Legal Forms for Authors & Self-Publishers, by Tad Crawford (paper) $4.99
The Complete Guide to Self-Publishing, by Tom & Marilyn Ross (paper) $18.95
How to Write with a Collaborator, by Hal Bennett with Michael Larsen $1.00
How You Can Make $25,000 a Year Writing, by Nancy Edmonds Hanson (paper) $14.95
This Business of Writing, by Gregg Levoy $19.95

To order directly from the publisher, include $3.00 postage and handling for 1 book and $1.00 for each additional book. Allow 30 days for delivery.

Writer's Digest Books
1507 Dana Avenue, Cincinnati, Ohio 45207
Credit card orders call TOLL-FREE
1-800-289-0963
Stock is limited on some titles; prices subject to change without notice.

Write to this same address for information on *Writer's Digest* magazine, *Story* magazine, Writer's Digest Book Club, Writer's Digest School, and Writer's Digest Criticism Service.